Learning from Each Other

The publisher and the University of California Press Foundation gratefully acknowledge the generous support of the Atkinson Family Foundation Imprint in Higher Education

Learning from Each Other

Refining the Practice of Teaching in Higher Education

———

Edited by

Michele Lee Kozimor-King
and Jeffrey Chin

UNIVERSITY OF CALIFORNIA PRESS

University of California Press, one of the most distinguished university presses in the United States, enriches lives around the world by advancing scholarship in the humanities, social sciences, and natural sciences. Its activities are supported by the UC Press Foundation and by philanthropic contributions from individuals and institutions. For more information, visit www.ucpress.edu.

University of California Press
Oakland, California

Library of Congress Cataloging-in-Publication Data

Names: Kozimor-King, Michele, 1971- editor. | Chin, Jeffrey C. (Jeffrey Chuan-che), editor.
Title: Learning from each other : refining the practice of teaching in higher education / edited by Michele Kozimor-King and Jeffrey Chin.
Description: Oakland, California : University of California Press, [2018] | Includes bibliographical references and index. |
Identifiers: LCCN 2018024585 (print) | LCCN 2018027724 (ebook) | ISBN 9780520969032 (e-edition) | ISBN 9780520296589 (pbk.)
Subjects: LCSH: College teaching.
Classification: LCC LB2331 (ebook) | LCC LB2331 .L3927 2018 (print) | DDC 378.1/25—dc23
LC record available at https://lccn.loc.gov/2018024585

27 26 25 24 23 22 21 20 19 18
10 9 8 7 6 5 4 3 2 1

CONTENTS

ACKNOWLEDGMENTS

A book like this is the work of many hands. Thanks to the many people who helped bring this project to completion.

This project was made possible through the support of Alpha Kappa Delta (AKD), the international honor society for sociology. Since 2013, AKD has sponsored workshops on teaching and learning at the annual meetings of the regional sociology associations. Because these workshops have produced many wonderful ideas for teaching and learning, the next logical step was to capture these ideas, commit them to writing, and assemble them for the benefit of others who were unable to attend.

This project was launched by a conversation with Seth Dobrin, then editor at the University of California Press, at the 2015 annual meeting of the Pacific Sociological Association in Long Beach, California. Seth approached Wendy Ng, the Chair of the PSA Program Committee, who suggested that Seth, Jeff, and Michele get together to chat.

Mary Radford served as our local copy editor. Mary was the copy editor when Jeff was editor of *Teaching Sociology*. Mary's services were made possible by an Athanasius Kircher Senior Research Fellowship grant at Le Moyne College.

Andrea Golembiewski served as graduate student clerical assistant for the Department of Anthropology, Criminology, and Sociology at Le Moyne College, and in that role, she supported Jeff's work.

I, Jeff, dedicate this book to my mother, now 98, who does not consider herself a "real sociologist" because she does not think she is very good with statistics. She earned a PhD in sociology from a small school in Cambridge, Massachusetts and studied with some guy named Talcott Parsons.

I, Michele (Koz), dedicate this book to the many inspirational teachers whom I have learned from. I would like to thank my mother for modeling relationship-centered learning before it was mainstream. Mrs. Nancy Kozimor gets the credit for teaching the first set of students to refer to themselves as "Koz Kids" when she was a sixth grade teacher in Carteret, New Jersey. Dr. Caleb Rosado was the prophet who first put the notion of becoming a sociologist into my head. Thank you for not letting me drop Social Theory my first year at Elizabethtown College and for planting the seeds that have grown into meaningful life work. I am grateful to Dr. Donald Kraybill for seeing through my rebellious facade in Methods of Social Research enough to offer me teaching and research assistant opportunities as an undergraduate student. Many of his pedagogies have formed the foundation of my teaching philosophy, including the importance of student research. There are many more individuals who have shaped the educator I have become, but I would like to end with a special thanks to the amazing students (past and present) at Elizabethtown College, Messiah College, and The Pennsylvania State University. You have transformed my teaching in immeasurable ways. Each time I interact with you inside or outside of the classroom, I learn from you. I am very grateful to be able to pass the lamp of learning on to Barbara Prince, who has chosen to embrace the scholarship of teaching and learning. You have already become an amazing teacher.

Michael Reder

One of the many things I like about *Learning from Each Other* is that the essays it contains present a wide range of approaches to teaching that are all informed by evidence. This collection has teaching ideas for everyone, from the beginning graduate teaching assistant to the experienced full professor. The variety of approaches is important, because just as there is no single "right way" to learn, I believe there is no single "right way" to teach—except, perhaps, "effectively."

How you teach is shaped by your individual identity (race, gender, age, sexuality, experience, etc.) and your personality, as well as by the nature of your discipline, the difficulty of the material, the size of your course, the experiences of the learners, and even the space in which you are teaching. Moreover, the variables related to effective teaching only increase as students, disciplines and subjects, learning contexts, and faculty identities shift and change. Given the diversity of possible approaches to teaching, we need to move beyond habit and instinct into practices that are informed not only by our expertise and experiences, but also by evidence, including new knowledge about the neurobiology of learning, the most recent theories of effective teaching, and assessment of our students' experiences.

The twenty-one essays that Michele Lee Kozimor-King and Jeffrey Chin have assembled, written by faculty across their career stages at institutions ranging from two-year community colleges to R1 doctoral universities, are wide in scope. They address a large variety of teaching topics, spanning from global approaches to teaching, such as co-teaching, community research, and internationalizing the curriculum, to more specific classroom techniques, including strategies for engaging students with difficult topics, using games and simulations, and learning in teams. This volume also includes brief sections on approaches to helping students prepare more effectively for class, as well as easy approaches for including assessment in your course and assignment design. So whether you are interested in refining a teaching technique you already use—such as discussion, lecture, or community research—or learning about something new, such as "flipping" an introductory course or the latest research on the science of learning, there is something in this volume for you.

Becoming familiar with the wide range of teaching options is in many ways the first step toward becoming a more effective teacher. We need to understand the opportunities and challenges related to different approaches to course design and teaching in order to make informed choices about our teaching practices.

What these diverse essays have in common is that they offer us the opportunity, as the apt title proclaims, to learn from each other. In many ways this volume represents a "community of practice" in a book, an opportunity to share and critically reflect upon collective wisdom about teaching and learning. It re-creates the origins of these chapters: the many discussions and workshops on effective teaching held across the country.

I believe that we can create more effective and equitable learning experiences for our students by making intentional, evidence-informed decisions about our assignments, course design, and teaching techniques. Because these essays present an opportunity to learn about the specific research related to a given teaching practice, they not only have the potential to improve student learning, they also can help us develop as teachers by nurturing the habits of mind needed for improvement: thinking critically and intentionally about our teaching.

Connecticut College
New London, CT

Introduction

Michele Lee Kozimor-King and Jeffrey Chin

Widespread accessibility to working teachers matters a great deal, especially if we consider the incredibly diverse range of contexts in which higher education operates these days.

—JAMES M. LANG, *SMALL TEACHING* (2016:5)

The quote by Dr. James M. Lang speaks to the aim of this book, which is to bring the most current, vital teaching practices together into one resource enabling both new and experienced faculty to learn from each other. Of course, the topic itself is a familiar one—a proliferation of books examining the best practices in teaching and learning, the science of learning, and assessment techniques line the shelves of centers for teaching excellence and the office desks (and floors) of our colleagues. Book discussion groups on teaching topics have become a staple of professional development programming (often found convening at campus coffee shops). Still, for many faculty or graduate student instructors, reading and digesting over a dozen new texts (not to mention journal articles) each year in the scholarship of teaching and learning is just not possible. This book attempts to bring together, in one volume, a collection of the tried-and-true best practices and most recent innovations in scholarly teaching. Over 20 instructors have shared their experiences, knowledge, challenges, assessment strategies, and practical tips to ensure that graduate students in courses on teaching, adjuncts, and new and tenured faculty can benefit from and refine the practice of scholarly teaching. To meet the goal of accessibility for those from diverse educational contexts, the authors represent a multitude of institutional settings and rank, including educational developers, junior, mid-, and late-career faculty, community college faculty, faculty at private institutions, and those from research-based state systems.

We have compiled original chapters from faculty who are active scholars in the field of teaching and learning to provide insights into the most effective strategies and evidence-based best practices. Furthermore, to be included in the volume, chapters had to meet three basic criteria. First, the topic of the chapter had to be grounded in the scholarship of teaching and learning beyond the disciplinary journals of the author's field of study. With over 400 scholarly journals within the scholarship of teaching and learning, this requirement was essential to avoid discipline-specific contexts and enable the reader to locate the application of the subject more broadly. Next, each chapter needed to include an assessment strategy or evidence of effective implementation of the teaching technique, theory, or framework. This criterion ensures that the chapters in this book model best practices in the scholarship of teaching and learning. In addition, evidence of effectiveness helps the reader determine whether a specific practice would align with the outcomes of their particular course as well as larger institutional goals. Finally, all chapters provide concrete tips and practical resources that instructors can use in their own teaching and learning environment. Many of the tips in the chapters reflect Lang's (2016) small teaching approach whereby instructors can make small changes to their current course structure. Other chapters require more time, reflection, and planning to apply the pedagogy being introduced.

The idea for this volume grew out of a series of teaching and learning workshops, organized by the editors, where both the participants and facilitators learned from each other. The workshops were sponsored and organized by a small group of members of Alpha Kappa Delta (AKD), the International Sociology Honor Society. Held just prior to the annual regional sociology meetings throughout the United States, the workshops created a transformative experience by bringing faculty and graduate students who were passionate about scholarly teaching together in a collaborative environment. In order to build a community of learners, we held sessions facilitated by individuals who incorporated the best practices of teaching, innovative assignments, and effective assessment strategies in their courses.

Feedback from workshop participants further encouraged us to find a way to share the learning from each other's experiences on a wider scale. Nearly all of the participants from the workshops indicated that throughout the sessions they considered overarching processes and ideas that would inform their future teaching choices, and they were able to identify other scholarly teachers. Additionally, nearly all of the participants believed that the workshop met or exceeded their expectations. Participants stated that they especially enjoyed the conversations with each other and the sense of community that developed from the peer-learning format.

While largely successful at networking and providing inspiration, these workshops present challenges to the dissemination of the scholarship of teaching and learning. One challenge is that attendees desired more details about the topics presented beyond the one-page handouts and brief sessions. They also wanted information on the teaching techniques and strategies from the sessions they were unable to attend. Another challenge of the workshop format for long-term learning is what participants actually do with the materials, tips, and techniques gained. Very often, attendees return to their home institutions inspired and armed with the intention of incorporating the material they learned into their courses or sharing ideas with colleagues. Unfortunately, we know that the excitement often ends when the reality of the needs of the current semester or demand for research productivity hits. By mid-semester, most of us file away (or more aptly pile away) those handouts and notes from the attended workshop. Such materials often resurface much later during an office makeover or a transitional move. By that time, the innovation is outdated or the notes are indecipherable.

Attendance at the workshops continues to be robust, and AKD has made every attempt to keep the registration fees affordable for all teachers in higher education (including offering travel awards). Still, we know that funding for teaching and learning workshops is becoming more difficult to secure, and additional time away from teaching in the middle of a semester is a challenging hurdle for many faculty, instructors, and graduate students. Given the positive feedback and success of the pre-conference workshops and the challenges associated with a workshop format, we began discussing how to bring the accessibility with working teachers of the pre-conference model to a larger audience. That is when the idea for this edited volume took flight. Some of the chapters in this volume are authored by the initial workshop participants. All chapters are written by individuals we can learn from. While many of our contributors are from sociology, and the majority are from disciplines in the social sciences, their allegiance is to improving teaching and learning for all.

Our contributors focus on a number of different aspects of teaching: starting from understanding how learning happens, to specific ideas on pedagogical techniques, and ending with the dissemination of information through the scholarship of teaching and learning. We have divided the book into four sections: curricular innovations, classroom techniques, out-of-class situations, and assessment. We could have placed many of the chapters into multiple units as the topic and methods naturally overlap. Our greatest hope for this book is that it will assist us in learning from each other.

PART 1: CURRICULAR INNOVATIONS

- Chapter 1, "The Science of Learning in a Social Science Context" by Melinda Messineo, provides an overview of the science of learning to help readers address common learning challenges in their social science classes. Readers will explore how the brain learns, ways to help students improve their focus to more effectively retain information, and how to enhance the social aspects of learning.

- Chapter 2, "Pedagogical Techniques for Creating a Community of Inquiry in Online Learning Environments" by Andrea N. Hunt, describes the findings from a survey of undergraduate students regarding their perceptions and preferences for course delivery and provides a conceptual model (i.e., the Community of Inquiry framework) that connects social interaction, critical thinking, and effective course design to promote deep and integrated learning.

- Chapter 3, "Co-Teaching: Risks and Rewards" by Renee Monson and Kristy Kenyon, provides a review of the scholarship on student and faculty experiences in co-taught courses and includes the reflections of the authors on experiences in co-teaching a bi-disciplinary course. The authors demonstrate that co-teaching can foster intellectual engagement and growth for students and faculty alike. They offer practical advice for those considering co-teaching, including recommendations for seeking institutional support, course planning, classroom dynamics, assessing student learning, and course assessment.

- Chapter 4, "A Collaborative Affair: Connecting Students with the Community through Research" by Michele Lee Kozimor-King and Barbara Prince, provides a summary of the literature on the benefits and challenges of community-based research (CBR), presents background information and assessment of a CBR project embedded within a research methods and statistics course sequence, and ends with a practical guide on how to implement a CBR project into a new or existing course.

- Chapter 5, "Strategies and Resources for Internationalizing the Curriculum" by Christine K. Oakley, provides a context for understanding current campus internationalization initiatives and useful strategies to adapt to specific student populations and institutional settings. She presents a discussion of the ideal institutional environment for internationalizing the curriculum, strategies to assess how well a program of study meets globally focused student-learning outcomes, and ways to infuse intercultural and global dimensions into courses. The chapter includes a brief discussion of strategies for faculty to become globally engaged.

- Chapter 6, "Flipping Out: Understanding the Effects of a General Education Flipped Classroom on Student Success" by Craig Douglas Albert, Stacie K. Pettit, and Christopher Terry, investigates the effects a flipped classroom has on student success. They tested the relationships between the flipped design on student performance and content knowledge in Introductory American Government using grades and withdrawal rates as a measure of student performance. In addition, they administered a 15-question pre- / post-test content knowledge instrument. Finally, they provide results from the data and suggestions for implementation.

- Chapter 7, "Reaching and Teaching 'Nontraditional' Students in Community Colleges and Beyond" by Sara Parker, provides an introduction to teaching community college students by identifying four characteristics of this population: academic under preparedness, significant percentages of first-generation and / or immigrant students, complicated attendance patterns, and heterogeneity. The chapter includes a review of literature on increasing student success and provides evidence of a successful classroom intervention.
- Chapter 8, "Addressing Learner Variability on Campus through Universal Design for Learning" by Shannon Haley-Mize, provides an overview of the principles of universal design for learning (UDL) theory and a review of the literature on UDL in higher education. She provides an application of UDL to course design, including online learning environments and suggestions for implementation.

PART 2: CLASSROOM TECHNIQUES

The second section of the volume is rich with suggestions on ways to improve specific pedagogical techniques that we typically use in our classrooms.

- Chapter 9, "Without Apology: Reclaiming the Lecture" by Diane L. Pike, draws on the scholarship of teaching and learning (SoTL) literature and professional experience to support four key behaviors (accompanied by the appropriate attitudes and knowledge) that can strengthen lecture: a new kind of preparation, embedded action, eradication of traditional PowerPoint, and playback. The chapter provides guidance on how to utilize the lecture successfully.
- Chapter 10, "Scribes in the Classroom: Effectively Using PowerPoint to Enhance the Classroom Experience" by Monica R. Sylvia and Brenda J. Kirby, explores how to use PowerPoint to facilitate the best learning environment from both the instructor's and students' perspectives. They review the literature on effective PowerPoint use and examine the results from their empirical study that investigates the differences between text-intensive and bulleted-outline PowerPoint slide formats.
- Chapter 11, "Discussion in the Social Science Classroom" by Jay R. Howard, examines classroom norms that present challenges in engaging students as well as lead to the domination of discussion by a small group of students. The chapter provides strategies for overcoming these classroom norms to encourage participation and involvement in discussion.
- Chapter 12, "Facilitating Learning and Leadership in Student Team Projects" by Dennis O'Connor, provides an overarching model for creating successful student teams and building team leadership from project development and management to evaluation. This chapter includes tips and tools for implementing student team projects designed to increase the learning that occurs through group work.

- Chapter 13, "Courting Controversy and Allowing for Awkward: Strategies for Teaching Difficult Topics" by Mari Plikuhn, explores the range of topics that are currently considered difficult to teach, reviews the literature on classroom management strategies for structuring productive discussions of controversial material, discusses techniques for creating safe student interactions, and provides examples of policies designed to develop a respectful classroom culture.
- Chapter 14, "Becoming a Culturally Inclusive Educator" by Dena R. Samuels, examines the role that faculty members play in creating a diverse and inclusive classroom. She presents results from her own national research study that examines faculty perceptions of and education on being culturally inclusive. The chapter provides strategies for implementation so faculty can transform themselves and their classroom into a more culturally inclusive environment.
- Chapter 15, "The Value of Games and Simulations in the Social Sciences" by Amanda M. Rosen, explores the benefits and challenges of using simulations and games in the social science college classroom. She presents the results from an analysis of 66 publications on games and simulations in political science along with an interdisciplinary discussion of the literature discussing the conditions under which simulations and games are effective. She also provides best practices and tips for the use of simulations and games in the classroom.
- Chapter 16, "Putting the Student at the Center: Contemplative Practices as Classroom Pedagogy" by Tracy Wenger Sadd, provides an introduction to the use of contemplative practices in academic courses ranging from physics, chemistry, biology, and environmental science to literature, law, social work, economics, and sociology. She provides a summary of the research on student outcomes related to the use of contemplative practices, basic guidelines for integrating these practices into the classroom, and several examples from the implementation into two academic disciplines.

PART 3: OUT-OF-CLASS SITUATIONS

The third section of the volume covers two topics that largely affect students' preparation outside of the classroom: reading and engagement with the material.

- Chapter 17, "Student Reading Compliance and Learning in the Social Sciences" by Jay R. Howard, examines one of the key challenges in virtually all college-level courses: getting students to read. The chapter provides a review of the literature on the effects of motivation and use of classroom time with regard to students completing reading assignments. He also provides suggestions of best practices for ensuring students read and benefit from the reading.
- Chapter 18, "Cultivating Engagement and Deepening Understanding While Leaving the Textbook Behind" by Robin G. Isserles, chronicles the decision to

abandon the use of a traditional textbook in an introductory sociology course and provides concrete tips for implementation of the practice. She discusses the literature on textbook use and the impetus for the decision to leave the textbook behind. She explains the results from her analysis of student survey data and student work.

PART 4: ASSESSMENT

The final section focuses on assessment strategies, including backward design and the development and use of rubrics. The last chapter provides a discussion on how to transform innovative assessment techniques and pedagogies into research consistent with the scholarship of teaching and learning.

- Chapter 19, "(Re-)Creating Your Course: Backward Design and Assessment" by Melinda Messineo, discusses backward course design using a step-by-step process suitable for new course development or revision of an existing course. Instructors will develop transferable strategies by examining concepts important to backward design and course assessment, including alignment, active learning, and formative and summative assessments. She provides tips and techniques for implementation.
- Chapter 20, "'Am I Grading Consistently and Effectively?': Developing and Using Rubrics" by Shirley A. Jackson, provides an examination of how rubrics can be useful tools to help faculty provide feedback to students that is meaningful, efficient, and consistent with grading standards. She presents a discussion of the benefits of and challenges to using rubrics. This chapter includes suggestions and tips for novice users of rubrics.
- Chapter 21, "Defining and Implementing the Scholarship of Teaching and Learning" by Jeffrey Chin, examines the area of study referred to as the scholarship of teaching and learning (SoTL), distinguishes Sot from scholarly teaching, and provides a short history of the field. He provides strategies and tips for ways to transform scholarly teaching into Sot research. The chapter also explains how faculty can use Sot to fulfill the demands for assessment of the curriculum.

REFERENCE

Lang, James M. 2016. *Small Teaching: Everyday Lessons from the Science of Learning*. San Francisco: Jossey-Bass.

PART I

Curricular Innovations

The Science of Learning in a Social Science Context

Melinda Messineo

Perhaps you have heard the quote attributed to William Glasser suggesting that we learn 10 percent of what we read, 20 percent of what we hear, 80 percent of what we experience, and 95 percent of what we teach others.[1] Possibly an adaptation of Dale's *Cone of Experience* (1969), the percentages are merely symbolic and are meant to illustrate the importance of engagement in the learning process. Research shows that the more active you are in the learning process, the more it "sticks" and the more capable you are at applying and adapting what you have learned to other contexts (Meyers and Jones 1993). The last 30 years have witnessed a significant push for higher education to employ active-learning strategies (Pascarella and Terenzini 2005; see also the journal *Active Learning in Higher Education*).[2] Instructors in higher education have moved toward highly diverse delivery formats that involve a myriad of assessment strategies (Angelo and Cross 1993; Barkley and Major 2016). At the heart of these approaches is active learning.

ACTIVE LEARNING

Active learning is an umbrella term that describes a variety of learning experiences in which the learner demonstratively engages in the learning process (Bonwell and Eison 1991; ERIC thesaurus). Active learning focuses more on what the student is doing in the learning process as opposed to the behaviors of the instructor. If the instructor is the most active person in the classroom, the odds are that the students are at risk of being disengaged from the learning experience. As a result, learner-centered pedagogies that increase the engagement of students have emerged as the most effective for learning and retention. Research across many fields documents the positive impact that active strategies have on student engagement and learning outcomes (Michael 2006; Prince 2004). Learner-centered strategies are more likely to lead to active learning. As a result, the justification for the shift toward learner-centered strategies is based on evidence that active learners learn more (Bransford, Brown, and Cocking 2000).

The challenge of interpreting learning outcome data, however, lies in deciding how to actually measure improvement. Some studies focus on the degree to which students master objective exams (Hake 1998; Martin, Grimbeek, and Jamieson-Proctor 2014). Other studies focus on more subjective measures of improvement (see examples in Prince 2004). In many cases, typical assessments are ill equipped to measure the value added through these more complex approaches. For example, cooperative and problem-based strategies often create benefits in students in terms of teamwork and improved interpersonal skills. However, change in these areas is difficult to measure (Terenzini et al. 2001). Despite these challenges, research shows that active-learning strategies increased learning and affective outcomes. Specifically, the active student engaging in more authentic learning experiences learns and retains more (Fink 2013). Changes in brain scanning technology and cognitive science can now provide an explanation for why it is that student-centered active learning works.

THE SCIENCE BEHIND ACTIVE LEARNING—
HOW THE BRAIN LEARNS
Recording, Sorting, and Storing

Learning involves change in the learner's brain, and this change occurs through electrical and chemical processes (Clay 2007; Ford 2011; Learner Centered Teaching n.d.; Stroman 2016). External stimuli activate specific patterns in the brain that allow for the recording and storage of information. We are generally aware that different parts of the brain do different things and that the reactivation of patterns strengthens the pathways across these parts and assists in recall.[3] Learning occurs through the development of connections between existing patterns and new patterns. As babies, our brains have no established patterns or constructs. However, once we have some existing patterns, it is easier to store new information because we have something to attach it to. The more the pathways are fired or activated, the stronger the paths and patterns become, and the learner has an easier time with future recall and connections (Ford 2011). This explains why older memories are the most stable patterns in the brains of individuals with dementia and Alzheimer's disease. Having been fired the most, they are the strongest and most stable in the brain (Smith and Squire 2009). The challenge with learning is that you can only fire neural pathways for a brief period of time before the brain fatigues. Involving other parts of the brain can extend the learning time block, but a very narrow, focused task usual tires the brain in four to eight minutes (Perry 2000). The brain needs to rest for a few minutes and then can work on finding patterns and making connections again. This intense firing of electricity and chemicals means the brain also burns a fair amount of energy in the process.[4] Learning is work.

The initial storage capacity of short-term memory is rather small. The classic research by Miller (1956) solidified the idea that we can remember seven items at a time, give or take two items. These items can be without context and can be recalled fairly easily. What is useful to note, however, is that the items can be clustered together as "chunks," and then the chunks can become the seven items (plus or minus two) that can be recalled. Chunks that consist of three pieces of information are the most manageable, and this feature is evident in the way that we remember Social Security numbers. Instructors can help student learning by clustering material and by helping students to use the technique themselves.

APPLYING THE SCIENCE OF LEARNING TO TEACHING
Practice and Context Matter

Given that neural pathways fire, and that they strengthen the more they fire, the use of *practice* as part of the learning experience becomes extremely important. Practice helps to strengthen pathways for improved learning and recall (Ambrose et al. 2010). However, the practice activity cannot be simply "time on task" or "busy work." It needs to be deliberate practice on authentic problems that is guided by an expert. Unfortunately, practice inadvertently fell out of favor when the critique of rote learning and memorization hit its stride. Bloom's taxonomy lists "remembering" as the least complex type of learning that can occur (Bloom et al. 1956). The problem with rote learning (i.e., the process of reviewing discrete facts over and over until they are memorized) is that it is too narrow and often without context. The critique is justified since decontextualized memorization is not an effective way to learn material if you hope to apply it to other contexts. Think of those neural pathways again. Rote memorization fires between two regions over and over until the path is well set. That path, however stable, is not connected to other areas of the brain, which means it is difficult to connect that idea to other ideas. In contrast, practice in general, and deliberate practice in particular, is important to the learning process (Ericsson and Lehmann 1996). With more areas of the brain engaged while learning occurs, retention increases, as does the flexibility to use that information in other places and other ways.

Emotion and Learning

Developments in brain science have helped us better understand the role of emotion in the learning experience. Connecting with emotion centers is especially important for learning; therefore, enjoyment, pleasure, wonder, and fear can be powerful forces in the learning process. Positive first contact with people and ideas impacts the brain differently than negative experiences (Tendler and Wagner 2015). Research shows that peptide neurotransmitters (biologically occurring peptide chemical chains) are a critical element in how the body experiences emotions (Tendler and Wagner 2015). Focusing on just two for this conversation, instructors can benefit from understanding the roles of cortisol, often called the stress hormone, and endorphins, frequently associated with positive emotions. Research shows that cortisol heightens attention and focus in the classic "fight or flight" response system. It can also contribute to a sense of euphoria when control is established. However, chronically high cortisol levels can eventually compromise the neurons associated with learning and memory (Vincent 1990). Gazzaniga's work (1989) shows that even short-term, stress-related elevation of cortisol in the hippocampus can prevent learners from effectively determining what is important in a learning environment. Thus, stress can heighten awareness, but if chronic, it can impede learning (see also D'Mello and Graesser 2012). It is not that stress and confusion are always bad; rather, it is about moderation.

Endorphins, in contrast, are opiate peptide pain inhibitors and can increase focus and retention, resulting in a sense of euphoria. The positive feelings associated with endorphin release can increase learning and retention. Instructors can facilitate endorphin release through physical activity and positive social contact (Levinthal 1988). Laughter and play are mechanisms that can produce endorphins. In fact, learning itself can release positive-feeling neurotransmitters like dopamine, which the body experiences as a reward. This positive feeling reinforces the motivation in many learners to keep learning. Together, all of these pieces illustrate why active learning in a positive social classroom environment can lead to better learning outcomes and increased motivation to learn.

Novelty Matters

The brain is quite proficient at distinguishing the familiar from the novel. Some research suggests that our ancestors used this strategy for survival. Early humans would scan their environment to distinguish between what was new or unusual (and a possible threat) and what was known and already classified. As a result, the brain actually seeks out novelty and moves focus or attention away from the familiar (Ford 2011; Perry 2000). Combine this novelty-seeking strategy with an easily fatigued brain and it becomes clear why attention spans are not particularly long.

This explains why students have difficulty retaining a long recitation of facts. Even if the facts themselves are not familiar, the sameness or lack of variation in the experience itself will lull the listener into losing focus.

At times the facts are so novel that the student has no familiarity with the idea or concept and thus no cognitive constructs with which to connect the new information. In these situations, the instructor needs to create experiences that help the learner connect to their preexisting understandings. To connect with a preexisting understanding, a student needs to be aware that the understanding even exists in the first place. Faculty can help students become aware of their preexisting understandings through reflection activities, pre-tests, cognitive maps, and storytelling. If done well, lectures that involve engaging stories that help the listener connect the content to their own lives can be an effective teaching strategy (Bligh 2000). Add some social engagement, and you have the ingredients for an effective learning environment. The challenge lies in finding the links that can keep everyone engaged. If students are not inherently engaged with a topic, they can learn strategies to help reset their attention.

Novelty and the Learning Environment

Using classroom and study spaces intentionally also helps improve learning. The brain responds to place and time sensations, and scent and feeling markers impact recall. Do you remember your location when you were studying for an important exam, and upon recalling that space, do you remember the information you learned? These unique markers are extremely valuable to the learning process and can facilitate recall. However, unless you plan to only recall a piece of information in the location where you studied, it is better to vary your study location (Bjork and Yan 2014).

Expert and Novice Learners

Learning changes the brain. The more patterns or constructs that we have in our brains, the more paths we can explore and the more insights we can discover. Dreyfus and Dreyfus (1986) outline the progress of the learner from novice to expert and note that the way in which learners perceive problems and their potential solutions vary greatly. Novice learners fail to see the role of context in their own learning, and they have different motivations and different decision-making approaches.

At the brain level, we know that learners make memories and connections using existing constructs. Research comparing the fMRI scans of experts versus novices shows that their approaches to tasks and their impact of learning differ significantly (Solso 2001). In the novice brain, the limbic area or emotional center of the brain fires intensely as the learner attempts to learn and master new skills.

These limbic processes can increase learning through endorphin and dopamine processing, but can also impede learning when cortisol inhibits retention and recall.

The expert brain, however, is in a less emotionally engaged place and is more likely to achieve a state that is often experienced as "flow" (Csikszentmihalyi 1997). As expert learners, instructors often forget what it was like to experience the struggle and confusion of forming those new pathways. Some experts move too quickly to the solution, while others struggle to see where the error is coming from in the first place (Mathan and Koedinger 2005). Assuming that your students learn and experience information just like you do can create barriers in the classroom context.

Metacognition

Another advantage that expert learners have over novices is that they have better metacognitive skills (Bransford et al. 2000). Metacognition, or "thinking about thinking," is a powerful strategy for increased learning. It is the process of applying evaluative criteria to one's thinking processes and the outcomes of one's thinking to decide if one should employ new learning strategies. Expert learners know when they "are not getting it." If they read a paragraph and are not able to make connections, they prompt themselves to reread the paragraph. If that intervention does not help, expert learners know how to break the material down into the elements that they do understand and the elements they do not understand. Then, these learners know how to use other resources to obtain clarification. Importantly, expert learners can usually distinguish between confusion resulting from the introduction of *new information* and confusion based on *contradictory information* (Masson et al. 2014). It is one thing to not understand something you have no experience with, but it is a different issue if the confusion results from this new information indicating your previous understanding of something is incorrect. Experts are prepared to explore their own understanding to determine whether or not they need to adapt old understandings to new information. In contrast, novice learners experience this tension as confusion and need guidance through the clarification process.

Attention Matters

Expert learners are also skilled at paying attention. Part of effective metacognition is knowing when you are focused and knowing when your mind is wandering. The literature on mind wandering indicates that this brain state is an important mechanism for sorting information and making connections. Some research suggests that this default state is how the hypothalamus transitions information from short-term to long-term memory. Focus is necessary for learning to occur, and the brain can only focus on one thing at a time (Ophir, Nass, and Wagner 2009). Controlling your focus is a critical element in self-directed learning, and in a fast-paced cultural context, the expectation to do more and do it faster conflicts directly with effective learning.

There is also the blind spot concerning multitasking to consider, in that most of us think we are better at multitasking than we actually are. Research shows that multitasking reduces accuracy and efficiency.[5] Importantly, it dramatically reduces learning and retention (Rubinstein, Meyer, and Evans 2001). The brain cannot focus on two things at the same time. What we think of as multitasking is actually rapid-task shifting or rapid-serial tasking (Rubinstein et al. 2001). We move back and forth quickly between two foci. At each switch there is a tiny gap where information is lost and the resulting connections between ideas are fragile. We end up in this state of continuous partial attention, which means nothing receives our full attention. Instructors can use many videos online to help reveal to students their inability to effectively multitask. One activity is to have students write down the alphabet while they count out loud from 1–26. Some students can go further than others, but the point is that it is a challenge for most to switch back and forth quickly in any meaningful way. Once students realize that they are actually wasting time by multitasking instead of being more efficient, they can give themselves permission to change the way they approach learning.

Unlearning and Relearning

As novices progress in their skill and understanding, they run the risk of making errors because of the underdeveloped constructs they bring to new situations. For example, some learners find that reading something once is enough exposure to ensure accurate recall of that information at some later time. Repeated success with this strategy causes the advanced beginners to overestimate their reading comprehension and retention skills. When faced with a more complex task, they may not be able to monitor their likely success and are thus surprised by failure. Where the complete novice has no previous experience to base their expectations on, the more advanced beginner may have developed some bad habits that will get in the way of future success. In these contexts, the learner's errors need to be revealed to them so that they can unlearn the incorrect information and relearn the correct information. Activities where students are pushed beyond their ability help make explicit the errors in their understanding. Cognitive scientists describe these as situations of "desired difficulty" (Bjork and Linn 2006). For example, having a student recall information improves learning over simply having the student continue to study. The act of retrieval, whether successful or not, when coupled with instruction, improves the student's ability to recall the correct information in the future.

Expert learners know to test themselves for understanding and risk the possibility of failure in order to reveal their errors in understanding. Novice learners are hesitant to face this failure and lack the skills needed to correct their errors when encountered. On the brain side of the equation, once you have created a neural pathway, there is really no way to un-create it, though illness and injury do block or impede pathways (Jagust et al. 2009). The brain has to create new pathways between existing and new patterns or understanding. The "unlearning" happens more in the disuse of the old pathway than any actual dismantling of that connection (Mauk and Ohyama 2004). The more the new path is used, the more quickly it becomes integrated into the workings of the brain.[6]

COMMON LEARNING ERRORS UNDERSTOOD THROUGH BRAIN SCIENCE

Poor student performance in class may partially come from students' lack of understanding of how learning happens. Cramming, poor nutrition, lack of sleep and exercise all make the brain's job of learning and recall much more difficult. Beyond the proper care and keeping of their brains, there are other ways that we can help students understand how to be more effective learners. Brain science can assist us in gaining a better understanding of five common learning errors: inattention, decontextualization, conflicts with previous knowledge, absent or ineffective practice, and isolated learning. By thinking about how these errors manifest themselves in our students, we may more easily understand these concepts.

Manifestation 1: The incredulous test-taker. Common sentiment—"I studied for four hours and knew everything, but I still got a bad grade."

I remember when I first heard a student utter these words. My initial reaction was, "Are you sure?" I could not imagine that a sincere effort of four hours would result in such a poor outcome. As instructors we often attribute students' poor performance to lack of motivation, so we are somewhat incredulous when students report that they studied a great deal and were not successful. But taking the students at their word, I now know that four hours could produce poor learning outcomes for a variety of reasons even with high motivation.

First, instructors will want to ask students about their multitasking behaviors. Multitasking reduces learning outcomes dramatically and is a frequent "user error." Instructors will also want to assess the students' metacognitive skills. A high time investment with low outcomes could suggest that the students are reviewing the material but are not cognizant of their failure to understand and/or retain the material. Next, instructors will want to see the material the students were actually studying. I ask students to bring in their books, notes, study guides, flash cards, or whatever they used while studying. Some students have nothing to offer for review, which, in many ways, is a positive thing because instructors can easily address this.

If students bring in resources for inspection, I often see that the students were studying the wrong information. I commonly see this in the form of flashcards containing inaccurate definitions or examples. This is a slightly bigger challenge because students have to unlearn the earlier effort and learn the new material on top of whatever new learning experiences are coming their way. Last, I ask students about how they study. Did they give themselves enough time between study sessions to rest and for their brains to draw connections and correctly store information? If a student only has four hours to study, they would be better served by doing shorter blocks of time more frequently and include numerous opportunities to practice with feedback. If students have trouble retaining information, was it due to a lack of adequate practice or a lack of engagement of the multiple parts of the brain during the learning process?

Manifestation 2: The overwhelmed reader. Common sentiment—"The readings / assignments are too difficult."

The other "fixes" identified above may help this student as well. Multitasking is devastating to reading comprehension. Also, reading with low metacognitive skills may produce low reading comprehension as well. If students are concerned about difficulty, instructors may want to assess the degree to which assignment elements are scaffolded. Try not to be lulled into the mindset that the smartest student in class is doing fine so it must be well scaffolded. That high achieving student is not your best indicator, just as you, as an expert learner, are probably not the best judge of difficulty. This concern may also reflect that the learner is not practicing enough. Sometimes students need to reread texts or discuss them with others for clarification. Designing practice with feedback into the course may help. If students remain confused about a topic or are surprised by errors, perhaps the default patterns in their brains resort to these misunderstandings when distracted in stressful testing environments.

Manifestation 3: The skeptical writer. Common sentiment—"I do not know what you want on your assignments."

This concern raised by students potentially reflects many of the user errors listed above. The student's experience of the assignments may include low levels of scaffolding because either the student missed the classes earlier in the curriculum where this scaffolding was to occur or it was lacking in the course itself. There may have been insufficient practice with the concepts or skills so the student was not able to clarify the ambiguities at the formative assessment stage and thus was not successful at the summative assessment stage. Such students may also be exhibiting low metacognition as well since it appears that they are not able to articulate where the confusion lies. The instructor can help them by having clear objectives, by providing scaffolding that includes opportunities for practice, and by assisting in developing metacognitive strategies.

WHY THIS MATTERS FOR THE SOCIAL SCIENCES

Learning is changing the brain. When you distill the types of change instructors seek in learners, they fall into three basic categories: change in the content knowledge, change in skills, and change in behavior/affect. In order to create these changes, we must impact the student brain. All disciplines focus on all three areas of change, but the social sciences often encounter students who see the content and skills we ask them to master as "common sense" and therefore less challenging. Because students feel like experts in the social sciences by virtue of having a lifetime of experience as members of society, they tend to discount the need to develop mastery in these areas and are reluctant to change. As a general rule, a student facing physics for the first time is more likely to recognize their novice learner status when confronted by the laboratory and the periodic table despite having lived in a world governed by the laws of physics. The terminology and context is novel, and their attention is heightened. The complexity of the lab prevents, to some degree, multitasking, and mastery of the content, terminology, and skills demands deliberate practice.

In contrast, the apparent familiarity of the topics of social sciences makes them appear easy and less rigorous. As a result, students often draw faulty conclusions. For example, students commonly commit ecological and exception fallacies. With ecological fallacies, students make inferences about the experience of individuals based on information they have on the group to which those individuals belong. An exception fallacy occurs when you reach a group conclusion on the basis of exceptional cases. This faulty logic is common in everyday life. However, students feel like the work of social science is common sense.

The social sciences are also quite interested in impacting students' behavior/affect, which is a different learning task than skills and content mastery. Learning the facts or statistics about poverty and inequality is rarely the entire goal of a course. We often want our students to experience empathy for those experiencing social injustice and would even like students to consider taking action. Again, understanding the science of learning can help instructors reach these goals.

Recall how connecting information to emotional centers helps students learn, retain, and recall information. This strategy works for learning empathy as well. Research using fMRI on study participants found that watching individuals experience joy as well as suffering activates those centers in the brain of the participants as well, often as if they were experiencing the emotion themselves. Feeling someone's pain is possible to the degree that empathy is experienced neurologically and is not entirely egocentric (cited in Bergland 2013). Emotions and thoughts about how a person feels in a situation are powerful teaching tools. In fact, empathy can be taught through role playing and the integration of first-person narratives into our coursework (Weng et al. 2013). Social science instructors can use role playing and brain science to more effectively reach the behavioral affective goals of their curricula.

The social sciences often emphasize the socially constructed nature of knowledge. Facts are constructed through social agreement (Berger and Luckmann 1967), and in order to understand a person's experience, it is important to know how *they* understand their experience (Collins 2005). Learning with others helps to stimulate different parts of the brain, which, as described previously, helps with learning and retention. Who you learn with plays a critical role in what you learn, how you are socialized, and who you become in adulthood. Much of this empowerment of the individual is related to the values of the social sciences as they relate to equity. However, the science of learning offers physiological support for how the learner creates knowledge through brain activity. Context, community, and environment are critical to knowledge construction because those are precisely the mechanisms through which the brain works.

The manner in which empathy is learned along with the emphasis on the social aspects of learning and the socially constructed nature of knowledge makes brain science and the social sciences critical partners in pedagogy.

Based on these findings, there is a great deal that instructors can apply from brain science in their classes. I asked a cognitive psychologist if her students aced all of their classes because their discipline empowered them with the understanding of how learning happens. She jokingly said that "even dentists get cavities" and then elaborated by saying that "knowing something is not the same as applying something." We need to apply what we know about the science of learning to our classes, and we can help our students apply this knowledge as well. Instructors can use intentional pedagogical choices to help students be more mindful about their own learning and help them develop metacognitive skills that improve learning outcomes. What is especially intriguing about this rapidly changing field is that there is so much more to know. Imagine the learning possibilities.

NOTES

1. Quote retrieved January 17, 2016 (http://thinkexist.com/quotation/we-learn-of-what-we-read-of-what-we-hear-of-what/397216.html); see also http://wglasser.com/. Benjamin Franklin, perhaps an early proponent of active learning, is credited with having said, "Tell me and I forget. Teach me and I remember. Involve me and I learn." Quote retrieved January 17, 2016 (http://www.americanhistorycentral.com/entry.php?rec=469&view=quotes).

2. A search for "'active learning' in 'higher education'" in Google Scholar produced 266 results for 1970–80, 924 results for 1981–90, 7,960 results for 1991–2000, 22,400 results for 2001–10, and 19,300 results for 2011 to January of 2016.

3. Some evidence suggests that we have been misinterpreting the "right-brained as creative versus left-brained as logical" lateralization. Yet the fact that different parts of the brain do different things still remains. Another misconception is that the average human only uses 10 percent of their brain capacity, suggesting that we are not very talented at using this resource. The error may come from our understanding that neurons make up about 10 percent of our brains compared to the glial cells that support these systems and make up a much larger portion of the brain. This white matter versus gray matter confusion may be related to the myth (Boyd 2008).

4. While it makes up only 2 percent of our body weight, the brain uses 20 percent of the oxygen and 25 percent of the glucose in our systems (Mink, Blumenschine, and Adams 1981).

5. Multitasking should not be confused with the concept of interleaving. Interleaving is the strategy whereby the learner breaks up studying time across a range of topics as opposed to focusing in depth for hours on just one topic. This focused, interspersed approach helps extend the effectiveness of studying sessions (Birnbaum et al. 2013).

6. We still do not know a great deal about the brain (Eagleman 2007). For example, we do not know much about how the brain stores information, and we know even less about the retrieval mechanism. It is not clear how the information is actually coded onto neural activity. We are not sure what emotions are or what intelligence means in terms of brain structure, or how different parts of the brain communicate with each other. We do not even completely understand why we sleep and dream, though it may be a time for the brain to clean up (Xie et al. 2013). We do know that sleep is extremely important to learning, and it is not your imagination that you came up with a solution in a dream (Tamaki 2013). Someday we hope to know why this happens and whether or not it is possible to leverage this brain activity for more effective problem-solving.

REFERENCES

Ambrose, Susan A., Michael W. Bridges, Michele DiPietro, Marsha C. Lovett, and Marie K. Norman. 2010. *How Learning Works: 7 Research-Based Principles for Smart Teaching.* San Francisco: Jossey-Bass.

Angelo, Thomas, and Patricia Cross. 1993. *Classroom Assessment Techniques: A Handbook for College Teachers.* 2nd ed. San Francisco: Jossey-Bass.

Barkley, Elizabeth F., and Claire Howell Major. 2016. *Learning Assessment Techniques: A Handbook for College Faculty.* San Francisco: Jossey-Bass.

Berger, Peter, and Thomas Luckmann. 1967. *The Social Construction of Reality: A Treatise in the Sociology of Knowledge.* Norwell, MA: Anchor.

Bergland, Christopher. 2013. "The Neuroscience of Empathy: Neuroscientists Identify Specific Brain Areas Linked to Compassion." *Psychology Today.* Retrieved January 18, 2016 (https://www.psychologytoday.com/blog/the-athletes-way/201310/the-neuroscience-empathy).

Birnbaum, Michael, Nate Kornell, Elizabeth Bjork, and Robert Bjork. 2013. "Why Interleaving Enhances Inductive Learning: The Role of Discrimination and Retrieval." *Memory and Cognition* 41:392–402.

Bjork, Robert, and Marcia Linn. 2006. "The Science of Learning and the Learning of Science: Introducing Desirable Difficulties." *APS Observer* 19:29–39.

Bjork, Robert, and V. X. Yan. 2014. "The Increasing Importance of Learning How to Learn." Pp. 15–36 in *Integrating Cognitive Science with Innovative Teaching in STEM Disciplines,* edited by M. A. McDaniel, R. F. Frey, S. M. Fitzpatrick, and H. L. Roediger, III. Saint Louis, MO: Washington University in St. Louis Libraries.

Bligh, Donald A. 2000. *What's the Use of Lectures?* San Francisco: Jossey-Bass Higher and Adult Education.

Bloom, Benjamin, M. D. Engelhart, E. J. Furst, W. H. Hill, and David Krathwohl. 1956. *Taxonomy of Educational Objectives: The Classification of Educational Goals. Handbook I: Cognitive Domain.* New York: David McKay.

Bonwell, Charles, and James Eison. 1991. "Active Learning: Creating Excitement in the Classroom." *ASHEERIC Higher Education Report No. 1.* George Washington University, Washington, DC.

Boyd, Robynne. 2008. "Do People Only Use 10 Percent of Their Brains? What's the Matter with Only Exploiting a Portion of Our Gray Matter?" *Scientific American,* February 7. Retrieved January 17, 2016 (http://www.scientificamerican.com/article/do-people-only-use-10-percent-of-their-brains/).

Bransford, John D., Ann L. Brown, and Rodney R. Cocking, eds. 2000. *How People Learn: Brain, Mind, Experience and School.* Washington, DC: National Academies Press.

Braxton, John M., Jeffrey Milem, and Anna Shaw Sullivan. 2000. "The Influence of Active Learning on the College Student Departure Process: Toward a Revision of Tinto's Theory." *Journal of Higher Education* 71(5):569–90.

Clay, Rebecca. 2007. "Functional Magnetic Resonance Imaging: A New Research Tool." *Association Booklet.* American Psychological Association, Washington, DC. Retrieved January 17, 2016 (http://www.apa.org/research/tools/fmri-adult.pdf).

Collins, Randall 2005. *Interaction Ritual Chains.* Princeton, NJ: Princeton University Press.

Csikszentmihalyi, Mihaly. 1997. "Intrinsic Motivation and Effective Teaching: A Flow Analysis." Pp. 72–89 in *Teaching Well and Liking It: Motivating Faculty to Teach Effectively,* edited by J. J. Bass. Baltimore, MD: Johns Hopkins University Press.

D'Mello, Sidney, and Arthur Graesser. 2012. "Dynamics of Affective States during Complex Learning." *Learning and Instruction* 22:145–57.

Dale, Edgar. 1969. *Audio-Visual Methods in Teaching.* 3rd ed. New York: Holt, Rinehart & Winston.

Dreyfus, Hubert, and Stuart Dreyfus. 1986. *Mind over Machine: The Power of Human Intuition and Expertise in the Era of the Computer.* New York: Free Press.

Eagleman, David M., Arielle D. Kagan, Stephanie S. Nelson, Deepak Sagaram, and Anand K. Sarma. 2007. "A Standardized Test Battery for the Study of Synesthesia." *Journal of Neuroscience Methods* 159:139–45.

Ericsson, K. Anders, Ralf Krampe, and Clemens Tesch-Römer. 1993. "The Role of Deliberate Practice in the Acquisition of Expert Performance." *Psychological Review* 100:363–406.

Ericsson, K. Anders, and Andreas Lehmann. 1996. "Expert and Exceptional Performance: Evidence on Maximal Adaptations on Task Constraints." *Annual Review of Psychology* 47:273–305.

Fink, Dee. 2013. *Creating Significant Learning Experiences: An Integrated Approach to Designing College Courses.* 2nd ed. San Francisco: Jossey-Bass.

Ford, Donald. 2011. "How the Brain Learns." *Training Industry.* Retrieved January 17, 2016 (http://www.trainingindustry.com/contentdevelopment/articles/how-the-brain-learns.aspx).

Gazzaniga, Michael. 1989. *Mind Matters: How Mind and Brain Interact to Create Our Conscious Lives.* Boston: Houghton Mifflin.

Hake, Richard. 1998. "Interactive-Engagement Versus Traditional Methods: A Six-Thousand Student Survey of Mechanics Test Data for Introductory Physics Courses." *American Journal of Physics* 66:64.

Jagust, William J., S. M. Landau, L. M. Shaw, J. Q. Trojanowski, R. A. Koeppe, E. M. Reiman, N. L. Foster, et al. 2009. "Relationships between Biomarkers in Aging and Dementia." *Neurology* 73(15):1193–99.

Learner Centered Teaching. N.d. "A Brain Based Explanation of Learning." Retrieved January 17, 2016 (https://learnercenteredteaching.wordpress.com/teaching-resources/brain-research/a-brain-based-explanation-of-learning/).

Levinthal, Charles. 1988. *Messengers of Paradise: Opiates and the Brain.* New York: Doubleday.

Major, Claire H., and Betsy Palmer. 2001. "Assessing the Effectiveness of Problem-Based Learning in Higher Education: Lessons from the Literature." *Academic Exchange Quarterly* 5(1):4.

Martin, David, Peter Grimbeek, and Romina Jamieson-Proctor, 2014. "Measuring Problem-Based Learning's Impact on Pre-Service Teachers' Mathematics Pedagogical Content Knowledge." 2nd International Higher Education Teaching and Learning Conference, 2013, Curtin University, Sarawak, Malaysia.

Masson, Steve, Patrice Potvin, Martin Riopel, and Lorie-Marlène Brault Foisy. 2014. "Differences in Brain Activation between Novices and Experts in Science during a Task Involving a Common Misconception in Electricity." *Mind, Brain, and Education* 8(1):44–55.

Mathan, Santosh, and Kenneth Koedinger. 2005. "Fostering the Intelligent Novice: Learning from Errors with Metacognitive Tutoring." *Educational Psychologist* 40(4):257–65.

Mauk, Michael D., and Tatsuya Ohyama. 2004. "Extinction as New Learning Versus Unlearning: Considerations from a Computer Simulation of the Cerebellum." *Learning and Memory* 11(5):566–71.

Meyers, Chet, and Thomas B. Jones. 1993. *Promoting Active Learning: Strategies for the College Classroom.* San Francisco: Jossey-Bass.

Michael, Joel. 2006. "Where's the Evidence That Active Learning Works?" *Advances in Physiology Education* 30(4):159–67.

Miller, George. 1956. "The Magical Number Seven, Plus or Minus Two: Some Limits on Our Capacity for Processing Information." *Psychological Review* 63:81–97.

Mink, Jonathan, Robert Blumenschine, and D. B. Adams. 1981. "Ratio of Central Nervous System to Body Metabolism in Vertebrates: Its Constancy and Functional Basis." *American Journal of Physiology* 241(3):203–12.

Nielsen, Jares, Brandon Zielinski, Michael A. Ferguson, Janet E. Lainhart, and Jeffrey S. Anderson Young He, eds. 2013. "An Evaluation of the Left-Brain vs. Right-Brain Hypothesis with Resting State Functional Connectivity Magnetic Resonance Imaging." *PLoS One* 8(8):e71275.

Ophir, Eyal, Clifford, Nass, and Anthony Wagner. 2009. "Cognitive Control in Media Multitaskers." *Proceedings of the National Academy of Sciences for the United States of America* 106(37):15583–87.

Pascarella, Ernest T., and Patrick T. Terenzini. 2005. *How College Affects Students: A Third Decade of Research*. 1st ed. San Francisco: Jossey-Bass.

Perry, Bruce. 2000. "How the Brain Learns Best." *Instructor* 110(4):34–35.

Prince, Michael. 2004. "Does Active Learning Work? A Review of the Literature." *Journal of Engineering Education* 93(3):223–31.

Rubinstein, Joshua, David Meyer, and Jeffrey Evans. 2001. "Executive Control of Cognitive Processes in Task Switching." *Journal of Experimental Psychology: Human Perception and Performance* 27(4):763–97.

Smith, Christine, and Larry Squire. 2009. "Medial Temporal Lobe Activity during Retrieval of Semantic Memory Is Related to the Age of the Memory." *Journal of Neuroscience* 29:930–38.

Solso, Robert. 2001. "Brain Activities in a Skilled Versus a Novice Artist: An fMRI Study." *Leonardo* 34(1):31–34.

Stroman, Patrick W. 2016. *Essentials of Functional MRI*. Boca Raton, FL: CRC Press.

Tamaki, Masako, Tsung-Ren Huang, Yuko Yotsumoto, Matti Hämäläinen, Fa-Hsuan Lin, José E. Náñez Sr., Takeo Watanabe, and Yuka Sasaki. 2013. "Enhanced Spontaneous Oscillations in the Supplementary Motor Area Are Associated with Sleep-Dependent Offline Learning of Finger-Tapping Motor-Sequence Task." *Journal of Neuroscience* 33(34):13894–902.

Tendler, Alex, and Shlomo Wagner. 2015. "Different Types of Theta Rhythmicity Are Induced by Social and Fearful Stimuli in a Network Associated with Social Memory." *eLife* 2015:4.

Terenzini, Patrick, Alberto Cabrera, Carol Colbeck, John Parente, and Stephanie Bjorklund. 2001. "Collaborative Learning vs. Lecture / Discussion: Students' Reported Learning Gains." *Journal of Engineering Education* 90:1.

Vincent, Jean Didier. 1990. *The Biology of Emotions*. Cambridge, MA: Basil Blackwell.

Weimer, Maryellen. 2013. *Learner-Centered Teaching: Five Key Changes to Practice*. 2nd ed. San Francisco: Jossey-Bass.

Weng, Helen, Andrew S. Fox, Alexander J. Shackman, Diane E. Stodola, Jessica Z. K. Caldwell, Matthew C. Olson, Gregory M. Rogers, and Richard J. Davidson. 2013. "Compassion Training Alters Altruism and Neural Responses to Suffering." *Psychological Science* 24(7):1171–80.

Xie, Lulu, Hongyi Kang, Qiwu Xu, Michael J. Chen, Yonghong Liao, et al. 2013. "Sleep Drives Metabolite Clearance from the Human Brain." *Science* 342(6156): 373–77.

2

Pedagogical Techniques for Creating a Community of Inquiry in Online Learning Environments

Andrea N. Hunt

Online learning is an extension of what was previously referred to as distance education, which was originally developed to provide educational opportunities for students who were geographically separated from a college or who had to work full-time. Since the 1960s, distance education evolved from an independent correspondence study to an online delivery (both synchronous and asynchronous) format using learning management systems or course websites. Online learning still serves the traditional distance education student population, but is increasingly seen as an option for on-campus students. The most recent data reported by Allen and Seaman (2015) suggest that 70 percent of academic leaders see online learning as critical for their long-term strategy. Because of this, the growth in online learning continues and is especially salient among two- and four-year public institutions that may be struggling with cost-effective ways to increase enrollment at their institutions.

As online learning has grown in the last several decades, scholarship in this area has also proliferated. Much of this research focuses on asynchronous classes and compares the effectiveness of online learning to face-to-face learning. While there is research that suggests that students in face-to-face classes outperform online classes in terms of grades (Logan, Augustyniak, and Rees 2002; Utrel 2008), other research has found little significant differences in academic outcomes between online learning and face-to-face learning when courses are designed according to best practices (Driscoll et al. 2012). However, even with similar outcomes, student satisfaction is often lower in online courses (Summers, Waigandt, and Whittaker 2005). The lower levels of satisfaction are often associated with less interpersonal interaction between students and professors (Delaney et al. 2010).

Since the literature has shown that one weakness of online learning is a lack of relational connections (see Tichavsky et al. 2015), then how do we create innovative and engaging online learning experiences to overcome this? First, this chapter will review the literature on students' perceptions and preferences for course delivery. Second, a conceptual model (i.e., the Community of Inquiry framework) for online learning is presented that connects social interaction, critical thinking, and effective course design to promote deep and integrated learning.

STUDENT PERCEPTIONS OF ONLINE LEARNING

Students who prefer online courses consistently report that it is more convenient for their schedules and allows for more flexibility than traditional classes (Daymont, Blau, and Campbell 2011; Picciano, Seaman, and Allen 2010; Tichavsky et al. 2015). In addition to the convenience and flexibility of online learning, some students prefer more independent learning experiences and are more comfortable writing on discussion forums than speaking in class (Tichavsky et al. 2015). Yet, students still cite negative learning experiences in online courses and a lack of satisfaction due to perceptions of disrespectful treatment by instructors, delay in instructor feedback, lack of community, and feelings of isolation from the instructor and peers (Bergstrand and Savage 2013; Delaney et al. 2010). Students who prefer face-to-face courses have concerns about self-motivation and more independent learning, which is central to success in online classes. In Tichavsky et al.'s (2015) research, students framed independent learning in a negative manner and expressed a need for more direct instruction than what they perceived occurs in online courses. Their preference for face-to-face classes was rooted in a "sage on the stage" model of teaching where a professor disseminates information to them and tells them the exact information they need to know. Instructors also report a sense of detachment from students in the online learning environment and are cautious about the value and legitimacy of online learning (Allen and Seaman 2015; Picciano et al. 2010).

Hybrid or blended learning integrates the benefits associated with the convenience and flexibility of online learning along with the interactional elements of face-to-face learning. Tichavsky et al. (2015) found that students took hybrid courses for the convenience but needed the extrinsic motivation that they perceived as coming from their instructors in the form of constant reminders about course work. While these students do mention the need for interaction, this interaction is not framed as mutual, but rather the physical presence of someone else in the classroom and information dissemination is perceived as interaction. Clayton, Blumberg, and Auld (2010) found that students preferred hybrid courses because of the emphasis on augmented learning. Further, Riffell and Sibley (2004) cite increased attendance during scheduled class meetings as a result of using a hybrid format.

To summarize, students take online courses primarily for the convenience and ability to self-pace, while other students cite the lack of interaction and motivation as obstacles to online learning. Given these findings, how do we create innovative and engaging online learning experiences that foster relational connections while also encouraging more self-directed learning? I would argue that the Community of Inquiry framework (Garrison, Anderson, and Archer 2000) provides a conceptual basis from which instructors can work to develop courses with opportunities for critical thinking, social interaction between students, and instructor feedback.

THE COMMUNITY OF INQUIRY FRAMEWORK

Online learning is often guided by e-learning frameworks or learning design theories that focus on instructional strategies without offering a comprehensive theoretical framework. Adult learning theories have also been widely applied to online learning (Cercone 2008) and conceptualize learning as encompassing the adult learners' self-concept, their experiences and resources for learning, readiness to learn, orientation (i.e., immediate need for knowledge rather than long-term application), and internal motivation. This approach does provide a more comprehensive attempt at understanding online learning than e-learning frameworks; however, the assumptions of the theory are solely grounded within the characteristics of adult learners and not college students of various ages.

A team of Canadian teacher-scholars developed the Community of Inquiry (CoI) framework (Garrison et al. 2000) as a conceptual tool for online learning. While this framework is not the only model of online learning, it is one of the most fully developed and empirically assessed frameworks to date. The CoI framework suggests that educational experiences are embedded within a community of inquiry composed of teachers and students. This notion of a community of inquiry stems from Dewey (1933) and Lipman (2003), who suggest that knowledge formation and scientific inquiry happen within a group and are embedded within larger social contexts. Thus, online classes can serve as a community of inquiry, and the separation of teacher and student should not concede the necessity of sustained and purposeful communication.

The CoI framework is a process model that addresses the purposeful connections between students, teachers, and course content. The CoI framework conceptualizes that learning occurs within the community of teacher and students through three different components of online learning: cognitive presence, social presence, and teaching presence. Cognitive presence is the most fundamental element of the CoI framework and refers to students' ability to construct meaning through sustained communication that is vital to critical thinking. Social presence is the ability of students and teachers in a community of inquiry to interact with others through different communication mediums and to know that "real" people are in the class with you. Teaching presence involves the design, facilitation, and direction of both cognitive and social presence to achieve the desired student-learning outcomes. The intersection of each of these three elements creates worth-while educational experiences, contributes to deep and integrated learning, and enhances metacognitive skills (Garrison and Akyol 2015; Lambert and Fisher 2013).

Elaboration of Cognitive Presence

Jaffee (2003) argued in *Teaching Sociology* that online classes need the active proc-ess of engagement, application, synthesis, and authentic understanding. This is essentially what happens when there is a cognitive presence in online classes. Cog-nitive presence encompasses course assignments and activities that use inquiry, exploration, reflection, and resolution (i.e., problem-solving) that focus on critical thinking. Cognitive presence might be one of the most difficult areas of the CoI framework because it depends on the development of higher-level thinking skills in the online environment. This means that instructors must use assignments that require critical thinking and reflection rather than rote memorization.

To achieve cognitive presence, there are phases of the inquiry process that must first begin with a *triggering event* that introduces an issue to be studied and explored. For example, Hauhart (2007) describes introducing students to Hoch-schild's (1989) study of working women's unpaid labor in the household and how this contributes to larger patterns of societal inequality. This serves as the point of entry (i.e., triggering event according to Garrison et al.'s [2000] framework) into the topic of inequality. Through *exploration,* students search for information about the issue both individually and collaboratively, and they use reflection and dis-course during this process. Hauhart (2007) accomplished this through the imple-mentation of a survey of household labor in his online course that became the basis of larger class discussions and student reflections about inequality.

To achieve the next step of cognitive presence, the instructors should provide prompts, probe the learning that has taken place, and allow for *integration* of the course material. This is akin to having students connect findings to course read-ings or comparing and contrasting arguments or evidence as a way to generate meaningful discussion. The final phase of cognitive presence is *resolution,* or the application of what students have learned to different settings (e.g., the workplace). Using Hauhart's (2007) exercise as an example, students see inequality in their everyday life and can become more mindful about the practices that reproduce inequality in interactions and social institutions.

Elaboration of Social Presence

Social presence refers to the ability of students to project personal characteristics and present themselves as "real" in mediated communication (Garrison et al.

2000). Social presence includes affective/personal communication, open communication (interaction), and group cohesion through collaboration (Vaughn and Garrison 2006). The focus is not on the type of technology per se, but on how technology facilitates meaningful interactions among students in online learning environments. Social presence is also a way for instructors to decrease the type of miscommunication that impedes learning in online contexts. To do so, interaction should be structured and systematic to help meet the student-learning outcomes.

Persell (2004) developed a structured approach to interaction in a sociology class to further the development of a community of learners and to encourage a deeper understanding of sociological ideas and thinking (i.e., cognitive presence). Although Persell's class was not fully online, she illustrates how online components can facilitate more meaningful dialogue and interaction between students. Students were required to participate in three web-based discussions throughout the semester and were assigned a role in the discussion forum. Those referred to as the *Staters* posted on the course website what they had learned from a reading, what was most difficult about the reading, and new sociological questions that were raised as a result of the reading. *Responders* addressed the difficulties posted by the *Staters* and responded to the questions the latter posted while also posing further sociological questions. Two days later, the *Integrators* synthesized and integrated what they had learned from the discussion posts, readings, and seminar discussion, and then they raised additional questions. Persell (2004) found that students showed an increase in engagement with ideas and readings. Students also showed a more complex understanding of the sociological perspective. Persell (2004) suggests that certain processes contributed to these outcomes that are consistent with the CoI framework: facilitating student access and review, providing all students with a voice, and presenting opportunities to engage in metacognition (Garrison and Akyol 2015). Persell's (2004) work demonstrates how online discussions in sociology can simultaneously increase social and cognitive presence.

Richardson and Swan (2003) found that students who perceived a higher social presence in the course also had higher perceptions of learning and course satisfaction. Their open-ended responses indicated that students perceived writing assignments to be the most beneficial for their learning in an online course because it offered opportunities for faculty and peer feedback and the ability to see other students' perspectives. Hostetter (2013) also assessed whether discussion forums, PowerPoint presentations, and weekly graded papers on readings affected social presence. Each pedagogical method had a significant effect on students' perception of social presence. Similar to Richardson and Swan (2003), discussion forums had a stronger effect on perceptions of social presence, which suggests that students see discussion forums as more effective for increasing interaction and a sense of community in online courses. Akyol and Garrison (2008) found that social presence was associated with higher course satisfaction but had no impact on students' perception of learning. Their findings might be due to the small sample size and less overall interaction on discussion forums because of these reduced numbers or differences in the survey instruments used across studies. However, teaching and cognitive presence did have a significant effect on students' perceptions of learning.

Joksimovic et al. (2015) used a different approach to studying social presence and examined 1,747 online discussion posts. They found that open communication was a significant predictor of final courses grades. Similar to Akyol and Garrison (2008), Joksimovic et al. (2015) found that teaching presence moderated the association between social presence and academic performance, which suggests that interaction alone does not positively affect students' academic performance, but rather the use of effective course design and opportunities for higher-order thinking skills in online classes.

Elaboration of Teaching Presence

Teaching presence is the part of the CoI framework that focuses on course design and facilitation and enables both social and cognitive presence. In semi-structured interviews with faculty, teaching presence ranked as the most important part of online course development because it enables the development of cognitive and social presence (York and Richardson 2012). Teaching presence has three components. First, instructional design and organization includes time parameters, utilizing technology effectively, and establishing "netiquette." This also includes how you plan on "chunking" content and assessments to create modules. Clark-Ibáñez and Scott (2008) describe using thematic content modules, for example, "What Is Sociology" for an introductory-level course, which would include a lecture, discussion prompts, assignments, and web links on the topic. Each module for the course should have a consistent layout and time parameters. Are they weekly modules, and when are assignments due each week? Ice et al. (2011) found that instructional design and organization were related to high student satisfaction and low disenrollment at a large, online university.

Second, facilitating discourse involves setting the climate for learning, prompting discussions, encouraging student involvement and engagement, and assessing the learning process. Clark-Ibáñez and Scott (2008) suggest that learning is most successful when students interact with their peers. Instructors can use ice-breaker discussion forums that are similar to ones they might use in a face-to-face classroom. This sets the tone that interaction is vital in online courses as well. Since most interaction in online classes takes place in discussion forums, it is imperative that instructors provide explicit prompts to explain the type of interaction expected from students. The lack of facilitation and prompt feedback is related to issues with online student retention (Ice et al. 2011).

Rusche and Jason (2011) describe one format of structured reflective writing that instructors can easily integrate into online social science classes. The structured reflection follows a Quotation, Concept, Comparison, Questions (QCCQ) format using the discussion forum tool provided in learning management systems. The students provide a quotation (2–4 sentences) that they feel represents the main idea of one of the readings assigned for that week. Students interpret and summarize the concept or idea in the quotation. Students then compare or contrast their selected reading to another reading from that week or in that unit. This can be challenging because it requires students to use higher-level thinking skills and move through the phases of cognitive presence by integrating course material. Students then pose their own critical thinking questions as part of the process of deep critical inquiry. The questions are intended to extend the class discussion by leading to deeper learning. To facilitate social presence, students respond to the questions posed by their fellow classmates and integrate course material in their replies. Instructor responses / interaction and grading the discussion forums is efficient because of the structured nature of the assignment, and direct and early feedback is essential for students to improve their quality of writing (Clark-Ibáñez and Scott 2008; York and Richardson 2012).

Protocols for discussion forums such as those offered by Rusche and Jason (2011) and Persell (2004) are effective in balancing cognitive, social, and teaching presence because they create more shared group cognition and student ownership of the discussion (Zydney, deNoyelles, and Seo 2012). Protocols also provide some structure for instructors as they give comments and feedback that push the discussion further. Clarke and Bartholomew (2014) examined instructor feedback on three different one-week modules from five courses and found that instructors did not use cognitive codes—that is, they were not supporting higher-order thinking in their comments and responses to students. However, their analysis did show that instructors were validating student comments, which set the tone for increased participation.

Last, direct instruction is the presentation of content and the resolution of technical issues (Garrison et al. 2000; Shea and Bidjerano 2008). Will material be presented through PowerPoints, Prezis, and course readings? Will material be presented by the instructor themselves through a video recording tool such as Mediasite (http://www.sonicfoundry.com/mediasite/) or Screencast-o-matic (https://screencast-o-matic.com)? What types of multimedia will be most effective in illustrating the course concepts? Direct instruction also involves troubleshooting any technical issues that might arise. Shea, Li, and Pickett (2006) found that effective instructional design and "directed facilitation" predicted students' sense of a learning community. This is likely due to the types of activities that are used to help students develop a sense of community in online courses (Shea et al. 2005) and the types of interactive technologies (e.g., audio feedback) that instructors integrate into courses (Ice et al. 2007).

APPLICATION OF THE COMMUNITY
OF INQUIRY FRAMEWORK

The CoI framework was influenced by John Dewey's (1933) work on the distinction between levels of learning. Critical thinking is often equated with higher-level thinking (Geertsen 2003). However, Dewey (1933) suggested that higher-level thinking is not synonymous with critical thinking, but that critical and reflective thought are both part of higher-level thinking. The use of structured writing assignments is consistent with the CoI framework and can increase critical and reflective thinking through the integration of social, cognitive, and teaching presences. In online courses, structured writing is often the primary way that students articulate their mastery of the course material. In doing so, they are cultivating skills in independent and creative thinking through the development of thesis statements and supporting those thesis statements with logical, rational, and appropriate evidence (Roberts 2002). Structured writing in online classes is also consistent with the CoI framework by providing opportunities to interact with classmates, the instructor, and the course material.

Maples and Taylor (2013) provide a creative, yet structured, writing assignment to teach social problems to undergraduate students. While they used the assignment in a face-to-face class, it can be easily implemented in online classes. For this assignment, students write a children's book about a social problem. The project gives students an opportunity to use their sociological imagination to understand social problems, gain research skills through the use of empirical evidence, and disseminate their findings in an alternative format. As Maples and Taylor (2013) note, this project can be modified for other courses and disciplines. For example, I used this assignment in an online Family Diversity and Social Change course in Fall 2014. The course included students from sociology, psychology, social work, criminal justice, and interdisciplinary studies. I used Susan Ferguson's *Shifting the Center* (2007) for the course readings, and the student-learning outcomes focused on cultural competence and information literacy. As such, this project provided multiple measures of the student-learning outcomes.

Maples and Taylor (2013) provide a set of handouts for the project; however, I modified the assignment to fit the purposes of my online course. The first step of the children's book project required students to choose a topic. This is akin to the triggering event according to the basic tenets of cognitive presence. Similar to Maples and Taylor (2013), I encouraged students to choose a topic that they were interested in or that was meaningful to them. I directed students to the Teaching for Change Bookstore (http://www.tfcbooks.org/) to find ideas for their topics and also shared video recordings of me showing them different children's books that had acceptable themes for the course. My assistance with the topic choice and use of video recordings helped establish teaching presence. Students submitted their topic on a discussion forum for others to see and included information on the angle that they would take with their topic, the reason for selecting the topic, and the benefit that this book would have to others. Students chose topics such as families in transition, same-sex families, foster children, multiracial families, military families, families and mental health, and families with special needs children.

After choosing a topic, students entered into the exploration phase of cognitive presence and found peer-reviewed research that they could use as evidence to shape their storyline. Students completed an article evaluation where they summarized a journal article, addressed how the article defined families and related families to other social institutions, described what they learned about their topic, and discussed how the article would help them approach writing their children's book. This was the integration phase of cognitive presence where students synthesized information that they previously had on their topic with new, empirically based information. Several weeks after submitting their topics, students submitted a draft of their children's book and participated in a peer-review process through Canvas (learning management system). Maples and Taylor (2013) suggest using a writing workshop as a way to establish connections and increase interactions with students. Since this was an online class, we accomplished this through peer review, which provided students a greater sense of social presence.

At the end of the semester, students submitted their final product—a completed book with a full storyline and illustrations (students used hand-drawn illustrations, photos of their own families, and clipart)—online for the entire class to view. Along with the story, the final project included an author's note that stated the topic clearly, explained the relevance of the book (i.e., the resolution phase of cognitive presence), provided a brief summary of the story, and explained the book's sociological perspective. The children's book project moves students through the phases of cognitive presence where they connect and apply new ideas to disseminate to their peers.

I implemented the children's book project in a Family Diversity and Social Change course with student-learning outcomes focused on cultural competency and information literacy. Students completed a pre-test and post-test related to cultural competency and information literacy. All self-reported measures of cultural competency increased between pre- and post-tests. Example statements included: "Even though my professional or moral viewpoints may differ, I accept the family/parents as the ultimate decision makers for services and supports for their children"; "I generally understand other cultures and cultural values. I know about the basic ways in which cultures are similar and the ways they are different"; and "I recognize and accept that individuals from culturally diverse backgrounds may desire varying degrees of acculturation into the dominant culture." Self-reported skill level in all domains of information literacy (i.e., information search, information evaluation, information processing, and information communication and dissemination) increased between pre- and post-tests. The change could be due to multiple factors other than the children's book project, such as the readings in Ferguson's *Shifting the Center* (2007). Nonetheless, students did attribute much of this change to the children's book project and commented on open-ended survey questions how they had to really know about their topic to explain it to a child-aged audience. Similar to the comments cited by Maples and Taylor (2013), students appreciated the different format for the writing assignment, and many involved their own children in the project. Several students commented that they would be able to use the children's book in their work settings.

While an assignment like the children's book project integrates cognitive, social, and teaching presence, it is not without challenges. This is a nonnormative assignment and students may have some resistance to it. It is necessary to show students that while it is a creative writing assignment, it is very structured and will be completed in different stages. Grading student work can always be challenging, especially with an assignment like this. Therefore, a teaching presence is imperative in establishing clear and detailed instructions and a grading rubric (see Maples and Taylor [2013] for more information on the children's book project including instructions and grading rubric).

CONCLUSION

The growth in online courses in the last decade is undeniable. Research on online education originally focused on comparability of student-learning outcomes. We have learned a great deal in this area, with research demonstrating that comparability in student-learning outcomes can be achieved across course delivery formats. Another area of growing research is on student perceptions of online learning and how this affects their preferences for course delivery. Findings show that students prefer online learning for very specific reasons (e.g., flexibility and control over pace of learning), while other students perceive online learning as lacking the relational connections that they seek. The Community of Inquiry framework is particularly helpful in shaping course design and the facilitation of online courses to increase the sense of community among learners. It calls for purposeful or intentional interactions between students, the student/instructor, and the student/course content. While students and instructors often perceive the online environment as lacking an interactional element (Tichavsky et al. 2015), the CoI framework gives instructors the tools to develop courses that have high levels of social, cognitive, and teaching presence. This chapter provided an overview of the CoI framework and practical pedagogical examples that are consistent with the CoI framework. The challenge for all instructors, no matter the learning mode, is to create student buy-in, design activities that encourage interaction and engagement, and create opportunities for students to integrate course material and apply it to real-world problems. While more work is still needed in this area, the CoI framework does give us a lens or conceptual model for developing courses that engage students with the content, other learners, and the instructor in order to create meaningful educational experiences.

REFERENCES

Akyol, Zehra, and D. Randy Garrison. 2008. "The Development of a Community of Inquiry over Time in an Online Course: Understanding the Progression and Integration of Social, Cognitive and Teaching Presence." *Journal of Asynchronous Learning Networks* 12(3–4):3–22.

Akyol, Zehra, and D. Randy Garrison. 2011. "Understanding Cognitive Presence in an Online and Blended Community of Inquiry: Assessing Outcomes and Processes for Deep Approaches to Learning." *British Journal of Educational Technology* 42(2):233–50.

Allen, I. Elaine, and Jeff Seaman. 2015. *Grade Level: Tracking Online Education in the United States*. Retrieved May 15, 2016 (http://www.onlinelearningsurvey.com/reports/gradelevel .pdf).

Bergstrand, Kelly, and Scott V. Savage. 2013. "The Chalkboard Versus the Avatar: Comparing the Effectiveness of Online and In-Class Courses." *Teaching Sociology* 41(3):294–306.

Cercone, Kathleen. 2008. "Characteristics of Adult Learners with Implications for Online Learning Design." *AACE Journal* 16(2):137–59.

Clarke, Lane Whitney, and Audrey Bartholomew. 2014. "Digging beneath the Surface: Analyzing the Complexity of Instructors' Participation in Asynchronous Discussion." *Online Learning* (formerly *Journal of Asynchronous Learning Networks*) 18(3):1–22.

Clark-Ibáñez, Marisol, and Linda Scott. 2008. "Learning to Teach Online." *Teaching Sociology* 36:34–41.

Clayton, Karen, Fran Blumberg, and Daniel P. Auld. 2010. "The Relationship between Motivation, Learning Strategies and Choice of Environment Whether Traditional or Including an Online Component." *British Journal of Educational Technology* 41(3):349–64.

Daymont, Thomas, Gary Blau, and Deborah Campbell. 2011. "Deciding between Traditional and Online Formats: Exploring the Role of Learning Advantages, Flexibility, and Compensatory Adaptation." *Journal of Behavioral and Applied Management* 12(2):156–75.

Delaney, Jerome, Albert Johnson, Trudi Johnson, and Dennis Treslan. 2010. *Students' Perceptions of Effective Teaching in Higher Education*. St. John's, Newfoundland: Distance Education and Learning Technologies.

Dewey, John. 1933. *How We Think*. Rev. ed. Boston: D.C. Heath.

Driscoll, Adam, Karla Jicha, Andrea N. Hunt, Lisa Tichavsky, and Gretchen Thompson. 2012. "Can Online Courses Deliver In-Class Results? A Comparison of Student Performance and Satisfaction in an Online Versus a Face-to-Face Introductory Sociology Course." *Teaching Sociology* 40(4):312–31.

Esterberg, Kristin G. 2002. *Qualitative Methods in Social Research*. Boston: McGraw-Hill.

Ferguson, Susan J. 2007. *Shifting the Center: Understanding Contemporary Families*. New York: McGraw-Hill.

Garrison, D. Randy, and Zehra Akyol. 2015. "Toward the Development of a Metacognition Construct for Communities of Inquiry." *Internet and Higher Education* 24:66–71.

Garrison, D. Randy, and Terry Anderson. 2003. *E-Learning in the 21st Century: A Framework for Research and Practice.* London: Routledge / Falmer.

Garrison, D. Randy, Terry Anderson, and Walter Archer. 2000. "Critical Inquiry in a Text-Based Environment: Computer Conferencing in Higher Education." *Internet and Higher Education* 2:87–105.

Geertsen, H. Reed. 2003. "Rethinking Thinking about Higher-Level Thinking." *Teaching Sociology* 31(1):1–19.

Gunawardena, Charlotte N., and Frank J. Zittle. 1997. "Social Presence as a Predictor of Satisfaction within a Computer Mediated Conferencing Environment." *American Journal of Distance Education* 11(3):8–26.

Hauhart, Robert C. 2007. "Teaching about Inequality in a Distance Education Course Using 'The Second Shift'." *Teaching Sociology* 35:174–83.

Hochschild, Arlie, with Ann Machung. 1989. *The Second Shift.* New York: Viking Press.

Hostetter, Carol. 2013. "Community Matters: Social Presence and Learning Outcomes." *Journal of the Scholarship of Teaching and Learning* 13(1):77–86.

Ice, Philip, Reagan Curtis, Perry Philips, and John Wells. 2007. "Using Asynchronous Audio Feedback to Enhance Teaching Presence and Students' Sense of Community." *Journal of Asynchronous Learning Networks* 11(2):3–25.

Ice, Philip, Angela M. Gibson, Wally Boston, and Dave Becher. 2011. "An Exploration of Differences between Community of Indicators in Low and High Disenrollment Online Courses." *Journal of Asynchronous Learning Networks* 15(2):44–69.

Jaffee, David. 2003. "Virtual Transformation: Web-Based Technology and Pedagogical Change." *Teaching Sociology* 31(2):227–36.

Joksimovic, S., D. Gasevic, V. Kovanovic, B. E. Riecke, and M. Hatala. 2015. "Social Presence in Online Discussions as a Process Predictor of Academic Performance." *Journal of Computer Assisted Learning* 31:638–54.

Lambert, Judy L., and Juenethia L. Fisher. 2013. "Community of Inquiry Framework: Establishing Community in an Online Course." *Journal of Interactive Online Learning* 12(1):1–16.

Lipman, Matthew. 2003. *Thinking in Education.* 2nd ed. Cambridge: Cambridge University Press.

Logan, Elisabeth, Rebecca Augustyniak, and Alison Rees. 2002. "Distance Education as Different Education: A Student-Centered Investigation of Distance Learning Experience." *Journal of Education for Library and Information Science* 43(1):32–42.

Maples, James N., and William V. Taylor. 2013. "Writing Children's Books in Sociology Class: An Innovative Approach to Teaching Social Problems to Undergraduate Students." *International Journal of Teaching and Learning in Higher Education* 25(3):1–11.

Persell, Caroline Hodges. 2004. "Using Focused Web-Based Discussions to Enhance Student Engagement and Deep Understanding." *Teaching Sociology* 32(1):61–78.

Picciano, Anthony G., Jeff Seaman, and I. Elaine Allen. 2010. "Educational Transformation through Online Learning: To Be or Not to Be." *Journal of Asynchronous Learning Networks* 14(4):17–35.

Richardson, Jennifer C., and Karen Swan. 2003. "Examining Social Presence in Online Courses in Relation to Students' Perceived Learning and Satisfaction." *Journal of Asynchronous Learning Networks* 7(1):68–88.

Riffell, Samuel K., and Duncan F. Sibley. 2004. "Can Hybrid Course Formats Increase Attendance in Undergraduate Environmental Science Courses?" *Journal of Natural Resources and Life Sciences Education* 33: 16–20.

Roberts, Keith A. 2002. "Ironies of Effective Teaching: Deep Structure Learning and Constructions of the Classroom." *Teaching Sociology* 30(1):1–25.

Rusche, Sarah Nell, and Kendra Jason. 2011. "'You Have to Absorb Yourself in It': Using Inquiry and Reflection to Promote Student Learning and Self-Knowledge." *Teaching Sociology* 39(4):338–53.

Shea, Peter, and Temi Bidjerano. 2009. "Measures of Quality in Online Education: An Investigation of the Community of Inquiry Model and the Next Generation." *Journal of Educational Computing Research* 39(4):339–61.

Shea, Peter, Chun Sau Li, and Alexandra Pickett. 2006. "A Study of Teaching Presence and Student Sense of Learning Community in Fully Online and Web-Enhanced College Courses." *Internet and Higher Education* 9:175–90.

Shea, Peter J., Chun Sau Li, Karen Swan, and Alexandra Pickett. 2005. "Developing Learning Community in Online Asynchronous College Courses: The Role of Teaching Presence." *Journal of Asynchronous Learning Networks* 9(4):59–82.

Summers, Jessica J., Alexander Waigandt, and Tiffany A. Whittaker. 2005. "A Comparison of Student Achievement and Satisfaction in an Online Versus a Traditional Face-to-face Statistics Class." *Innovative Higher Education* 29(3):233–50.

Swan, Karen P., Jennifer C. Richardson, Philip Ice, D. Randy Garrison, Martha Cleveland-Innes, and J. Ben Arbaugh. 2008. "Validating a Measurement Tool of Presence in Online Communities of Inquiry." *e-mentor* 2(24):1–12.

Tichavsky, Lisa, Andrea N. Hunt, Karl Jicha, and Adam Driscoll. 2015. "It's Just Nice Having a Real Teacher: Student Perceptions of Online Versus Face-to-face Instruction." *International Journal for the Scholarship of Teaching and Learning* 9(2). Retrieved April 29, 2016 (http://digitalcommons.georgiasouthern.edu/ij-sotl/vol9/iss2/2).

Urtel, Mark G. 2008. "Assessing Academic Performance between Traditional and Distance Education Course Formats." *Educational Technology and Society* 11(1):322–30.

Vaughan, Norman, and D. Randy Garrison. 2006. "How Blended Learning Can Support a Faculty Development Community of Inquiry." *Journal of Asynchronous Learning Networks* 10(4):139–52.

York, Cindy S., and Jennifer C. Richardson. 2012. "Interpersonal Interaction in Online Learning: Experienced Online Instructors' Perceptions of Influencing Factors." *Journal of Asynchronous Learning Networks* 16(4):81–96.

Zydney, Janet M., Aimee deNoyelles, and Kay Kyeong-Ju Seo. 2012. "Creating a Community of Inquiry in Online Environments: An Exploratory Study on the Effect of Protocols on Interactions within Asynchronous Discussions." *Computers and Education* 58(1):77–87.

3

Co-Teaching

Risks and Rewards

Renee Monson and Kristy Kenyon

WHAT IS CO-TEACHING?

In this chapter, we use the term "co-teaching" to refer to collaborative teaching: synchronous teaching partnerships between instructors of one or more college-level courses. These partnerships take a variety of forms, but all violate the norm of a solo instructor in a single, autonomous college course. The norm violation is particularly consequential at the micro level of classroom dynamics: in interactions between instructors, between instructors and students, and in the self-conscious (re)negotiation of the roles and identities that are taken for granted in solo college teaching (Preves and Stephenson 2009). Thus, we situate our discussion of what co-teaching is, how co-teaching affects students and faculty, and best practices for co-teaching within the "sociology of the college classroom" (Atkinson, Buck, and Hunt 2009; Macomber, Rusche, and Atkinson 2009).

Collaborative teaching's form and purpose vary along several axes. Most of the scholarship on teaching and learning (SoTL) literature explores the implications of how the faculty share the instructional spaces of the classroom / laboratory and syllabus. This ranges from the episodic integration of two or more distinct courses via multiple guest lectures and / or occasional joint class meetings (see Pharo et al. 2012; Todd and O'Brien 2016; Waltermaurer and Obach 2007), to alternating or hierarchically structured instructor presence and authority within one course (see Cordner, Klein, and Baiocchi 2012; Preves and Stephenson 2009), to an "equally co-authored" course and fully shared classroom space (see de Welde et al. 2014; Krometis et al. 2011; Vogler and Long 2003). Other sources of variation in co-teaching include whether the faculty are: peers or in a mentor-mentee relationship, a dyad or a larger team, and trained in the same or different disciplines. The wider SoTL literature focuses primarily on co-teaching across rather than within disciplines, and this chapter reflects that focus. A review of articles published in *Teaching Sociology* between 2000 and 2009 found that just 15 percent were authored or co-authored by nonsociologists and urged sociologists to participate more fully in interdisciplinary SoTL conversations (Paino et al. 2012). We respond to that call by grounding this chapter in accounts of co-teaching that do and do not include sociologists.[1]

This chapter also is informed by our experiences with twice co-teaching a bi-disciplinary course, The Politics of Reproduction. We designed the course to meet a perceived gap in the curriculum of Public Policy Studies, an interdisciplinary program at our institution with which we both were affiliated.[2] Our course addressed three broad policy areas in reproductive technology at the intersection of our two disciplines of sociology and developmental biology: preventing and interrupting pregnancy (contraception and abortion), facilitating pregnancy (IVF and surrogacy), and perfecting embryos, fetuses, and babies (sex selection, birth defects, and environmental impacts on fetal health). Our teaching partnership was a peer-peer dyad (both of us were tenured when we co-taught for the first time), and we mainly aimed for a fully collaborative approach. We discussed the structure and content of our lecture and in-class activities with each other in advance. On some days just one of us lectured; more often, one of us "took" the first part of the class and the other "took" the second part, or we jointly guided students through active-learning exercises (debates, role-plays, and small group discussions). When it was *not* "her" day, or when "her" part of the class had concluded, the other instructor typically sat among the students, took notes, and asked questions about the course readings, lecture material, and / or lab activities.

Finally, we incorporate evidence of student-learning experiences in our course, taken from end-of-term course evaluations and focus group discussions. In 2014 students completed the course evaluation using paper forms (response rate = 94 percent); in 2016 our institution used online forms (response rate = 74 percent). In both years, we asked two colleagues from the Center for Teaching and Learning (CTL) to conduct a 30–35-minute focus group discussion with our students in the penultimate week of the course to assess their learning experience.[3]

WHY CO-TEACH? EFFECTS ON STUDENTS AND INSTRUCTORS

Co-teaching, like most norm violations, is risky. Among other things, co-teaching means relinquishing "the authority [and protection] that being the sole teacher confers" (Allen, Floyd-Thomas, and Gillman 2001). Preves and Stephenson (2009) capture some of the uneasiness we may feel when we co-teach:

> Opening one's classroom up to the eyes of a colleague may provoke feelings of inse-curity and defensiveness about one's formerly unexplored and highly private class-room interactions. The fear of being viewed as incompetent may even prevent col-leagues from inviting each other into their classrooms for observation let alone teaming. It is strange and even a little disturbing how very private many of us are about what we do behind those (closed) classroom doors. (P. 248)

Preves and Stephenson (2009) argue that when we co-teach, we risk a less polished classroom performance and a more complex process of identity negotiation than when we teach solo. We risk the uncertainties of the unfamiliar terrain outside or even within our discipline. We risk conflict with or the judgment of our esteemed colleague (Shibley 2006). Students also may feel unsettled by the various ways that a co-taught course interrupts their normative expectations (Allen et al. 2001; Preves and Stephenson 2009; Vogler and Long 2003; Wilson and Kwilecki 2000), and so we risk unfavorable judgments or even hostility from our students as well. Why do it, then?

One argument is that co-teaching has positive effects on student learning and student attitudes toward course material. Vogler and Long (2003) found that most students in their two sections of a co-taught course perceived co-teaching to be effective for their learning. Instructors have claimed that co-teaching fosters criti-cal thinking (Borg and Borg 2001), depth of learning (Rooks and Winkler 2012), and / or integrative learning within and across disciplines (de Welde et al. 2014; Helms, Alvis, and Willis 2005; Krometis et al. 2011; Todd and O'Brien 2016; Wal-termaurer and Obach 2007). Claims about student learning and experiences in co-taught courses often rely on students' self-reports, either on course evaluations or through surveys or interviews, but occasionally student learning in co-taught courses is measured directly (Todd and O'Brien 2016).

How Does Co-Teaching Foster Student Learning?

If co-teaching is effective in fostering student learning, what are the mechanisms by which this is accomplished? The literature points to several interrelated mecha-nisms; each reveals the classroom as a social site that sociological theory can illu-minate (Halasz and Kaufman 2008).

Co-teaching can counteract the rationalization of higher education. It, like other violations of classroom norms (Albers 2009), disrupts predictable, efficient, stand-ardized, McDonaldized pedagogy (Ritzer 2004). This can enhance student engage-ment with course material and foster and maintain their "epistemological curios-ity" (Halasz and Kaufman 2008:304). However, some students will continue to prefer the more conventional mode of solo instruction (Vogler and Long 2003; Wilson and Kwilecki 2000). Other students' eventual engagement (or experience of "ecstasy" [Albers 2009]) may be preceded by a period of vigorous resistance to the norm violation of co-teaching (Allen et al. 2001; Vogler and Long 2003).

In our bi-disciplinary course, this pattern of initial student resistance often emerged as a claim of disciplinary identity. Students often claimed, "I'm not a science person" when explaining their failure to demonstrate understanding of developmental biology concepts on an exam, or they protested, "I'm pre-med" when complaining about their paper grade having been docked for writing errors. We read these claims as defenses of "college as usual" in which the natural sciences, social sciences, and humanities occupy separate silos, and students are permitted to "live" and perform in one silo at a time. But by the end of the course, students often described a journey toward acceptance of a different, integrated way of learning.

> I'm a sociology major and I've always had trouble in science and biology. So coming to this, when I can make a connection with a frame of mind that I struggle with— that's always my "a ha!" moment, and I always feel really accomplished for being able to do that. It's not like if you're a biology major you can just make this class about biology or if you're a soc major you can just make this about sociology. You're forced to go with both and develop either frame of mind that you're deficient in.

Co-teaching across disciplines (and across subfields within sociology) creates opportunities to interrogate language and epistemology as the tools of power they are (Halasz and Kaufman 2008). As instructors dialogically present different perspectives within sociology (Waltermaurer and Obach 2007) or across disciplines (Borg and Borg 2001; Krometis et al. 2011; Rooks and Winkler 2012; Shibley 2006), students gain an appreciation for the epistemological and methodological underpinnings of knowledge claims in particular disciplines and subdisciplines. They develop an awareness of how power operates discursively (Bourdieu 1999) and the ability to navigate this aspect of power more effectively themselves (Halasz and Kaufman 2008).

We witnessed several instances of this in our course, one in the context of a laboratory exercise in which students observed the process of fertilization and early development of *Xenopus laevis* (South African clawed frogs). This is a species in which fertilization and development happen externally and are thus observable. In the lab, we had students manually fertilize frog eggs with a small piece of testes from a male frog. Students then used a microscope to compare the physical properties of these "in vitro fertilized eggs" with those of unfertilized eggs, and of fertilized eggs produced through frogs' typical mating, as the embryos developed. Students were required to write up their observations, describing as concretely as possible what they actually saw under the microscope, and then propose an experiment for future study. In conjunction with this lab report assignment, we asked them to read Emily Martin's (1991) classic piece, "The Egg and the Sperm," which analyzed the gendered language used in scientific textbooks to describe conception.

It is remarkable how "femininely" the egg behaves and how "masculinely" the sperm. The egg is seen as large and passive. It does not *move* or *journey,* but passively "is transported," "is swept," or even "drifts" along the fallopian tube. In utter contrast, sperm are small, "streamlined," and invariably active. They "deliver" their genes to the egg, "activate the developmental program of the egg," and have a "velocity" that is often remarked upon. (P. 489)

A pre-med biology major wrote to us the night before her lab report was due:

Frustrated that as I am writing my experiment proposal I am using language that reinstates the active role of sperm and passive role of egg: "sperm must navigate through the layers of the egg to initiate fertilization." Awesome that I now recognize what the language perpetuates. Not so awesome that I will be spending twice the time trying to figure out ways to manipulate that language in a gender neutral way.

For this pre-med student, the frustrating experience of trying to express her scientific observations and questions in a "gender neutral way" sharpened her sociological understanding of how language constrains as well as expresses knowledge, and thus creates as well as reveals gendered worldviews.

Co-teaching across disciplines or subdisciplines encourages independent and critical thinking and models constructive disagreement. As Borg and Borg (2001) point out, students who

see two "experts" in the classroom who often disagree with one another and see issues in contrasting lights ... are less likely to mimic the professor's thoughts as their own in the hopes of getting a good grade because no matter which professor they mimic, the other professor disagrees with them! (P. 21)

Co-instructors' airing of their fields' epistemological and methodological differences models for students how peers can disagree in a collegial and productive fashion (de Welde et al. 2014) and how to "debate assertively" rather than "disagree disparagingly" (Letterman and Dugan 2004:79).

For example, the clashing ontological assumptions of our two disciplines initially came into view as we were planning out a "first day of class" exercise. We decided to ask our students why they thought The Politics of Reproduction was a bi-disciplinary course, and to brainstorm a list of "things we need to know" in order to engage with policy debates about reproductive technologies. We had in mind a vague notion that students would generate lists of "biological things" and "sociological things" that could be useful when engaging with these policy debates. As we continued to plan this exercise, it became clear that much more was at stake. Renee suggested that after the students had created their list of "things we need to know," we should organize the list into a kind of diagram or schematic, so as to draw the topics into relation with one another. To illustrate, she sketched a three-pointed triangle, with culture, social structure, and social institutions at each of the points, and with arrows going back and forth between each of the points. Kristy cocked her head and inquired, "Where is biology in this diagram?" Renee pointed to social institutions (e.g., modern medicine) and culture (e.g., the beliefs underlying positivism). "So," Kristy asked, "biology is just a subset or a subtopic in this frame?" Renee cocked *her* head, genuinely puzzled, and said, "Where else would it be? *Everything* is a subset in this frame." Kristy pointed out that the frame itself was a sociological one. Fair enough! Renee asked, "What diagram would you draw to organize the list of 'things we need to know'?" Kristy drew two overlapping circles and labeled them "the physical" and "the social." Renee's eyebrows shot up. "But nothing is outside the social, not even the physical world!"

The clashing ontological assumptions of sociology and biology entered the public space of the classroom when the Martin article, which our pre-med student found both "frustrating" and "awesome," triggered an impromptu in-class debate between the two of us on the social construction of scientific knowledge. Renee explained that for sociologists, the world *is* social, because humans are fundamentally social beings. "Think of an onion," she said, "where the layers are 'the social,' but if you peel all the layers of the onion away there is nothing left, and that is what humans are. So too with human efforts to apprehend the world around them: what we (think we) know about the world cannot be separated from the social nature of the knower." Kristy explained that for biologists, the world *is* physical: an apple, with a "real" core beneath the skin and flesh of the social. "Human efforts to know the physical world are affected by their social locations, of course," she said, "but there is still a real world that can be known and which exists independently of humans' (flawed) descriptions and analyses of it."

We relished our in-class debates, but worried about the advisability of "fighting in front of the children." Would our students misinterpret our disagreements as animus rather than animated intellectual engagement? We need not have worried. Two students once stopped into Renee's office hours and announced that "our favorite thing is when you and Professor Kenyon fight." Evidence from the course evaluations also suggests that airing our disciplinary disagreements had a positive effect on our students' learning. Two students responded to the question, "Convey to each instructor his/her most significant contribution to the course," with these comments:

The ability that you both have to portray to us when you were confused or disagreed. It made me feel more comfortable.

Loved the dialogue between the professors.

Co-teaching can challenge the conventional meaning of learning. Students have been socialized to believe that they are empty vessels waiting to be filled by a teacher (Freire 1998). To the extent that the co-instructors are learners, co-teaching can pull students into an alternative understanding of learning as a dialogic, lifelong, and joyful practice (Blanchard 2012; Shibley 2006). In our course, we decided not to try to master the other's discipline prior to the beginning of the term. Because we also aimed for a fully collaborative model of co-teaching we often moved back and forth between the roles of instructor and student in the classroom, but we did so in a particular way. When one of us sat among the students, took notes, and asked questions, our questions were similar to other students' questions in that they revealed a novice's confusion about the material our colleague was communicating. But our questions also were different, in that they evidenced the particular interests of an expert from a *different* discipline about *this* discipline. Thus we were not *either* an "expert" *or* a "novice-learner" in the classroom; instead, we moved back and forth between the roles of "expert" and "expert-*as*-novice-learner." Two students responded to the question, "Convey to each instructor his / her most significant contribution to the course," with references to this aspect of our classroom roles:

> I could tell that both instructors loved teaching this course and really wanted to be here and loved learning with us.

> Experienced much growth as a student and thinker because of the way the professors interacted.

How Does Co-Teaching Benefit Faculty?

The corporatization and commercialization of higher education can contribute to feelings of anomie among faculty (Halasz and Kaufman 2008). Co-teaching can combat these anomic tendencies by promoting what Durkheim termed organic solidarity among faculty across discipline, rank, or status (Allen et al. 2001; Letterman and Dugan 2004; Preves and Stephenson 2009). For example, Pharo et al. (2012) formed a collaborative cross-disciplinary network involving eight instructors who taught into each other's classes on the topic of climate change; they report that "the most positive aspects of the project were the collegiality and support for teaching innovation provided by peers" (p. 497). This kind of support also could be useful for less experienced instructors who collaborate with more senior instructors (see Cordner et al. 2012; Smollin and Arluke 2014), particularly if the senior colleague offers diagnostic rather than summative feedback (i.e., not intended for use in tenure or promotion reviews).

We found that co-teaching gave rise to many of the most joyful and deeply meaningful moments of our teaching careers. Because we were grappling with so many new concepts, arguments, bodies of evidence, and epistemological assumptions, we often commented, gleefully, that we felt like we were in graduate school again. In addition, we drew support, sustenance, and inspiration from each other's teaching. Like de Welde et al. (2014:118–19), we came away from the experience with greater clarity about "our own pedagogical styles and how we might grow in the classroom," and this led us to rethink some of our approaches to the material in our solo-taught courses. For example, Kristy now includes in her developmental biology course more explicit discussions of how biological research findings (and science more generally) are represented in political discourse in ways that scientists themselves would not endorse. After co-teaching with a developmental biologist, Renee now has a different and deeper understanding of Connell's (2009) theory of how social embodiment recreates gender relations over time. This has enriched the way she teaches Sociology of Sex and Gender. Finally, after co-teaching we began to collaborate on scholarly projects (on the curricular practice of interdisciplinarity, and on the place and purpose of the natural sciences in twenty-first century liberal education). In short, our co-teaching experience created rich opportunities for *our* learning and growth as teacher-scholars. As Shibley (2006) observed, the best team teaching experiences capitalize on the potential for colleagues to learn from each other.

HOW TO CO-TEACH WELL: CONSIDERATIONS AND BEST PRACTICES

Identifying Sources of Institutional Support

Early in the planning process, faculty should consider the impact of co-teaching on department and program staffing plans, and identify institutional commitments and resources that could support co-teaching pedagogy (Blanchard 2012; de Welde et al. 2014). At our institution there is a long history of institutional investment in interdisciplinarity. Until 2015–16, students had been required to complete both a major and a minor, one of which had to be disciplinary and one of which had to be interdisciplinary; an earlier iteration of the general curriculum had required that students take two different bi-disciplinary courses. In 2011–12, our provost and dean of faculty made funds available for new cross-disciplinary faculty collaboration, and we used one of these internal grants to develop our bi-disciplinary course.

We also leveraged our institution's curricular commitment to study-abroad programs to support our co-teaching. Our bi-disciplinary course counted as an intermediate-level elective for sociology but not for biology, so Kristy had to negotiate a way to teach outside of the biology curriculum in the face of considerable enrollment pressures in biology courses. Her department chair received adjunct support to replace this course by making the case that Kristy's co-teaching of our bi-disciplinary course contributed to the institution's curricular mission in ways that were comparable to faculty members leading study-abroad programs (and those faculty typically were replaced with adjunct support). Several authors report that they co-taught in response to institution-wide curricular initiatives aimed at enhancing the first-year student experience, fostering interdisciplinary learning,

developing online courses, or preparing students for postbaccalaureate employment (Goodman and Huckfeldt 2014; Heath and White 2013; Krometis et al. 2011;
Pharo et al. 2012). In short, co-teaching pedagogy can be incorporated in a variety
of institutional curricular priorities, particularly when new initiatives are proposed or trialed.

Course Planning and Preparation

Virtually all of the literature on co-teaching emphasizes the time-intensive nature
of course planning and preparation. Institutional constraints and other pressures
may truncate the planning timeline, but this likely will have negative effects on
both students and instructors (Goodman and Huckfeldt 2014). Devoting considerable time to course planning has important side benefits in building the mutual
trust, regard, and respect between instructors that will be crucial during the teaching of the actual course (Vogler and Long 2003).

Letterman and Dugan (2004) recommend that course planning include a focus
on pedagogy as well as course content: co-instructors should talk with other faculty who have co-taught, review the SoTL literature on co-teaching, and become
acquainted with one another's teaching styles. Shibley (2006:272) emphasizes that
the success of co-teaching hinges on negotiating differences in pedagogical styles
during the planning phase rather than in the classroom and addresses three
aspects of pedagogy as particularly important to clarify in advance: learning objectives, how to share leadership in the classroom itself, and how to resolve or close
each classroom session. One issue related to learning objectives involves thinking
through how prepared for and receptive to the co-taught course your students are
likely to be. Will the course be required or an elective, and what will be the prerequisites? Some of the most difficult co-teaching experiences reported in the literature involved interdisciplinary courses that were required (Goodman and Huckfeldt 2014) and / or enrolled students whose choice of major predisposed them to
resistance or hostility to different disciplines (Wilson and Kwilecki 2000). Todd
and O'Brien's (2016) account of their otherwise successful collaboration across
introductory environmental ethics and geoscience courses notes that some geoscience students were unprepared to engage with ethics as an academic discipline,
and that this had a negative effect on learning outcomes.

Our own experience suggests that a common prerequisite for all students
enrolled in a co-taught course may be beneficial. In 2014, the course prerequisite
was introductory sociology; in 2016, students could use either introductory biology or introductory sociology as a prerequisite. In 2016, we observed a more
muted level of class participation, and the focus group discussion at the end of the
course revealed more widespread anxiety about the relative disadvantage experienced by students with only one of the two permitted prerequisites. The next
time we teach the course, we plan to revert to the original design of requiring

introductory sociology so that all enrolled students have at least one disciplinary "language" in common.

The workload of course planning increases with the number of instructors and disciplines involved and the extent to which each instructor attempts to become acquainted with unfamiliar content in advance.[4] Letterman and Dugan (2004) recommend sampling the relevant literature of your co-instructor's field prior to co-teaching. Rooks and Winkler (2012) describe in detail how a co-teaching team of two sociologists and two social workers negotiated the selection of assigned course readings for a course on hunger and homelessness; this process revealed the depth and breadth of several theoretical and methodological differences between their disciplines. Pharo et al. (2012) found the use of a part-time facilitator essential to their eight-person team for bridging disciplinary language differences (as well as for relaying communication across subgroups when not everyone could meet at the same time). Krometis et al. (2011:77) reported that their four-person team devoted a full two years to course development; much of this focused on teaching each other basic vocabulary and tenets of their disciplines, which they found important for developing a "unified front" in the classroom.

Although we agree that being on the same page pedagogically with your co-instructor(s) is important to a successful co-teaching experience, we are less persuaded that it is crucial to front-load an in-depth exposure to your co-instructor's field in the course planning stage. We did not attempt to learn the fundamentals of each other's discipline in advance, and we think this choice had important benefits for our students' experience. Our approach to developing the course was akin to the construction of a suspension bridge, which is supported by cables attached to the ground and to the tops of two pylons built on either end of the central portion of the bridge's main span. The stages involved in building such a bridge include surveying the site, excavating for and pouring the two pairs of pylons, building the bridge spans, and finally attaching the cables. Our years of working together in the Public Policy Studies program were a crucial aspect of "surveying the site" of the future bridge. Once we decided to co-teach, we mainly stayed on our "own riverbanks" (disciplines) as we "excavated for and poured the pylons" (reviewed relevant literatures, chose texts, and planned laboratory exercises). It was not until we "built the bridge spans" (by writing the syllabus) and then "attached the supporting cables" (by actually teaching together) that we really began to learn the key concepts and epistemological assumptions of each other's disciplines. Thus, a good deal of our learning happened in the public space of the classroom, which allowed us to model learning for our students in a highly authentic way.

Classroom Dynamics

Every classroom, like every social site, is inflected by relations of power. Because co-teaching engenders different power dynamics than a solo-taught course, co-instructors should discuss their expectations and experiences regarding class-room management and authority during course planning. Part of this is about turf: whose course is it and / or which portions of the course belong to whom, and how will that be telegraphed to students?

Co-teaching also requires that co-instructors attend to how their *relative*, as well as particular, social positions will affect classroom dynamics (Allen et al. 2001; Preves and Stephenson 2009). Letterman and Dugan (2004:79) advise faculty to cultivate a keen awareness of their co-instructor's concerns about how their gen-der, race, class, age, and so on will be perceived by students, and to develop some mutual agreements about how to present themselves and respond to students in the classroom. In addition, co-teaching is an opportunity to diversify the instruc-tional perspective and expert identity that is presented to students (Halasz and Kaufman 2008; Wilson and Kwilecki 2000). De Welde et al. (2014) and Allen et al. (2001) draw on the insights of feminist standpoint theory in their recommenda-tion to be mindful of how the interaction between co-instructor(s) is part of what students are taught about what counts as knowledge, who is a knower, and how knowledge claims are legitimated or challenged.

No matter how carefully we try to plan in advance how to handle classroom dynamics among co-instructors and between students and co-instructors, unex-pected issues will come up in the classroom and will have to be addressed on the spot. Some of these will have to be navigated with your co-instructor in front of your students, exposing aspects of classroom management that usually happen "backstage" to students' gaze and evaluation (Goffman 1959, 1971). Preves and Stephenson's (2009) deeply thoughtful analysis explores how co-teaching inher-ently "blurs the distinction between front and back regions" of our teaching per-formances (p. 247). They comment that the ensuing "mess" was uncomfortable for each of them as well as for their students and speculate that it may have negatively affected students' evaluations of that course. As a solution, Preves and Stephenson (2009) recommend intensive and careful backstage planning in order to achieve and maintain a consistent "shared definition of the [classroom] situation," but urge co-instructors to recognize that

> a fair amount of front region classroom improvisation on the part of the teaching team will still be required. Furthermore, the teaching team will be far more effective in maintaining a consistent and convincing definition of the situation if they not only expect but also welcome improvisation as a regular feature of their performance rep-ertoire. (P. 255)

We wholeheartedly agree. We think that improvisation in the co-taught classroom—indeed in any classroom—is an important means of challenging the rationalization of higher education.

Assessing Student Learning

Being evaluated by multiple instructors with multiple perspectives (even if within a single discipline) can be stressful for students (Vogler and Long 2003). Dugan and Letterman (2008:14) found that some students in co-taught courses criticized co-instructors' lack of communication or organization, particularly when this made it difficult to "ascertain the professors' expectations and the way to earn good grades." Preves and Stephenson (2009) also comment that they exercised insufficient foresight about how to grade student work, and this caused them, as well as their students, some anxiety. One way to address these anxieties is to be especially explicit about learning goals and grading rubrics.[5] Another option, if the teaching collaboration is across multiple courses, is for each instructor to grade the students in their own course (Bakken, Clark, and Thompson 1998).

If co-instructors choose to each grade all of their students, it is important to think through how to handle the process of commenting on student work as well as the process and rubrics by which grades are actually assigned. In particular, co-instructors should consider the tradeoffs involved in grading separately or "with one voice." When we graded papers or exams, we each did a separate read of the work, assessed it a tentative overall grade, and then met to reconcile any differences in our grades through lengthy discussion and rereadings. But as we did our initial reads and made substantive comments directly on the paper or exam, we used different color pens that "marked" our comments explicitly as either Professor Kenyon's or Professor Monson's even more emphatically than did our different handwriting. Renee took the additional step of using a third color pen to designate students' writing errors in their papers. We did not discuss this with each other in advance, but simply applied the marking / commenting process we had developed in our solo-taught courses to our co-taught course. If we thought about it at all, we probably expected our students to experience this as a laudable effort at transparency in evaluating their work. Although some students may have had that reaction, many responded with confusion, defensiveness, and heightened anxiety about how to achieve "good" grades given the clearly distinctive ways that each of us assessed their work. The next time we co-teach, we may experiment with a more "unified front" approach to grading by utilizing online course management technology (see Heath and White 2013:26).

Assessing the Course

Dugan and Letterman (2008) found that students' appraisals of co-taught courses do not differ from their appraisals of conventional solo-taught courses. Their comparison of student evaluations of solo-taught courses and several types of co-taught courses used the same data collection instrument for all courses: a standard form developed by the Individual Development and Educational Center (IDEA)

that has been used to create a national "benchmark" database of course evaluations (Dugan and Letterman 2008:12–13). Yet they do not discuss whether and
how the same course evaluation structure may be appropriate for solo-taught and
co-taught courses. Many studies of the effectiveness of co-teaching for student
learning also rely on course evaluation data to support their claims, but most of
these are similarly silent on the question of whether and how standard course
evaluations should be used to evaluate a co-taught course.

In solo-taught courses, one form generally is used to evaluate both the course
as a whole and the instructor, and the evaluation form's structure typically pre-
sumes that "the two are one." But this is not the case for co-taught courses, no
matter what model of co-teaching is utilized. Various approaches can be used to
assess co-taught courses and co-instructors. Helms et al. (2005:32) chose to have
their students use separate evaluations for each member of the teaching team to
give feedback on their particular teaching style, but one evaluation for rating the
course content, materials, and testing. Despite their objections, the policy at Wilson and Kwilecki's (2000) institution "dictated that each instructor would be evaluated only by students registered for the [interdisciplinary] course in her department" (p. 148). Whether the evaluation of teaching at your institution is done via
peer observations of the classroom, student course evaluations, or some other
means, think through how you and your co-instructor(s) should be evaluated—as
one unit, as fully separate, or as some hybrid of these? Ask how these evaluations
will be used for tenure and promotion reviews at your institution.

IN SUM
Good Co-Teaching Is Good Teaching

Best practices for solo teaching also apply to co-teaching, if anything even more so.
Keep student learning at the center of your joint efforts. Clarify your learning
goals, use diverse pedagogies and modes of assessment, give frequent, useful, and
prompt feedback on student work, and make adjustments midstream as well as
before teaching the course again.

Good Co-Teaching Is Collaborative Teaching

However, choices about course content, pedagogy, and assessment have to be worked
out together, implemented in a coherent fashion across co-instructors, and evaluated
and adjusted as a team. You will need to work together on the form, substance, and
logistics of the collaboration before and throughout the term, regardless of the co-
teaching's type or purpose. A high level of mutual trust, regard, and respect is essential
for a successful collaboration between faculty, and a strong and transparent collaboration helps students to lean into rather than resist the nonnormative experience of a

co-taught course. Clear, thoughtful course structures, classroom routines, and expectations for student work are important for students' confidence that all is not chaos and that the complexity of a co-taught course need not be overwhelming.

Good Co-Teaching Is Collaborative Learning

In the best co-teaching experiences, we learn from and with our co-instructor. Risk-taking and vulnerability are inherent in the practice of collaborative teaching, as in all learning. Practice self-awareness and anticipate potential problems as much as possible, but realize you cannot anticipate them all precisely because— and to the extent that—you are a learner as well as an instructor in co-teaching. In the end, co-teaching is an unparalleled opportunity for faculty to model risk-taking, inquiry, disagreement, and dialogue, and thus inspire a lifelong love of learning in our students (Blanchard 2012).

NOTES

1. We direct readers who are especially interested in how sociologists engage in co-teaching to Cordner, Klein, and Baiocchi 2012; de Welde et al. 2014; Heath and White 2013; Letterman and Dugan 2004; Preves and Stephenson 2009; Rooks and Winkler 2012; Waltermaurer and Obach 2007.

2. There is a long tradition of co-taught, bi-disciplinary courses at our small liberal arts institution, and about a half-dozen are offered each year. The enrollment cap for bi-disciplinary courses typically ranges from 20–40 students; our cap was 25 students. The annual teaching load at our institution is 3–2; this course counted as a full unit in the teaching load for each of us. We discuss how to identify institutional resources to support co-teaching below.

3. We left the classroom while our CTL colleagues led and recorded this discussion; they later transcribed the recording, ensured that students were not identified by name in the transcript, and gave us the transcripts after we had turned in final course grades. We received permission from our institution's IRB to use the course evaluation and focus group data for research purposes.

4. Dugan and Letterman (2008) find that students preferred co-taught courses with just two instructors over those with three or more instructors. Such courses can feel "overwhelming" to students (Allen, Floyd-Thomas, and Gillman 2000:318; Krometis et al. 2011:73).

5. For an explication of how to conceptualize and assess levels of student learning in a co-taught interdisciplinary course, see Gouvea et al. 2013.

REFERENCES

Albers, Cheryl. 2009. "Teaching: From Disappointment to Ecstasy." *Teaching Sociology* 37(3):269–82.

Allen, Katherine R., Stacey M. Floyd-Thomas, and Laura Gillman. 2001. "Teaching to Transform: From Volatility to Solidarity in an Interdisciplinary Family Studies Classroom." *Family Relations* 50(4):317–25.

Atkinson, Maxine P., Alison R. Buck, and Andrea N. Hunt. 2009. "Sociology of the College Classroom: Applying Sociological Theory at the Classroom Level." *Teaching Sociology* 37(3):233–44.

Bakken, Linda, Frances L. Clark, and Johnnie Thompson. 1998. "Collaborative Teaching: Many Joys, Some Surprises, and a Few Worms." *College Teaching* 46(4):154–57.

Blanchard, Kathryn D. 2012. "Modeling Lifelong Learning: Collaborative Teaching across Disciplinary Lines." *Teaching Theory and Religion* 15(4):338–54.

Borg, J. Rody, and Mary O. Borg. 2001. "Teaching Critical Thinking in Interdisciplinary Economics Courses." *College Teaching* 49(1):20–25.

Bourdieu, Pierre. [1991] 1999. *Language and Symbolic Power.* Edited by John Thompson and translated by Gino Raymond and Matthew Adamson. Cambridge, MA: Harvard University Press.

Connell, Raewyn. 2009. *Gender in World Perspective.* 2nd ed. Cambridge, UK: Polity Press.

Cornder, Alissa, Peter T. Klein, and Gianpaolo Baiocchi. 2012. "Co-Designing and Co-Teaching Graduate Qualitative Methods: An Innovative Ethnographic Workshop Model." *Teaching Sociology* 40(3):215–26.

de Welde, Kristine, Nicola Foote, Michelle Hayford, and Martha Rosenthal. 2014. "Team Teaching 'Gender Perspectives': A Reflection on Feminist Pedagogy in the Interdisciplinary Classroom." *Feminist Teacher* 23(2):105–25.

Dugan, Kimberly, and Margaret Letterman. 2008. "Student Appraisals of Collaborative Teaching." *College Teaching* 56(1):11–15.

Fobes, Catherine. 2006. "Practicing Critical Pedagogy in Travel–Study Abroad: Teacher-as-Learner in Cusco, Peru." Pp. 7–13 in *Critical Pedagogy in the Classroom,* 2nd ed., edited by P. Kaufman. Washington, DC: American Sociological Association.

Freire, Paulo. 1998. *Pedagogy of Freedom: Ethics, Democracy and Civic Courage.* Lanham, MD: Rowman and Littlefield.

Goffman, Erving. 1959. *Presentation of Self in Everyday Life.* New York: Doubleday.

Goffman, Erving. 1971. *Relations in Public.* New York: Basic Books.

Goodman, Barbara E., and Vaughn E. Huckfeldt. 2014. "The Rise and Fall of a Required Interdisciplinary Course: Lessons Learned." *Innovative Higher Education* 39(1):75–88.

Gouvea, Julia Svoboda, Vashti Sawtelle, Benjamin D. Geller, and Chandra Turpen. 2013. "A Framework for Analyzing Interdisciplinary Tasks: Implications for Student Learning and Curricular Design." *CBE—Life Sciences Education* 12:197–205.

Halasz, Judith R., and Peter Kaufman. 2008. "Sociology as Pedagogy: How Ideas from the Discipline Can Inform Teaching and Learning." *Teaching Sociology* 36(4):301–17.

Heath, Sarah E., and Eva Roa White. 2013. "Walking the Line: Lessons in Online Interdisciplinary Instruction." *Currents in Teaching and Learning* 6(1):18–29.

Helms, Marilyn M., John M. Alvis, and Marilyn Willis. 2005. "Planning and Implementing Shared Teaching: An MBA Team-Teaching Case Study." *Journal of Education for Business* 81(1):29–34.

Krometis, Leigh-Anne H., Elena P. Clark, Vincent Gonzalez, and Michelle E. Leslie. 2011. "The 'Death' of Disciplines: Development of a Team-Taught Course to Provide an Interdisciplinary Perspective for First-Year Students." *College Teaching* 59(2):73–78.

Lattuca, Lisa R. 2001. *Creating Interdisciplinarity: Interdisciplinary Research and Teaching among College and University Faculty.* Nashville, TN: Vanderbilt University Press.

Letterman, Margaret, and Kimberly Dugan. 2004. "Team Teaching a Cross-Disciplinary Honors Course: Preparation and Development." *College Teaching* 52(2):76–79.

Macomber, Kris, Sarah E. Rusche, and Maxine P. Atkinson. 2009. "From the Outside Looking In: The Sociology of the College Classroom." *Teaching Sociology* 37(3):228–32.

Martin, Emily. 1991. "The Egg and the Sperm: How Science Has Constructed a Romance Based on Stereotypical Male-Female Roles." *Signs* 16(3):485–501.

Paino, Maria, Chastity Blankenship, Liz Grauerholz, and Jeffrey Chin. 2012. "The Scholarship of Teaching and Learning in *Teaching Sociology*: 1973–2009." *Teaching Sociology* 40(2):93–106.

Pharo, Emma J., et al. 2012. "Can Teacher Collaboration Overcome Barriers to Interdisciplinary Learning in a Disciplinary University? A Case Study Using Climate Change." *Teaching in Higher Education* 17(5):497–507.

Preves, Sharon, and Denise Stephenson. 2009. "The Classroom as Stage: Impression Management in Collaborative Teaching." *Teaching Sociology* 37(3):245–56.

Ritzer, George. 2004. *The McDonaldization of Society.* Revised New Century Edition. Thousand Oaks, CA: Pine Forge Press.

Rooks, Daisy, and Celia Winkler. 2012. "Learning Interdisciplinarity: Service Learning and the Promise of Interdisciplinary Teaching." *Teaching Sociology* 40(1):2–20.

Shibley, Ivan A. Jr. 2006. "Interdisciplinary Team Teaching: Negotiating Pedagogical Differences." *College Teaching* 54(3):271–74.

Smollin, Leandra M., and Arnold Arluke. 2014. "Rites of Pedagogical Passage: How Graduate Student Instructors Negotiate the Challenges of First-Time Teaching." *Teaching Sociology* 42(1):28–39.

Todd, Claire, and Kevin J. O'Brien. 2016. "Teaching Anthropogenic Climate Change through Interdisciplinary Collaboration: Helping Students Think Critically about Science and Ethics in Dialogue." *Journal of Geoscience Education* 64(1):52–59.

Vogler, Kenneth E., and Emily Long. 2003. "Team Teaching Two Sections of the Same Undergraduate Course: A Case Study." *College Teaching* 51(4):122–26.

Waltermaurer, Eve, and Brian Obach. 2007. "Cross Course Collaboration in Undergraduate Sociology Programs." *Teaching Sociology* 35(2):151–60.

Wilson, Loretta S., and Susan Kwilecki. 2000. "Economics and Religion: A Bridge Too Far?" *College Teaching* 48(4):147–50.

4

A Collaborative Affair

Connecting Students with the Community through Research

Michele Lee Kozimor-King and Barbara Prince

Community-based learning (CBL), with its strong pedagogical tradition, has grown in popularity and practice as a way to increase student involvement in the community as part of the learning process. However, for those unfamiliar with CBL, navigating the literature on the topic can be overwhelming, in part because of the nomenclature typically used. Numerous scholars have noted the multiplicity of terms (service-learning, community-based learning, community-based research, etc.) used interchangeably, or with minor differences, throughout the literature (e.g., Stoecker 2016; Wickersham et al. 2016). For example, according to Mooney and Edwards (2001) community-based learning "refers to any pedagogical tool in which the community becomes a partner in the learning process" (p. 182). There are numerous teaching pedagogies that are routinely included under the broad category of CBL, including out-of-class activities, volunteering, service add-ons, internships, service-learning, and service-learning advocacy (Mooney and Edwards 2001). More specifically, Wickersham and colleagues (2016) classify CBL as "a learning in which significant field work is guided by and grounded in academic reflection, differentiating this pedagogy from field-based learning that is not academically guided; for instance, many work-based internships and volunteer or co-curricular service activities" (p. 18).

One specific type of CBL with a long history of use in nursing and public health fields is community-based research (CBR). CBR has recently been gaining momentum within the social science classroom. Kerry Strand and colleagues (2003) define CBR as: "A partnership of students, faculty, and community members who collaboratively engage in research with the purpose of solving a pressing community problem or effecting social change" (p. 3). The Centre for Community-Based Research

(2016) describes CBR as *community-situated* because it begins with a research topic of relevance to the community partner and is carried out in community settings, as *collaborative* in that both community members and researchers share control of the research agenda, and as *action-oriented* because the process and results are useful to community members.

According to Strand et al. (2003) there are three core principles of CBR. First, CBR is meant to be a collaborative experience between the researchers and community members, not a situation in which one group is helping the other. Second, CBR aims to achieve social action and social change, which ultimately results in social justice. Third, CBR is meant to validate multiple sources of knowledge, encourage various methods of discovery, and share the knowledge obtained from the research. These core principles are what differentiate CBR from service-learning.

The National Service-Learning Clearinghouse defines service-learning as "a method of teaching and learning that connects classroom lessons with meaningful service to the community." CBR and service-learning are similar in that they use meaningful work with a community partner as a teaching and learning tool; however, they differ in their relationship with the community partner. According to Berman (2006), service-learning does not always achieve mutually collaborative relationships, but instead will sometimes emerge as volunteerism or charity (Lewis 2004). Furthermore, Wade (1997) points out that service-learning can sometimes widen the gap between students and the organization by highlighting the boundaries between the two. More specifically, the "server" (students) versus "served" (the community partner) mentality can emerge (Wade 1997). In contrast, CBR, when successful, involves capacity building and maintaining long-term collaborative relationships (Wallerstein and Duran 2006). Throughout the rest of this chapter we use CBR to refer to our projects. We start with a review of the literature, followed by examples and assessment from successful CBR projects, and then conclude with a step-by-step guide for designing and implementing your own CBR project.

WHY DO COMMUNITY-BASED RESEARCH?

The effects of CBL on outcomes for students, faculty, and community have been extensively examined across a variety of contexts (e.g., Celio, Durlak, and Dymnicki 2011; Eyler et al. 2001; Wickersham et al. 2016) and found to be beneficial (see Eyler et al. 2001). As with CBL more generally, CBR has been found to have numerous benefits for students, faculty, and the community partner (i.e., Bach and Weinzimmer 2011; Chapdelaine and Chapman 1999; Strand et al. 2003; Stocking and Cutforth 2006). Community-based organizations are often overworked, face enormous challenges, and are limited in their ability to address underlying causes of problems or affect structural changes within their organization (Strand et al. 2003). In addition, organizations are increasingly being asked to collect quantitative data to assess their success as an organization (Strand et al. 2003). CBR partnerships can help by taking pressure off of the community partner and acting as an important resource by designing, collecting, and assessing data for the organization. CBR partnerships can also benefit the community by helping the organization develop skills, expand resources, provide energy and expertise, and assist with the identification and securing of funding (Strand et al. 2003). Overall, CBR assists community organizations with capacity building in both the short and long term (Stocking and Cutforth 2006; Strand et al. 2003). In addition, the community partner receives assistance and becomes better equipped to improve their community as a result of the project (Bach and Weinzimmer 2011). CBR is a hands-on way of making a difference within a community (Chapdelaine and Chapman 1999).

Research shows that CBR projects directly benefit the students and faculty involved in the project. CBR provides students with a better understanding of the research process through the application of social science research to real-world settings (Bach and Weinzimmer 2011; Chapdelaine and Chapman 1999; Strand et al. 2003; Stocking and Cutforth 2006). Chapdelaine and Chapman (1999) found that the CBR project helped to improve students' writing skills, increase critical thinking, and solidify understanding of research method–specific skills. In addition, participating in the CBR project increased students' awareness of social issues, and students reported the experience as highly positive (Chapdelaine and Chapman 1999). Students also learned team-building skills, problem-solving skills, and interpersonal relationship skills (Stocking and Cutforth 2006).

CBR also provides benefits and opportunities for faculty. As Stocking and Cutforth (2006) state, "CBR provides the unique opportunity for faculty to integrate research, teaching, and service activities expected and valued in university settings. This integration is increasingly recognized as a criterion for promotion and tenure related to the scholarship of engagement" (p. 57). CBR has the potential to benefit faculty as it includes elements of research (often absent from traditional service-learning) that increase its credibility in some disciplines (Stocking and Cutforth 2006). CBR complements research agendas and allows faculty to apply their knowledge and skills in an applied way through collaboration with a community agency (Chapdelaine and Chapman 1999; Stocker and Cutforth 2006). Additionally, Chapdelaine and Chapman (1999) found that both faculty and students benefit from recognition of service by the university and community and from the rewarding collaborative interactions.

CBR PROJECTS AT ELIZABETHTOWN COLLEGE

Elizabethtown College is a private liberal arts college located in south central Pennsylvania with approximately 1,900 undergraduate students. For the past seven years the first author of this chapter has successfully integrated a CBR project into a required 300 level two-course sequence, Research Methods and Statistical Analysis, with six different community partners. The first project was conducted during the 2008–09 academic year.

Starting with the 2013–14 academic year, we began to formally assess student outcomes associated with the CBR project. We received IRB approval during August of 2013. During the first week of the methods course, all students complete a questionnaire consisting of 67 questions that examine satisfaction with experiences in the department, involvement and participation in the department, confidence in research skills, expectations of research methods and statistics, knowledge and excitement about working with the community partner, importance of the goals of the course, and basic demographics. Students receive the same questionnaire at the completion of the Research Methods course (fall semester) and again at the completion of the Statistical Analysis course (spring semester). This chapter presents the quantitative results from the pre-test and last post-test (collected at the end of the spring semesters) of all students enrolled in the Research Methods and Statistical Analysis courses at Elizabethtown College during the 2013–14, 2014–15, and 2015–16 academic years.

Beginning in the 2014–15 academic year, the Research Methods and Statistical Analysis course sequence received the Signature Learning Experience CBL designation. At the completion of the Statistical Analysis course, the Elizabethtown College Center for Community and Civic Engagement requires students to complete a short assessment of their Community-Based Learning experience to receive credit for the experience (in addition to successfully passing the class). The student quotes used throughout the remainder of this chapter are taken from the student reflection part of this assessment from the 2014–15 and 2015–16 academic years.

Benefits We Have Found

Consistent with the literature, we have found numerous positive outcomes for students as a result of participating in a CBR project. First, CBR has been a transformative experience for our students. For example, participation in the CBR project has contributed to increased graduate school applications and enrollment, led to changes in a concentration within the major, and introduced the possibility of research as a career. For example, a senior History and Sociology / Anthropology double major stated, "To experience first-hand everything that goes into this type of research will benefit me for the rest of my life."

Data from an end of semester survey suggest that the CBR project indirectly contributed to increased integration, social interaction, and a stronger tie to the departmental community. At the end of the CBR project, compared to the start of the CBR project, students reported being significantly more satisfied with interactions with fellow majors (t = −2.572; p = .013) and mentoring relationships with a faculty member or student teaching assistant (t = −2.557; p = .012). They also felt significantly more involved in the department (t = −4.761; p = .000).

Consistent with previous research, we found that participating in the CBR project develops professional skills and creates a culture of professionalism. At the conclusion of the CBR project, students reported feeling significantly more confident in specific research skills, such as assessing a client's research needs and making recommendations to a client. Students also noted in their written responses that one of the most positive experiences of working on the CBR project was the skills they developed. For example, a sophomore Sociology / Anthropology major stated, "I felt that the CBL project we conducted as a class allowed me to apply skills I learned in class in a real-world setting. I value these skills much more now because I can see first-hand how useful they are in life outside of Elizabethtown College." These skills such as working in teams, taking meeting minutes, giving presentations, and making recommendations to a community-partner are all transferrable to nearly all work environments.

Implementing a CBR project can assist with cohort career advising, including how the applicability of the skills acquired during the class is important for specific careers in the discipline. Students reported being significantly more satisfied with the quality of career advising after participating in the CBR project (t = −2.814; p = .006). Although we cannot say for certain that the CBR project caused these changes, qualitative responses from students indicate that their experiences in the CBR project helped shape their knowledge and decisions about careers. For example, a junior Mass Communications and Sociology / Anthropology double major stated, "The experience also allowed me to reflect on future career choices, and I am excited for further opportunities with the project."

DEVELOPING A CBR PROJECT

Now that we have identified the potential benefits associated with using CBR, both within the literature and from our personal experience, we intend to guide faculty through the steps needed to conceptualize, design, implement, and assess an effective CBR project. Despite the well-documented benefits of using CBR projects, such benefits are largely dependent on successful integration of these pedagogies into the course (Garouttee and McCarthy-Gillmore 2014). Although we will continue to use examples from the successful implementation of a CBR project in a Research Methods and Statistical Analysis course sequence, it is important to note that nearly any type of course can utilize CBR projects. As Strand et al. (2003) point out, one "rather obvious" place to use CBR to teach discipline-specific course content is in the social sciences (p. 125). The most important component is being able to connect the project to course content.

Step 1: Finding a Community Partner

The first step is to find a community partner willing to collaborate on a project. When looking for a community partner, it is important to broaden your definition of "community." As Strand et al. (2003) point out, community partners include, but are not limited to, educational institutions, community-based organizations, and any other type of group or agency that may not be in close proximity to the college / university but has similar values and goals. For example, we have partnered with a local living history museum in the same town as the college (Winters Heritage House Museum), groups / programs on campus (Elizabethtown College Student Senate and the Sophomore Year and Faculty / Staff Purposeful Life Work Retreats), a historical society approximately 30 minutes from the college (LancasterHistory.org), an honor society whose headquarters is four hours away from the college (Alpha Kappa Delta [AKD] International Sociology Honor Society), and a global partner whose headquarters is located over 8,500 miles away from the college (Mindanao Peacebuilding Institute Foundation). For your first CBR project it is important to choose locally, not globally. Global partnerships add a whole new layer of challenges: time differences, language barriers, international IRB, etc.

All of our partnerships developed from situations where each of the community partners expressed a need for or interest in the completion of research of some kind. Another option is for the instructor to approach a community partner to inquire about research needs. In our current assessment-based society, many organizations are deficient in the skills and resources needed to conduct assessment and analyze data. We have found community partners to be both enthusiastic and grateful for free or low-cost assistance, and they have been dedicated to providing an experiential learning opportunity for students. Interestingly, our community partners have been just as concerned about what the students have learned through the project as they have been about the recommendations made in the final report.

Initially, you may not be able to find a partner who expresses an interest in having research conducted for their specific organization. Another way to find a potential partner is through a center at your institution that is dedicated to civic engagement, service-learning, teaching and learning, or global citizenship. These types of centers often have connections with organizations in the local community, and they are a good place to start looking for community partners, especially for your first time implementing a CBR project in your course.

When choosing a community partner it is also important to match the topic of research to the course subject. For example, if you are implementing a CBR project in a social work class focused on aging, you will want to partner with an organization that deals with aging either directly (like a nursing home) or indirectly (like Meals on Wheels). If you implement a CBR project into a Research Methods course, the type of community partner or topic of research is not as important since the topic of interest for your students is everything research methods.

Another important consideration includes building a meaningful relationship between the students and the community partner. The degree of involvement by the community partner varies by their location, availability, and desire. Since students may not be doing much (or any) of their CBR work at the location of the community partner, creating connections will encourage greater investment in the project. For example, during the Winters Heritage House Museum and Lancaster-History.org projects, all students in the class took tours of the facilities. Alternately, when it is not possible for all students to physically meet with the community partner, it is important to find other ways to connect. For example, with the AKD project, several students volunteered to represent the class at the Eastern Sociological Society Annual Meeting, where they presented preliminary results of the project and met representatives of the community partner. Upon their return, the students related their experience to the rest of the class including the expectations the community partner had for the final product. All of our projects began with an initial research design meeting, in person, with the community partner.

Step 2: Learning about the Community Partner and Setting Goals

To design the most effective CBR project, it is imperative to fully understand the community partner's expectations of the project. This requires early, clear communication between the instructor and the community partner. Ideally, three to six months prior to the start of the CBR project, the instructor should establish the research question(s), anticipated research design, project objectives, and funding requirements with your community partner. The challenge is to anticipate the needs and barriers inherent in the project so you can help your students authentically navigate the discovery and problem-solving process. Having the research design and important details set up ahead of time with the community partner will allow you to guide your students through the important steps while alleviating high levels of stress and uncertainty during the project.

After you have learned about and communicated with your community partner, it is important to establish the specific student learning outcomes and project objectives. Both faculty (Polanyi and Cockburn 2003; Stocking and Cutforth 2006) and students (Willis et al. 2003) have attested to the importance of setting clear outcomes or goals at the beginning of a CBR project. It is essential to have student-learning outcomes, community-partner outcomes, and specific objectives for the project. This is also where you will establish the connection between the project and course content.

Step 3: Organizing Work Teams

Our version of CBR uses a team-based approach. Therefore, the next step is to create the work teams for the project. The number and type of teams will depend on the number of students in the class, the structure and needs of the community partner, and the project goals for the specific course. It is important that all teams have a roughly equal workload, even though the busy time may occur during different parts of the semester. For example, the IRB team will do most of its work early in the semester while the Report / Writing and Editing team will have more work toward the end of the semester.

A challenge with any type of group activity or assignment is determining how to create teams. Individuals enrolled in the methods course are required to complete a 30-minute online strengths assessment called the Clifton StrengthsFinder developed by StrengthsQuest and the Gallup Education Practice (focused on higher education). The StrengthsQuest inventory can be found at www.strengthsquest.com and costs approximately $10. The inventory identifies the top five talent themes, out of a possible 34, for each individual based on research within the field of positive psychology. Furthermore, the talent themes can be categorized according to four domains of leadership including executing, influencing, relationship building, and strategic thinking. Research by Rath and Conchie (2009) found that teams excel when strengths in each of the four domains existed; although each individual team member need not have strengths in a particular domain, the team should be well rounded. We used the collective results to group individuals into teams, with each team having members fitting within the four domains. Furthermore, using research examining Clifton StrengthsFinder and attending workshops held by a Strengths coach, we carefully distributed particular strength themes. The themes of competition, command, and social intelligence were carefully distributed to ensure that none of the teams would have more than one individual with those strengths to avoid conflict and allow for a greater likelihood of collaboration.

As Stocking and Cutforth (2006) point out, students' personal characteristics play a critical role in the success of CBR projects. Utilizing the StrengthsQuest inventory also helps you, as the instructor, to understand your class more holistically and know where you may need to allocate more time or resources. For example, if your class has no or very few executors, you may need to build in extra deadlines to help them get tasks completed in a timely manner. Similarly, if the class has few relationship builders, you may need to spend more time on relationship-based skills such as conflict management or ways to build cohesion and collaboration within the class.

In addition, if resources allow, it is ideal to have undergraduate or graduate teaching assistants (TAs) assist with the project. For our projects, we assign undergraduate TAs to each group, and they act as the liaison between the teams and the professor. This helps structure the project more like a "real world" consulting firm and allows for TAs to become more experienced on certain aspects of the project. TAs are responsible for meeting with teams, collecting and providing feedback on meeting minutes, keeping track of the tasks that need to be completed by each group, as well as being a resource for the project and community partner. This type of structure also helps alleviate some of the faculty workload.

Step 4: Establishing Professional Norms

It is vital to establish the professional norms for the course. One way we chose to do this is through the creation of a CBR resource guide. We titled this guide *The Research Methods Playbook* (because of our emphasis on teams and teamwork). We use it to help facilitate collaboration both within and between teams and the community partner. The TAs created our playbook, we update it every year, and we distribute it to the class during the first week of the semester. While our playbook has "Research Methods" in the title, the information included is applicable to any course containing a CBR project after some modification. Basically, your guide should contain resources that you think students need to be successful in the project, from general information about the structure of the project to specific templates. The playbook provides a more holistic approach to teaching that focuses on the whole student and helps provide additional information on "real world" skills, like collaboration, business casual attire, and writing meeting minutes. Previous research has noted the importance of providing students with clear support systems throughout the project (Stocker and Chapman 2006; Willis et al. 2003). Our playbook is one way we accomplish this.

Another way we establish professional norms throughout the project includes the keeping of meeting minutes. In order to foster greater accountability and transparency, and to track the decisions that have been made, we require that each team submit professional meeting minutes after each meeting. Even if your campus is not residential, students could meet as a team briefly during, before, or after class. All meeting minutes have to follow the same template and must be submitted to the supervising TA for approval within 48 hours of the meeting. At the conclusion of the project, we include all minutes in the final report that is submitted to the community partner.

Next, it is important to educate students about the difference between CBL, CBR, service-learning, and volunteering. Stocker and Chapman (2006) refer to this as "ensuring student readiness" that "relates to the extent which students are familiar with and sensitive to the community; understand the principles of CBR, and possess the relevant research skills and substantive knowledge" (p. 62). We accomplish this in our class by assigning required reading that includes specific articles on CBL and CBR. Students then have to answer questions about the definitions, benefits, and perceived challenges during the first group meeting. Not only does this help students become familiar with the different terms, we also use the assigned journal articles to discuss strategies for reading scholarly work. Finally, using the resources in the Playbook, the journal articles, and research about the community partner, the class develops an "elevator talk" summarizing the project that everyone in the class memorizes.

Step 5: Developing an Assessment Plan

Faculty will need to develop a project assessment plan that includes an evaluation of student performance. Evaluation of student performance has been identified as one of the most challenging aspects of implementation of CBR (Stoker and Curforth 2006). Some ways that student learning has been assessed in the literature include the evaluation of written components (Chapdelaine and Chapman 1999; Stoker and Curforth 2006) and field notes (Wickersham et al. 2016), as well as in-class and formal public presentations (Stoker and Curforth 2006).

At the conclusion of Research Methods, we base students' grades for the CBR project on several components: completion and quality of group tasks, submission and quality of group status reports and meeting minutes, the mid-project or final project report, and an end of semester assessment. We give the end of semester assessment to students during the last week of class, and structure it like a take-home final exam. The final assessment requires students to answer questions about all areas of the project, from research design and IRB to sampling and data collection, as well as provide a 250-word reflection on what they learned and their overall experience with the project.

While students may consult with each other and specific teams for answers to the questions, they are expected to write their reactions independently. The purpose of this assignment is threefold. First, this assignment allows us to evaluate who has been engaged with the material during class throughout the semester and to determine overall retention of material. Relatedly, this assignment rewards individuals and teams who have been collaborating and working diligently all semester. Third, the reflection piece serves as an assessment of learning, personal growth, and the value of CBR in the classroom.

It is important to note that in the six years we have been using a CBR project in the course sequence, not a single student has ever asked about how they are being graded for the project. In fact, it does not seem like the grade is the motivating factor for completion of the project. The students seem to care more about their team representing the college in the community. Additionally, students seem highly concerned that their final product accurately exemplifies the class and each individual's work ethic. Similarly, undergraduates from a variety of institutions stated, "As students, we were devoted to our projects well beyond just receiving grades" (Willis et al. 2003:40).

Students' grades on the CBR project during Statistical Analysis are based on several of the same criteria (completion and quality of group tasks, submission and quality of group status reports and minutes, and the final project report), but instead of an end of semester assessment, all students in the class present the project at Elizabethtown College Scholarship and Creative Arts Day (http://www.etown.edu/programs/scad/); present it at an additional conference, such as the Mid-Atlantic Undergraduate Social Research Conference or Eastern Sociological Society Annual Meeting; and participate in a presentation to the community partner (in some format). These presentation-type assessments align more closely with the "real world" skills and desired outcomes for the course. In addition, requiring students to present the project at the end of the semester keeps them motivated and on task to finish the project in a timely manner.

CHALLENGES

As with executing any project, creating a CBR project inevitably runs into at least one challenge. Every CBR project, no matter how well planned, is a work in progress. We have identified a few of the main challenges we have faced when implementing a CBR project.

Relationships

Although the CBL literature documents the benefits to students, faculty, and the community partner of collaboration, it has been our experience that students finish the project feeling more negative toward the community partner than at the start of the project. More specifically, while students were significantly more likely to think the community partner was important for the community ($t = -2.991$; $p = .004$), feel confident that they know a great deal about the community partner ($t = -7.023$; $p = .000$), and feel confident that they know a lot about the people who are serviced by the community partner ($t = -6.721$; $p = .000$), they were not significantly more excited about working with the partner. Students often voiced negative feelings about the community partner in class as well as in written feedback. For example, as a sophomore Sociology/Anthropology major stated, "It was also very time consuming and frustrating when the group we were working with wouldn't respond in a timely manner." While we do not suggest implementing a CBR project for the sole purpose of getting students to care about the community partner, we do believe collaborating with a community partner provides a rare opportunity to learn about patience and working in the "real world."

Time

As with any successful pedagogy, CBR projects are incredibly time- and work-intensive, for both faculty members and students (Chapdelaine and Chapman 1999; Polanyi and Cockburn 2003; Stocking and Cutforth 2003; Willis et al. 2003). On the part of faculty members, organizing and coordinating a CBR project often means 3–6 months of planning before the semester even begins. In addition, although this project is supposed to simulate a real-world work environment, these are still college students, so the normal 9–5 workday will not apply. You may have to make yourself available to meet with students outside of normal business hours.

CBR projects are often more time-consuming and demanding for students than traditional modes of assessment, such as exams. When asked to rate their agreement with the following statement, "I expect to view the course as involved, time consuming and / or demanding" on a scale from 1 (strongly disagree) to 5 (strongly agree) the students averaged a 4.18 at the pre-test, which increased to a 4.72 by the post-test ($p = .004$). So while students were expecting the course to be time-consuming and demanding, it ended up being even more so than they expected. As one senior English and Sociology / Anthropology double major stated, "The time commitment was my biggest challenge. Between other classes, two jobs, and an internship it took serious time management to get everything done."

Uncertainty

Another obstacle for faculty before (and while) implementing a CBR project is the high level of uncertainty (Chapdelaine and Chapman 1999; Stocking and Cutforth 2003; Willis et al. 2003). What if the community partner quits during the project? What if we do not complete the project? These same questions cause us to lose sleep every semester, even after successfully completing numerous CBR projects in the past. We have never had a partner quit nor have we ever failed to complete a project. Remember, no matter how much you plan, *something will go wrong*. For example, the day we launched the questionnaire for one of our CBR projects, the first author was sick at home and began receiving multiple emails from individuals trying to take the survey about an issue with one of the questions. She had to contact the class from home, who then had to figure out how to fix the problem remotely. Fortunately, the TAs were responsible, and the students had plenty of resources to problem solve. It ended up being a confidence-building experience for all involved. During another CBR project, students were supposed to interview individuals who participated in specific programs at a museum, but none of those who agreed to be interviewed beforehand showed up for the workshops. We had to make an onsite decision to interview anyone who was at the museum that day, eliminating some workshop-specific questions from the interview guide. Once you begin a CBR project, you must see it through to completion. Be prepared to assure students, and yourself, that through hard work and diligence, the project will come to a successful conclusion.

One problem we have encountered consistently is that the class fails to complete (to our standards) the final report. This is not to say that students did not do a great deal of work or that they just did not complete the project. Rather, it is our experience that students get busy with other tasks at the end of the semester and do not compile the final reports as carefully as we would like. Furthermore, previous research on CBR has stated over and over again that because of format, depth, and time commitments, CBR projects do not fit well within the traditional semester format (Stocking and Cutforth 2003; Willis et al. 2003). Since these reports are often all the community partner reads about the process, we want the final reports to be of the highest quality. We now plan for and expect to be editing the final report for the community partner over winter and summer break before we send it out. In addition, when funds are available, we have hired students to work as research assistants over break to finish the project. We are not alone; research shows that other faculty have had different students take over projects (Stocking and Cutforth 2006) or have had students finish on their own after the end of the semester either through grants, independent studies, honors projects, or being hired as research assistants (Stocking and Cutforth 2006; Willis et al. 2003).

FINAL THOUGHTS

CBR improves student learning, increases confidence in research skills, fosters professionalism, encourages relationship building, and increases interest in social issues. Furthermore, we have found CBR to be transformative, cohort building, skill developing, and rewarding. CBR has the potential to be successfully incorporated into any type of course using the steps identified in this chapter.

One unexpected benefit we have recently identified has been watching students use CBR and the skills they developed from the project independently in applied settings. We would like to close with a story of one particularly rewarding example. The past two years, the first author served as the faculty sponsor of an institutional team of students who participated in the Client Problem Solving Competition (formerly the Judith Little Problem Solving Competition) at the Association of Applied and Clinical Sociology (AACS) Annual Meeting. Prior to the meetings each year, the student team researched and co-authored a grant proposal that secured funding for the trip from the Dean of Faculty at Elizabethtown College. The proposal construction incorporated many skills and professional norms gained from the CBR project. Once at the AACS annual meeting, the student teams were well prepared for the intense 48-hour experience. The competition requires student teams to meet with a client where they were given a "problem" to solve, including the compilation of a literature review, data collection, writing an executive summary, and then presenting a "solution" to the client. This format closely resembled the CBR project described in this chapter. With a truncated timetable to work with for the competition, both student teams were able to use the skills they developed to successfully present their solution to a panel of eight judges including the client representative. The Elizabethtown College team was named the winning team both years. Another team will be competing this year to continue the tradition and once again test their skills obtained from the CBR project. We never anticipated that students from the course sequence would want to spend their Fall Break working 48 hours to complete a CBR project. Furthermore, the end goal for both teams was not to win; rather, it was to develop a viable solution for the community partner and provide the best possible supporting data. Without the CBR project, the team would not be prepared or interested in such a competition.

This chapter had three main goals: to provide a foundation of scholarship on CBR for faculty interested in pursuing and implementing their own CBR project; to provide background and assessment of our own CBR project in order to illustrate the benefits to students and faculty; and to serve as a practical guide for explaining how to successfully integrate a CBR project into a course. We hope you use information from this guide to create your own journey that will enable you to experience the benefits for yourself, your students, and your community beyond what we describe in this chapter.

REFERENCES

Bach, Rebecca, and Julianne Weinzimmer. 2011. "Exploring the Benefits of Community-Based Research in a Sociology of Sexualities Course." *Teaching Sociology* 39(1):57–72.

Berman, Sally. 2006. *Service Learning: A Guide to Planning, Implementing, and Assessing Student Projects.* Thousand Oaks, CA: Corwin Press.

Celio, Christine I., Joseph Durlak, and Allison Dymnicki. 2011. "A Meta-Analysis of the Impact of Service-Learning on Students." *Journal of Experiential Education* 34(2):164–81.

Chapdelaine, Andrea, and Barbara L. Chapman. 1999. "Using Community-Based Research Projects to Teach Research Methods." *Teaching of Psychology* 26(2):101–5.

Eyler, Janet, Dwight E. Giles Jr., Christine M. Stenson, and Charlene J. Gray. 2001. "At a Glance: What We Know about the Effects of Service-Learning on College Students, Faculty, Institutions, and Communities, 1993–2000: Third Edition." *Higher Education,* Paper No. 143. Retrieved September 15, 2016 (http://digitalcommons.unomaha.edu/cgi/viewcontent.cgi?article = 1137&context = slcehighered).

Garoutte, Lisa, and Kate McCarthy-Gillmore. 2014. "Preparing Students for Community-Based Learning Using an Asset-Based Approach." *Journal of the Scholarship of Teaching and Learning* 14(5):48–61.

Lewis, Tammy L. 2004. "Service Learning for Social Change? Lessons from a Liberal Arts College." *Teaching Sociology* 32(1):94–108.

Mooney, Linda A., and Bob Edwards. 2001. "Experiential Learning in Sociology: Service Learning and Other Community-Based Learning Initiatives." *Teaching Sociology* 29(2):181–94.

National Service-Learning Clearinghouse. N.d. "What Is Service-Learning?" Retrieved September 19, 2016 (https://gsn-newdemo2.s3.amazonaws.com/documents/1250/original/what-is-service-learning.pdf?1397836188).

Polanyi, Michael, and Lynn Cockburn. 2003. "Opportunities and Pitfalls of Community-Based Research: A Case Study." *Michigan Journal of Community Service Learning* 9(3):16–25.

Rath, Tom, and Barry Conchie. 2009. *Strengths Based Leadership: Great Leaders, Teams, and Why People Follow.* New York: Gallup Press.

Stocking, Vicki B., and Nick Cutforth. 2006. "Managing the Challenges of Teaching Community-Based Research Courses: Insights from Two Instructors." *Michigan Journal of Community Service Learning* 13(1):56–65.

Stoecker, Randy. 2016. *Liberating Service Learning and the Rest of Higher Education Civic Engagement.* Philadelphia: Temple University Press.

Strand, Kerry J., Nicholas Cutforth, Randy Stoecker, Sam Marullo, and Patrick Donohue. 2003. *Community-Based Research and Higher Education: Principles and Practices.* San Francisco: John Wiley & Sons.

Wade, Rahima C. 1997. *Community Service-Learning: A Guide to Including Service in the Public School Curriculum.* Albany: State University of New York Press.

Wallerstein, Nina B., and Bonnie Duran. 2006. "Using Community-Based Participatory Research to Address Health Disparities." *Health Promotion Practice* 7:312–23.

Wickersham, Carol, Charles Westerberg, Karen Jones, and Margaret Cress. 2016. "Pivot Points: Direct Measures of the Content and Process of Community-Based Learning." *Teaching Sociology* 44(1):17–27.

Willis, Jason, Jennifer Peresie, Vanessa Waldref, and Deirdra Stockmann. 2003. "The Undergraduate Perspective on Community-Based Research." *Michigan Journal of Community Service Learning* 9(3):36–43.

5

Strategies and Resources for Internationalizing the Curriculum

Christine K. Oakley

Anthony Giddens (2002) characterized globalization not as something solely "out there" (e.g., global financial systems, geopolitics, climate change), but included what is "in here" (sexuality, intimacy, work, family). Reimers (2016) reminds us that we live in a world where "[l]ocal and global affairs are deeply intertwined, and technology has transformed the ways in which most people interact, access knowledge, work, and participate civically." According to the American Council on Education's (2011) Blue Ribbon Panel on Global Engagement, colleges and universities are obligated to prepare students for the realities of living and working in a globalized environment "so that they can meet their responsibilities as citizens" (p. 14).

Yet only slightly more than half of colleges and universities identify some aspect of preparing students to engage and excel in a globalized world among their top five strategic priorities; less than a third have a comprehensive plan for integrating global learning into curricular and co-curricular offerings (American Council on Education 2012). The purpose of this chapter is to provide tools and strategies to educators who want (or have been asked) to "internationalize the curriculum." I begin with a brief discussion of historical and contemporary contexts in which higher education has been viewed as strategic in educating students for global engagement. I then introduce specific tools available to educators to "internationalize the curriculum," beginning with a more macro examination of a discipline's program of study, then identifying various ways to infuse globally related material into a specific course. The chapter ends with some tips for becoming more international as an educator, teaching students abroad, and teaching in an internationally diverse classroom.

HIGHER EDUCATION AS A SITE FOR INTERNATIONAL EDUCATION

It is important to understand the historical context of the contemporary internationalization movement in higher education to appreciate it as an ongoing process. The challenges posed by internationalizing our own approaches to teaching, research, and service are worth the effort, if the outcome is "informed, open-minded, and responsible [students] who are attentive to diversity across the spectrum of differences, [who] seek to understand how their actions affect both local and global communities, and [who] address the world's most pressing and enduring issues collaboratively and equitably" (Association of American Colleges and Universities n.d.).

Although higher education has always been "international," as travelers sought "learning, friends and leisure" in university cities in the Middle Ages (de Wit 2002:5), recognition of the value of global learning, as it is carried out on U.S. college campuses today, began in the twentieth century shortly after World War I. The founding of two present-day organizations, the Institute for International Education (IIE) in 1919 and the German Academic Exchange Service or DAAD (Deutscher Akademischer Austauschdienst) in 1925, to foster peace through understanding between nations through international educational exchange (de Wit 2002), marks the onset of this movement. After World War II, the Fulbright Act was passed to "[foster] bilateral relationships in which citizens and governments of other countries work with the U.S." (Fulbright 2016). Yet it was the Cold War and the success of the Soviet satellite Sputnik that crystallized the relationship between national defense and international education with rare federal dollars for education secured through the National Defense Education Act (NDEA) in 1958 for science, math, and foreign language training. In the following decade, Congress appropriated over a billion dollars to fund NDEA programs, resulting in a doubling of college enrollments between 1960 and 1970 (U.S. House 2016). However, the failure of the 1966 International Education Act, designed "[to] provide for the strengthening of American educational resources for international study and research" (IEA 1966), prompted one of the leading scholars on global issues in higher education, Hans de Wit, to conclude that the inherent value of an international education in and of itself is not strong enough to secure the type of economic and institutional support needed to transform colleges and universities into global institutions (2002).

Comprehensive Internationalization

De Wit's cautionary remarks are instructive for today's educators in two significant ways. Regardless of whether you want to infuse global content into a course or participate in assessing your department's curriculum for indicators of global

TABLE 5.1 Adapted from CIGE Model for Comprehensive Internationalization (2012)

Institutional Features	Areas of Inquiry
Articulated institutional commitment	Do mission statements, strategic plans, and formal assessment mechanisms express an institution's commitment to internationalization?
Administrative structure and staffing	Are there administrative / faculty positions dedicated to internationalization? Is there an International Office? Does it report to Student Affairs, the Provost, or the President?
Curriculum, co-curriculum, and learning outcomes	Are international opportunities, courses, and programs reflected in the general education and language requirements, co-curricular activities and programs, and specified student-learning outcomes?
Faculty policies and practices	Is there support for hiring international faculty? How well is international travel supported? Are international collaboration, study abroad, and international grant awards reflected in tenure and promotion policies?
Student mobility	What percent of students study abroad? What percent of students are international? Are there incentives for student-incoming and -outgoing mobility?
International collaboration and partnerships	Are there joint-degree or dual / double-degree programs with international partners? Are there incentives to form international collaborations?

SOURCE: American Council on Education. 2012. "Mapping Internationalization on U.S. Campuses: 2012 Edition." Washington, DC: American Council on Education. Retrieved December 30, 2016 (http://www.acenet.edu/newsroom/Documents/2011-CIGE-BRPReport.pdf).

learning, first learn about your institution's strategic, financial, and / or academic investment in internationalizing itself. Second, discover ways to become a part of that investment. By doing so, you may be able to access resources and collaborate with like-minded colleagues, who can assist you in this process. This section highlights some of those institutional elements that support comprehensive campus internationalization.

Hudzik (2011) defines comprehensive internationalization as "a commitment, confirmed through action, to infuse international and comparative perspectives throughout the teaching, research, and service missions of higher education" (p. 6). Over the past three decades much has been written about the value, barriers, structure, and politics of internationalization in higher education; for example, see Parcells, O'Brien, and Wordruff's (2013) comprehensive bibliography, in addition to Altbach and Knight (2007), de Wit (2002), Green (2012), Hudzik (2011), and Mestenhauser and Ellingboe (1998). The National Association for International Educators (NAFSA) and the American Council on Education's Center for Internationalization and Global Engagement (CIGE) have provided useful guides for initiating comprehensive internationalization. Altbach and Knight (2007) recognize, however, that while comprehensive internationalization appears to be a central influence in today's institutions of higher education, certain trends may affect its pace. Changes in national security and immigration policies that impact visa accessibility, for example, could affect both study abroad and international student recruitment, faculty exchange, and other factors impacting the cross-border academic initiatives that contribute to internationalization.

The general features in Table 5.1 can assist you in learning about the degree of internationalization on your campus. Ideally each feature should be both integrated throughout an institution's general policies, programs, and initiatives, and, of course, adequately resourced. Best practices recognized as notable achievements in comprehensive internationalization are available through NAFSA's Simon Internationalization Best Practices Index (2016).

INTERNATIONALIZING THE CURRICULUM

Given that the national averages for students studying abroad approximate the percent of international students studying in the United States (both around 5 percent) (Farrugia and Bhandari 2015), many institutions are looking for "at home" strategies to internationalize. Cogan (1998) asserts that until the curriculum is internationalized, "all other efforts [at campus internationalization] will be secondary" (p. 106). Leask (2013) defined internationalization of the curriculum broadly as "the incorporation of an international and intercultural dimension into the content of the curriculum as well as the teaching and learning arrangements and support services of a program of study" (p. 106). This definition allows for the internationalization of an entire program of study, as well as the individual course.

Curriculum Mapping

Internationalization of the curriculum is ideally accomplished by establishing general education and disciplinary-specific student-learning outcomes that contribute to global learning. One tool to evaluate the degree to which a program of study is internationalized is a curriculum map or curriculum matrix. Based on Jacobs's (1997) foundational work to foster curricular integration in K–12 settings, comprehensive curriculum maps are designed to graphically display: (1) an institution's expected undergraduate learning outcomes, (2) how these outcomes are operationalized in discipline-specific programs of study and / or the institution's general education curriculum, (3) which courses provide students with opportunities to accomplish these outcomes, and (4) what activities in those courses assess the degree to which a student achieves a level of competency of a given outcome. Institutions of higher education vary in their goals for constructing curriculum maps. For examples of discipline-specific curriculum maps, see Florida International University's online compendium of assessment rubrics and curriculum maps. For those seeking a simplified process, Carney (2015) offers easy-to-follow tips for map designs that identify gaps in the curriculum to fulfill student-learning outcomes. The CIGE has developed an Internationalization Tool Kit that offers extensive examples of internationalized curricula, co-curricula, and global learning outcomes.

The value of curriculum mapping to internationalization is twofold. It enables the examination of both institutional and disciplinary learning outcomes with global learning goals in mind. A map may also show the degree to which a program of study provides opportunities for students to gain global perspectives and intercultural skills by identifying which courses meet specific outcomes. If an introductory course, for example, is the only course in a program of study that provides "global content," to what extent would that curriculum be considered internationalized?

Course Content Infusion

Many of us may not have the opportunity to become involved with internationalizing the curriculum at that level, but would still like to internationalize a current course in our teaching portfolios. Cogan (1998) and others support this approach over the creation of new "global" courses. Groennings and Wiley (1990) reported an inattention to international content in courses they examined across the seven humanities, social science, and communication disciplines. They discovered that faculty with international interests and experience across these disciplines genuinely understood the positive relationship between global learning and student success after graduation, but that international content was isolated to a few general education courses and not incorporated throughout the curriculum.

Cogan (1998) offers three simple suggestions for infusing international content into existing courses. While he notes that these simple strategies are not "new or earthshaking . . . curricular infusion does require some international experience so that one's assumptions about the world and the way in which we do things are challenged" (p. 116).

1. Assign globalized reading material to ensure a variety of cultural perspectives and methodological approaches are used to explore a specific topic.
2. Construct assignments that enable cross-cultural perspectives and international foci, or require students to work with students from different cultural backgrounds. Baldassar and McKensie (2016), for example, incorporated the investigation of international students' lived experiences into the teaching of qualitative research methods. Through this course, students not only gained practical research experience, but by engaging with international students, they learned cultural perspectives from their peers in meaningful ways that served to advance campus internationalization. Bernardo and Deardorff's *Building Cultural Competence* (2012) is an excellent resource for intercultural communication activities and skill development. Written in a workbook format, this text offers explicit

classroom and professional development activities on topics such as understanding difference, navigating identity, building global teams, and managing cultural transitions. Each activity includes learning outcomes, facilitation tips, and debriefing strategies.

3. Use authentic globally related examples in lectures, discussion prompts, and visuals drawn from one's own international experiences. In my Global Leadership Capstone Course, I show videos from students who have traveled with me to share their research about a complex global issue. It is empowering for students to see their peers in Bangladesh, for example, discussing water filtration systems with villagers negatively affected by contaminated wells. Other examples of global infusion include inviting visiting international faculty to guest lecture or rewarding students for participating in relevant international activities on campus, such as International Women's Day or celebrating the Chinese New Year. It is important to note, however, that Cogan is not suggesting an "add global and stir" approach. Infusing global content into any course must enable a student to achieve a global competency objective established in the course's student-learning outcomes.

Another strategy for infusing global learning into existing coursework is to draw from the Association of American Colleges and Universities' VALUE rubrics. Although these 16 rubrics were designed for assessment purposes (VALUE = Valid Assessment of Learning in Undergraduate Education), they provide a wealth of ideas for curricular innovation and course revision. For example, the VALUE rubric for Intercultural Knowledge and Competence frames topics such as culture, empathy, and intercultural experience within the wider contexts of self-knowledge and personal and social responsibility. I use the Global Learning VALUE rubric as a scaffolding for my leadership course. Beginning with an examination of the self, the students have an opportunity to explore how culture influences certain aspects of their personal identity. The rubric enables me to systematically move from the micro (self-awareness), through intercultural skill development, to understanding the global systems and the importance of applying knowledge for social change. The VALUE rubrics can be especially useful in internationalizing the core requirements in a discipline such as introductory, research skills, theoretical foundations, and capstone courses.

Virtual Intercultural Exchange

The State University of New York was one of the first to experiment with using online technologies to enable intercultural learning between U.S.-based classrooms and students in classrooms abroad. Their resulting practice was termed Collaborative Online International Learning (COIL) (Rubin and Guth 2015).

COIL should not be considered a specific technology or set of technologies, but a framework that institutions can adapt to a wide variety of courses, disciplines, and levels of faculty expertise. The basic components include: (1) an international faculty partnership, (2) a collaborative assignment or project, and (3) online tools easily accessible in both countries. Some international faculty partners team-teach a course from a syllabus they co-designed within the context of the COIL framework, while others incorporate intercultural learning through one project or assignment using simple online technologies. Two excellent online resources that provide valuable information on the development and implementation of COIL courses are SUNY's COIL Center and the University of Washington's COIL Initiative.

Levinson and Davidson (2015) examined another approach to international education through the use of online learning. They observed parallel increases in two similar experiential learning trends: online learning and study abroad. They identified three different types of course offerings that combine these two trends to provide cross-cultural experience: virtual study abroad (no international travel), a hybrid of international travel and online learning, and comprehensive offerings that extend beyond a semester. Although they emphasize the need for rigorous student-learning outcome data, they suggested that such studies would best be collaborative efforts among international educators, experts in online learning, and researchers in the scholarship of teaching and learning.

Barriers to Faculty Engagement in International Work

Lisa K. Childress identified a number of barriers that impede faculty engagement in internationalization of the curriculum, as well as the mechanisms that institutions can use to overcome these barriers (cited in Leask 2013). She found a lack of financial resources for faculty international engagement as a commonly cited barrier, and she suggested that the provision of even small grants for international work, including those for internationalizing teaching and learning, can increase faculty involvement. She also identified a lack of recognition for international work in tenure and promotion and suggested that institutions not only reward international research, but also international fellowships and service. Goodwin and Nacht (1991) identified challenges posed to faculty who conduct work abroad. Their work relays some obvious, and a few subtle, costs of international travel. Even when the travel is for research purposes, faculty cited interruptions in graduate student mentoring, participation in departmental decision-making, and on-campus service obligations as "costs" of being abroad. While technology has mitigated some of the challenges to overseas communication, time differentials and in-country technical limitations still pose difficulties. They also mentioned the burden that international travel has on family, especially if a partner or child is unable to accompany the faculty abroad.

Despite these challenges, Ellingobe (1998) identified faculty engagement as one of six components that administrators, faculty, and staff indicated as key to campus internationalization. In her University of Minnesota case study, she found that faculty engagement contributed significantly to the availability of globally focused courses across the disciplines, to international collaborations, and to a more inclusive campus climate that fostered faculty interactions with international students and scholars. I have selected two additional ways faculty can foster global learning.

Faculty-Directed Study Abroad

Shari Becker Albright defines the global classroom as "one that creates a global vision and culture, recruits and prepares internationally-oriented teachers, transforms curriculum and instruction by integrating international content, emphasizes language proficiency, and expands student experiences through harnessing technology, international travel and partnerships, and international service learning and internships" (cited in West 2012:3). While this description is of a brick-and-mortar classroom, we can apply it to the study abroad classroom of a faculty-directed program. Faculty-directed (or faculty-led) study abroad programs are applicable to all disciplines from animal science to accounting. Faculty-directed study abroad programs are a form of experiential learning in which a faculty member directs the educational experience of students abroad, most commonly, for four to eight weeks during the summer. These programs often include teaching credit-bearing courses in a given program of study, facilitating excursions to in-country sites relevant to the course material, and providing opportunities for service learning or career development. Faculty, for example, might take a group of students to Brazil to study from-farm-to-cup coffee production, a crop not easily studied in the United States, or travel to Jordan to experience the history and preservation of the architectural wonders of Petra.

Many faculty engaged in this type of teaching and learning design programs for locations where they have international partnerships or collaborations, taking advantage of existing networks to design student-learning opportunities. This type of teaching, however, requires the same attention to student learning as does the development and delivery of an on-campus course. It is imperative that the academic rigor, course contact hours, and adherence to an itinerary that maps activities to student-learning outcomes is equal to or even exceeds that of a traditional class.

While there are inherent challenges engaging in international travel with undergraduates, with the proper training, support, and program design, directing a study abroad program provides a learning experience for both faculty and students that is not achievable in a campus classroom. It enables faculty to explore alternative teaching styles and develop assessment tools for experiential learning. It also provides students the opportunity to learn course material in a culturally relevant environment (Hulstrand 2006).

While NAFSA and the Forum on Education Abroad have resource materials on faculty-directed programs, the best resource for faculty interested in this type of international engagement is their institution's study abroad office.

International Pedagogy

In 2014–15, the number of international students studying in the United States increased by 10 percent, bringing the number of students from all over the world to 975,000 (Farrugia and Bhandari 2015). Although student mobility is an essential element of comprehensive internationalization, faculty may not be prepared to teach a diverse array of international learners. While much has been written about the institutional and pedagogical impact of international students and scholars on campus (Parcells et al. 2013), the University of Michigan Center for Research on Learning and Teaching offers accessible online resources for effectively engaging international students in the classroom. These practical approaches are effective in creating a safe and supportive environment for diverse student learners. The following examples are among the simplest to incorporate into current teaching practices:

- Slow down; use a lecture pace that allows time for note-taking
- Provide an agenda or outline for each class
- Post PowerPoint slides
- Illustrate key points with visual material
- Create study guides and study questions to help students prioritize reading material
- Ask all students to write responses to questions asked in class; ask students to read their responses
- Use pairs so all students can talk about an idea
- Clarify idioms and cultural references when used
- Question generalizations and cultural stereotypes
- See difference as a valuable resource in the classroom to facilitate learning from various cultural perspectives

CONCLUDING THOUGHTS

As professional educators, faculty have an obligation to prepare students to lead and excel in a global society. Although efforts to internationalize the curriculum require time and resources, pedagogical change, and in some cases a disciplinary stretch, the potential impact on student learning and the development of intercultural competency cannot be understated. While much work needs to be done to assess the relationship between our work to internationalize the curriculum and our students' global competency, it has been my experience as an international educator that our work has contributed to the development of global citizens. I have been privileged to see this transformation in many of my students, whether they have studied abroad or gained their global perspectives "at home." Their willingness to learn, their commitment to social justice, and their courage to bridge cultural and language differences inspires me to continue to be engaged in this rewarding work.

REFERENCES

Altbach, Philip, and Jane Knight. 2007. "The Internationalization of Higher Education: Motivations and Realities." *Journal of Studies in International Education* 11(3–4):290–305.

American Council on Education. 2011. "Strength through Global Leadership and Engagement." Washington, DC: ACE. Retrieved December 30, 2016 (http://www.acenet.edu /news-room/Documents/2011-CIGE-BRPReport.pdf).

American Council on Education. 2012. "Mapping Internationalization on U.S. Campuses: 2012 Edition." Washington, DC: ACE. Retrieved December 30, 2016 (http://www.acenet .edu/news-room/Documents/2011-CIGE-BRPReport.pdf).

American Council on Education. 2016. "CIGE Model for Comprehensive Internationalization." Washington, DC: ACE. Retrieved December 30, 2016 (http://www.acenet.edu /news-room/Pages/CIGE-Model-for-Comprehensive-Internationalization.aspx).

Association of American Colleges and Universities. N.d. "VALUE Rubric Development Project." Washington, DC: AACU. Retrieved January 8, 2017 (https://www.aacu.org /value/rubrics).

Association of International Educators (NAFSA). 2016. "Simon Internationalization Best Practices Index." New York: Association of International Educators. Retrieved January 2, 2017 (http://www.nafsa.org/SearchExcerpt.aspx).

Baldassar, Loretta, and Lara McKenzie. 2016. "Beyond 'Just Being There': Teaching Internationalization at Home in Two Qualitative Method Units." *Teaching Sociology* 44(2): 84–95. Retrieved August 28, 2016 (http://journals.sagepub.com/doi/abs/10.1177 /0092055X16631126).

Bernardo, Kate, and Darla Deardorff, eds. 2012. *Building Cultural Competence: Innovative Activities and Models.* Sterling, VA: Stylus.

Carney, Elizabeth. 2015. "Curriculum Mapping: A Quick Guide for Programs." Pullman: Washington State University. Retrieved January 2, 2016 (https://atl.wsu.edu/documents /2015/03/curriculum-mapping.pdf).

Cogan, John. 1998. "Internationalization through Networking and Curricular Infusion." Pp. 106–17 in *Reforming the Higher Education Curriculum: Internationalizing the Campus,* edited by Josef Mestenhauser and Brenda Ellingboe. Phoenix, AZ: Oryx Press.

Deutscher Akademischer Austauschdienst (DAAD). 2016. "From the Very Beginning." Bonn, Germany: DAAD. Retrieved December 30, 2016 (https://www.daad.de/der-daad /ueber-den-daad/portrait/en/32996-from-the-very-beginning/).

de Wit, Hans. 2002. *Internationalization of Higher Education in the United States of America and Europe.* Westport, CT: Greenwood Press.

Ellingboe, Brenda. 1998. "Divisional Strategies to Internationalize a Campus Portrait." Pp. 198–228 in *Reforming the Higher Education Curriculum: Internationalizing the Campus,* edited by Josef Mestendauser and Brenda Ellingobe. Phoenix, AZ: Oryx Press.

Farrugia, Christine A., and Rajika Bhandari. 2015. *Open Doors 2015 Report on International Educational Exchange.* New York: Institute of International Education.

Florida International University. 2017. "Rubrics and Curriculum Maps." Retrieved January 2, 2017 (https://assessment.fiu.edu/resources/rubrics-and-curriculum-maps/index.html).

Fulbright U. S. Student Program. 2016. "History." New York: Institute of International Education. Retrieved December 30, 2016 (https://us.fulbrightonline.org/about/history).

Giddens, Anthony. 2002. *Runaway World: How Globalization Is Reshaping Our Lives.* New York: Routledge.

Goodwin, Craufurd, and Michael Nacht. 1991. *Missing the Boat.* New York: Cambridge University Press.

Green, Madeleine. 2012. "Measuring and Assessing Internationalization." Washington, DC: Association of International Educators. Retrieved August 28, 2016 (http://www.nafsa.org/_/File/_/downloads/measuring_assessing.pdf).

Groennings, Sven, and David Wiley, eds. 1990. *Group Portrait: Internationalizing the Disciplines.* New York: American Forum.

Hayward, Fred. 2000. *Internationalization of U. S. Higher Education.* Washington, DC: American Council of Education. Retrieved January 4, 2017 (http://www.nyu.edu/classes/jepsen/internationalreport2000.pdf).

Hudzik, John. 2011. "Comprehensive Internationalization." Washington, DC: Association of International Educators. Retrieved August 28, 2016 (https://www.nafsa.org/uploadedFiles/NAFSA_Home/Resource_Library_Assets/Publications_Library/2011_Comprehen_Internationalization.pdf).

Hulstrand, Janet. 2006. "Abroad on the Fast Track." *International Educator* (May–June):47–55. Retrieved January 9, 2016 (https://www.nafsa.org/_/File/_/education_abroad_fast.pdf).

Institute of International Education. 2016. "A Brief History of IIE." New York: Institute of International Education. Retrieved December 30, 2016 (http://www.iie.org/Who-We-Are/History#.WGbL933Auj4).

International Education Act of 1966, Public Law 89–698. U. S. Government Printing Office. Retrieved October 29, 2016 (http://uscode.house.gov/statutes/pl/89/698.pdf).

Jacobs, Heidi Hayes. 1997. *Mapping the Big Picture: Integrating Curriculum and Assessment K–12.* Alexandria, VA: ASCD.

Leask, Betty. 2013. "Internationalizing the Curriculum in the Disciplines—Imagining New Possibilities." *Journal of Studies in International Education* 17(2). Retrieved August 15, 2016 (http://journals.sagepub.com/doi/abs/10.1177/1028315312475090).

Levinson, Nanette, and Kaitlin Davidson. 2015. "Linking Trajectories: On-line Learning and Intercultural Exchanges." *International Journal for the Scholarship of Teaching and Learning* 9(2). Retrieved August 28, 2016 (http://digitalcommons.georgiasouthern.edu/ij-sotl/vol9/iss2/3/).

Mestenhauser, Josef, and Brenda Ellingboe, eds. 1998. *Reforming the Higher Education Curriculum: Internationalizing the Campus.* Phoenix, AZ: Oryx Press.

Parcells, C., M. K. O'Brien, and G. Woodruff. 2013. "Bibliography: Internationalizing Higher Education." University of Minnesota: GPS Alliance. Retrieved December 31, 2016 (https://global.umn.edu/icc/documents/bibliography_intlz_higher_ed.pdf).

Peltier, Kathryn. 2015. "Engaging Global Challenges: The Interconnected Effects of Individual Actions." *Diversity and Democracy* 18(3). Retrieved January 2, 2017 (https://www.aacu.org/diversitydemocracy/2015/summer/editor Jan 4).

Reimers, Fernando. 2016. "Turning Students into Global Citizens." *Education Week* 35(37):21. Retrieved August 28, 2016 (http://www.edweek.org/ew/articles/2016/08/03/turning-students-into-global-citizens.html).

Rubin, Jon, and Sarah Guth. 2015. "Collaborative Online International Learning: An Emerging Format for Internationalizing Curricula." Pp. 15–27 in *Globally Networked Teaching in the Humanities: Theories and Practices,* edited by Alexandra S. Moore and Sunka Simon. New York: Routledge.

United States House of Representatives. 2016. "History, Art, & Archives." Washington, DC: U.S. House of Representatives. Retrieved December 30, 2016 (http://history.house.gov/HouseRecord/Detail/15032436195).

University of Michigan. 2016. "Teaching International Students: Pedagogical Issues and Strategies." Ann Arbor: University of Michigan. Retrieved August 28, 2016 (http://www.crlt.umich.edu/internationalstudents).

West, Charlotte. 2012. "Toward a Globally Competent Pedagogy." Washington, DC: Association of International Educators. Retrieved August 14, 2016 (https://pdfs.semanticscholar.org/b301/362dfbb5a05820dd71a41f36095d8743c64c.pdf).

6

Flipping Out

Understanding the Effects of a General Education Flipped Classroom on Student Success

Craig Douglas Albert, Stacie K. Pettit, and Christopher Terry

The authors would like to thank Taylor Thompson for her technical support in the completion of this chapter.

The present study investigates the effects a flipped university classroom has on student success. It seeks to investigate the relationship between the flipped design on student performance and content knowledge in an introductory American Government core curriculum class. Specifically, this chapter addresses the question, "Does a flipped classroom model improve performance and content knowledge?" We expect to find that this model does indeed improve student success in both areas. The expectation is that a high correlation exists between the flipped model and an increase in student performance measured by a decrease in Ds, Fs, and student withdrawal (DFW) rates and an increase in student performance measured by end-of-course grades (As and Bs particularly, or AB rates). We also expect the findings to show that students in this pedagogical environment improve their general knowledge content at a level higher than students taking the same course, but with a traditional lecture format.

This study is the result of a two-phased process. The first phase, or the pilot study of the class, was run in the Spring semester of 2015 and generated mixed results on the relationship between the flipped classroom and student engagement, performance, and satisfaction (Albert, Pettit, and Terry 2016). Importantly, Phase I produced a valuable "lessons-learned" study that helped the investigators redesign the course taking into account those lessons. The present chapter seeks to incorporate results from Phase II, measuring the effectiveness after designing the pilot study and implementing changes based on the pilot-study findings. Essentially, we posit that the flipped model engages students far better than other class-room techniques and argue that to increase student persistence rates, end-of-course grades, and general content knowledge, and to decrease DFW rates, this pedagogy should be more widely implemented, especially in required core classes throughout the general education curriculum. We proceed in four main sections. The first section contains a brief review of the literature pertinent to the flipped classroom pedagogy. Second, this chapter discusses the methodology, research design, and university/class dynamics and course design. Third, this chapter delivers the results of Phase II, comparing them to the Phase I data. Last, it con-cludes with a discussion of the results of, and limitations to, the flipped pedagogy and the direction for future research. This section concludes with ideas for satis-factorily implementing a flipped classroom. Although this study is specific to a political science course, we believe it is generally applicable to any social science course. To begin, this chapter examines the flipped concept in the literature.

THE FLIPPED PEDAGOGY

This literature review begins with defining flipped pedagogy and listing similar models of teaching and learning. Although there is no single way to flip a class-room, the main purpose of flipping is to shift responsibility for learning from the teacher to the student. According to Bergmann and Sams (2012), flipping a class is more of a mindset than a formula, with the goal being for students to learn instead of just completing assignments. Instead of the traditional model of listening to a lecture in class and working on problems at home, students read material and view videos before coming to class. The at-home assignments prepare students for in-class activities that engage students in active learning such as case studies, labs, games, simulations, or experiments (Herreid and Schiller 2013). Other similar models include blended learning, hybrid learning, reverse instruction, and the 24/7 classroom. Nearly every discipline and major in higher education has attempted to integrate flipping in some way.

Researchers have varying thoughts on what aspects are crucial to flipped class-rooms. Although they found few studies that met the criteria, according to Bishop and Verleger's model (2013), flipped classrooms must have interactive group-learning activities inside the classroom and direct computer-based individual instruction outside the classroom. To counter some misconceptions about flipped learning, the Flipped Learning Network (2014) has identified four pillars of F-L-I-P: Flexible environment (students choose where and when they learn), Learning culture (shift from instructor-centered to student-centered), Intentional content (what is taught directly or self-taught), and Professional educator (planning and expertise are crucial). These pillars combine to form the definition of flipped learning as "a pedagogical approach in which direct instruction moves from the group learning space to the individual learning space, and the resulting group space is transformed into a dynamic, interactive learning environment where the educator guides students as they apply concepts and engage creatively in the subject matter" (p. 1). Interestingly, Bishop and Verleger (2013) believe flipped classrooms must use computers, but the pillars of F-L-I-P do not include that as a criterion. The present study is consistent with addressing the elements from all aforementioned definitions of flipped classrooms by including interactive activities for group learning in the classroom, individual instruction outside class using technology, as well as student choice and flexibility that comes from thoughtful planning by a professional educator.

Although it is not a requirement to use technology such as YouTube, textbook publishing ancillaries, or learning management systems to create learning outside of the designated classroom time, we believe these technologies are effective in utilizing the flipped classroom model. The SAMR model—substitution, augmentation, modification, redefinition—is a useful lens through which to evaluate flipped classroom practice. According to the hierarchal SAMR model, which helps educators infuse technology into teaching and learning (Puentedura 2012), flipped learning should occur at the modification (third) level of technology use and student engagement. In the SAMR model, the lower two levels merely enhance an existing activity. Meanwhile, the higher two levels are actually transformational in nature because the technology is being used to do things not otherwise possible without the implementation, instead of just being used to substitute or augment an activity that already exists. Specifically in our context, the opportunities provided for in-depth class explorations as a result of flipped learning would not be possible without the flipped implementation, in which case the current example successfully falls into the targeted modification level of SAMR.

Research on flipped classrooms has yielded positive results across disciplines on student learning and engagement (Bishop and Verleger 2013). These positive interdisciplinary results have come from Programming, Physical Therapy, Nursing, History, Chemistry, Architecture, and Calculus, among others (Alpaslan, Cavlazoglu, and Zeytuncu 2015; Harrington et al. 2015; Murphree 2015; Murray, McCallum, and Petrosino 2014; Souza and Rodrigues 2015; Yestrebsky 2014; Zappe et al. 2009;). Flipped classrooms have also been utilized with positive results in courses that were not previously "lecture-heavy" and with English Language Learners (ELLs) (Hung 2015; Kvashnina and Martynko 2016). Kvashnina and Martynko (2016) found that ELLs demonstrated a positive reaction to the flipped classroom model and benefited from being able to work at their own pace, the amount of materials at various levels of English difficulty, and the development of autonomous learning skills.

Some researchers claim that since beginning college students do not have much exposure to online learning, they are potentially receptive to "new methods, tools, and interventions to help them navigate this evolving environment" (Lang and O'Connell 2015). Additionally, others contend that students are accustomed to digital learning, so instructors are speaking their language through the implementation of flipped learning (Bergmann and Sams 2012). Taken either way, flipped learning opens possibilities for innovative and motivating classrooms in the twenty-first century.

The literature on flipped classrooms includes a variety of benefits found with use of the model, such as an increase of student interaction and a strengthening of relationships (Bergman and Sams 2012). Other benefits include differentiation, elimination of many classroom management issues, and making the instructors' objectives transparent (Bergmann and Sams 2012). Additionally, results from a chemistry course using flipped instruction showed increased performance with higher exam scores and overall class success (Ruddick 2012). Furthermore, Nouri (2016) focused on students' perception of the flipped classroom model within the context of a postsecondary research methods course and found statistically significant differences between low achievers and high achievers in evaluations of the use of video components, the sense of increased learning, and the perception of *more effective* learning in the flipped model; low achievers reported a stronger positive perception of these elements and outcomes in their own learning. The flipped classroom model can also be a way to encourage the development of community as a tool to create student involvement (McCallum et al. 2015). For example, one student participant reported, "If we didn't have so much activity, I wouldn't be able to know her (the instructor) so well. Otherwise, I would just be staring at the board and taking notes" (Nouri 2016:49). Another student says of the classroom environment, "There is more bonding. . . . You don't get that when you have a bunch of lecture classes. I mean, we actually enjoyed it because you were trying to compete with other people and you're not thinking about it, but you are actually learning about some of the terms" (p. 49). The class time created through online learning at home can be used to create "student-centered activities that require communication and collaboration—necessary components of a community of inquiry" (Tucker 2012:198).

In summary, flipped learning has the possibility of deepening concept learning in mathematics, providing time for practical use of language in a foreign language class, focusing on inquiry learning in science, and allowing for integration of more current events in social studies. Bergman and Sams (2012) provide a helpful question to frame decisions concerning flipped learning: "Which activities that do not require my physical presence can be shifted out of class time to activities that are enhanced by my presence?" (p. 96). Hopefully, using this guiding question can help ensure the use of flipped learning in meaningful ways across courses of higher education. This chapter next discusses the structure of the experimental class used in both phases of this project, focusing on best pedagogical practices in a flipped design. This section also discusses the study's research design and methodology.

CLASSROOM DESIGN, RESEARCH DESIGN, AND METHODS

Before beginning to describe the research design and methodology, it is first necessary to describe how the flipped model was used in this particular class, which we developed from best practices. With some modifications, it can be implemented in any general curriculum course. We would like to convey that the following is not meant to be a fully inclusive review of how a flipped pedagogy can be utilized; rather, it is one of many ways to do so successfully, especially in the social sciences and humanities. For the sake of brevity, we cannot fully explain all the methods associated with flipping, but we would like to emphasize that Socratic-based classrooms, those with little to no use of technology, and the use of in-class applications activities all work in addition to what follows. There are many ways to flip effectively. What proceeds is a quasi case-study example. The university where we used this model is located in the Deep South and has approximately 8,500 students, including undergraduate, graduate, and medical students. It is a public research institution. The institution has recently merged two separate universities into one; one was formerly a standalone medical college, the other, a commuter liberal arts college. Currently, and during all phases of this study's investigation, the university has focused on becoming a tier-1 research institute. Most students live off-campus, but around a thousand students live in campus residence halls. The course under investigation (Introduction to American Government) is required by the state legislature for all students in order to earn a degree. Therefore, each class has a mixed population of majors and nonmajors, military, and a few nontraditional students (over the age of 25). Most students are underclassmen, but it is not unusual to have a few upperclassmen. Typically, each class is capped at 30 students, though combined sections of up to 75 students are not rare and were included in the control and experimental sections for the purposes of this study.

Learning from best practices in the literature, as well as data from Phase I, the primary investigator (PI) decided to implement the flipped design in several ways. First, the professor recorded all course lectures via video, but rather than recording an actual lecture, the professor recorded voice-over PowerPoint presentations. The decision was made to keep these around 20 minutes in order to maintain student attention. To assess student understanding from the lectures, the PI created short, multiple-choice online assessments of the PowerPoint presentations. There was one assessment per PowerPoint lecture, totaling about 20 for the entire semester. Additionally, the PI provided the written notes upon which the lectures were based, though they were not complete (for example, specific examples provided in the lectures were not recorded in the notes, therefore giving reasons for students to watch the presentations rather than just reading the notes). These assignments were untimed, allowing students to have a fairly stress-free environment in which to complete the assignments, though there was a specific due date. Generally, all assignments were uploaded through weekly modules, so students knew what had to be completed for the week and allowed them the entire week to work.

In addition to these low-impact, lecture-based assignments, the PI decided to work with a textbook publishing company, Norton, to offer online modules and assignments associated with their text, *We the People: 10th Essentials Edition*. Norton created an online platform to help keep students engaged with different assessment assignments that the professor easily integrated to the university's Learning Management System, Desire2Learn. The professor generally gave these assignments a week in advance and listed all of them individually on the syllabus to help students keep track of the multiple, daily assignments. These were broken into several categories (by the publishers) and included under the syllabus "grades" section so students would know precisely what assignment counted for what portion of the course grade. Assignments were untimed but had specific due dates. Six different online modules were offered, including textbook chapter post-tests. The PI counted the remaining five modules as class participation, allowing for formative assessment, weekly data to discover which students were at-risk by retrieving individual student data to see the students who were failing to complete assignments as well as those performing consistently at lower than 80 percent total grade level. The PI would then send out emails to students determined to be at-risk, in an effort to help them improve. These assignments were all generally multiple-choice in nature, although a few included open-ended, short-answer/essay questions, and some involved student analysis of graphs, charts, videos, and text depending on the module, all provided by the publishing company for use in conjunction with the textbook.

Additionally, the PI required the students to discuss three topics online via Desire2Learn. The three topics were the lectures and module assignments, current events, and the readings (textbook and additional reading discussed below). The syllabus, provided to each student, contained the rubric for number of posts required per letter grade, so students would know beforehand how much participation was required for them to earn an A on this portion of the class. The non-textbook readings consisted of typically 5–8 pages per class night of Alexis de Tocqueville's *Democracy in America*, which Albert and Ginn (2014) demonstrated as achieving higher student success and satisfaction in introductory American Government classes than using traditional textbooks or other sources. The students were expected to read the selections prior to class and complete online assignments over the readings each week. These quizzes were short answer/essay and were untimed, although they had specific due dates. As with all assignments above, the PI generally gave the students a week to complete the quizzes. To help prepare students for class time, and to help them do well on the reading assignments, the PI provided students with guided reading questions for each class day's reading selection. The students were not required to answer these questions, which were only given to help them with the reading material and to help them have informed answers for discussions in class that stemmed from these guided-reading questions.

Class time was then spent mainly in Socratic dialogue, encouraging debate and understanding from the lectures, modules, and readings. The PI tended to devote more time to the readings than lecture since we believed that this practice would help develop more higher-order thinking. Socratic dialogue involves questioning the students in discussion format, rather than typical lecturing. It usually involves answering a question with a question, but with enough clarifying information that the student is more capable of finding the answer independently. It also focuses more on the professor as question-asker while the student becomes the expert. In other words, the PI asks thematic, analytical questions, and the students provide the answers. The classroom thus becomes a student-centered discussion forum rather than an instructor-focused lecture. In order to force students to be engaged and to bring technology into the classroom, which has been demonstrated to help in-class engagement (Heiberger and Junco 2011), the PI used an iPhone application (iLEAP Pick A Student) to randomly call on students to answer professor-guided discussion questions on the lectures and readings. Once the original respondent provided an answer (or could not provide an answer), the PI allowed random students to participate. In so doing, the PI forced students who may not otherwise pay attention in class or participate to be on their toes, constantly anticipating the random student generator. It also, however, allowed the more ambitious students ample time to express themselves.

Additionally, the PI tried to incorporate real-time polling in the classroom, which has also been demonstrated to increase student engagement (Burkhardt and Cohen 2012). To save money and to make it more interactive, the professor utilized another phone application, Poll Everywhere. This application allows the PI to create several types of polls, including open-ended questions, multiple-choice, and true-false, and they are projected onto the screen for students to view. They then vote either through their phones or other online platforms such as laptop or touchpad, and they can respond via the website itself linked by the professor, via text or Twitter account, which has also been demonstrated in the literature to promote student engagement and motivation (Lederer 2012; Mazer, Murphy, and Simonds 2007). Notably, these in-class techniques would not be possible in the Socratic fashion without teaching through a flipped method. Most of these methods would require too much time if combined with an in-class lecture, and something would have to be left out of the learning environment. By using the flipped method, the student does not lose valuable information, and more engaged practices are utilized during class time as a result. It is precisely this method that allowed different pedagogical practices to occur during class time to also focus on engagement. Thus, the class focused on increasing engagement online and during actual face-to-face time. Now that we have described the classroom design, we can discuss the research design and methods.

RESEARCH DESIGN AND METHODS

This study's research question is, "Does a flipped classroom model improve student performance and content knowledge?" To investigate this question, this study has two hypotheses.

Hypothesis 1: The flipped pedagogical model increases student performance in the course more than traditional lecture-based classes.

Hypothesis 2: The flipped pedagogical model increases students' course content knowledge more than traditional lecture-based classes.

To test these hypotheses, we needed to test the experimental course described above (run in Fall 2015 and Spring 2016) against the same professor's classes run in the previous years not using the flipped model (Fall 2013 and Fall 2014). We also compared Phase II to Phase I results to see if any meaningful difference emerged from the two distinct phases of the study. We also needed to test the flipped course against the rest of the department's Introduction to American Government classes run in Fall 2015 and Spring 2016 and against the entire department's Introduction to American Government classes in the previous two years.

To test the first hypothesis, we decided to utilize two tools as a measure of student performance: DFW (grades of D or F and withdrawals) and AB (grades of A or B) rates. Certainly, course withdrawals have a direct relationship with student performance. Therefore, a decrease in course Ws would demonstrate a higher rate of student performance. It can also be surmised that a decrease in the number of Ds and Fs in a course corresponds to an increase in student performance. We expected to find that the flipped model increased student performance of the experimental course over all control courses, including department-wide and professor-specific controls. We also decided to compare end-of-course grades of either an A or B in the experimental course to the same control courses described above. We expected that the flipped model would result in an increase in AB rates when compared to all control courses, including department-wide and professor-specific courses, thus demonstrating that the experimental course improves student performance when compared to traditional lecture-based classes.

To test hypothesis 2, all participating professors administered a 15-question pre/posttest content knowledge instrument on the first and last days of class. The instrument was given to both the experimental and control sections of the course. The instruments were all anonymous, with students providing only their birthdays (in eight-digit format) for paired analysis purposes. We expected that students in the experimental course would improve the total number of correct answers pretest to posttest when compared to students in the control sections of the same course.

RESULTS

Grade distribution data was gathered from the university's database. As noted previously, concerning hypothesis 1, student performance, we considered DFW rates as a measure of student performance. A reduction in DFW rates would be a sign of increased student performance.

The data in Table 6.1 show that the PI's DFW rates tend to be higher than the DFW rates of the department as a whole. However, when two-sample proportion tests were run on these data, the only time a difference was statistically significant was in Spring 2015. Both the PI's and the rest of the department's DFW rates show a general downward trend.

Comparing the PI's DFW rates during the control semesters to Phases I and II when the flipped approach was used, some interesting patterns emerge. The DFW rate from the Phase I semester is fairly high, the second highest of the semesters considered. This could have happened for a variety of reasons. The PI was teaching with the flipped method for the first time and likely had some problems to work out. Adopting a new teaching style may have also frustrated the expectations of some students who enrolled in the PI's classes expecting a traditional lecture style. By Phase II, the PI's DFW rates are the lowest of the semesters considered, but the differences from previous semesters do not come out statistically significant, except when the Fall 2015 rate is compared to the Fall 2013 rate. The practice with the new method in Phase I and the revisions in the method from Phase I to Phase II likely contributed to the reduction in DFW rates. Although results are not statistically significant, we believe that with more semester data collected, better results will emerge. Regardless, it is clear that the method is getting DFW rates to decline, which is progress, even if not yet significant.

We also used AB rates as a measure of student performance. An increase in these rates would suggest better student performance in the course (see Table 6.2). The PI's AB rates are quite similar to those of the rest of the department, with the PI's sometimes being higher and sometimes lower. When two-sample proportion tests were run comparing the rates, the difference was never statistically significant. There is an overall upward trend in both sets of AB rates, which is not surprising as this mirrors the downward trend in the DFW rates.

The pattern in the PI's AB rates suggests that students' performance is increasing. While the PI was using a traditional lecture approach, the rates were

TABLE 6.1 DFW Rates

DFW Rates	Fall 2013 Control	Fall 2014 Control	Spring 2015 Phase I	Fall 2015 Phase II	Spring 2016 Phase II
PI	24.6%	18.6%	23.5%	12.1%	16.0%
	n = 61	n = 70	n = 66	n = 66	n = 50
Rest of Department	17.0%	12.6%	13.7%	8.0%	9.3%
	n = 507	n = 555	n = 306	n = 450	n = 291

Two proportion tests done using α = 0.05.
SOURCE: Craig Douglas Albert, Stacie K. Pettit, and Christopher Terry

TABLE 6.2 AB Rates

AB Rates	Fall 2013 Control	Fall 2014 Control	Spring 2015 Phase I	Fall 2015 Phase II	Spring 2016 Phase II
PI	60.7%	71.4%	62.7%	75.8%	80.0%
	n = 61	n = 70	n = 51	n = 66	n = 50
Rest of Department	64.3%	70.5%	70.3%	79.3%	77.0%
	n = 507	n = 555	n = 306	n = 450	n = 291

Two proportion tests done using α = 0.05.
SOURCE: Craig Douglas Albert, Stacie K. Pettit, and Christopher Terry

quite similar to that of the department as a whole. The AB rate during Spring 2015, when the PI used the flipped method for the first time, was somewhat low, again likely reflecting the struggles involved in trying out a radically different approach to teaching. However, when we ran statistical tests comparing his AB rates, none of the differences come out as significant. In Phase II, when the PI was using the flipped approach for the second and third times, the PI achieved the highest AB rates of the semesters under consideration. The rates for both Fall 2015 and Spring 2016 come out as statistically significantly higher at a 10 percent level than that for Fall 2013, and the rate for Spring 2016 is statistically significantly higher than the rate from Fall 2015 (the first attempt at flipped). This, coupled with the content knowledge data considered next, suggests that the flipped teaching style is having a positive effect on student performance.

Hypothesis 2, student content knowledge, was tested through a pre/posttest. During the two semesters of Phase II, Fall 2015 and Spring 2016, all students enrolled in a section of Introduction to American Government received a 15-question political science general knowledge test at the beginning of the semester. The same test was administered at the end of the semester. We analyzed the Fall 2015 data in two ways. We looked at changes in individual students' scores from the pretest to the posttest as well as the change in percentage correct on each question from pretest to posttest. The mean change in score from pretest to posttest for students being taught by the PI using the flipped method was 2.083 additional questions correct. For the rest of the department, who all used a traditional lecture style, the mean change in score was 1.185 additional questions correct. A two-sample t-test comparing these means results in a p-value of 0.0056, which is evidence that the students learning through the flipped method had, on average, a greater increase in score from pretest to posttest, suggesting their content knowledge had improved. The change was greater for the flipped students on 12 of the 15 questions, and the mean change in percentage correct was 13.9 percent as compared to 7.5 percent for students taught using traditional lecture. Here, there is clear evidence that the flipped method increases student content knowledge. However, the results for Spring 2016 confuse this conclusion.

The Spring 2016 data and results were not as encouraging. The flipped students improved on only 5 of the 15 questions. Strangely, the change in percentage correct was negative on 7 of the 15 questions, meaning students did worse on the posttest than the pretest on those questions. The mean change in percentage correct was −0.7 percent for the flipped students as compared to a mean change of 8.8 percent for students taught using traditional lecture. The investigators are not sure why there is such a drastic difference in the two semesters under consideration. With such a high improvement in the first semester, coupled with negative results in the flipped sections for the second semester, the investigators believe that more testing is needed, and data collection is underway to have more semesters taken into account for the purposes of future studies. It is possible the data were somehow contaminated in one of the semesters, biasing the results. Ongoing data collection will resolve this puzzle in future research.

DISCUSSION AND CONCLUSION

To date, the pedagogical literature analyzing data from flipped courses compared to traditional courses has demonstrated promising results. Concerning this chapter's results, there are reasons for optimism that flipping works, though the results generated herein are mixed. The first hypothesis was that flipping would improve student performance, measured by DFW and AB rates. We believed flipping would decrease DFW rates, thus demonstrating an increase in student performance. After statistical analyses, however, there are no significant results, thus, the hypothesis is not supported. Although the data seem to discount the hypothesis, the flipped method clearly lowers the DFW rates for the PI from Phase I to Phase II.

Although results are not significant, the data are trending toward better results and are substantial. With more data collection underway, we believe that statistically significant results will appear in future studies.

The investigators hypothesized that the flipped method would increase student performance as measured by AB rates. We believed that the flipped method would result in higher AB rates when compared to the rest of the department, acting as a control, and when compared to the PI's nonflipped courses. Here, the results are more promising than for DFW rates. When testing the flipped courses against the department's control courses, no statistically significant results appear. However, the data demonstrate that the rates for the flipped course do correlate and trend with the department's rates overall. Both are increasing, though not at statistically significant levels. At the least it can be asserted that flipping does not hurt student success when compared to more traditional forms of learning. The results are better when analyzing only the PI's experiment courses with the PI's control courses. Data demonstrate that AB rates are increased at statistically significant levels when comparing the PI's flipped courses to the PI's nonflipped courses. These results demonstrate that flipping does work, at least at the instructor level. The results are trending positively, increasing student performance as measured in AB rates. More students earned As and Bs in the first phase of the experiment compared to the PI's control courses; Phase II also showed an increase over Phase I. Thus, the results are mixed. When compared to the rest of the department, the data match overall, with no significant differences. However, the hypothesis is confirmed at the instructor level. We are confident that future research will continue to demonstrate an increase in AB rates at significant levels. Further data collection is ongoing.

For hypothesis 2, we believed that the flipped method would increase course content knowledge more so than nonflipped courses. As with hypothesis 2, the results are mixed. For Phase I of the experiment, there are substantial and significant results to confirm the hypothesis. However, rather alarming results were illustrated in Phase II. For some questions, students actually performed worse than in the control courses. Although alarming, we think there were some unaccounted factors that affected the results. First, the Phase II data do not match Phase I data; second, Phase II data demonstrate a decrease in DFWs and an increase in AB rates. This would lead one to believe that, logically, one could expect an increase in content knowledge since DFW rates were lower and AB rates were higher. Additionally, it could be that because of the flipped classroom, students were experiencing more higher-order thinking that caused multiple-choice assessments to be oversimplified.[1] In other words, the posttest was not an effective measurement of the analytical thinking students were discovering in the new environment, and thus, results were not as positive. We are confident that future research will provide positive, statistically significant results concerning content knowledge. As such, we can neither confirm or deny hypothesis 2, but do believe the results are promising and warrant future research and experimentation.

Although the data produce mixed results, we believe that more professors should experiment with the flipped pedagogical design. Especially with millennials, it is critical to provide differentiated and sophisticated course design for technologically savvy students who are inundated with social media. Students no longer "stay tuned" to traditional lecture-style courses. In fact, in qualitative data being analyzed for future research, a plurality of students stated that the flipped method was their favorite part of the course. Most stated that this was true because: (1) they had time to work on their own and at their own pace with online work; and (2) class time was exciting and engaging because of the debates, discussion, and dialogue that a flipped course allowed. Because of this, we encourage more professors in different courses to study and implement the flipped pedagogy.

Many publishing companies are developing online material that lends itself to the flipped classroom. One of the modules used in this study, Norton's "InQuizitive" feature, is being developed and rolled out in many disciplines. For sociology alone, there are over 6,000 students participating in Fall 2016. Overall, there are over 80,000 students who have answered 75,000,000 quiz questions, with over 2 million grades recorded.[2] These numbers demonstrate that higher education is moving toward a flipped method where more work is done online and outside of class than ever before. As such, it is critical to investigate how this is affecting student success. More research is needed to understand clearly the relationship between student success and the flipped pedagogy. For now, this chapter demonstrates mixed results. But now that we have established a base, there is optimism for future growth concerning flipped pedagogy, and evolution of material in future courses, we believe, will continue to illustrate substantial and significant results.

The question remains, after reading this chapter: How should a professor wanting to try this pedagogy begin? It is important to understand three main points. First, an instructor new to this format will want to become immersed in the scholarship of teaching and learning (SoTL) concerning flipped, hybrid, and blended learning to try to get a more complete picture of what it all entails. As with research agendas, starting a new teaching practice should begin with an intense review of the literature. We hope this chapter lends itself to this endeavor. Second, and perhaps the most important tip for implementing a flipped course, is time management. A flipped course demands that the professor spend a significant amount of time in preparation and implementation to ensure success. In fact, when beginning implementation, the PI in this study spent far more hours designing the flipped classroom than any other class. It was far more time-consuming than even the first course prep of the PI's career. This does not make it unworthy, however.

When an instructor sees the type of increased engagement within the classroom, all the extra hours pay off. In fact, this study's investigator's future research is looking solely at how this pedagogy affects student engagement. Additionally, and perhaps more importantly for student success, an instructor must be cognizant of the time demands that a flipped pedagogy places on the student as well. One of the more serious lessons learned from this study's evolution was that even though course work is completed at home, professors must not inundate students with copious amounts of work. It is important to keep in mind that students have other courses that require their time and effort, and to understand that to keep students engaged, ambitious, and determined, one cannot kill their morale by assigning too much work.

Third, it is extremely helpful to network with a publishing company you trust, which has an online learning platform attached to a book you find appropriate for your course. Many companies, for instance in this study, Norton, have very useful online modules paired with books to help in a flipped environment. These are usually paired out by chapter and directed at fulfilling different Student-Learning Outcomes (SLOs) based on Bloom's taxonomy. Work with a representative or figure out which publisher is a great fit for your purposes. However, one cannot rely solely on these types of platforms. Students will grow tired of the same type of assignments. Therefore, it is useful to have additional readings that are completely different from the textbook; as mentioned earlier, the PI for this study uses a book on political philosophy in addition to the text. In-class assignments are thus mixed between discussing Tocqueville one day, current events the next, and assignments from the textbook and its accompanying online learning platform. This is why, in addition to the SoTL research, time management is so important. A novice professor to this pedagogy must understand how much time a mini-simulation will take, how much preparation is needed, what materials to assign out of class to make sure in-class time is used efficiently, etc. After doing a simulation, switch to a week of Socratic discourse based on a theoretical book. Next, have open discussion on current events relevant to one's course. The fourth week, have student debates based on an assignment in the textbook. I often have Socratic discourse on *Democracy in America* one week, followed by student debates on marijuana legalization the next (an assignment over this topic is included in the Norton modules).

Beside the above three meta-concerns when implementing a flipped course, several smaller issues could also help ease a new professor, as well as students, into this design. First, write a letter to the students or dedicate a significant part of the syllabus to explain the flipped pedagogy to them, the reasons you are using it, and the expected benefits of it. Provide some data on how it potentially helps serve student success over more traditional lectures. Transparency is perhaps one of the most undernoted virtues of a talented professor. The PI for this study included a few pages on the syllabus about the flipped pedagogy;[3] added a section about being new to the format and asked for patience with any mistakes, and gave a low impact online quiz over the syllabus to ensure the students read it in detail and understood the PI's reasoning. Based on qualitative evaluations, this earned respect from the students. Additionally, allow room for online discussions. Post your own questions based on readings, for instance, and heated classroom topics, but also provide an open forum for students—in other words, one that they control and direct and in which they decide the topics to discuss. Read all of these at least cursorily, and respond with comments to encourage critical, creative thinking. Foster honest academic debate as well as higher-order thinking. Do not nitpick if details are fuzzy; rather, encourage the thought process over specifics in this type of forum. Class time can be devoted to any serious confusion over details.

The most important piece of advice on implementing the flipped pedagogy we can offer is to try and overcome the fear of failure. Anything worth doing is going to face unexpected challenges and pitfalls. Do not be discouraged when a simulation does not work, when students are not engaged on a particular topic, or when the entire semester just did not work! This happens. Focus on discovering why something did not work—learn from and improve on the experience. One method to limit failed attempts or to evolve less successful ones is student evaluations. The PI gives monthly student evaluations (and adds a little extra credit to them to alleviate any concerns that the professor will penalize a student for criticism) that ask students to name three strengths and three weaknesses of the class so far. These evaluations allow the student to feel included in the process and allow a modicum of transparency. Additionally, the professor can see what really works and what does not. These evaluations will help inform instructors on what to evolve, what to keep, and what to throw out. Not to mention that if one does this monthly throughout the semester, the final university-administered evaluations will perhaps be better because problems have been addressed all semester. Have thick skin, however, and do not respond negatively to criticism. Finally, based on these evaluations, make course improvements and explain them to the students before implementing them. Anecdotally, doing so seems to increase student respect for the instructor and helps deliver the message of professor empathy to student concerns. And always remember—not trying is the only consequential failure.

NOTES

1. The authors would like to thank an anonymous reviewer for this insight.
2. Data provided by Norton at PI's request.
3. Please contact the PI for a copy of the syllabus.

REFERENCES

Albert, Craig Douglas, and Martha Humphries Ginn. 2014. "Teaching with Tocqueville: Assessing the Utility of Using 'Democracy' in the American Government Classroom to Achieve Student-Learning Outcomes." *Journal of Political Science Education* 10(2):166–85.

Albert, Craig Douglas, Stacie K. Pettit, and Christopher Terry. 2016. "WTF (What the Flip)? Preliminary Results of a Flipped-Hybrid Classroom Model on Student Success." *Questions in Politics* (3):1–23.

Alpaslan, Sahin, Baki Cavlazoglu, and Yunus E. Zeytuncu. 2015. "Flipping a College Calculus Course: A Case Study." *Journal of Education Technology and Society* 18(3):142–52.

Bergmann, Jonathan, and Aaron Sams. 2012. *Flip Your Classroom: Reach Every Student in Every Class Every Day.* International Society for Technology in Education.

Bishop, Jacob Lowell, and Matthew A. Verleger. 2013. "The Flipped Classroom: A Survey of the Research." Presented at the 120th ASEE Annual Conference and Exposition, Atlanta, GA.

Burkhardt, Andy, and Sarah Faye Cohen. 2012. "'Turn Your Cell Phones On': Mobile Phone Polling as a Tool for Teaching Information Literacy." *Communications in Information Literacy* 6(2):191–201.

Flipped Learning Network (FLN). 2014. "The Four Pillars of F-L-I-P." Retrieved December 10, 2016 (http://flippedlearning.org/definition-of-flipped-learning/).

Harrington, Susan Ann, Melodee Vanden Bosch, Nancy Schoofs, Cynthia Beel-Bates, and Kirk Anderson. 2015. "Quantitative Outcomes for Nursing Students in a Flipped Classroom." *Nursing Education Perspectives* 36(3):179–81.

Heiberger, Greg, and Rynol Junco. 2011. "Meet Your Students Where They Are: Social Media." *NEA Higher Education Advocate* 28(5):6–10.

Herreid, Clyde Freeman, and Nancy A. Schiller. 2013. "Case Studies and the Flipped Classroom." *Journal of College Science Teaching* 42(5):62–66.

Hung, Hsiu-Ting. 2015. "Flipping the Classroom for English Language Learners to Foster Active Learning." *Computer Assisted Language Learning* 28(1):81–96.

Kvashnina, O. S., and E. A. Martynko. 2016. "Analyzing the Potential of Flipped Classroom in ESL Teaching." *International Journal of Emerging Technologies in Learning* 11(3):71–73.

Lang, Guido, and Stephen D. O'Connell. 2015. "Learning about Learning about Learning: Insights from a Student Survey in a Hybrid Classroom Environment." *Issues in Information Systems* 16(3).

Lederer, Karen. 2012. "Pros and Cons of Social Media in the Classroom." *Campus Technology,* January. Retrieved January 10, 2015 (http://www.campustechnology.com/articles/2012/01/19/pros-and-cons-of-social-media-in-the-classroom.aspx?page = 1).

Mazer, Joseph P., Richard E. Murphy, and Cheri J. Simonds. 2007. "I'll See You on 'Facebook': The Effects of Computer-Mediated Teacher Self-Disclosure on Student Motivation, Affective Learning, and Classroom Climate." *Communication Education* 56(1):1–17.

McCallum, Shelly, Janel Schultz, Kristen Sellke, and Jason Spartz. 2015. "An Examination of the Flipped Classroom Approach on College Student Academic Involvement." *International Journal of Teaching and Learning in Higher Education* 27(1):42–55.

Murphree, Daniel. 2015. "Flipping the History Classroom with an Embedded Writing Consultant: Synthesizing Inverted and WAC Paradigms in a University History Survey Course." *Social Studies* 106(5):218–25.

Murray, Leigh, Christine McCallum, and Christopher Petrosino. 2014. "Flipping the Classroom Experience: A Comparison of Online Learning to Traditional Lecture." *Journal of Physical Therapy Education* 28(3):35–41.

Nouri, Jalal. 2016. "The Flipped Classroom: For Active, Effective, and Increased Learning—Especially for Low Achievers." *International Journal of Educational Technology in Higher Education* 13(1):33.

Puentedura, Ruben R. 2012. "The SAMR Model: Background and Exemplars." Retrieved January 10, 2015 (http://www.hippasus.com/rrpweblog/archives/000073.html).

Ruddick, Kristie Winfield. 2012. "Improving Chemical Education from High School to College Using a More Hands-on Approach." PhD dissertation, Department of Chemistry, University of Memphis.

Souza, Manoj Joseph D., and Paul Rodrigues. 2015. "Investigating the Effectiveness of the Flipped Classroom in an Introductory Programming Course." *New Educational Review* 40(2):129–39.

Tucker, Catlin. 2012. *Blended Learning in Grades K–12*. Thousand Oaks, CA: Corwin.

Yestrebsky, Cherie L. 2014. "Flipping the Classroom in a Large Chemistry Class—Research University Environment." *Procedia—Social and Behavioral Sciences* 191:1113–18.

Zappe, Sara, Robert Leicht, John Messner, Thomas Litzinger, and Hyeon Woo Lee. 2009. " 'Flipping' the Classroom to Explore Active Learning in a Large Undergraduate Course." *Proceedings of the 2009 American Society for Engineering Education Annual Conference and Exhibition*, Austin, TX.

7

Reaching and Teaching "Nontraditional" Students in Community Colleges and Beyond

Sara Parker

The community college system was established in the early twentieth century. Since its inception, it has been tasked with an eclectic mix of mandates. Community colleges provide open access education, a foothold to the promise of higher education, vocational training and occupational retraining, personal educational enrichment for lifelong learners, an alternative educational path for students under the age of 18, and a community engagement center. They are deeply embedded in the communities they serve and play an important civic engagement role (Cohen, Brawer, and Kisker 2014).

Today, over 12 million Americans (approximately 7.5 million for credit and 5 million not for credit) take advantage of the accessible, affordable, and quality education that the 1,123 community colleges in America provide. Credit-seeking students at community colleges accounted for 46 percent of all American undergraduates in the United States in 2013 (AACC 2015). Further, community colleges are vibrant and diverse institutions whose students disproportionately represent first-generation college students, minority students, parents, and other "nontraditional" students as compared to four-year institutions (AACC 2015).

The "traditional student"—the student who enrolls in college immediately after high school, is financially supported by their parents, whose primary "job" is attending school, and is between the ages of 18 and 22—is a minority in higher education (Giancola, Munz, and Trares 2008). In this respect, the "new majority" (Svanum and Bigatti 2006) is composed of "nontraditional students." Mounsey, Vandehey, and Diekhoff (2013) use the umbrella term of "nontraditional" to capture all students who fall into one or more of these groups: "(a) postpone entering college, (b) enroll part-time, (c) work full-time, (d) rely on selves financially, (e) financially support others, (f) single parent, (g) did not earn a high school diploma . . . (h) received education from a two-year program, and (i) is female" (p. 379). Community colleges serve these students, and they do it well. Students who begin their higher education at community colleges have a higher likelihood of completing a bachelor's degree within eight years than students who start at four-year institutions (Shapiro et al. 2013). Close to half of all students who complete degrees at a four-year institution were enrolled at a two-year institution during the previous 10 years (National Student Clearing House 2015). Four-year college faculty should understand the diversity and challenges of teaching community college students both because community college transfer students *become* their students and because community colleges are a microcosm of contemporary America. Therefore, they are a preview of what students across the higher education system will look like in the near future.

This chapter provides an introduction to teaching community college students by identifying four significant and overarching characteristics of this population: (1) academic underpreparedness, (2) significant populations of first-generation and / or immigrant students, (3) complicated attendance patterns, and (4) heterogeneity. In each of these categories, I summarize the existing literature about how to increase success for these students.[1] The last section of the paper presents evidence from a successful classroom intervention using best practices.

ACADEMIC UNDERPREPAREDNESS

Students entering community college arrive with divergent levels of academic preparedness, and we know that this is a strong predictor of baccalaureate attainment (Wang 2009). According to Barr and Schuetz 2008, "underprepared refers to a constellation of factors that together indicate that a student is not yet emotionally, socially, or academically prepared for college-level work" (p. 8). About 60 percent of all entering community college students need at least one remedial course (Deil-Amen 2011). In California community colleges, 90 percent of incoming freshman are below preparedness in transfer-level math and 73 percent are below preparedness for transfer-level English (Brown and Niemi 2007). As Perin (2013) cites, the list of explanatory factors for under preparedness is long: "inadequate instruction during the K–12 years, low English language proficiency, learning disabilities, low motivation, and barriers associated with low socioeconomic status and minority race and ethnicity" (p. 119).

Historically, the task of addressing basic skills deficiencies has been relegated to English, math, and English as a Second Language (ESL) departments. But, of course, students do not limit their course loads to these classes, so all instructors must be prepared: "If community colleges continue to provide an academic environment largely designed for prepared students with the view that the underprepared students are the problem, there should be little expectation of any significant improvement in outcomes for students" (Barr and Schuet 2008:15). In today's higher education, it is appropriate for all instructors to view themselves as "basic skills" educators.

A concerted focus on the integration of basic skills into discipline-specific curricula does not "water it down." In fact, research has shown that enrolling in remedial courses can significantly inhibit student progress (Suárez-Orozco et al. 2011:157); placement assessments "severely misplace" about one third of all students (Belfield and Crosta 2012), and students who bypass the development system are more likely to pass college-level English and math courses (Hayward and Willett 2014). We help community college students succeed in all of their courses when we embed basic skills across the curriculum.

What Works in the Classroom? Embedding Developmental Education

There are many models for improving student reading and writing skills. The most common include: the incorporation of developmental reading and writing instruction into content-area courses to enable students to access disciplinary texts, enhancing literacy and / or writing skills, and / or referring underprepared students to supplemental instruction or tutoring (Perin 2011, 2013).

Studies do not find widespread use of these models in the community college system (Perin 2011); however, a policy shift supportive of embedding developmental skills into college coursework is underway (Barr and Schultz 2008; Perin 2013). One such example is the Reading Apprenticeship Program, a program that supports instructors to "develop advanced academic literacies, including disciplinary specific ways of reading, writing, researching and problem solving" (Reading Apprenticeship n.d.). The Writing Across the Curriculum (WAC) movement (also known as Writing in the Disciplines) has been around for decades and has achieved strong success at four-year institutions. However, just 33 percent of community colleges utilize a WAC model (McMullen-Light 2010). An instructional approach called Content Comprehension Strategy Intervention (CCSI) supplements classroom instruction with reading comprehension and writing skills instruction using content-specific texts, also known as "contextualization" (Perin et al. 2013). Educational technologies designed to increase academic writing skills are increasingly common.

Another common pedagogical technique is "scaffolding" (Browne, Hough, and Schwab 2009). Scaffolds are "forms of support provided by the teacher (or another student) to help students bridge the gap between their current abilities and the intended goal" (Rosenshein and Meister 1992:26). This technique is often associated with ESL education but can be used for any skill and may be particularly useful for higher-order critical thinking.[2]

A 2005 study of first-generation community college students found that they perceived "life skills" such as time management, focus, and self-advocacy as contributing to their success (Byrd and MacDonald). Cox (2009) suggests that some of the best ways to help students include addressing their fears of failure through incorporating encouragement and examples of quality coursework into classroom instruction. Recent scholarship on "Habits of Mind" encourages instructors to broaden their focus on what a student knows and encourages instructors to help students evaluate their own work critically, learn from others, and think "flexibly" (Costa 2008).

IMMIGRANT AND / OR FIRST-GENERATION STUDENTS

It is estimated that immigrants make up 15 percent of the U.S. population and they are 20 percent more likely to begin their postsecondary education at community colleges (Conway 2010). Immigrant students face financial need, but are less likely to apply for student loans and spend more hours per week on family responsibilities than their native-born peers (Teranishi, Suárez-Orozco, and Suárez-Orozco 2011). Limited language proficiency can negatively impact students' experience applying to college, and immigrant and ESL students may fear interacting with native-born students in the classroom (Bledsoe and Baskin 2014). Limited English proficiency affects a significant number of immigrant students and is correlated with educational outcomes among immigrants (Baum and Flores 2011).

Those who would be the first in their families to attend college are far less likely to enroll when compared to students whose parents attended college: 54 percent versus 82 percent (Choy 2001). It is estimated that first-generation students comprise 36 percent of all community college students (AACC 2015).

In addition to being at greater risk of academic underpreparedness (Engle 2007; Teranishi et al. 2011), immigrants and first-generation college students are considerably more likely to lack the skills necessary to navigate college successfully, often referred to as "cultural capital" (Baum and Flores 2011). "Students who lack cultural capital are less integrated in both academic and social aspects of college life and may lack the support networks that other students can rely on as they learn to navigate higher education" (Mekolichick and Gibbs 2012:40).

According to Mekolichick and Gibbs (2012), "cultural capital" accounts for the difference between the experiences and relevance of higher education to students from privileged versus working-class families. The difference in median income between freshmen whose parents attended / did not attend college is extreme: $99,635 to $37,565 (Mangan 2015).[3] Research shows that immigrant and minority students may self-select into institutions below their qualifications and/or prefer to remain closer to home (Baum and Flores 2011; Conway 2010). They tend also to be more risk averse (Mangan 2015). The combination of these factors may contribute to the significantly increased likelihood of first-generation college students going on academic probation (Conway 2010).

Finally, there is a growing number of undocumented students in the American community colleges, particularly in those states where they are allowed to pay instate tuition (Baum and Flores 2011).[4] Already stigmatized and disenfranchised, these students face even greater challenges than their documented immigrant peers.

What Works? Regular, Positive Interactions with Students, among Students

As with academic skills, classroom instructors can nurture "college skills." When instructors create a supportive classroom environment for all students, their' feelings of anxiety lessen (Bledsoe and Baskin 2014). Tovar's 2015 study on nearly 400 Latino/a students in a diverse, urban community college in California found that regular, positive interactions with faculty outside of class increased GPA among Latino/as. Lundberg (2014) cites evidence that faculty mentorship increases student persistence, positive interactions boost student confidence and help students improve their skills, and procedural assistance is particularly valuable for first-generation students. Suárez-Orozco, Pimentel, and Marin looked at the relationship between immigrant students and school personnel (including faculty) and also found that relationships increased student engagement, student effort, and stronger grades (as cited in Baum and Flores 2011:175).

When students engage with faculty outside of the classroom, such as during office hours, extracurricular events, or in learning communities, it deepens their relationship to the institution and reinforces perceptions of themselves as legitimate college students. Weaver and Qi (2005) find that faculty interactions help students "learn professionalism, view criticism in a constructive way, and enhance students' confidence in the classroom" (p. 587). These interactions carry over beyond individual faculty-student exchanges, because "personal relationships between students and instructors can create inroads of trust in the classroom" (Bledsoe and Baksin 2014:38). Even a small but critical mass of allies in the classroom can create a supportive culture that improves student work ethic and engagement.

Faculty can utilize demonstrated pedagogical techniques in the classroom to encourage students to get to know their classmates. Because first-generation and immigrant students are more likely to have significant off-campus responsibilities, they spend less time on campus (Bickerstaff, Barragan, and Rucks-Ahidiana 2012). Therefore, the classroom may be one of the only places they can develop the social connections that make them feel like inclusive members of the campus community. Faculty can integrate community-building activities into their courses, facilitate the creation of study groups, mix up students during partner and group activities, and make choices to ensure their classrooms are centered around student learning.

COMPLICATED ATTENDANCE PATTERNS

Some of the most important and predictive characteristics of community college students have to do with attendance patterns. Community college students are more likely than not to start and stop their education or to attend erratically (Crosta 2014). The fluidity of community college students is extreme.

"Upward transfer" is when students move from community colleges to four-year institutions. This is the stated goal of two-thirds of community colleges students and a central mission of the community college, yet actual transfer rates remain between 20 and 30 percent (Conway 2010). Students frequently "lateral transfer" between community colleges. One of the largest studies conducted on transfer students focused on the California Community College system and found that 27 percent of first-time students transferred between community colleges within six years of enrolling (Bahr 2009). Students at four-year institutions increasingly "reverse transfer" or dual-enroll in community colleges, and students at community colleges "reverse transfer" to trade or certificate programs (Bahr 2012).

Community college students are very likely to work, and to work long hours, yet only 2 percent receive federal work-study funds (NPAS 2013). "The average public 2-year collegian works extensively (27.7 hrs / week for dependents and 34.9 hrs / week for independents).The majority of students work to pay their tuition fees, and living expenses (55.7 percent for dependents and 77.4 percent for independents) as opposed to being employed for relevant job experience or spending money" (Perna, Cooper, and Li cited in Wood, Harrison, and Jones 2016:328). Working long hours can contribute to heightened stress and reduced success rates (Dundes and Marx 2006; Mounsey et al. 2013; Wood et al. 2016).

The vast majority of community college students enroll part-time. "Despite empirical evidence indicating that continuous, full-time enrollment is the optimal scenario for degree completion, many community college students find that route impossible to follow. . . . Only 31 percent of community college students enroll exclusively full time; indeed, 26 percent enroll less than half time" (Goldrick-Rab 2010:454). While Crosta's (2014) research suggests that frequent switching between full-time and part-time status does not appear to have a negative impact, we know that students characterized by part-time or discontinuous enrollment have lower transfer rates and are less likely to earn credentials.

What Works? Establishing a Classroom Culture and Using Course Design to Encourage and Reward Attendance

Many of the teaching techniques already discussed in this chapter, such as forming supportive relationships and keeping students engaged, can increase the likelihood that students prioritize their attendance. For students who are new to a campus, spend little time on campus, and / or are already coming to class overwhelmed by obligations outside of school, a welcoming classroom environment is particularly important. "Stress and anxiety levels also go down when students feel they have regular opportunities to provide feedback on what they [are] learning—or not—in the classroom" (Bledsoe and Baskin 2014:38). Bickerstaff et al. (2012) cite research that "if a student does not expect to achieve success, he or she is less likely to engage in positive, self-regulatory behaviors related to academic performance" (p. 2 citing Oyserman, Bybee, and Terry 2006).

Cox (2009) notes that lack of confidence among community college students may lead to attrition and poor performance. A study on confidence among community college students found that confidence fell when students received negative feedback on their work, low grades, and realized they would need to invest more time to be successful in college than they had in high school. On the flip side, students gained confidence when instructors recognized their potential, which Bickerstaff et al. (2012) refer to as "experiences of earned success." Faculty members can proactively create earned success opportunities for their students.

Research also substantiates the link between test anxiety and poor academic performance (Hancock 2001). Hancock finds that this phenomenon is acutely exacerbated by classroom conditions "perceived as highly evaluative." Her 2001 findings suggest that test-anxious students are far more sensitive to competitive, teacher-centric environments than those students who do not suffer from text anxiety (p. 288). Furthermore, a competitive environment lowers performance even for students who have low levels of test anxiety. She advises professors to reduce the degree in which students feel they are competing with one another.

An area where faculty choice can make a significant difference for students is in their textbook/course materials. One study found that far more students *do not* read before coming to class than do, another found that as many as 64 percent of students at one university did not purchase the required textbooks (Hilton III 2016). Although I am not aware of any study that assesses how many community college students drop or fail courses because they do not have access to a textbook, this is a common phenomenon among my students. Hilton's (2016) analysis of 16 studies cautiously suggests that the use of open educational resources does not appear to decrease student learning.

EXTREME HETEROGENEITY

As previously detailed, community colleges are more ethnically, racially, and linguistically diverse than four-year institutions, include more first-generation and immigrant students, and increasingly, have greater age diversity (Maxwell et al. 2003). The life experiences of community college students differ: they are more likely to be married, come from low-income families, take care of others, and commute (Lundberg 2014). In addition, 49.1 percent of all unmarried student parents attend community colleges, where they make up about 16 percent of the student population (most of those parents attend full-time *and* work at least 15 hours a week) (Goldrick-Rab and Sorensen 2010). Aspirational differences among students dependent upon income, parental education, and immigration status also exist (Conway 2010).

On the one hand, this generates the potential for diverse interactions among students (Lundberg 2014). The chance to engage with peers who are different from you has been shown to provide positive educational benefits (Gurin et al. 2002). On the other hand, this heterogeneity can pose challenges. For example, instructors cannot assume common reference points in terms of cultural or historical knowledge. Students may perceive their own experiences, circumstances, or educational goals as too unique from their classmates to connect with them. The following are introductions provided by three students that aptly capture the reality of the community college classroom:

> I am currently a full-time student . . . as I am a full-time employee . . . I am 21, live on my own. I am willing to put all the effort I can into all my classes even though it is very hard at times balancing sleep, meals, school, and work. But my dreams are big so giving up / quiting [sic] is not an option . . . I try my best not to let my obstacles take away my focus from school. It's really my priority because it's the only way I excape [sic] the reality of where I come from not many reach to see my age, therefore I want to suceed [sic] for me, my family, and for all those children that don't have an opportunity to education.

> I just turned 33 years old. I have a husband and son. My Mom stays with us. I served almost 10 years in the U.S. Navy as a Military Police Officer. I met my husband in Japan while we were stationed there. I am excited about this class . . . I still feel like a new college student. It's great to be here.

> I have been in the nursing field since 1975 and decided to go back to college to study forensic medicine. Since I work full time it has taken a few years but I have enjoyed the classes . . . I really only have one concern about the class and that is, because I'm older, I will have much different perspectives on current events. I know many of my fellow students have never worked or owned property.

Wyatt (2011) recommends that faculty adapt their teaching methods in ways that respond to the learning styles of nontraditional students. Options for doing this include culturally responsive teaching, contextualized teaching, and active-learning strategies, all of which capitalize on social capital to benefit student learning.

What Works? Culturally Responsive, Contextualized Teaching and Active Learning

A 2014 Center for Community College Student Engagement Report found that Latino and African American men experienced some of the lowest educational outcomes despite the fact that they were among the more engaged students. "The

Center attributes this in part to stereotype threat and emphasizes that community colleges must devote specific efforts to actively counteract threats through effective culturally relevant pedagogy, narratives focusing on belonging, and student-agent relationships characterized as positive, supportive, and demanding" (Tovar 2015:52). Some of the pedagogical techniques that have been shown to be highly beneficial for student performance are "learner-centered activities, personalized instructions, relating learning to students' experiences, assessing student needs, climate building, encouraging student participation in the learning process, and maintaining 'flexibility'" (Bledsoe and Baskin 2014). When instructors ask students to work on shared goals and explicitly encourage students to bring their own experiences to bear on tasks at hand, they "enter a new world of academia together" (Bonet and Walters 2016:227).

The Research and Planning Group for California Community Colleges (Center for Student Services 2013) produced a primer titled "Contextualized Teaching and Learning," a concept that connects subject content to the real world with the goal of improving both students' marketability as well as "their capacity and confidence in themselves as life-long learners who can adapt to the changing demands of the workplace" (p. 5). Two of the report's many recommendations are: employ a hyper-focus on curriculum relevance through the use of real-world examples that are of interest to students, and empower students to identify issues of importance and concern to inform the curriculum. The practice of including diversity content has been shown to increase success for minority students (Sweat et al. 2013).

Just as positive faculty interactions can improve student learning (Lundberg 2014), student collaboration also contributes to engagement and learning (Braxton, Hirschy, and McClendon 2004). Although the proportion of in-class time students spend listening to lecture has declined over the years, it remains the most dominant instructor approach in higher education (Panacci 2015). A meta-analysis of 225 studies on lecturing and active learning in the STEM fields found that students in traditional lecture-based courses were one and a half times more likely to fail (Freeman et al. 2014). Research shows that women, minorities, and adult learners, specifically, are more likely to benefit from group and peer learning, interactivity in the classroom, and hands-on learning (Panacci 2015; Ramsay 2005; Sweat et al. 2013;).

"Active learning" is a term used to refer to a wide range of pedagogical techniques including the integration of videos, group work, student presentations, and simulations. Group work is among the most common strategies used in the classroom to engage students (Bledsoe and Baskin 2014), yet "'Active learning' is more than just cobbling together questions for class discussions or small group work: it is about developing a clearly-sequenced teaching strategy that weaves together 'information and ideas, experiences, and reflection' where experiences are comprised of 'doing' and 'observing'" (Fink 2003:106).

EVIDENCE FROM THE CLASSROOM

Years ago, interested in creating a classroom environment that integrates as much of "what works" for teaching community college students as possible, I began building a cache of small-scale, active-learning activities that could be integrated into the curricula of my introductory International Relations course. In Fall 2014 and 2015, I incorporated structured active-learning experiences to illustrate specific course concepts into every other week of the course (eight in total). For example: to introduce the composition and structure of the United Nations, students were assigned a country and provided information to act out several real-world scenarios. These activities supplemented regular classroom interactions, such as partnering and group discussion activities. Loggins (2009) identifies a series of components that define effective simulations: being oriented toward the real world, loosely structured and complex, generative of multiple hypotheses, consistent with desired learning outcomes, built upon previous knowledge and experience, and helping to promote the development of higher order cognitive skills. Four additional criteria defined the small-scale activities I used: (1) use 20 minutes of class time; (2) reconfigure students physically in the classroom to enable them to interact with one another; (3) do not require advance preparation (other than regular outside-of-class expectations); (4) lead students through an experience to bring a concept to life.

The use of these activities addressed best practices for teaching community college students by helping to build community (*regular, positive interactions*), enable students to practice and build academic and college skill sets such as communication, critical thinking, and problem solving (*embedding basic and college skills*), require participation for scheduled exercises (*emphasize in class work*), and create opportunities for students to demonstrate their unique knowledge (*contextualized, active learning*). This pedagogical approach positively influenced course outcomes by: increasing student attendance and participation, creating a more welcoming classroom culture, and improving student-learning and course outcomes.

In February 2016, I sent a survey to students from my Fall 2014 (31 students) and Fall 2015 (29 students) classes asking them to reflect on the use of these activities in my course. The combined response rate to the survey was 37 percent. While the sample would have been larger if I gave the survey to students in class at the end of the semester, I would not have been able to assess whether these activities had any long-term impact. Table 7.1 shows the survey results pertaining to the role these activities played in improving classroom culture.

The survey asked students to comment on the overall value of doing these activities as related to their education in the course. One student wrote: "These small learning actives [*sic*] helped emphasize and visualize the material. Not

TABLE 7.1 Survey Results of Classroom Activities

These activities . . .	Not really	A little bit	Definitely
. . . made me more likely to come to class (n=22)	0%	9%	91%
. . . helped me get to know my classmates better (n=22)	4.5%	32%	62.5%
. . . were fun (n=22)	0%	14%	86%
. . . were unique (n=22)	0%	0%	100%
. . . were inclusive (n=22)	0%	9%	91%

SOURCE: Sara Parker

TABLE 7.2 Student Outcomes Data

	Fall 2011	Fall 2012	Fall 2014	Fall 2015
Average Final Participation Grade	76%	86%	89%	89%
Success Rate ("C" or better; excludes students who withdrew from the class)	60%	66%	84%	85%
N =	33	41	31	29

SOURCE: Sara Parker

only did they help reaffirm the material but also created a sense of community within the class in which everybody was safe to share ideas or opinions." Another wrote, "I also liked it because it made the class get to know each other more instead of everyone being quiet & uncomfortable. It's always nice when the teacher tries to include everyone & have fun." And, "These small activities are largely positive for understanding IR concepts and definitely promoted attendance; without being engaged the way I was, I wouldn't have really understood the theories section, much less the other key concepts taught. Plus given the nature of IR [International Relations] major, in hindsight it is a great way to network during these activities."

Student success data supports the impact this approach had on course outcomes: both student participation and passing rates increased from Fall 2011 and 2012, prior to the regularized use of learning activities, as compared to 2014 and 2015 (see Table 7.2).

In reading student comments I realized that these activities served as building blocks, giving students confidence in their understanding of the material in ways that helped them mentally and emotionally. Students were able to retain knowledge about key concepts. The literature tells us that students remember only a fraction of what they learn. One scholar cites several research findings that show: "'students retain 10 percent of what they read, 20 percent of what they hear, 30 percent of what they see, 50 percent of what they see and hear, 70 percent of what they say, and 90 percent of what they do and say together'" (Asal 2005:359). To evaluate this more concretely, I asked students to recall learning outcomes associated with five activities identified only by title. Over half of the students surveyed were able to correctly identify an intended learning outcome in *at least* four referenced activities. Students believed these activities helped them learn the material. As one student wrote, "When you learn about something, you don't really understand it until you've been placed in a situation where you're conducting an activity and learning material, because only then does it become a personal experience, which is more likely to be remembered." Eighty-two percent of students said that these activities *definitely helped them to understand the material better.*

IMPLICATIONS

Teaching "nontraditional" students is extremely rewarding largely due to the life experiences they bring to the classroom. Students reference native countries and cultural traditions, and they draw on everyday relationships with children and extended family, work experiences, stories of struggle, triumph, and future goals. As the demographics of the United States continue to shift to a minority-majority country, we can expect to see the entire landscape of American higher education reflect this degree of diversity.

Pedagogically grounded, innovative, passionate teaching serves *all* students, but first-generation students, underrepresented minorities, returning students, and others who fall into the "new majority" particularly deserve our focused efforts to teach in ways that respond to their unique needs.

NOTES

1. Although many of the ideas introduced herein may be effective in an online setting, the scope of this chapter focuses on classroom teaching.

2. For an excellent overview of scaffolding, see Rosenshein and Meister 1992.

3. Note that these figures include both two-year and four-year students.

4. Currently, 18 states allow undocumented students to pay in-state tuition; six states allow them to receive financial aid; three states prohibit undocumented students from enrolling (http://www.ncsl .org/research/education/undocumented-student-tuition-overview.aspx).

REFERENCES

AACC (American Association of Community Colleges). 2015. *2015 Fact Sheet*. Retrieved January 16, 2017 (http://www.aacc.nche.edu/AboutCC/Pages/fastfactsfactsheet.aspx).

Asal, Victor. 2005. "Playing Games with International Relations." *International Studies Perspectives* 6(3):359–73.

Bahr, Peter Riley. 2009. "College Hopping: Exploring the Occurrence, Frequency, and Consequences of Lateral Transfer." *Community College Review* 36:271–98.

Bahr, Peter Riley. 2012. "Student Flow Between Community Colleges: Investigating Lateral Flow." *Research in Higher Education* 53:94–121.

Barr, Jim, and Pam Schuetz. 2008. "Overview of Foundational Issues." *New Directions for Community Colleges* 144:7–16.

Belfield, Clive, and Peter M. Crosta. 2012. "Predicting Success in College: The Importance of Placement Tests and High School Transcripts." Community College Research Center, Working Paper No. 42.

Bickerstaff, Susan, Melissa Barragan, and Zawadi Rucks-Ahidiana. 2012. "'I Came in Unsure of Everything': Community College Students' Shifts in Confidence." Community College Research Center, Working Paper No. 48.

Bledsoe, T. Scott, and Janice J. Baskin. 2014. "Recognizing Student Fear: The Elephant in the Classroom." *College Teaching* 62:32–41.

Bonet, Giselle, and Barbara R. Walters. 2016. "High Impact Practices: Student Engagement and Retention." *College Student Journal* 50(2):224–35.

Braxton, John M., Amy S. Hirschy, and Shederick A. McClendon. 2004. "Understanding and Reducing College Student Departure." *ASHE-ERIC Higher Education Report* 30(3). San Francisco: Jossey-Bass.

Brown, Richard S., and David N. Niemi. 2007. *Investigating the Alignment of High School and Community College Assessment in California*. San Jose, CA: National Center for Public Policy and Higher Education.

Browne, Laurie, Melissa Hough, and Keri Schwab. 2009. "Scaffolding: A Promising Approach to Fostering Critical Thinking." *Schole: A Journal of Leisure Studies and Recreation Education* 24:22–28.

Byrd, Kathleen, and Ginger MacDonald. 2005. "Defining College Readiness from the Inside Out: First-Generation College Student Perspectives." *Community College Review* 33(1):22–37.

Center for Student Services. 2009. *Contextualized Teaching and Learning: A Faculty Primer*. Research and Planning Group for California Community Colleges. Retrieved January 16, 2017 (http://www.cccbsi.org/websites/basicskills/images/ctl.pdf).

Choy, Susan. 2001. *Students Whose Parents Did Not Go to College: Postsecondary Access, Persistence, and Attainment*. Washington, DC: National Center for Education Statistics.

Cohen, Arthur M., Florence Brawer, and Carrie B. Kisker. 2014. *The American Community College*. San Francisco: Jossey-Bass.

Conway, Katherine M. 2010. "Educational Aspirations in an Urban Community College: Differences between Immigrant and Native Student Groups." *Community College Review* 37(3):209–42.

Costa, Arthur L. 2008. "Describing the Habits of Mind." Pp. 15–41 in *Learning and Leading with Habits of Mind,* edited by Arthur L. Costa, and Bena Kallick. North Garden, VA: Association for Supervision and Curriculum Development.

Cox, Rebecca D. 2009. "Promoting Success by Addressing Students' Fear of Failure." *Community College Review* 37(1):52–80.

Crosta, Peter M. 2014. "Intensity and Attachment: How the Chaotic Enrollment Patterns of Community College Students Relate to Educational Outcomes." *Community College Review* 42(2):118–42.

Deil-Amen, Regina. 2011. "Beyond Remedial Dichotomies: Are 'Underprepared' College Students a Marginalized Majority?" *New Directions for Community Colleges* 155:59–71.

Dundes, Lauren, and Jeff Marx. 2006. "Balancing Work and Academics in College: Why Do Students Working 10 to 19 Hours per Week Excel?" *Journal of College Student Retention* 8:107–20.

Engle, Jennifer. 2007. "Postsecondary Access and Success for First-Generation College Students." *American Academic* 3:25–48.

Freeman, Scott, Sarah L. Eddy, Miles McDonough, Michelle K. Smith, Nnadozie Okoroafor, Hannah Jordt, and Mary Pat Wenderoth. 2014. "Active Learning Increases Student Performance in Science, Engineering, and Mathematics." *Proceedings of the National Academy of Sciences of the United States of America* 11(23):8410–15.

Fink, L. Dee. 2003. *Creating Significant Learning Experiences: An Integrated Approach to Designing College Courses.* San Francisco: Jossey-Bass.

Giancola, Jennifer Kohler, David C. Munz, and Shawn Trares. 2008. "First-Versus Continuing-Generation Adult Students on College Perceptions: Are Differences Actually Because of Demographic Variance." *Adult Education Quarterly* 58(3):214–28.

Goldrick-Rab, Sara. 2010. "Challenges and Opportunities for Improving Community College Student Success." *Review of Educational Research* 80(3): 437–69.

Goldrick-Rab, Sara, and Kia Sorensen. 2010. "Unmarried Parents in College." *Future of Children* 20(2):179–203.

Gurin, Patricia, Eric L. Dey, Sylvia Hurtado, and Gerald Gurin. 2002. "Diversity and Higher Education: Theory and Impact on Educational Outcomes." *Harvard Educational Review* 72(3):330–66.

Hancock, Dawson R. 2001. "Effects of Test Anxiety and Evaluative Threat on Students' Achievement and Motivation." *Journal of Educational Research* 94(5):284–90.

Hayward, Craig, and Terrance Willett. 2014. *Curricular Redesign and Gatekeeper Completion: A Multi College Evaluation of the California Acceleration Project.* Berkeley: Research and Planning Group for California Community Colleges.

Higher Education Research Institute. "Undergraduate Teaching Faculty: The 2013–14 HERI Faculty Survey." Retrieved January 16, 2017 (http://heri.ucla.edu/monographs/HERI-FAC2014-monograph.pdf).

Hilton III, John. 2016. "Open Educational Resources and College Textbook Choices: A Review of Research on Efficacy and Perceptions." *Educational Technology Research and Development* 64(4):573–90.

Loggins, Julie A. 2009. "Simulating the Foreign Policy Decision-Making Process in the Undergraduate Classroom." *PS: Political Science and Politics* 42(2):401–7.

Lundberg, Carol. 2014. "Peers and Faculty as Predictors of Learning for Community College Students." *Community College Review* 42(2):79–98.

Mangan, Katherine. 2015. "The Challenge of the First Generation Student." *Chronicle of Higher Education* 61(36):1–9.

Maxwell, William, Linda Serra Hagedorn, Scott Cypers, Hye S. Moon, Phillip Brocato, Kelly Wahl, and George Prather. 2003. "Community and Diversity in Urban Community Colleges: Coursetaking among Entering Students." *Community College Review* 30(4): 21–46.

McMullen-Light, Mary. 2010. "Great Expectations: The Culture of WAC and the Community College Context." *Across the Disciplines* 7 (November 30).

Mekolichick, Jeanne, and Michael Gibbs. 2012. "Understanding College Generational Status in the Undergraduate Research Mentored Relationship." *Council on Undergraduate Research Quarterly* 33(2):40–46.

Mounsey, Rebecca, Michael A. Vandehey, and George M. Diekhoff. 2013. "Working and Non-Working University Students: Anxiety, Depression, and Grade Point Average." *College Student Journal* 47(2):379–89.

National Center for Education Statistics. 2014. *Digest of Education Statistics, 2014* (NCES 2016–006). U.S. Department of Education. Retrieved January 16, 2017 (https://nces .ed.gov/programs/digest/d14/index.asp).

National Postsecondary Student Aid Study. 2013. *2011–12 National Postsecondary Student Aid Study (NPSAS: 12)*. Washington, DC: U.S. Department of Education, National Center for Education Statistics.

National Student Clearing House. 2015. "Snapshot Report: Contributions of Two-Year Institutions to Four-Year Completions." Retrieved October 17, 2016 (https://nscresearchcenter .org/wp-content/uploads/SnapshotReport17-2YearContributions.pdf).

Panacci, Adam G. 2015. "Adult Students in Higher Education: Classroom Experiences and Needs." *College Quarterly* 18(3):1–17.

Perin, Dolores. 2011. "Facilitating Student Learning through Contextualization: A Review of Evidence." *Community College Review* 39(3):268–95.

Ramsay, Nancy J. 2005. "Teaching Effectively in Racially and Culturally Diverse Classrooms." *Teaching Theology and Religion* 8(1):18–23.

Reading Apprenticeship at WestEd. N.d. "Overview" (College & Career). Retrieved October 16, 2016 (http://readingapprenticeship.org/our-approach/college-career/).

Rosenshein, Barak, and Carla Meister. 1992. "The Use of Scaffolds for Teaching Higher-Level Cognitive Strategies." *Educational Leadership* 49(7):26–33.

Shapiro, Doug, Aftet Dundar, Mary Ziskin, Yi-Chen Chiang, Autumn Harrell, and Vasti Torres. 2013. *Baccalaureate Attainment: A National View of the Postsecondary Outcomes of Student Who Transfer from Two-year to Four-year Institutions*. National Student Clearinghouse Research Center, Signature Report.

Suárez-Orozco, Carola, Hirokazu Yoshikawa, Robert T. Teranishi, and Marcelo M. Suárez-Orozco. 2011. "Growing Up in the Shadows: The Developmental Implications of Unauthorized Status." *Harvard Educational Review* 81(3):438–72.

Sweat, Jeffrey, Glenda Jones, Suejung Han, and Susan M. Wolfgram. 2013. "How Does High Impact Practice Predict Student Engagement? A Comparison of White and Minority

Students." *International Journal for the Scholarship of Teaching and Learning* 7(2): Article 17.

Teranishi, Robert T., Carola Suárez-Orozco, and Marcelo Suárez-Orozco. 2011. "Immigrants in Community Colleges." *Future of Children* 21(1):153–69.

Tovar, Esau. 2015. "The Role of Faculty, Counselors, and Support Programs on the Latino / a Community College Students' Success and Intent to Persist." *Community College Review* 43(1):46–71.

Wang, Xueli. 2009. "Baccalaureate Attainment and College Persistence of Community College Transfer Students at Four-Year Institution." *Research in Higher Education* 50:570–88.

Weaver, Robert R., and Jiang Qi. 2005. "Classroom Organization and Participation: College Students' Perceptions." *Journal of Higher Education* 76(5):570–601.

Wood, J. Luke, John D. Harrison, and T. Kenyatta Jones. 2016. "Black Males' Perceptions of the Work-College Balance: The Impact of Employment on Academic Succession the Community College." *Journal of Men's Studies* 24(3):326–43.

Wyatt, Linda G. 2011. "Nontraditional Student Engagement: Increasing Adult Student Success and Retention." *Journal of Continuing Higher Education* 59(1):10–20.

Addressing Learner Variability on Campus through Universal Design for Learning

Shannon Haley-Mize

Universal Design (UD) is a term used to describe the process of planning with intentional consideration of usability, accessibility, and inclusion for a wide range of users with variable skills and characteristics (Burgstahler 2015a). Initially used in the field of architecture to describe structure and space that is designed to be accessible to those with a range of physical capacity, UD has translated into several theoretical models that are applicable to education. These include Universal Instructional Design (UID; see Chickering and Gamson 1987), Universal Design for Instruction (UDI; see Burgstahler 2015a), and Universal Design for Learning (UDL; see Meyer, Rose, and Gordon 2014). Despite many features shared among the three models and similarities in the recommended instructional practices, some distinctions exist between them (see Burgstahler 2015c). Each of these frameworks can assist institutions in moving closer to the goal of equitable access and full inclusion in higher education.

The primary focus of this chapter is on UDL because the recommendations for implementation draw on research and strategies that align with this model; however, the chapter also includes some review of research and projects that use either one of the other models or the broader term UD. After a review of UDL theory and its relationship to diversity, this chapter examines the research on UD in higher education, application of UDL to various elements of course design, and briefly considers UDL's application to online learning environments and appropriate supports for college students with mental health issues. The chapter concludes with suggestions for implementation.

OVERVIEW OF UDL

Universal Design for Learning (UDL), developed by the Center for Applied Special Technology (CAST), is a framework for learning experiences and programs that are intentionally designed to meet the widest range of individual needs to allow universal access (Meyer et al. 2014). The UDL model is composed of the three principles of representation, action and expression, and engagement, and it espouses the notion that enhancing access for one group of individuals will ultimately benefit all. Each of the three principles, based on research in cognition and neuroscience, is associated with an area of the brain and align with what we know about how individuals learn. For each principle, CAST provided checkpoints that provide further detail on specific teaching and design approaches that support the three principles. These checkpoints can be invaluable tools for evaluating and improving current practice. CAST (2011) defines the UDL principles as follows:

1. *Representation*—The principle of representation is associated with the recognition network of the brain and is the "what" of learning. It includes how learners gather and categorize information perceived by the senses. To support recognition, instructors should present content in a variety of ways to facilitate learning. This includes multiple options for perception through different modalities (e.g., vision, hearing, or touch); options for language, mathematical expressions, and symbols to avoid inequalities in how students perceive content and support comprehension; and options for comprehension that include any scaffold necessary to ensure all learners have access to knowledge.

2. *Action and expression*—Action and expression is the domain of the strategic network of the brain and encompasses the "how" of learning. The principle of action and expression considers how learners organize and express ideas to plan and perform tasks. This domain incorporates options for physical action as well as expression and communication. Action and expression encompasses assessment of learning and includes providing options for students to demonstrate their knowledge, use of multiple media for communication, and support of executive functions such as goal setting.

3. *Engagement*—The principle of engagement is aligned with the affective networks of the brain and includes the "why" of learning. This principle examines why certain learners become engaged and are able to sustain motivation during the learning process. To achieve learner engagement, instructors should consider options for recruiting interest, sustaining effort and persistence, and self-regulation. Options that support engagement include optimizing choice and fostering collaboration, among other considerations.

UDL AND DIVERSITY

UDL is a potentially powerful tool to address equity and access issues that are presented by the growing diversity in the student body at institutions of higher education. UDL fills a void in research-based practice on equitable access for postsecondary students with disabilities. In contrast to the lack of research on students with disabilities in higher education, there is a growing body of work that deals with the impact of a racially and ethnically diverse educational community, and this research helps to guide campus supports. Disability is examined less frequently (McCune 2001), prompting some scholars to point out that even in conversations about inclusion, disability is marginalized (Higbee, Katz, and Schultz 2010).

UDL has the potential to impact all learners, but given the dearth of research on appropriate access for students with disabilities and the numbers of individuals with disabilities, it is imperative to eradicate barriers for this population specifically. Approximately 11 percent of college students report having a disability (NCES 2016). One study that examined types of disabilities reported approximately 31 percent of these students indicated a learning disability, 18 percent reported attention deficit, and 15 percent cited mental health conditions (NCES 1999). A variety of other disabilities such as autism were reported less frequently. There is a significant difference in achievement for this group when compared to peers who do not have a disability or other at-risk status. For example, college students with disabilities are far less likely to graduate when compared to peers without disabilities. About 38 percent of students with disabilities who begin attending will finish, compared to 51 percent of students who do not have a disability (Sanford et al. 2011). Both individual and institutional factors influence these poorer outcomes (Burgstahler 2015b). One example of an individual factor is self-determination skills, such as the ability to advocate for accommodations that remove barriers to access of facilities, services, and content. Institutional factors that impact these outcomes include accessibility of services and courses (Burgstahler and Cory 2008).

Many individuals with disabilities who go on to postsecondary institutions face barriers that contribute to the lower rates of retention and graduation. There is evidence that many students with disabilities do not enroll in campus disability services and, thus, do not request accommodations and modifications (Getzel 2008). The large number of students who do not access these services is likely partially attributable to the stigma surrounding disability as a construct. The model of requiring students to self-identify as having a disability and to request accommodation perpetuates the idea that the individual has a deficit and, thus, needs a "fix" to be able to participate. In contrast, UDL is aligned with the social model of disability that "posits that it is not an individual's impairment or adjustment but the socially imposed barriers—the inaccessible buildings, the limited modes of transportation and communication, the prejudicial attitudes—that construct disability as a subordinate social status and devalued life experience" (Berger and Lorenz 2015:1). Advocates for a UDL approach to course and service design recognize that addressing accessibility and inclusion during the planning process communicates that difference, or learner variability, is the expectation—the rule rather than the exception. As Burgstahler (2015b) intimates:

> focusing on difference rather than deficit supports the social model of disability and other integrated approaches within the field of disability studies that consider variations—such as those with respect to gender, size, socioeconomic status, race, ethnicity, and ability—a normal part of the human experience. Thus, disability is viewed simply as one aspect of a spectrum of human variations. (P. 7)

UDL theory also exemplifies a social justice perspective because it ideally results in "full and equal participation of all groups in a society that is mutually shaped to meet their needs" (Adams, Bell, and Griffin 2007:1). This perspective makes UDL especially relevant to the teaching across disciplines that demonstrate a "long disciplinary history of engagement with social issues" (Petray and Halbert 2013:441) and allows faculty and support staff at institutions of higher education to assume and model the role of change agents. Additionally, UDL encourages examination of both environmental and individual characteristics employing sociological imagination to contextualize experience in terms of social structures to avoid confinement in the individual experience (Mills 2000). This inspires a transformative mindset. This view insists that the environment is the source of the disability and, thus, should be the focus of interventions (Evans 2008).

Accommodations vs. UDL

The American with Disabilities Education Act (1990) defines a reasonable accommodation as one that renders existing facilitates accessible and useable by individuals with disabilities. This includes modifications to equipment, examinations, and content materials. It also includes provision of accessible documents and qualified readers or interpreters. Providing accommodations for individual students in a reactive fashion has disadvantages beyond perpetuating the idea that the disability is a problem or individual deficit and requires a solution. Institutions only provide accommodations to students that self-identify as having a disability and articulate that the course or service is inaccessible. This is a problem because, as previously noted, research shows that most college students with disabilities do not reach out to disability service offices, which makes them ineligible for supports (Wagner et al. 2005). Securing accommodations requires that the student make an extra effort that is not necessary for other students. This process of seeking out accommodations to access course materials and other campus services marginalizes students with disabilities. Accessible documents and materials may not be readily available and require time to produce, which may result in the student not having access to content in the same time frame as other students. In addition, providing accommodations to individual students does not have the potential to benefit all students.

In contrast, UDL is a proactive approach that involves designing courses and other student services in a manner that deliberately analyzes and removes barriers that may be present for a wide variety of learners. The UDL process prompts faculty and staff to think like designers and to create content, experiences, services, and environments that are more likely to be accessible to all. This represents a paradigm shift from a narrow focus on a "normal" user to instead consider a wide range of human characteristics and variability (Myers, Lindburg, and Nied 2013).

RESEARCH

As Edyburn (2010) articulated, there is a lack of empirical research on the application of UDL in learning environments. The existing, relatively small foundation of empirical research is more robust if the examination includes the broader term of UD as search criteria. Most of the work examined in the published reviews and in additional studies cited in this section is qualitative, including action research. This section includes a few examples of quasi-experimental studies (e.g., Davies, Schelly, and Spooner 2013) and one experimental study (Spooner et al. 2007).

A review of current research on UD in educational settings conducted by Rao, Ok, and Bryant (2014) identified only 13 journal articles that empirically evaluated application of UD to the teaching and learning process. A review by Roberts et al. (2015) included 19 articles, with five studies overlapping between the two reviews. Overall, results indicated that studies reported gains in specific academic outcomes, improved access for students with reading difficulties, increased student engagement, fostered formation of community, and increased interaction in college courses. Rao et al. (2014) warn that "the evidence should be interpreted with caution as a set of preliminary positive results based on varied methods of analysis" (p. 162).

A recent study by Black, Weinberg, and Brodwin (2015), not included in either of the aforementioned reviews, examined the perspectives of college students with disabilities on teaching methods and pedagogy that they perceived as being supportive of their learning. The researchers then determined if the strategies identified by the students as beneficial were aligned with UDL. Students reported that they experienced barriers to learning and that UDL practices were helpful. One interesting theme that emerged was the students' belief that faculty and staff would benefit from basic awareness training and professional development on how to work with students with disabilities. In a similar vein, students reported that some accommodations were not appropriately executed.

Some evidence exists that faculty professional development (PD) is effective in improving application of UD to course design and instruction. For example, a study by Zhang (2005) found that sustained and targeted PD was effective in improving participants' growth and use of technology. Faculty identified UDL as a high-need training topic, and web-based, self-paced PD increased participants' self-efficacy in meeting the needs of students with a wide variety of needs (Izzo, Murray, and Novak 2008). Davies et al. (2013) also reported that students perceived UDL professional development had significant positive effect on teaching methods employed by faculty.

The research investigating UD application to online course development demonstrates a positive impact on a variety of student factors and perceptions of learning. Ye He (2014) found that student self-efficacy in teaching and learning online improved after participation in a course using UD principles. Participants reported that pacing and flexibility were the most impactful elements in the course.

APPLICATION

UDL is a powerful academic design tool when employed in higher education. Consideration of several components of course construction using a UDL lens is advantageous, and resources for instructors are readily available. The following recommendations were compiled using resources available at CAST's UDL on Campus site (www.udloncampus.cast.org) and the DO-IT program housed at the University of Washington (http://www.washington.edu/doit).

Syllabus

The syllabus serves as a roadmap for the course and shapes the students' initial impressions of the type of learning environment that the instructor will establish in the classroom. Therefore, at a minimum, the syllabus should be an accessible document. Because UDL is best integrated during the design of the course, the syllabus is the perfect starting point for constructing a UDL course. The course instructor can use the syllabus to set the climate of the course, to articulate expectations, and to give information about options and accessibility. There are several modifications that can be made to syllabus design to support a broader range of individuals and improve access. For example, the course calendar can list the readings and media in all formats available and give guidance on how to access the content. The syllabus also usually outlines how learning will be assessed and allows another opportunity to articulate the UDL options embedded in the course by highlighting options for action and expression.

The syllabus should serve as a personal introduction of the instructor. A section in the syllabus should be dedicated to introducing the instructor, and this section can be used to engage students through use of a photo and video. This type of enhanced introduction allows students to get to know the instructor, the expectations, and the structure of the course. Several methods of communication and options for obtaining answers to questions should be provided such as email, phone, text, discussion boards dedicated to course questions, and links to any instructor, professional social media accounts.

The course syllabus should include the statement on accommodations, a description of the course, and course objectives. Instructors can apply UDL considerations to each of these syllabus components. First, consider putting the disability statement and available supports at the beginning of the syllabus rather than at the end. This ensures that students see the information, and it communicates that the instructor prioritizes their success in the course. Second, the course description should identify clear goals for the course and establish relevance to the students. Third, carefully articulate the objectives and connect them directly to the assignments. This makes the purpose of each assignment in the course explicit. To clarify the course material, divide objectives by topic. Utilizing a graphic organizer helps to display how course objectives relate.

Course Materials

During course design, instructors can also assemble course materials using the UDL approach. A UDL course designer considers a wide variety of materials beyond printed text. Content can be provided in different formats such as digital versions of class presentations. Videotaping the course sessions and making the videos available on the online course platform ensures multiple pathways to the content. Designers can also make any materials such as handouts, videos, and PowerPoint presentations accessible online. These alternatives allow for multiple sources of representation of the same content and increase engagement. Designers can invite students to contribute to a collection of materials related to the course content to encourage shared ownership. These materials might include online resources such as streaming video, related social media accounts, or links to pertinent professional agencies that extend the course content. As materials are amassed, the instructor should ensure that included material is accessible to all learners. For example, videos should have closed captioning, documents should be compatible with screen reader technology, and images should have captions.

Assignments and Assessments

Course assignments and assessments are under the purview of the UDL principle of action and expression. This principle prompts course designers to consider choices for physical actions, expression and communication, and executive functions. Potential barriers, including construct-irrelevant factors, should be identified. Instructors must differentiate the actual content that they want to test, from construct-irrelevant factors that potentially act as barriers. For example, if the purpose of an assessment is to analyze the student's content knowledge on a specific topic, it may be that requiring an essay response on an assessment includes factors that are irrelevant to the learning objective but are nonetheless required for the response. If part of the learning objective is to assess the student's ability to synthesize information, then an essay response may be appropriate, but perhaps spelling ability or the speed at which the student completes the response are construct irrelevant, so the designer could eliminate those potential barriers by allowing access to a dictionary and unlimited time for completion.

A course that incorporates dependable routines and expectations assists students with planning and prioritizing. Instructors should explicitly state assignment deadlines in the course schedule and incorporate feedback into a predictable routine. These routines can be outlined in the syllabus with weekly content and connections with the course objectives. A well-designed, UDL course also allows numerous opportunities for the instructor to detail expectations for learners. Instructors can articulate these expectations in the introductory video and revisit them frequently at different intervals over the length of the semester.

Course Delivery

Course delivery is a vital consideration from a ULD perspective. There are some general recommendations in this realm. For face-to-face classes, provide a digital space for collecting accessible artifacts and materials and to extend the discussion. Artifacts and materials include captioned photos of products created during class, digital versions of notes and presentations, and links to streaming or other videos used during class. Opportunities to extend the dialogue in the online course space might include discussion boards, designed boards for questions about the course content, or links to online platforms that include forums. For online courses, offer at least one opportunity for a meeting in person. The students may not take advantage of it or may not be able to meet due to factors such as distance, but it is a consideration when feasible.

Considerations for Online Learning

In order to meet the requirements of federal law and to provide equitable access, UDL should also be applied to online learning experiences (Case and Davidson 2011). There are some affordances of online learning for students with disabilities. In general, digital text is more flexible and malleable than printed material. Digital spaces can support multiple media and hyperlinked text that allow options for representation of content and scaffolding. Digital content can be varied in order to facilitate and support student engagement. Many digital platforms also support collaboration, allowing for options for action and expression.

To realize the potential of these affordances, instructors should create accessible materials and documents. The Web Content Accessibility Guidelines (WCAG 2.0 2016) provide guidance in the form of four principles to consider when creating accessible, web-based content.

In addition to the WCAG 2.0 guidance, data from studies conducted with students with disabilities identify priorities for UDL-designed, online learning experiences. For example, Catalano (2014) collected interview data from students with disabilities who were participants in a course using a UD design. The common themes that emerged from this examination included the need for clear expectations, frequent interaction with the professor, audio accompaniment for tutorials and presentations, and feedback on assignments. The students also highlighted a video introduction of the instructor, an invitation to meet in person, and timely answers to emails as essential components.

These student recommendations are consistent with CAST's suggestions on how to design effective online courses for a wide variety of learners. CAST also emphasizes the need for executive functioning support in an online environment. Executive functioning includes setting appropriate goals, planning and organizing, developing steps to achieve a goal, and using strategies for problem solving. Other executive functions are prioritizing, self-discipline, and monitoring progress (Huizinga, Dolan, and van der Molen 2006). Executive functioning is essential for success in all learning experiences, but becomes especially critical in an online environment. Designers can provide the necessary supports by incorporating clear, interactive course headings and icons; grouping content into small, logical modules; incorporating checklists for monitoring progress; and providing self-check quizzes and activities with immediate feedback. Students also benefit from options to create notes in various ways, annotate material, and organize resources.

Students with Mental Health Needs

Although it is difficult to discern exact statistics due to reliance on self-disclosure, evidence does exist that the number of college students with mental health issues is increasing, and these learners often experience educational challenges (Rickerson, Souma, and Burgstahler 2012). One estimate indicates that despite this growth in enrollment, as many as 86 percent of students with psychiatric disabilities withdraw before completing their degrees (Collins and Mowbray 2005). Teaching strategies consistent with UD can address various characteristics of this type of "invisible disability." Application of UD principles is especially important for these students because studies have found that as few as 10 percent access accommodations, which is likely due to the stigma associated with mental illness (Koch, Mamiseishvili, and Higgins 2014). Another contributing factor may be the lack of awareness of services.

Several components of the traditional college classroom may present barriers for these students. They may struggle with paying attention to the lecture and class discussion while simultaneously taking adequate notes. Pacing of courses may require that students grasp concepts quickly and that students navigate complex interactions with the instructor and their peers—especially if the instructor employs a variety of pedagogical strategies and uses flexible grouping.

Applying UDL to course design to reduce barriers for students with mental health issues also means that instructors should give consideration to testing and class assignments. These students may struggle with heightened test anxiety, which may impact performance. Poor time management and limited ability to organize multiple assignments can further negatively impact performance. Because of these factors, instructors must consider a variety of alternative assessment strategies that encourage students to express their knowledge in a variety of ways. Examples include portfolios, presentations, research assignments, peer and self-evaluations, and creative projects that align with the learning objectives. Digital tools provide a wealth of options for multiple means of expression from digital storyboards to comic strips. Class assignments can also include multiple means of expressing and gaining knowledge. These alternatives can incorporate activities such as debates, case studies, and discussion. Other tools include brainstorming sessions and cooperative projects. Students might also benefit from scaffolding for more complex assignments and frequent due dates for smaller portions of a large project.

IMPLEMENTATION

Institutional Level

Professional development (PD) to raise awareness for faculty and staff across campus has been demonstrated to be effective in establishing a foundation for greater accessibility and inclusion of students with disabilities in higher education (Lombardi and Murray 2011; Murray, Lombardi, and Wren 2011). To support faculty in making meaningful changes in course design and teaching practices, PD should include specific action steps (Edyburn 2010). Assessment tools are available to evaluate inclusive teaching practices (Lombardi, Murray, and Gerdes 2011) and guide PD topics.

Change Process at a Course Level

Nelson (2014) suggests the following steps to integrate UDL into instruction:

1. Reflect on the needs of students. Ask yourself, "What are my students struggling with?"
2. Identify a principle or a specific checkpoint that addresses the student need identified. Ask, "How might I use this checkpoint to meet the needs of learners?"
3. Investigate and create new pedagogical methods or strategies. Pose the question, "What brings this principle or checkpoint to life?"
4. Teach a lesson with the new method / strategy. Prompt yourself to think about "What does this principle or checkpoint look like in my teaching environment?"

5. Assess the method / strategy by asking, "In what ways did my students demonstrate knowledge or skills?"
6. Reflect on how the new method / strategy worked by considering, "How did the principle or checkpoint enhance student outcomes?"

CONCLUSION

The impetus for using the UDL framework is multifaceted and grounded in the social model of disability that conceptualizes learner variability as the expectation, rather than a problem to be rectified. UDL shifts the traditional deficit-based view of disability to a critical analysis of the curriculum as a source of potential barriers and provides guidance on ways to ameliorate those barriers. UDL has the potential to benefit all learners and is applicable to online learning environments. UDL also provides solutions for faculty and staff struggling to meet the needs of the growing population of students with mental health needs. Campuses can build capacity for the use of UDL across academic and student services by providing professional development and supporting a gradual implementation that includes incremental changes and reflection.

REFERENCES

Adams, Maurianne, Lee Anne Bell, and Pat Griffin. 2007. *Teaching for Diversity and Social Justice*. New York: Routledge.

Americans with Disabilities Act of 1990, Public Law 101-336, 104 U.S. Statutes at Large 328 (1990).

Berger, Ronald J., and Laura S. Lorenz. 2015. *Disability and Qualitative Inquiry: Methods for Rethinking an Ableist World*. New York: Routledge.

Black, Robert D., Lois A. Weinberg, and Martin G. Brodwin. 2015. "Universal Design for Learning and Instruction: Perspectives of Students with Disabilities in Higher Education." *Exceptionality Education International* 25(2):1–16.

Burgstahler, Sheryl E. 2015a. *Equal Access: Universal Design of Instruction*. Seattle: University of Washington.

Burgstahler, Sheryl E. 2015b. "Universal Design in Higher Education." Pp. 3–28 in *Universal Design in Higher Education: From Principles to Practice*, edited by S. E. Burgstahler. Cambridge, MA: Harvard Education Press.

Burgstahler, Sheryl E. 2015c. "Universal Design of Instruction: From Principles to Practice." Pp. 3–28 in *Universal Design in Higher Education: From Principles to Practice*, edited by S. E. Burgstahler. Cambridge, MA: Harvard Education Press.

Burgstahler, Sheryl E., and Rebecca C. Cory. 2008. *Universal Design in Higher Education: From Principles to Practice*. Cambridge, MA: Harvard Education Press.

Case, D. Elizabeth, and Roseanna C. Davidson. 2011. "Accessible Online Learning." Pp. 47–58 in *Fostering the Increased Integration of Students with Disabilities: New Directions for Student Services*, edited by M. Huger. San Francisco: Jossey-Bass.

Center for Applied Special Technology (CAST). N.d. *UDL on Campus*. Retrieved January 20, 2017 (http://udloncampus.cast.org/home#.WHZvx7GZPUo).

Center for Applied Special Technology (CAST). 2011. *Universal Design for Learning Guidelines version 2.0*. Retrieved January 20, 2017 (http://www.udlcenter.org/aboutudl/udlguidelines /principle1).

Catalano, Amy. 2014. "Improving Distance Education for Students with Special Needs: A Qualitative Study of Students' Experiences with an Online Library Research Course." *Journal of Library and Information Services in Distance Learning* 8(1):17–31.

Chickering, Arthur W., and Zelda F. Gamson. 1987. "Seven Principles for Good Practice in Undergraduate Education." *AAHE Bulletin* 39(7):3–7.

Collins, Mary Elizabeth, and Carol T. Mowbray. 2005. "Higher Education and Psychiatric Disabilities: National Survey of Campus Disability Services." *American Journal of Orthopsychiatry* 75(2):304–15.

Davies, Patricia L., Catherine L. Schelly, and Craig L. Spooner. 2013. "Measuring the Effectiveness of Universal Design for Learning Intervention in Postsecondary Education." *Journal of Postsecondary Education and Disability* 26(3):195–220.

Edyburn, Dave L. 2010. "Would You Recognize Universal Design for Learning if You Saw It? Ten Propositions for the Second Decade of UDL." *Learning Disability Quarterly* 33(1):1–41.

Evans, Nancy. 2008. "Theoretical Foundations of Universal Instructional Design." Pp. 11–24 in *Pedagogy and Student Services for Institutional Transformation: Implementing Universal Design in Higher Education*, edited by J. L. Higbee and E. Goff. Minneapolis: Regents of the University of Minnesota, Center for Research on Developmental Education and Urban Literacy, College of Education and Human Development. Retrieved January 25, 2017 (http://www.cehd.umn.edu/passit/docs/PASS-IT-Book.pdf).

Getzel, Elizabeth E. 2008. "Addressing the Persistence and Retention of Students with Disabilities in Higher Education: Incorporating Key Strategies and Supports on Campus." *Exceptionality* 16(4):207–19.

He, Ye. 2014. "Universal Design for Learning in an Online Teacher Education Course: Enhancing Learners Confidence to Teach Online." *MERLOT Journal of Online and Teaching* 10(2):283–98.

Higbee, Jeanne L., Rachel E. Katz, and Jennifer L. Schultz. 2010. "Disability in Higher Education: Redefining Mainstreaming." *Journal of Diversity Management* 5(2):7–16.

Huizinga, Mariette, Conor V. Dolan, and M. W. Maurits van der Molen. 2006. "Age-Related Change in Executive Function: Developmental Trends and a Latent Variable Analysis." *Neuropsychologia* 44(11):2017–36.

Izzo, Margaretha V., Alexa Murray, and Jeanne Novak. 2008. "The Faculty Perspective on Universal Design for Learning." *Journal of Postsecondary Education and Disability* 21(2):60–72.

Koch, Lynn C., Ketevan Mamiseishvili, and Kirstin Higgins. 2014. "Persistence to Degree Completion: A Profile of Students with Psychiatric Disabilities in Higher Education." *Journal of Vocational Rehabilitation* 40(1):73–82.

Lombardi, Allison R., and Christopher Murray. 2011. "Measuring University Faculty Attitudes Toward Disability: Willingness to Accommodate and Adopt Universal Design Principles." *Journal of Vocational Rehabilitation* 34(1):43–56.

Lombardi, Allison R., Christopher Murray, and Hilary Gerdes. 2011. "College Faculty and Inclusive Instruction: Self-Reported Attitudes and Actions Pertaining to Universal Design." *Journal of Diversity in Higher Education* 4(4):250–61.

McCune, Pat. 2001. "What Do Disabilities Have to Do with Diversity?" *About Campus* 6(2):5–12.

Meyer, Anne, Derek H. Rose, and David Gordon. 2014. *Universal Design for Learning: Theory and Practice.* Wakefield, MA: CAST Professional.

Mills, C. Wright. [1959] 2000. *The Sociological Imagination.* Oxford: Oxford University Press.

Murray, Christopher, Allison Lombardi, and Carol T. Wren. 2011. "The Effects of Disability-Focused Training on the Attitudes and Perceptions of University Staff." *Remedial and Special Education* 32(4):290–300.

Myers, Karen A., Jaci J. Lindburg, and Danielle M. Nied. 2013. *Allies for Inclusion: Disability and Equity in Higher Education.* Hoboken, NJ: Wiley Periodicals.

NCES (National Center for Educational Statistics). 1999. "An Institutional Perspective on Students with Disabilities in Postsecondary Education." *Postsecondary Education Quick Information System.* U.S. Department of Education. Retrieved September 8, 2017 (https://cms.hutchcc.edu/uploadedFiles/StudentServices/DisabilityServices/instpers .pdf).

NCES (National Center for Education Statistics). 2016. *Digest of Education Statistics 2014* (2016–006). U.S. Department of Education. Retrieved January 21, 2017 (https://nces .ed.gov/fastfacts/display.asp?id = 60).

Nelson, Loui L. 2014. *Design and Deliver: Planning and Teaching Using Universal Design for Learning.* Baltimore, MD: Brookes.

Petray, Theresa, and Kelsey Halbert. 2013. "Teaching Engagement: Reflections on Sociological Praxis." *Journal of Sociology* 49(4):441–55.

Rao, Kavita, Min Wook Ok, and Brian R. Bryant. 2014. "A Review of Research on Universal Design Educational Models." *Remedial and Special Education* 35(3):153–66.

Rickerson, Nancy, Alfred Souma, and Sheryl Burgstahler 2012. *Psychiatric Disabilities in Postsecondary Education: Universal Design, Accommodations, and Supported Education.* Seattle: DO-IT, University of Washington.

Roberts, Kelly, Hye Jin Park, Steven Brown, and Bryan Cook. 2015. "Universal Design for Instruction in Postsecondary Education: A Systematic Review of Empirically Based Articles." *Journal of Postsecondary Education and Disability* 24(1):5–15.

Sanford, Christopher, Lynn Newman, Mary Wagner, Renée Cameto, Anne Marie Knokey, and Debra Shaver. 2011. *The Post–High School Outcomes of Young Adults with Disabilities Up to 6 Years after High School: Key Findings from the National Longitudinal Transition Study-2 (NLTS2)* (NCSER 2011–3004). Menlo Park, CA: SRI International. Retrieved January 26, 2017 (https://ies.ed.gov/ncser/pubs/20113004/pdf/20113004.pdf).

Spooner, Fred, Joshua N. Baker, Amber A. Harris, Lynn Ahlgrim-Delzell, and Diane M. Browder. 2007. "Effects of Training in Universal Design for Learning on Lesson Plan Development." *Remedial and Special Education* 28(2):108–16.

Wagner, Mary, Lynn Newman, Renée Cameto, Nicolle Garza, and Phyllis Levine. 2005. *After High School: A First Look at the Postschool Experiences of Youth with Disabilities. A*

Report from the National Longitudinal Transition Study-2 (NLTS2). Menlo Park, CA: SRI International. Retrieved January 29, 2017 (http://www.nlts2.org/reports/2005_04/nlts2 _report_2005_04_complete.pdf).

Web Accessibility Initiative. 2016. "How to Meet WCAG 2.0." Retrieved January 20, 2017 (https://www.w3.org/WAI/WCAG20/quickref/.).

Wisbey, Martha E., and Karen S. Kalivoda. 2011. "College Students with Disabilities." Pp. 347–370 in *Multiculturalism on Campus,* edited by M. J. Cuyjet, M. F. Howard-Hamilton, and D. L. Cooper. Sterling, VA: Stylus.

Zhang, Yixin. 2005. "A Collaborative Professional Development Model: Focusing on Universal Design for Technology Utilization." *ERS Spectrum* 23(3):32–33.

PART II

Classroom Techniques

9

Without Apology

Reclaiming the Lecture

Diane L. Pike

On the way to my roundtable at the Midwest Sociological Society AKD work-shop, a colleague whom I knew slightly asked me what my topic was.

"How to give better lectures," I answered.

She raised her chin, actually snorted, and declared, "I never lecture in my courses."

Seriously?

"Of course you lecture," I thought to myself, as I faked a smile and let her go ahead—clearly not on her way to join my group.

This encounter illustrates an enduring 30-plus year trend in higher education to bash, dismiss, question, and declare dead the lecture as a meaningful pedagogy in college learning. Such assertions often appear anchored in some purported moral high ground. Particularly, but not exclusively, in the natural sciences and professional studies, there persists an approach to lecture that is reminiscent of the Queen of Hearts' tendency to pronounce "Off with their heads!" (Fortunately, the King quietly pardons the condemned when the Queen is not looking.)

The problem, however, is *not* lecture per se. Lecture remains the dominant modality in undergraduate college and university teaching, despite the attention to active and experiential learning and to the integration of technology (Cashin 2010; Weimer 2014). Most of us continue to spend significant time explaining in depth, presenting ideas, crafting arguments, imparting information to students, and engaging in what is called "direct instruction." Walk down most any hallway and peer into classrooms to confirm this pattern. You might also track for a week or two the amount of time spent lecturing in your own courses and see what these data reveal.

The problem is lousy lectures, too much lecture, and lecture for the wrong purposes. Whether we lecture for 20 or 80 percent of a class session or an entire course, it matters that we lecture so that students are engaged and learning; such an approach to lecture is commonly understood to be "interactive lecture." The traditional college classroom lecture has been defined as everything from "the professor speaking for most of the period" (Wiggins 2014) to "more or less continuous expositions by a speaker who wants an audience to learn something" (Bligh 2000) to "a special form of communication in which voice, gesture, movement, facial expression, and eye contact can either complement or detract from the content" (Cashin 2010). For our purposes here, lecture refers to face-to-face, oral delivery by the professor of prepared course-relevant material. Done well, lecture is one valuable way to establish relationships between people and ideas, engage with new material, model thinking, and create a classroom environment that works.

Yet we are in a moment in higher education when lecture alternatives are being aggressively marketed and put into practice. This trend is a result of both pressures to adopt new technologies and therefore different pedagogies, as well as the cyclical realization that we need to take teaching seriously and keep our teachings current. Nearly wholesale rejection of lecture is being promoted in many places, but it fails to serve either the students or instructors very well.

My hope is that this chapter succeeds in helping us reclaim a pedagogy that endures for at least the foreseeable future. I make three claims that, while neither wholly original nor even new, nevertheless bear repeating, are worth acting upon, and contain some valuable insights into our teaching. First, we must pay more attention to when and how we lecture. Second, we must simultaneously understand that "the lecture" continues to morph to fit the current educational context to which we must adapt. Third, there are better and worse ways to execute this pedagogy. We should try for better.

THE TENACITY OF LECTURE

"Why lectures are dead (or soon will be)" (Bates 2014). This dramatic statement by a British educator and author in his blog / open textbook is just one example of the sweeping claims made about lectures and lecturing. Nary does a week go by without someone in the *Chronicle of Higher Education,* on blogs, in university leader press conferences, or in TED talks boldly disdaining lecture and advocating for its replacement. They rarely advocate for its improvement. The claims are frequently made by faculty and nonfaculty (publishers, politicians, pundits) who embrace digital learning as the solution to every problem in higher education (Christensen, Horn, and Johnson 2008; DeMillo and Young 2015; Skonnard 2015).[1] Bates writes that technology in lecture (e.g., tablets in class, clickers, PowerPoint) is just "lipstick on a pig" because all lecture can do is transmit information. He closes his discussion suggesting that institutions might better spend their money, not on classrooms and lecture theatres, but "on digitizing the curriculum and making it openly available" since lectures, in the future, will likely be "'special events' that are multi-media, synchronously and asynchronously delivered" (2014).

To physics Nobel laureate Carl Wieman, the college lecture is the educational equivalent of bloodletting (Westervelt 2016). By all accounts a brilliant research scientist, Wieman appears to have discovered midcareer that teaching could be improved if faculty did not lecture all the time. At the broadest level, the shift appeared to be that having students observe a professor work a problem on the board in a huge lecture hall was less useful than having the students work the problem in class with peers. Wieman became focused in his rejection of lecture and in his affection for clickers, leading to the Science Education Initiative while still teaching at CU Boulder (http://www.colorado.edu/sei/). Today at Stanford, holding a joint appointment in physics and the graduate school of education, Wieman and his partners continue to apply a scientific approach to teaching.

Similarly, Harvard's Eric Mazur, who like Wieman gives lots of lectures about not lecturing, helped revolutionize the teaching of physics.[2] As recently as June 2016 the lead article in the *Chronicle of Higher Education* characterized Mazur as a "teaching evangelist" who wonders "whether lecture (is) an ethical teaching choice (because) as the primary vehicle for teaching, it's completely outmoded" (Berrett 2016). Mazur fleetingly acknowledges the place of some lecture, some of the time, but the message is clear.

This awakening to the challenges of teaching well, and the resulting media attention on those individuals who are leading the charge, is what I have come to call the "Harvard Effect"—if someone at Harvard (or with a Nobel Prize) points it out, it gets attention. Think of this idea as a version of Merton's Matthew Effect—that scientists who have stature benefit disproportionally. Wieman, Mazur, and others promote good practices based on the scholarship of teaching and learning, and they add to the knowledge base with their own research. But their "discovery" that teaching is difficult to do well, and specifically that traditional lecture does not work as well as we think, is not new. Maybe it is like seeing snow for the first time if you grew up in Tahiti.

For decades, faculty developers and scholars of teaching and learning, as well as instructors in the trenches, have made the case for taking teaching seriously and building our skills with the same high-quality expectations we look for in disciplinary research. This movement has been especially strong in sociology. The deep body of cross-disciplinary work produced in the 1980s through today includes that of Wilbert McKeachie et al. (1987), Chickering and Gamson (1987), Kenneth Eble (1976), Maryellen Weimer (1990), Barr and Tagg (1995), Smith (1996), and Stephen Brookfield (1995). Sociologists Kathleen McKinney (1993, with Mary Graham-Buxton) and Daniel Chambliss (1999) have done seminal work in the scholarship of teaching and learning and on scholarly teaching. Many valuable ideas are included in the still relevant volume by Pescosolido and Aminzade, *The Social Worlds of Higher Education* (1999). Recent resources include the ASA journal *Teaching Sociology*, ASA's TRAILS digital library on teaching resources, *First Contact* (Greenwood and Howard 2011), and *In the Trenches* (Atkinson and Lowney 2016).

Acknowledging the existence of this wealth of accumulated knowledge and practice wisdom is important when we evaluate the present recommendations for change and when we identify new evangelists. There is no fault in Nobel laureates and Harvard professors doing more good work to promote good teaching. I just think that we should be clear that there was already snow.

To be sure, teaching in higher education today demands deep improvements, as do most other institutions (politics? banking? K–12? health care, anyone?). So, the effort here to reclaim lecture as an effective teaching and learning tool is not an assertion that lecture as it is currently practiced is just fine. Does some lecturing work pretty well? Yes. Does enough of our lecturing work pretty well? No. As critics have long pointed out, lecture in practice is in need of some serious upgrading (Bonwell and Eison 1991; Faust and Paulson 1998; Prince 2004). This upgrading requires more explicit attention to why, when, and how we lecture.

LECTURE TODAY

The settings of our teaching are in some ways unchanged from centuries of modern Western education—usually one professor, multiple students, a syllabus, a slate, a chalk- or whiteboard, a digital projector / laptop depending on the decade, readings, assignments, course units, and so on. There are things some of us have done for decades because they work.

There are things, of course, that have changed. Increased heterogeneity of student demographic profiles, evolving student motivations, digital learning opportunities and requirements, new knowledge and skills, and the stakeholder expectations as to what an education should and can be are all challenging our professional practices. These differences are significant, and they matter for our teaching. Thus, some of the things we did in the past (or still do) do not work today because the setting is changing. We can take more responsibility for what is working and what is failing.

So what should we pay attention to if we want to enhance our lecture practice? What features strengthen and improve this pedagogy? What should we avoid? Most importantly, how can effective, interactive lecture support the features of learning that really matter?

One distillation of the large body of scholarship on teaching and learning in this area is organized around the four dimensions in Table 9.1: the lecture, lecturing, the lecturer, and the lectured. The differentiations are not hard-lined and the characteristics are interrelated. It is one model for thinking through aspects of this pedagogy that we may fail to consider sufficiently when we sit down to prepare our lectures.

TABLE 9.1 A Heuristic Model for Reflecting on Lecture

	The Lecture	Lecturing: The Process	The Lecturer: The Instructor	The Lectured: The Students
Variables That Can Improve Lecture Practice	Quality content: determining what is worth knowing and why Well-organized materials Transparent links to learning goals Effective use of technology, e.g., "good" PowerPoint, audio, video, databases, whiteboards Appropriate visuals and props	Appropriate function: when to lecture and why Clear learning goals best suited for the lecture modality Controlled length and placement of the lecture in a session or a course	Characteristics of the instructor that can make a constructive difference: Gender Style Preparation Delivery Age Race / Ethnicity Expertise Experience	Appropriate levels of course work High level of student preparation Time of day (varies) Individual motivations (intrinsic and extrinsic) Previous relevant experiences Clear understanding of the goals
Variables That Can Weaken Lecture Practice	Tangential content Disorganization / too much freestyling Lack of clear goals Poor use of technology	Lecturing too long without active bridges Posting PowerPoint slides Bad rooms (lights, air, noise, seating) Distracting laptops/ cellphones	Tired / burned-out instructors Dislike of lecturing Inadequate preparation Boredom with content	Lack of sleep Required courses Failure to take notes Learning style fit with teaching style

SOURCE: Diane L. Pike

The Lecture

The content of the lecture is critical. Content may not always be king, but it should be front and center most of the time. Is the content worth knowing and more than just traditional "coverage"? Have we attended to the clarity of the lecture's structure—a beginning, middle, and an end? Have we considered the importance of the flow of the content, the relevance of the content to the learning goal of the session, and the relationship of the content to the effective use of technology? All these factors influence how the content of the lecture is experienced (Bligh 2000; Cashin 2010; Davis 1993).[3]

Paying attention to the importance of logically organized content—*what* we lecture on and in what order—can lead us to think more carefully about what we include at all. We may recognize that some of our "coverage" is really esoteric facts that will not be tested or used in analysis nor does it link to the main learning goals. The content included needs to have a connection to explicit learning goals for the course, the unit, and the session. ("Here's what we're doing today and *why*.") With content, sometimes less is more, and sometimes, slower is more. Especially in lecture when the goal is the story, the cognitive modeling, or the inspiration to know more or understand why. Let's make sure we have organized content that is worth having *the students* know.

It is also important to keep in mind that the best way to use face time with live human beings also speaks to differences in disciplines. While students working a tried-and-true problem set together during class can make sense in physics or math, much of social science learning is different from working problem sets. In sociology, we often guide students through an understanding of cultural relativism or the meaning of symbolic interaction theory. In an economics course examining the Great Recession, there is likely a need for scaffolded discovery by the instructor to complement small group discussions or individual reading. In psychology, lecture demonstration around classic findings, such as bystander issues or conformity, can be effective in multiple ways, both affective and cognitive. So we need to nuance ideas about lecture, as Hattie (2011) puts it, "to our intentions." It probably makes perfect sense not to ask students to sit still for 60 minutes watching someone else work a complex chemistry problem on the board or explain a detailed GDP slide, but that does not warrant the full-blown dismissal of lecture whether for chemistry or one of the social sciences. Lecture can be one of the reasons we are all in the room together, whatever the discipline.

As for the place of technology in lecture, the sheer quantity of attention to, research about, advocacy for, and resistance against the use of technology in teaching is both helpful and overwhelming. There are more opinions, research conclusions, daily practices, institutional policies, and products than one can manage. The jury is still out on what works and what does not. All we can do is go with our best understanding at any given time and work hard to separate the research findings from the personal preferences and from the sales pitches. With respect to technology in the lecture itself, two main ideas are offered here.

First, technology for technology's sake is a problem. So as with any tool—from whiteboard to smartboard, from clickers to online gaming to in-class exercises—make sure that the technology chosen adds value to the achievement of the learning goal. Like any tool, do not overuse it. The same strategy over and over wears thin for learners and instructors.

Second, be very careful with PowerPoint. A good image, map, or data *that are readable* for everyone in the room can enhance lecture by providing visual engagement, reference, or an opportunity for response by students. PowerPoint can be used effectively.[4] However, a text-based slide, especially when read aloud to students in case they cannot see it or apparently cannot read, is not an enhancement to lecture. (If you do not believe me, you have not been to a professional conference lately.) The research on PowerPoint shows that students generally find PowerPoint "boring" yet want the slides posted (Ralph 2015). Of course they want the slides—they are the teacher's notes. Used the way too many of us currently do (walk down that hallway again or look at your own slides), it makes lectures more boring rather than less. Let's agree that boring decreases learning. (Full disclosure: like Maryellen Weimer [2012], I am persuaded that PowerPoint is more often used poorly than effectively. In part, this failure resulted from early initiatives within faculty development and from instructional designers who encouraged faculty to use it for lectures without much training or thought behind how teaching a class with PowerPoint is different from a business presentation. Some research shows students do not learn more with PowerPoint in lecture despite their stated preference for it because slides organize and simplify course material [Hill et al. 2012]. As a faculty development director and in my SoTL work, I have pushed back hard on the notion that PowerPoint *by definition* is a good tool to use in lecture.)

The Lecture Process: What's the Function?

Most of the research on lecture—and there is a great deal of it—cites the bible on this topic, Donald Bligh's volume, *What's the Use of Lectures?* (2000). Based primarily on meta-analysis, Bligh sees the main function of lecture as effectively transmitting information; he argues that lecture is not effective for promoting thought, changing attitudes, or teaching skills (p. 3). There is a place for lecture done well and 20–30-minute lectures should be part of a range of activities in the classroom that vary stimulation (p. 56).

Newer work, however, has added to the discussion of what lecture actually accomplishes. For example, Wiggins (2014) thinks that lecture can model thought processes, share cognitive structures / mental models for understanding, provide context, and tell stories. Cashin's (2010) IDEA paper asserts that lecture can convey knowledge, communicate intrinsic interest, and demonstrate expertise, especially for graduate students (2011). Cashin also identifies the dysfunctional consequences of the lecture: the lack of usefulness for higher levels of critical thinking and the problem of the passivity of the "non-interactive" lecture.

One of the most intriguing, more recent pieces is John Hattie's chapter "Which Strategies Best Enhance Teaching and Learning in Higher Education." His work is a synthesis of 800 meta-analyses in Mashek and Hammer's edited volume, *Empirical Research in Teaching and Learning: Contributions from Social Psychology* (2011).[5] Hattie concludes that all typical teaching strategies do work in the appropriate contexts, but then adds what appears to be significant in terms of effect size (the measure of significance in meta-analyses): "What matters most are the transparency of the challenges and outcomes of the course, the use of multiple teaching strategies that emphasize student problem solving and engagement with the content, and the seeking by teachers of feedback about the impact of their teaching" (p. 139). So maybe the argument should not be about the pedagogy per se, but rather about how the chosen strategy in the right setting incorporates these features. How can lecture function to support these goals? Does the lecture achieve the learning goal for which you decided this was the best pedagogical road to travel?

The Lecturer: Individuals' Skills and Practices

We need to let go of the idea that most of us are somehow just naturally interesting to listen to. First, the literature is reasonably consistent in identifying what the lecturer should do to make for effective lectures.[6] Preparation, practice, delivery, and performance are the basics. Universal design is one idea that can help contextualize lecture pedagogy with its charge to provide multiple means of representation of the content of the learning, multiple means of action and expression of that learning, and multiple means of engagement and motivation to learn (National Center on Universal Design for Learning 2012). Thinking about these dimensions can be a good starting point.

Second, we also know that characteristics like gender, race, age, and social class can also influence how audiences perceive lecturers and how lecturers perceive themselves. How is one's status as a 30-year-old Asian female computer science professor different from a 60-year-old African American male history professor? For example, one study found that students perceived that females performed better using clickers in class, while males performed markedly better with lectures (Kang et al. 2012). While close examination of these variables is a separate chapter altogether, it makes sense to acknowledge and learn how these sociological variables make a difference.

So, letting go of assumptions about our natural charm and effectiveness is a good idea. Effective lecturing is learned behavior. (The belief that some of us are born lecturers simply fails to take us very far.) We can *unlearn* lecturing based on insufficient preparation on less important topics with little attention to delivery/performance and with the wrong focus on what students might need to hear rather than what we want to say. We all have strengths. Figure them out with the help of the scholarship, your peers, and your own analysis; then, work them.

The "Lectured"

The final category in Table 9.1 is one often only acknowledged perfunctorily. When working on lectures, the focus is typically on what to say and maybe what slides to prepare. For a long time, I did not think much about the characteristics of the audience and how this might shape what I do and why. Of course, we are all aware that the level of the course (intro or grad students) is important and that, over time, the particular character of the current cohort of students emerges. But there are other dimensions of audience / learners that we attend to less often.

Repeatedly, we assume that students are sufficiently similar in their readiness to learn. Yet, we know that the rate of learning, cognitive skills, relevant background knowledge, and subject matter interest (Cashin 2010) can be important variables in shaping what a student may learn from lecture (or from any pedagogy for that matter). While most successful instructors are aware of these variables, sociologists especially, we may need to act upon them as well.

We can add to this list the factors we all deal with daily: the amount of sleep students had, life-event distractions, hunger levels, social media pulls, mental health issues, and levels of intrinsic and extrinsic motivation (see Deci, Koesnter, and Ryan 1999). We cannot control most of these variables, but we can be more intentional about when lecture might work more or less effectively. Our clarity on the goals, our encouraging and rewarding student preparation, expectations of note-taking, and our demeanor with students can have a direct impact on the learners' success in the setting we create. In addition, our efforts at securing a classroom with good lighting, comfortable chairs, and decent airflow can also contribute to the readiness of the learners.[7]

Probably the most helpful thing to do is to get some sense of who the students are, why they are in the course, and what might be challenges for learning. We usually do this at the beginning of a course, but one can also incorporate this idea into lecture strategies. Start the lecture with a prompt or pair / share that might result in students assessing what they already know about a topic or an idea that is the learning goal for that lecture. Check in during the lecture to see how it is going, and be willing to adjust as needed.

GETTING BETTER ALL THE TIME . . .

This chapter closes by offering three ideas to consider to improve lectures. These recommendations are based on the research, my work in faculty development, and my experiences consulting with sociology departments over the years as a program reviewer for ASA. These three ideas are one contribution to this large and well-examined topic.

"It All Matters"

Three decades ago, one of the first panels I ever attended at a regional sociology meeting was a panel presentation by four award-winning teachers. Distinguished Professor Kathleen McKinney from Illinois State University, one of sociology's best and brightest in the scholarship of teaching and learning, talked specifically about giving high-quality lectures to very large classes (McKinney and Graham-Buxton 1993). As memory serves, McKinney bore no patience with the notion that large lectures could not be engaging, interactive, and enjoyable.

But what has stuck with me all these years was her response to a question from the audience about what matters in lecture. Her instant and forceful reply was, "It *all* matters . . . how you dress, how you prepare, what you deliver, how you follow up—everything." I took that advice to heart and it has served me well. For instance, some research shows that women cannot get away with dressing like they are doing yardwork in the way a charismatic male colleague can in history. Gender matters in numerous ways including, for example, that women are more likely to know and apply the SoTL research than men (see Miller 2016 for a recent summary of research).

Eye contact, good handouts, thoughtful content, and limited tangents are individual things that collectively strengthen or weaken a whole lecture-based experience.[8] So, even if we are not all naturally interesting, we can learn to improve lecture performance and delivery if we try to pay attention to what matters.

When my son was in medical school, he explained to me that lectures were video recorded so that if a student missed class, the lecture was available. (It was also available for review even if the student was present.) I asked him if most students went to class anyway. Most did, with a few outliers who seemed to excel in a highly individualized way and almost never went to any class. What then about the recorded lectures? He explained that students usually watched the videos instead of going to class when the instructor was not very good. When the lecture and lecturer were great, everyone was there in person. So perhaps we should think carefully about flipped classrooms, publisher-produced videos, and how we make the most of being in the room together.

It Should Almost Always Be "Lecture and . . . ."

No self-respecting faculty development person has advocated for anything other than what is more precisely called "interactive lecture" for decades; while those who vilify lecture usually cast an image of the 60-minute drone (not a good idea, no matter how rationalized by practitioners), that model has not been promoted by scholarly teachers since active learning came into vogue.[9]

So if the iconic view of the lecture is that we speak continuously for a long period, it seems reasonable to conclude that such a practice is at best a limited learning experience and sometimes a disaster. While few of us try to be ineffective, just ask students if you want to be assured that this model of lecture still exists in too many classrooms. The best lectures are ones where we intentionally stop talking for a while. I am not personally persuaded that lecture always needs to be limited to 6 or 17 minutes as some suggest. Rather, we need to support extending student attention spans, not capitulate to the idea that we need to be fast and furious because they watched too much *Sesame Street* as opposed to *Mr. Rogers*.

Lecture today means lecture and a brief pair / share: lecture and a three-minute video followed by two minutes of writing; lecture and responding to questions by clickers (or clickers, then lecture); lecture and a small group discussion; lecture and a one-minute paper; lecture and a break in the middle of a long class period; lecture and questions (to or from the instructor; to or from each other); lecture and collaboration on solving a problem or an equation; lecture and a demonstration . . . and so on.

New and existing technologies often improve lectures by helping to achieve the learning goal for which the instructor has chosen lecture as an effective means to that end. An image or short video as a lecture prompt, access to a database when a question arises during lecture that warrants an immediate response, whiteboards, chalk or markers, props or demonstrations are all possibilities within the lecture providing opportunities for engagement and contributing to the variety that Hattie identifies as crucial. Yet, whatever set of tactics we create, lecture is the dominant and critical thread that weaves the session and all its "interactions" together.

Closing the Lecture Loop

If lecture is going to be one of the tools that helps students learn and is a mainstay of our teaching practice, how can its impact be strengthened? One increasingly recognized idea is the importance of expecting students to take notes (by hand, not on laptops), showing them how to do it well, and reinforcing good note-taking.

While debate remains, recent articles make a strong case for good note-taking as part of learning (May 2014; Meyer 2014; Mueller and Oppenheimer 2014). It helps students think about what they are hearing and put it into their own words. It slows the pace in a positive way when we make space for students to take good notes. Therefore, we need to pause, use the board, ask them to repeat back an idea, trade notes with another student, and have students tell us what they think is the main point. Many of these ideas are versions of well-established classroom assessment techniques originally identified by Angelo and Cross (1993).[10] When we get caught up in something we feel passionately about, it is easy to forget about the listeners as note-takers.

One of the unintended consequences of PowerPoint is the diminishment of note-taking. If the professor is just going to post the text slides anyway, why bother? Often students do not bother, and it is a problem. As mentioned, the slide is the teacher's notes, not the student's. If one merely scans slides, the cognitive processing that typically comes with writing or summarizing or putting information into your own words is lost. This gap is one of the reasons that detailed text slides are generally not good lecture practice. Of course, all decisions must be contextualized in terms of accommodating students with learning disabilities and following principles of universal access.

One technique that instructors have found works well for lecture is the incomplete handout. In class, provide students a hard-copy outline that is not worth much on its own. Especially for more complex lectures, lecture outlines or lecture guides help clarify an instructor's thoughts (we need a meaningful structure if we are going to give a useful handout), and it helps the students see our logic for a given goal. As we lecture, give examples, explain, tell inspiring stories, or provide rationales that students write in their own notes. There are excellent resources on note-taking of different forms.

With some practice, clear expectation, and instruction by the faculty member to take good notes ("this idea / information is not in the books, so work to get it here"), this "closing the loop" can enhance both understanding and retention. Typically, students are more likely to remember what they write down; they then also have something of value to go back to and to study. We can guide our lecture style by making sure we recognize the value of this practice and make it easier, not harder, for students to get the most out of the lecture.

Laptops? With exceptions, laptops are generally not a good idea during lecture. (Law schools can create their own policies, and this issue is not taken up here.) In a traditional undergraduate class of any moderate size, it is nearly impossible for a student to adequately focus during a lecture while on one's laptop. Sure, anyone can tune out or daydream, but it moves the needle too far when checking Facebook, email, and websites. These distract the individual, anyone sitting near them, and often the instructor. It is a question of the type of respectful classroom learning environment we are largely responsible for creating. If we say, "You are an adult, do what you want when I am lecturing," that is a mistake. Low expectations, the risk of creating a disrespectful or distracting environment (the professor should not be checking their phone while a student is talking), and data that show that learning is decreased (see Fisher 2015) are negatives that outweigh the benefits of the argument that "students paid for this, so they can do what they want."[11]

The use of laptops or cell phones is also an issue where disciplines once again matter because of the goals or the intentions of the instruction (Hattie 2011). For example, in the same medical program referenced earlier, students were given iPads so they could have the image of the organ de jour on both the large screen, as the physician lectured, and on the tablet. Students then used a stylus to add their notes by hand while in class. This approach seems a good strategy given the focus on learning highly detailed content (as opposed to skills and attitudes about medical care executed with different teaching strategies). The parallel for the social sciences might be looking at complex data or even working a statistics problem.

CONCLUSIONS

1. We should lecture some and lecture well.
2. If we follow the advice above, we do not need to apologize for using this "dead," "unethical," "bloodletting" pedagogy.
3. The research, our peers, technology, and our own reflections can sustain and improve lecture practice.

The Queen of Hearts was characterized in Lewis Carroll's *Alice's Adventures in Wonderland* as a "blind fury." That is not a fair characterization of instructors working hard to improve learning. But we need to be careful not to aim for a Pyrrhic victory where the battle is won to nearly eliminate lecture but comes at too high a cost. We might lose the larger struggle for effective learning if we reject lecture completely—or even worse, ignore the need to expect good lecture practice—because it is not fashionable or because publishers want to replace lecture, textbooks, and in-class exercises with a digitized or automated product. We could very well find that we have failed to achieve the larger goal of enhancing learning between human beings because we rejected a useful tool that, like any other pedagogy, works when it promotes engagement, has a steady stream of feedback, and is linked to clear learning goals.

NOTES

1. The impact of technology in teaching and learning is a related but also independent topic for analysis. From MOOCs (massive open online courses) to clickers to flipped classrooms, technology is boldly offered as a solution to major problems in higher education; claims include the potential to address failing economic models for financial sustainability (online courses will bring in more revenue and cost less to offer), and promises are made by both for-profit and not-for-profit organizations as to the potential of new models of teaching and learning. Many of these assertions rest on a foundation of casting current higher education as dismal and ineffective. Technology / online learning / automated quizzes / asynchronous exchanges of typed text often look like hammers for which everything in higher education is now a nail. The role of technology in teaching is relevant to our discussion of lecture to the extent that the role of the live, face-to-face lecture is impacted when technology replaces it.

2. See "Confessions of a Converted Lecturer" at https://www.youtube.com/watch?v = WwslBP-j8GgI.

3. There are a gazillion websites, YouTube, and articles on lecture practice that typically address both lecture content and instructor delivery. One good place to start is Edutopia's "How to Build a Dynamic Lecture" by Todd Finley at http://www.edutopia.org/blog/how-to-build-dynamic-lecture-todd-finley.

4. Some suggested resources include Tufte 2006; McDaniel and McDaniel at http://cgi.stanford .edu/~dept-ctl/tomprof/posting.php?ID = 663.

5. Wiggins also cites Hattie's work in his article, so I feel affirmed in a Wallace and Darwin kind of way.

6. See the extensive bibliographies and resources at Vanderbilt University's Center for Teaching and Learning website (https://cft.vanderbilt.edu/guides-sub-pages/lecturing/) and Carnegie Mellon University's website (https://www.cmu.edu/teaching/designteach/design/instructionalstrategies/lectures .html).

7. These factors are important for all pedagogies, but perhaps more so with lecture given the note-taking and listening requirements.

8. I would suggest the same applies to our own conference presentations, which range from shar-ing of impressive scholarship to "please, tell me you don't teach like this?" (shuffling through pages highlighted in yellow, clearly not prepared, having two minutes left and still describing the methods section, slides that cannot be seen past the second row, and so on).

9. For an analysis of some of the most recent research on rejecting "traditional lecture" in the sci-ences see Freeman et al. 2014.

10. See also the recommendations made in the AVID program at http://www.avid.org/what-is-avid.ashx.

11. http://www.avid.org/what-is-avid.ashx.

REFERENCES

Angelo, Thomas A., and K. Patricia Cross. 1993. *Classroom Assessment Techniques: A Hand-book for College Teachers.* 2nd ed. San Francisco: Jossey-Bass.

Atkinson, Maxine, and Kathleen S. Lowney. 2016. *Teaching in the Trenches.* New York: W. W. Norton.

Bain, Kenneth. 2004. *What the Best College Teachers Do.* Cambridge, MA: Harvard Univer-sity Press.

Barr, Robert, and John Tagg. 1995. "From Teaching to Learning: A New Paradigm for Undergraduate Education." *Change* 27(6):12–25.

Bates, Tony. 2014. "Why Lectures are Dead (or Soon Will Be)." Online Learning and Dis-tance Education Resources. Retrieved May 22, 2016 (http://www.tonybates.ca/2014 /07/27/why-lectures-are-dead-or-soon-will-be/).

Berrett, Daniel. 2016. "The Making of a Teaching Evangelist." *Chronicle of Higher Education,* June 5.

Bligh, Donald A. 2000. *What's the Use of Lectures?* San Francisco: Jossey-Bass.

Bonwell, Charles C., and James A. Eison. 1991. *Active Learning: Creating Excitement in the Classroom.* ASHE-ERIC Higher Education Report No. 1. Washington, DC: George Washington University.

Brookfield, Stephen. 1995. *Becoming a Critically Reflective Teacher.* San Francisco, CA: Jos-sey-Bass.

Carroll, Lewis. [1865] 2002. *Alice's Adventures in Wonderland* and *Through the Looking Glass and What Alice Found There.* New York: Modern Library Classics.

Cashin, William. 1985. "Improving Lectures." Idea Paper No. 14. Center for Faculty Evalua-tion and Development, Kansas State University Press.

Cashin, William. 2010. "Effective Lecturing." Idea Paper No. 46. Retrieved July 3, 2016 (http://ideaedu.org/wp-content/uploads/2014/11/IDEA_Paper_46.pdf).

Chambliss, Daniel F. 1999. "Doing What Works: On the Mundanity of Excellence in Teaching." Pp. 422–34 in *The Social Worlds of Higher Education: Handbook for Teaching in a New Century,* edited by B. A. Pescosolido and R. Aminzade. Thousand Oaks, CA: Pine Forge Press.

Chickering, Arthur W., and Zelda F. Gamson, 1987. "Seven Principles for Good Practice." *AAHE Bulletin* 39(7):3–7.

Christensen, Clayton M., Michael B. Horn, and Curtis W. Johnson. 2008. *Disrupting Class.* Columbus, OH: McGraw-Hill Books.

Davis, Barbara Gross. 1993. *Tools for Teaching.* San Francisco: Jossey-Bass.

Deci, Edward L., Richard Koesnter, and Richard M. Ryan. 1999. "A Meta-Analytic Review of Experiments Examining the Effects of Extrinsic Rewards on Intrinsic Motivation." *Psychological Bulletin* 125(6):627–88.

DeMillo, Richard A., and Andrew J. Young. 2015. *Revolution in Higher Education: How a Small Band of Innovators Will Make College Accessible and Affordable.* Cambridge, MA: MIT Press.

Eble, Kenneth. 1976. *The Craft of Teaching.* San Francisco: Jossey-Bass.

Faust, Jennifer L., and Donald R. Paulson. 1998. "Active Learning in the College Classroom." *Journal on Excellence in College Teaching* 9(2):3–24.

Fisher, Beth. 2015. "Laptop Use in Class: Effects on Learning and Attention." Teaching Center, Washington University St. Louis. Retrieved April 3, 2016 (https://teachingcenter.wustl .edu/2015/08/laptop-use-effects-learning-attention/).

Freeman, Scott, Sarah L. Eddy, Miles McDonough, Michelle K. Smith, Nnadozie Okoroafor, Hanna Jordt, and Mary Pat Wenderoth. 2014. "Active Learning Increases Student Performance in Science, Engineering, and Mathematics." Retrieved July 2, 2016 (http:// www.pnas.org/content/111/23/8410.full.pdf).

Greenwood, Nancy, and Jay Howard. 2011. *First Contact: Teaching and Learning in Introductory Sociology.* Lanham, MD: Rowman & Littlefield.

Hattie, John. 2011. "Which Strategies Best Enhance Teaching and Learning in Higher Education." Pp. 130–42 in *Empirical Research in Teaching and Learning: Contributions from Social Psychology,* edited by Debra Mashek and Elizabeth Yost Hammer. Hoboken, NJ: Wiley-Blackwell.

Hill, Andrea, Tammi Arford, Amy Lubitow, and Leandra Smollin. 2012. "I'm Ambivalent About It: The Dilemmas of PowerPoint in the Sociology Classroom." *Teaching Sociology* 40(3):242–56.

Howery, Carla B. 2002. "The Culture of Teaching in Sociology." Pp. 153–69 in *Disciplinary Styles in the Scholarship of Teaching and Learning: Exploring Common Ground,* edited by M. T. Huber and S. P. Sherwyn. AAHE Publications. Retrieved May 9, 2016 (http://files .eric.ed.gov/fulltext/ED478800.pdf#page = 153).

Johnson, David W., and Roger T. Johnson. 1974. "Instructional Goal Structures: Cooperative, Competitive or Individualistic." *Review of Educational Research* 44:231–40.

Kang, Hosun, Mary Lundeberg, Bjorn Wolter, Robert del Mas, and Clyde F. Herreid. 2012. "Gender Differences in Student Performance in Large Lecture Classrooms Using Personal Response Systems ('Clickers') with Narrative Case Studies." *Learning, Media and Technology* 37(1).

Mauksch, Hans O., and Carla B. Howery. 1986. "Social Change for Teaching: The Case of One Disciplinary Association." *Teaching Sociology* 14(1):73–82.

May, Cindi. 2014. "A Learning Secret: Don't Take Notes with a Laptop." *Scientific American.* Retrieved March 11, 2016 (http://www.scientificamerican.com/article/a-learning-secret-don-t-take-notes-with-a-laptop/).

Mazur, Eric. 2012. "Twilight of the Lecture." *Harvard Magazine*, August 24. Retrieved April 12, 2016 (https://teachscience4all.org/2012/08/24/twilight-of-the-lecture-harvard-magazine/).

McKinney, Kathleen, and Mary Graham-Buxton. 1993. "The Use of Collaborative Learning Groups in the Large Class: Is It Possible?" *Teaching Sociology* 21(4):403–8.

McKeachie, William, Paul R. Pintrich, Yi-Guang Lin, and David A. Smith. 1987. *Teaching and Learning in the College Classroom: A Review of the Literature.* National Center for Research to Improve Postsecondary Teaching and Learning. Ann Arbor: University of Michigan.

Merton, Robert K. 1968. "The Matthew Effect in Science." *Science* 159(3810):56–63.

Meyer, Robinson. 2014. "To Remember a Lecture Better, Take Notes by Hand." *The Atlantic,* May. Retrieved May 2, 2016 (http://www.theatlantic.com/technology/archive/2014/05/to-remember-a-lecture-better-take-notes-by-hand/361478/).

Miller, Claire Cain. 2015. "Is the Professor Bossy or Brilliant? Much Depends on Gender." *New York Times,* February 6. Retrieved May 6, 2016 (http://www.nytimes.com/2015/02/07/upshot/is-the-professor-bossy-or-brilliant-much-depends-on-gender.html).

Mueller, Pam A., and Daniel M. Oppenheimer. 2014. "The Pen Is Mightier than the Keyboard: Advantages of Longhand over Laptop Note Taking." *Psychological Science* 1–10, May 22.

National Center on Universal Design for Learning. 2012. Retrieved April 4, 2016 (http://www.udlcenter.org/).

Pescosolido, Bernice A., and Ronald Aminzade, eds. 1999. *The Social Worlds of Higher Education: Handbook for Teaching in a New Century.* Thousand Oaks, CA: Pine Forge Press.

Prince, Michael. 2004. "Does Active Learning Work? A Review of the Research." *Journal of Engineering Education* 93(3):223–31.

Ralph, Paul. 2015. "Why Universities Should Get Rid of PowerPoint and Why They Won't." *The Conversation.* Retrieved June 22, 2016 (http://theconversation.com/why-universities-should-get-rid-of-powerpoint-and-why-they-wont-43323).

Science Education Initiative. 2016. Boulder: University of Colorado Boulder. Retrieved August 8, 2016 (http://www.colorado.edu/sei/).

Skonnard, Aaron. 2015. "5 Top Trends in Education Technology 2015." *Inc.* Retrieved May 22, 2016 (http://www.inc.com/aaron-skonnard/5-top-trends-in-education-technology-2015.html).

Smith, Karl A. 1996. "Cooperative Learning: Making 'Groupwork' Work." *New Directions for Teaching and Learning* 67:71–82.

Tufte, Edward. 2006. *The Cognitive Style of PowerPoint: Pitching Out Corrupts Within.* 2nd ed. Cheshire, CT: Graphics Press.

Weimer, Maryellen. 1990. *Improving College Teaching: Strategies for Developing Instructional Effectiveness.* San Francisco: Jossey-Bass.

Weimer, Maryellen. 2012. "Does PowerPoint Help or Hinder Learning?" *Faculty Focus,* Magna Publications. Retrieved March 29, 2016 (http://www.facultyfocus.com/articles /teaching-professor-blog/does-powerpoint-help-or-hinder-learning/).

Weimer, Maryellen. 2014. "Lecture Continues as the Dominant Instructional Strategy, Study Finds." *Faculty Focus,* Magna Publications. Retrieved May 6, 2016 (http://www .facultyfocus.com/articles/teaching-and-learning/lecture-continues-dominant-instructional-strategy/).

Westervelt, Eric. 2016. "A Nobel Laureate's Education Plea: Revolutionize Teaching." *National Public Radio,* April 14. Retrieved April 14, 2016 (http://www.npr.org/sections /ed/2016/04/14/465729968/a-nobel-laureates-education-plea-revolutionize-teaching).

Wiggins, Grant. 2014. "The Lecture." *Granted, and . . .: Thoughts on Education,* February 3. Retrieved April 22, 2016 (https://grantwiggins.wordpress.com/2014/02/03/the-lecture/).

10

Scribes in the Classroom

Effectively Using PowerPoint to Enhance the Classroom Experience

Monica R. Sylvia and Brenda J. Kirby

Although debate exists regarding its value in the classroom (e.g., McDonald 2004; Tufte 2003; Voss 2004; see especially Kernbach, Bresciani, and Eppler 2015 for an historical overview), instructors in higher education frequently use PowerPoint and similar presentation platforms (e.g., Prezi, Academic Presenter, etc.) to present course material. Recognizing this, most colleges and universities regularly outfit their classrooms with computerized projectors, and textbook publishers routinely include pre-packaged PowerPoint presentations with their supplementary materials. Students also have come to expect that their instructors will use PowerPoint, and often request that instructors make slides available outside of the classroom itself.

With the above in mind, it is interesting to note that neither students nor instructors may recognize the extent to which PowerPoint use can constrain the teaching and learning process. Indeed, a meta-analysis by Kernbach et al. (2015) identified three categories of constraining qualities that direct how information is delivered, received, and understood. From a cognitive perspective, they discuss research indicating that slides containing abbreviations and fragments may create obstacles when it comes to information processing. Likewise, because slide presentations tend to impose organization rather than allowing for a dynamic interchange between audience members and presenters, both groups may come to trivialize points not included on the slides. From an emotional and social perspective, Kernbach et al. (2015) point to research indicating that slide presentations may serve as a distraction and reduce audience investment in meaningful engagement with both the presenter and material at hand.

With the above discussion in mind, we acknowledge that there are instances when PowerPoint (and similar presentation technologies) should not be used, such as in upper-level seminar courses that require extended classroom discussions. Given the ubiquitous nature of this tool and the low likelihood that we will discontinue its use, however, this chapter explores how to facilitate the best learning environment from both the instructor's and student's perspectives when PowerPoint is used.

WHY INSTRUCTORS USE POWERPOINT

Instructors cite many different reasons for utilizing PowerPoint within their classrooms. One such reason is to alleviate anxiety about presenting complex information to students or audience members in a clear, concise, and understandable fashion. Hertz, Kerkhof, and van Woerkum (2016) surveyed social science academic conference speakers and found that those who had speech anxiety tended to use slides as speech notes. Although the slides were intended to help the speakers alleviate anxiety, the authors asserted that overreliance on them actually may reduce the quality of a presentation, with speakers becoming overfocused on the projected slides themselves; this, in turn, may reduce their attention to audience members. In another of their studies, Hertz and colleagues (2015) interviewed scholars from a variety of disciplines and at various stages of professional development. All seemed to use the tool, claiming among the advantages were that it serves as a memory support, focuses the attention of audience members on significant content, and fulfills audience expectations. They also identified disadvantages that included a tendency to use too much text, "loss of contact with the audience," and "fragmentation of the narrative" (p. 282).

In a study of sociology instructors, teachers expressed an understanding that many, perhaps even most, students expect slide presentations in their classes. Some noted that fulfilling these expectations may be driven in part by "institutional pressure to receive positive student evaluations of teaching" (Hill et al. 2012:253). Even so, many of these same teachers thought that using it helped them to keep a good pace and present information in an organized way.

STUDENTS' PERSPECTIVES ON POWERPOINT USE

Given its popularity, several studies also have investigated students' attitudes, perceived learning, and overall performance in courses where instructors used PowerPoint. In some cases, students reported feeling ignored or frustrated when instructors focused too much attention on the PowerPoint presentation itself or spent excessive amounts of time simply reading the slides (Voss 2004). Armour, Schneid, and Brandl (2016) report that 86.7 percent of a total of 1,905 students sampled over several years from physiology courses preferred having professors write on a whiteboard rather than use PowerPoint slides, and they indicated that this practice results in better class pacing, note-taking, and attention to class material.

In contrast to the above findings, students in some studies actually reported increased attention to classroom material presented via PowerPoint versus the use of a blackboard/whiteboard or overheads (Frey and Birnbaum 2002; Mantei 2000; Szabo and Hastings 2000). Indeed, a study examining sociology courses revealed that 84 percent of the students perceived PowerPoint use as making the classroom experience enjoyable, and 69 percent preferred classes where it was used (Hill et al. 2012). Students also reported benefits with regard to their ability to learn and recall class content during exams when their instructors used PowerPoint to present material (Frey and Birnbaum 2002; Mantei 2000). In certain cases, these benefits reportedly extended to exam performance, with students regularly exposed to PowerPoint in the classroom outperforming those exposed only to traditional lecture methods (Erwin and Rieppi 1999; Smith and Woody 2000). As Pike (2018) notes, such findings suggest that if used well, PowerPoint can serve to improve delivery of traditional lectures.

FORMATTING POWERPOINT SLIDES

Although evidence of students' preferences for PowerPoint presentations over traditional lecture methods exists (e.g., Frey and Birnbaum 2002; Smith and Woody 2000), few empirical investigations focusing on the format of the presentations themselves have been conducted (e.g., Collins and Massa 2006; Sylvia, Kirby, and DiTullio 2004). Hill et al. (2012) noted that such empirical evaluation may provide better guidance for how to use the tool. Instructors who use PowerPoint often do so in a variety of ways, ranging from the use of slides containing a great deal of text, thereby representing the emotionally constraining quality of "overloading" (Kernbach et al. 2015:306), to slides containing only brief, bulleted outlines (see Figure 10.1 for examples) or text-free photos, figures, or diagrams (Sylvia, Kirby, and DiTullio 2004). Although much has been written regarding the best ways to develop PowerPoint presentations (see Kosslyn 2007), most of the existing literature centers on helpful hints regarding how to construct and use slides appropriately (e.g., Quible 2002; Seaman 1998), rather than on identifying whether various formats differentially impact students' learning and classroom experiences.

EMPIRICAL COMPARISON OF POWERPOINT
SLIDE FORMATS

After casual discussions with students regarding their preferences and our own observations regarding the variety of PowerPoint slide formats used in the classroom, we decided to complete a study examining the impact of slide format on students' perceptions of this technology. We particularly were interested in examining the perceived versus actual benefits and/or drawbacks of using various slide formats when it came to understanding the course material.

In conducting our study, we each used PowerPoint slides on a regular basis while teaching two sections of a second-level course (i.e., two sections each of Child and Adolescent Development and Social Psychology); each section had an enrollment of approximately 25 students. These courses were standard offerings in the psychology department at Le Moyne College, a Jesuit college in Syracuse, New York, with an undergraduate enrollment of approximately 2,800 students. In one section of each course, we employed text-intensive slides with full definitions and / or examples of critical concepts, whereas in the second section, we each utilized bulleted-outline slides containing only a skeletal outline of the topics to be discussed at certain points in time (see Figure 10.1 for example slides). After several weeks, we surveyed students ($N = 99$) regarding their perceptions of how the slide presentations contributed to their learning, assisted them in preparing for an exam, and influenced their behaviors, including note-taking and ability to listen to the instructor.

Procedure

For the first unit of study (approximately four weeks), we presented the course material using only a traditional whiteboard. Following an exam on this material, we each used text-intensive PowerPoint slides in one section of our respective courses, and bulleted-outline slides in the remaining section for the entire second unit of study (approximately four weeks). We standardized the font size, typeface, background design, and number of slides between conditions, and none contained graphics (see Figure 10.1 for example slides). During this time, students did not have access to either hard or electronic copies of the slides. All classes were taught in the morning; however, we balanced the conditions across the two courses (i.e., Child and Adolescent Psychology and Social Psychology) based on which section was taught first by the given instructor.

During the class period following the second unit exam, we asked students to complete a survey designed to assess the effects of the two different slide formats on their perceived contributions to learning, classroom behavior, exam preparation, and anticipated grade on the second unit exam. Prior to completing the survey, we instructed students to focus exclusively on the PowerPoint used during the second unit of study only and not to generalize their responses to any additional experiences with PowerPoint outside of the course.

In completing the survey, each student provided basic demographic data, reported their anticipated grade on the exam, and then rated a series of 14 statements regarding the usefulness of the PowerPoint presentations. The ratings were on a 7-point Likert scale, with the end-points representing strong agreement or disagreement. We also asked students for permission to match their actual Unit 1 and Unit 2 exam scores to their survey responses; all but six agreed. Finally, as a manipulation check, we asked students to categorize the PowerPoint slide format that was used for the second unit of study as containing "mostly words and descriptions in text form" or "information presented in outline form."

Results

When asked to categorize the PowerPoint slide format used for the second unit of study, most students ($N = 77$) did so appropriately given their respective conditions. Because focusing our data analyses exclusively on these students did not significantly impact our results, the results that follow include those obtained from the full data set. In addition, we categorized students' responses as representing general agreement (i.e., responses ranging from 1–3), neutrality (i.e., responses of 4), or general disagreement (i.e., responses ranging from 5–7). We then analyzed this data using chi-square contingency tests with Bonferroni corrections for multiple comparisons (see Table 10.1 for frequencies).

Significant differences emerged with regard to student perceptions that Power-Point use made the course material more difficult to learn, $\chi^2(2) = 88.97$, $p < .001$. Follow-up analyses indicated that there were more students who disagreed than agreed with this statement, $\chi^2(1) = 41.78$, $p < .001$. Significant differences also emerged with regard to students' perceptions of their resulting notes, $\chi^2(2) = 67.82$, $p < .001$, with more students agreeing than disagreeing that the use of PowerPoint "helped them to take better notes in class," $\chi^2(1) = 28.58$, $p < .001$. Similarly, there were significant differences on their reported reliance on information presented via PowerPoint, $\chi^2(2) = 62.36$, $p < .001$, with more students agreeing than disagreeing that they "strongly relied on the information obtained from the PowerPoint presentation when preparing for exams," $\chi^2(1) = 33.91$, $p < .001$. The same was true with regard to the statement, "the use of PowerPoint helped me to recall course content during the exam," $\chi^2(2) = 22.06$, $p < .001$, with more students agreeing than disagreeing that this was the case, $\chi^2(1) = 25.21$, $p < .001$.

It is important to note that in each of the above instances, there were no differences between the PowerPoint conditions; students in both the bulleted-outline and text-intensive conditions reported similar attitudes. That was not the case, however, when it came to their classroom behavior. In this case, students reported significant differences regarding the amount of time spent listening to the professor, $\chi^2(2) = 15.01$, $p = .001$, with more students in the bulleted-outline than the text-intensive condition agreeing that the use of PowerPoint increased the amount of time spent listening to the professor, $\chi^2(1) = 9.26$, $p = .002$, and more students in the text-intensive versus the bulleted-outline condition disagreeing with this statement, $\chi^2(1) = 5.23$, $p = .02$. Likewise, when asked to express their preferences, 61 percent of students expressed agreement with statements indicating a preference for an outline format, whereas only 48 percent of students expressed agreement with statements indicating preference for a text-intensive format.

THE IMPACT OF SLIDE FORMAT ON THE ESTABLISHMENT OF AN INTERACTIVE LEARNING ENVIRONMENT

The results of the above study highlight a general perception among students that, regardless of actual slide format, the use of PowerPoint by an instructor assists them in taking quality notes. This belief may drive students' requests for instructors to use this classroom tool, which in turn might help to explain its increasing popularity over the past decade.

With the generally positive attitudes of students toward the use of PowerPoint, it is interesting to note that we found few tangible differences between the two format conditions, as the only significant difference came in the form of classroom behavior (i.e., amount of time spent listening to the professor). With that in mind, one casual observation we made was that students in the text-intensive condition seemed to spend more classroom time transcribing the PowerPoint slides than those in the bulleted-outline condition. We believe that this behavior may be due to the perception that text-intensive slides present the material in the instructor's "own words." When an instructor utilizes PowerPoint, students may feel obliged to copy all of the information presented on a slide. This effect may have been magnified in this study by the fact that we did not make copies of the slides available to students outside of class.

With regard to PowerPoint's usefulness in note-taking and exam preparation, it would seem reasonable that if students in both conditions simply copied the information on the slides, then the resulting notes in the text-intensive condition would have contained greater detail, which then could have been more useful in preparing for and taking the exam. This, however, was not the case, as there were no differences between the conditions when it came to students' anticipated or actual exam grades. Such findings stand in contrast to prior research indicating that taking notes from text-intensive PowerPoint presentations on blank pieces of paper, rather than on handouts of the actual slides, results in better transfer of learning between the classroom and subsequent exams (e.g., Collins and Massa 2006). In this case, although copying text-intensive slides may have provided students with an extensive opportunity to rehearse, in written form, the information presented in class, there actually was no difference between the text-intensive and bulleted-outline conditions with regard to their resulting exam grades. Therefore, although some might suggest that text-intensive PowerPoint slides facilitate students' abilities to process and later recall information, exam performance in this study suggests otherwise.

One of the major differences between the two format conditions involved the fact that the majority of students in the bulleted-outline condition agreed that the use of PowerPoint increased the amount of time they spent listening to the instructor, whereas the majority in the text-intensive condition disagreed with this statement. As noted earlier, we both observed a marked difference between the two conditions with regard to the amount of time that students spent copying the information presented on the slides. This suggests that one side effect of presenting students with text-intensive slides is that they may be distracted by the desire to transcribe the slides and, therefore, spend more time doing so rather than actively listening to the instructor, engaging in classroom conversation, and/or actively processing the material as it is presented.

To the extent that we seek active engagement on the part of students, the above issue raises an important question that college instructors must ask themselves regarding the usefulness of text-intensive PowerPoint slides over bulleted-outline slides: Are the perceived benefits of text-intensive over bulleted-outline slides by students worth the significant trade-off that must be made in terms of their attention and active participation in class? Given the lack of differences between the text-intensive and bulleted-outline conditions with regard to exam grades and students' general agreement that even bulleted-outline slides aid in note-taking and exam preparation, it would seem clear that the answer to this question is a resounding "no." A similar answer emerges when it comes to the question of whether instructors should dedicate more of their class preparation time to the design of text-intensive PowerPoint slides. Given the current data, it is clear that the increased amount of time that instructors and/or textbook publishers contribute to the construction of text-intensive versus bulleted-outline slides might better be spent on other areas of course preparation and the design of supplemental learning materials.

The suggestion that the use of text-intensive over bulleted-outline slides appears to decrease the amount of time that students spend actively listening and verbally participating in class also raises another key issue when it comes to the transfer of classroom information to exams and/or future learning. In this case, it is likely that students' efforts to transcribe text-intensive slides may affect their ability to note and/or remember novel classroom information that does not simply review and/or reinforce textbook readings or that is not presented in great detail on the slide. The extent to which exams focus on such information may lead to additional variation on exam grades as the result of varying slide formats and, therefore, should be the focus of future studies in this area. Using the bulleted slides instead may offer more opportunity for instructors to actively engage in the slide presentations—perhaps even participating in what Knoblauch (2008) referred to as a "performance of knowledge," standing at and pointing at the slides as a way to draw attention to the information and the instructor/student interaction.

BEST PRACTICES FOR CREATING SLIDES THAT SUPPORT STUDENT LEARNING

The results of our study indicate that when it comes to the use of PowerPoint in the classroom, less is definitely more. Although students clearly perceive the use of

TABLE 10.1 Categorization of Student Responses Based on Expressed Agreement, Neutrality, or Disagreement

Statement	Condition	Agree	Neutral	Disagree
The use of PowerPoint in this class made it more difficult to learn the course material.	Outline	5	6	39
	Text-Intensive	10	1	38
The use of PowerPoint helped me to take better notes during class.	Outline	35	7	8
	Text-Intensive	36	1	12
The use of PowerPoint increased the amount of time that I was able to listen to my professor.	Outline	29	7	14
	Text-Intensive	10	10	29
I strongly relied on the information that I obtained from the PowerPoint presentations when preparing for exams.	Outline	32	7	11
	Text-Intensive	38	6	5
The use of PowerPoint helped me to recall course content during the second exam.	Outline	23	16	11
	Text-Intensive	32	7	10

SOURCE: Monica R. Sylvia and Brenda J. Kirby

PowerPoint by instructors as an important learning and note-taking tool, we must be attentive to the critical balance between scaffolding students in their note-taking endeavors and providing them with both opportunities and incentives to engage in the learning process when designing our slides. Similarly, for those of us who use PowerPoint as a memory support for our lectures, avoiding the trap of simply reading from our slides and, instead, questioning and engaging in discussions with students about the material at hand is key.

With the above need for balance in mind, it becomes clear that PowerPoint slides designed to provide a skeletal outline format of the material best meet the needs of students and instructors alike. This format can assist students in their note-taking endeavors as it draws their attention to important vocabulary terms and / or concepts. As such, it simultaneously provides instructors with useful memory supports for their classroom presentations and discussions while helping them avoid the trap of reading from the slides. Moreover, unlike text-intensive slides that provide extended definitions and explanations in written form, bulleted-outline slides free students from their perceived need to copy the information presented and, instead, encourage them to listen and actively engage with the material being discussed as this is the only way to gain an understanding of the terms and concepts highlighted on each slide. Given the lack of differences between the two PowerPoint

FIGURE 10.1. Example of Text-Intensive and Bulleted Outline Powerpoint Slides.

MANUAL DEVELOPMENT

- **Posture and balance play an important role**
- **Pre-reaching:** inaccurate, uncoordinated attempts that do not end in success

  -Newborn reflex

- **Batting**: rapid, somewhat accurate attempts to touch, but not obtain object due to lack of hand shaping

  -3 months

- **Reaching:** accurate attempts to obtain object with hand pre-shaped and control over torso

  -5 months

MANUAL DEVELOPMENT

- **Role of Posture and Balance**

- **Pre-reaching**: newborn reflex

- **Batting:** 3 months

- **Reaching:** 5 months

SOURCE: Monica R. Sylvia and Brenda J. Kirby

formats when it comes to expected and actual exam performance and the desire for so many of us to engage students in our classrooms, using a bulleted-outline format clearly is the most beneficial format when it comes to supporting a dynamic and active-learning environment for students and professors alike.

Many individuals and organizations have published guidelines for best practices in creating PowerPoint slides. Most recommendations appear to be based on personal experience and anecdotal information. One such set of guidelines comes from the American Psychological Association (Rowh 2012), which recommends that presenters use large, easy-to-read fonts, figures rather than tables, and avoid using complete sentences on slides. Teaching centers at various universities such as Vanderbilt University and the University of Oregon also have published recommendations for presentation software use. Some recommendations include minimizing the number of slides, not reading from the slides themselves, providing verbal (rather than written) explanations for graphs or figures, and using the software as an accompaniment rather than a replacement for presentation of content (Teaching Effectiveness Program at the University of Oregon, Center for Teaching at Vanderbilt University N.d.). Few, however, report empirical research demonstrating support for their recommendations.

Future research must examine systematically the impact of certain PowerPoint effects, such as the use of animated graphics and sound effects, on students' attention to and interest in classroom material, as well as their overall attitudes toward the usefulness of such effects to their learning experience. Given that text-intensive slides can serve as a distraction from the instructor and classroom discussions, we caution that the use of such graphics and sound effects also may compete for students' attention and therefore should be used only sparingly and with great care. With this in mind, the results of the current study provide a strong first step in providing both instructors and textbook publishers with useful, student-centered information regarding two variations in PowerPoint slide formats.

REFERENCES

Armour, Chris, Stephen D. Schneid, and Katharina Brandl. 2016. "Writing on the Board as Students' Preferred Teaching Modality in a Physiology Course." *Advances in Physiological Education* 40(2):229–33.

Center for Teaching, Vanderbilt University. 2010. "Making Better PowerPoint Presentations." Retrieved August 31, 2017 (https://cft.vanderbilt.edu/guides-sub-pages/making-better-powerpoint-presentations/).

Collins, Heather R., and Laura J Massa. 2006. "PowerPoint Learning: Which Note-Taking Strategy Is Best?" Poster presented at the annual meeting of the Association for Psychological Science, May, New York, NY.

Erwin, T. Dary, and Ricardo Rieppi. 1999. "Comparing Multimedia and Traditional Approaches in Undergraduate Psychology Classes." *Teaching of Psychology* 26(1):58–223.

Frey, Barbara A., and David J. Birnbaum. 2002. "Learners' Perception on the Value of Pow-erPoint in Lectures." U.S. Department of Education, Office of Educational Research and Improvement, Educational Resources Information Center (ERIC), Document Repro-duction Service No. ED467192.

Hertz, Brigitte, Peter Kerkhof, and Cees van Woerkum. 2016. "PowerPoint Slides as Speak-ing Notes: The Influence of Anxiety on the Use of Text on Slides." *Business and Profes-sional Communication Quarterly* 79(3):348–59.

Hertz, Brigitte, Cees van Woerkum, and Peter Kerkhof. 2015. "Why Do Scholars Use Power-Point the Way They Do?" *Business and Professional Communication Quarterly* 78(3):273–91.

Hill, Andrea, Tammi Arford, Amy Lubitow, and Leandra M. Smollin. 2012. "I'm Ambivalent about It: The Dilemmas of PowerPoint." *Teaching Sociology* 40(3):242–56.

Kernbach, Sebastian, Sabrina Bresciani, and Martin J. Eppler. 2015. "Slip-Sliding-Away: A Review of the Literature on the Constraining Qualities of PowerPoint." *Business and Professional Communication Quarterly* 78(3):292–313..

Knoblauch, Hubert. 2008. "The Performance of Knowledge: Pointing and Knowledge in PowerPoint Presentations." *Cultural Sociology* 2(1):75–97.

Kosslyn, Stephen M. 2007. *Clear and to the Point: 8 Psychological Principles for Compelling PowerPoint Presentations.* Oxford: Oxford University Press.

Mantei, Erwin J. 2000. "Using Internet Class Notes and PowerPoint in the Physical Geology Lecture." *Journal of College Science Teaching* 29(3):301–5.

McDonald, Kim. 2004. "Examining PowerPointlessness." *Cell Biology Education* 3(3):156–57.

Pike, Diane L. 2018. "Without Apology: Reclaiming the Lecture." In *Learning from Each Other,* edited by J. Chin and M. Lee Kozimor-King. Oakland: University of California Press.

Quible, Zane K. 2002. "Maximizing the Effectiveness of Electronic Presentations." *Business Communication Quarterly* 65(2):82–85.

Rowh, Mark. 2012. "Power Up Your PowerPoint." *gradPSYCH Magazine,* January, p. 36.

Seaman, Michael. 1998. "Developing Visual Displays for Lecture-Based Courses." *Teaching of Psychology* 25(2):141–45.

Smith, Stephen M., and Paul C. Woody. 2000. "Interactive Effect of Multimedia Instruction and Learning Styles." *Teaching of Psychology* 27(3):220–23.

Sylvia, Monica R., Brenda J. Kirby, and Maria DiTullio. 2004. "When Less Is More: Student Atti-tudes toward Varying Formats of PowerPoint Presentations." Poster presented at the annual meeting of the American Psychological Society's Teaching Institute, May, Chicago, IL.

Szabo, Attila, and Nigel Hastings. 2000. "Using IT in the Undergraduate Classroom: Should We Replace the Blackboard with PowerPoint?" *Computers and Education* 35(3):175–87.

Teaching Effectiveness Program, University of Oregon. N.d. "Be Free to Teach: Presenting with PowerPoint." Retrieved August 31, 2017 (http://pages.uoregon.edu/tep/technology/powerpoint/docs/presenting.pdf).

Tufte, Edward R. 2003. *The Cognitive Style of PowerPoint.* Cheshire, CT: Graphics Press.

Voss, Diana. 2004. "PowerPoint in the Classroom: Is It Really Necessary?" *Cell Biology Edu-cation* 3(3):155–56.

Discussion in the Social Science Classroom

Jay R. Howard

Utilizing discussion as a pedagogical strategy is a risky endeavor. It requires that the instructor relinquish a significant amount of control in the classroom. One can never be certain that students will arrive in class having read the assignment, reflected upon the content, and prepared themselves to contribute to a productive discussion. There is also a risk that some students may express views that others find to be microaggressions or even overtly racist or sexist.[1] Students may introduce ideas that are, at best, tangentially related to the topic at hand. Of course, a chance exists that no one will say anything at all, leaving the class to endure painfully awkward stretches of silence. It is much safer for an instructor to take on the "sage on the stage" role and be the only voice heard in the classroom. Given these possibilities, why should an instructor risk utilizing discussion in the college classroom?

The short answer to the question is that discussion forces students to be engaged. An abundance of evidence demonstrates that engaged students learn more (see, for example, Pascarella and Terenzini 1991, 2005). Discussion is not the only strategy that assists with student engagement, but it is a commonly utilized strategy. However, effective discussions are rarely spontaneous outbreaks of student interest, enthusiasm, and reflection. Much more often, effective discussions occur because the instructor has reflectively considered how to structure a discussion and maximize the benefits.

Engagement in discussion forces students to move beyond superficial familiarity with content and rote memorization. In a well-designed discussion, students, along with their peers and the instructor, must deeply engage with the material, weigh the evidence in support of viewpoints, compare and contrast opposing perspectives, and apply insights to society and their own life experience. This entire process helps students develop critical-thinking skills (see, for example, Smith 1977). In the 2013–14 Higher Education Research Institute (HERI) survey of over 16,000 full-time faculty at 269 four-year colleges and universities, Eagan et al. (2014) found that 99 percent of faculty with undergraduate teaching responsibilities identified developing students' ability to think critically as a "very important" or "essential" goal. Therefore, it makes sense to utilize pedagogical strategies, like discussion, which have been shown to contribute to the development of these skills.

The benefits of a reliance on discussion in the college classroom are increasingly well documented and include increased student motivation, increased learning, development of communication skills, and even self-reported gains in character, as well as development of critical-thinking skills (see Rocca 2010 for a review of the literature). Across disciplines, when instructors structure their curriculum to encourage students to take responsibility for and to reflect on their own learning, students benefit more from the college experience including higher levels of self-reported intellectual and personal development and satisfaction with college (Laird et al. 2008). Sociology majors report that talking with others about the material, along with using application and real-world examples, are critical to their learning (McKinney 2008). Students prefer courses that include discussion over courses relying strictly, or primarily, on lecture (Aagaard, Conner, and Skidmore 2014). Given the overwhelming evidence that active-learning strategies promote student engagement and lead to greater learning and the development of critical-thinking skills, utilizing discussion is worth braving the associated risks. Yet the academic dimension of higher education is inextricably interwoven with the social dimension that can impact the nature and amount of discussion found in the college classroom (Aulls 2004).

DISCUSSION AS A SOCIAL PHENOMENON

Teaching and learning occur in a social context that is not entirely under the control of either the faculty member or students (Tiberius and Billson 1991). Students come to class with preconceived notions of what will and should occur, largely based upon prior experience in other courses. Students' expectations regarding participation in discussion are one component of the social context. If students (and faculty) view higher education as primarily being about information transmission, then engaging in the collective construction of knowledge and meaning through interaction may appear unnecessary, or possibly even counterproductive, in the view of students. This perception may cause students to resist instructors' efforts to engage them in discussion. Students may adopt a "student as customer" mentality, wherein the student / customer should never be made to feel uncomfortable or be required to assist in the creation of knowledge and understanding

(Howard and Baird 2000). Instead, such student / customers perceive that it is the instructor's job to be a "bank of knowledge" from which they make "withdrawals" by taking careful notes on the instructor's lecture (Freire [1968] 2006).

DISCUSSION NORMS IN THE COLLEGE CLASSROOM

Karp and Yoels (1976) were the first to identify a pair of college classroom norms that guide students' and faculty members' expectations regarding participation in discussion. These norms are so presumed that we are often unaware of them, at least until someone violates the normative expectations for participation in discussion.

Karp and Yoels (1976) labeled the first of these norms as *civil attention*. Rather than actually paying attention, the real norm in the majority of college classrooms is that professors expect students to pay civil attention. What is the difference? Civil attention involves creating the appearance of paying attention. Students do not have to actually pay attention as long as they appear to be doing so.

How is it that students in most college courses get away with paying civil attention instead of actually paying attention? Karp and Yoels (1976) place the responsibility for the situation largely on faculty members themselves. In most college courses, because faculty members view their students as responsible adults, students know that instructors will not call upon them to respond to a question or offer a comment unless the student signals a willingness to be called upon through such nonverbal actions as raising one's hand or making eye contact and holding the instructor's gaze. Most college faculty will not seek to embarrass students by directly questioning someone suspected of being unprepared for class. This enables students to "get away" with only paying civil attention. Students know they are unlikely to be "called out" if they are not paying attention in class. In this way, faculty members, through their unwillingness to directly call upon individual students who are not signaling a desire to speak, facilitate the norm of civil attention that allows students to avoid participation in classroom discussion.

The second college classroom discussion norm identified by Karp and Yoels (1976) is the consolidation of responsibility. Karp and Yoels (1976) and others (see, for example, Crombie et al. 2003; Fortney, Johnson, and Long 2001; Fritschner 2000; Howard, Zoeller, and Pratt 2006) have found that regardless of class size, five to eight students will account for 70 to 95 percent of all student verbal contributions during class. This norm is particularly deceptive for faculty members. An instructor can leave a class meeting convinced that the class was engaged in a wonderful discussion, when in reality the instructor and five students were engaged in a wonderful discussion, while the remainder of the students were observers of that discussion.

Which students are most likely to become the dominant talkers? Student gender is the most often studied variable when it comes to assessing student participation in discussion. This work was inspired by Hall and Sandler's (1982) "chilly climate" thesis, which contended that the higher education classroom was less welcoming to female students than males. Therefore, males will participate in discussion at a greater rate than females. However, the results of research on the relationship between participation in discussion and student gender have been mixed and inconsistent. For example, Earl-Novell (2001) found that while males contributed at a greater level than females, the proportion of men participating was less than that of women—in essence, the few men who talked, talked very frequently. In a study of large, lecture sections of biology courses, male and female students made an equal percentage of spontaneous, student-initiated comments (Eddy, Brownell, and Wenderoth 2014). However, in the same study, when it came to instructor-initiated interactions, males volunteered responses more often than did females (Eddy et al. 2014). Frequently, when researchers have found a gender effect, the study relied on student self-reports of levels of participation. Students tend to rate their own participation more highly than do their peers and instructor (see, for example, Burchfield and Sappington 1999). While all students tend to overestimate their participation in class discussion, male students tend to overestimate by a larger margin than female students. When researchers have relied on observations to count the number of interactions per student, student gender is much less likely to have a statistically significant relationship with participation. (For a review of the literature examining this relationship see Howard 2015 and Rocca 2010.)

Conversely, student age has consistently been found to have a statistically significant relationship with participation in discussion. Nontraditional students (25 years or older) participate at a much greater rate than traditional students (18 to 24 years old) in mixed-age classrooms (see Crombie et al. 2003; Fritschner 2000; Howard et al. 2006; Howard and Henney 1998; Howard, James, and Taylor 2002; Howard and Baird 2000; Howard, Short, and Clark 1996; Weaver and Qi 2005). Older students are most likely to become the dominant talkers in class. Perhaps because of their greater life experience, nontraditional students report more confidence in their ability to contribute to class discussion in comparison to their younger classmates (Loftin, Davis, and Hartin 2010).

Some evidence exists that nonwhite students and nonnative English speaking, international students participate at a lower rate in American college classrooms. The research on the impact of student race is quite limited, making it difficult to draw firm conclusions. But some preliminary studies suggest minority students participate differently (e.g., Howard et al. 2006; Packard 2011; Pitt and Packard 2012) and at a lesser rate (e.g., White 2011) than their white peers. There is somewhat more evidence to suggest that nonnative English speaking, international students hesitate to speak up in class due, at least in part, to cultural differences regarding respect for the instructor and due to a lack of confidence in their English language abilities (Bista 2011; Nakane 2005; Tatar 2005).

In addition to student characteristics that can impact participation in discussion, so can contextual factors such as course enrollment (class size), instructor gender, and classroom furniture/seating arrangements. While Karp and Yoels (1976) found the norm of the consolidation of responsibility in operation regardless of class size, it is possible that enrollment in a course may impact the overall number of contributions to discussion. Numerous studies have found that students are less likely to participate in larger classes (Crombie et al. 2003; Howard and Henney 1998; Howard et al. 2006; Loftin et al. 2010). Yet other studies (Howard et al. 2002; Nunn 1996) have not found a strong relationship between class size and levels of participation. Nunn's (1996) work suggests that rather than a direct, linear relationship between the number of students enrolled in a course and the amount of participation, there may be a "tipping point" around 35 students where the percentage of students willing to participate falls off markedly.

Instructor gender is another contextual factor that may impact students' willingness to participate in classroom discussion. Most recent studies have found that students participate more frequently in courses taught by female instructors than in courses taught by male instructors (Canada and Pringle 1995; Fassinger 1995; Howard and Baird 2000; Howard et al. 2002; Howard et al. 2006). However, this impact may be due to female faculty members' greater willingness to utilize pedagogical strategies that encourage discussion rather than due to the faculty members' gender per se (Auster and MacRone 1994).

Seating arrangements in the classroom can also impact student discussion. Loftin et al. (2010) found that students reported a greater willingness to speak up and ask for clarification in class if they could see their classmates' puzzled expressions. Thus, seating arrangements such as a circle or horseshoe appear to encourage greater participation than classrooms set up in rows facing the front of the room. Additionally, a number of studies have suggested that dominant talkers are more likely to be seated in the front third of the room (e.g., Howard et al. 2006), making it important that instructors be able to move to the middle and back of the room to engage additional students.

Research has demonstrated that both student characteristics and the social context of the classroom influence the amount and quality of participation in classroom discussion. What can instructors do to facilitate greater interaction?

ENCOURAGING CLASSROOM DISCUSSION

A couple of studies have attempted to identify which instructor behaviors lead to increased student participation in classroom discussion. Dallimore et al. (2004) asked students enrolled in graduate business courses to comment on ways their professors can increase the effectiveness of discussions. They identified six categories of behaviors that facilitate effective classroom discussions: (1) requiring/grading participation, (2) incorporating ideas and experiences, (3) active facilitation of discussion, (4) asking effective questions, (5) having a supportive classroom environment, and (6) affirming students' contributions and providing constructive feedback. The authors concluded that these results provide support for "cold calling" of students during class discussions. Of course, there are risks in attempting to generalize from a qualitative study of graduate students in business to undergraduates in general.

In a study of undergraduate students in introductory communications courses designed to build upon the findings of Dallimore et al. (2004), Finn and Schrodt (2016) developed an inventory that they titled the Teacher Discussion Facilitation Instrument (TDFI). This inventory measured discussion facilitation and assessed whether such behaviors impacted students' interest and engagement, leading to greater understanding. Finn and Schrodt (2016) found five dimensions of discussion facilitation behaviors that were positively associated with student interest and engagement. The first of these dimensions, which the authors labeled *affirms,* concerned affirmation of students' contributions and accounted for 45 percent of variance in student interest and engagement. An additional 10 percent of the variance was explained by students' perceptions of how well the instructor organized classroom discussion (*organizes*). The third dimension, *provokes,* accounted for just over five percent of the variance. Asking probing, open-ended questions (*questions*) that could lead students through the material was the fourth dimension that accounted for about three percent of the variance. The final dimension, *corrects,* which accounted for between three and four percent of variance, concerned the degree to which teachers gently corrected wrong answers while helping students understand why they were wrong and then provided constructive criticism. Finn and Schrodt (2016) concluded that effective classroom discussions can increase students' interest and engagement because effective discussions improve students' understanding. An effective discussion is characterized by the five teacher behaviors identified: affirms, organizes, provokes, questions, and corrects.

CLASSROOM STRATEGIES THAT CAN MAKE DISCUSSION MORE EFFECTIVE

Given Finn and Schrodt's (2016) findings, instructors can utilize specific strategies to facilitate classroom discussions that are likely to lead to greater student learning. Specifically, an instructor can develop strategies in response to each of Finn and Schrodt's (2016) five factors.

Affirms

Because these behaviors accounted for the greatest amount of variance, affirmation is a good starting point. Due to some salient experiences with professors who did not appreciate student contributions, or even showed impatience or hostility toward them, students need to be convinced that you, as the instructor, desire students' participation. There are some simple and basic ways to communicate your desire for student contributions to discussion and to affirm that input. Wait time is one strategy. Because we, like our students, are uncomfortable with silence in the classroom, we may fail to wait long enough for students to collect their thoughts and comment. If we ask for student input but only wait a second or two before jumping in and responding to our own question, we are communicating to students that we do not value their input sufficiently to wait for it. Instructors need to develop a tolerance for stretches of silence as students consider an invitation to participate.

Instructors must also create a safe atmosphere that welcomes discussion. One way to contribute to that atmosphere is to make an intentional effort to learn students' names. Many university registration systems now include student ID photos with course rosters. Instructors can review these, linking names with faces, prior to class to increase the likelihood of learning students' names. In larger classes, instructors could bring cardstock and markers on the first day. Ask students to fold the paper in half to make a "tent" and write their name in large letters on the front. Students then pick up their name tent at the start of each class and display it on their desk, enabling the professor to learn names more readily. It is also an unobtrusive attendance-taking strategy as the instructor can keep separate the unused name tents and record the owners as absent without taking time in class to read through a roster. Calling on students by name signals that the instructor values each student as an individual and wishes to help facilitate their success in class.

Instructors should also use the syllabus to both set the expectation for participation in discussion, communicating that civil attention and the consolidation of responsibility will not be the operative norms in this course, and to lay out some discussion ground rules. One example of an important ground rule is: listen carefully to the input of peers and recognize that one can criticize a position or perspective, but attacks on an individual are not allowed. So, for example, a student may say, "I find Marx's labor theory of value to be an insufficient accounting of how wealth is created because it fails to consider how technology, by itself, can increase productivity." However, a student may not say, "You are an idiot for agreeing with Marx's labor theory of value."

Instructors may also need to "slow down" the participation of dominant talkers in order to avoid the consolidation of responsibility. When it becomes apparent that the same few students are doing all the talking, one can say, "Let's hear from someone who has not spoken yet," "Let's hear from someone in the back half of the room," or "We've heard from a lot of the men in the room, what do women think about this topic?" This signals to the dominant talkers that they need to allow space for quieter students to contribute, and it signals to the quieter students that it is their opportunity to speak up.

When students are participating, instructors can show affirmation for their contributions in a variety of ways. Looking at the student who is speaking and nodding one's head indicates that you are paying attention and following the student's point. Smiling at students as they speak also shows appreciation for their effort to contribute. Asking nonthreatening follow-up questions to encourage students to expand their responses or to clarify also demonstrates that you, as an instructor, value their contributions.

Quieter students are more likely to be introverted personalities. While extroverts are willing to process aloud, figuring out their thoughts as they are speaking, introverts require time to collect their thoughts before speaking. A classic strategy that allows introverted students to collect their thoughts before joining a discussion is the think-pair-share classroom assessment technique (Lyman 1981). This strategy is particularly helpful in classes that students perceive as too large for safe participation in discussion. Begin by asking students to take one minute and write in response to a prompt. Then have students pair up and share their responses. Finally, instructors can ask for volunteers or call on pairs of students to share their thoughts. However, when seeking volunteers, the dominant talkers will most likely volunteer to share. Therefore, I prefer to ask students, "Whose partner had a good insight? If your partner made a particularly good point, call them out and have them share with the rest of us." This strategy makes it less likely that the same few dominant talkers will speak. Quieter students with valuable contributions have the opportunity to collect their thoughts, rehearse sharing them with one other person, and receive affirmation for the value of their thoughts. This makes it much "safer" for the introverted students to speak out in class.

Organizes

One often undervalued aspect of effective teaching is organization. As faculty, we often assume that discussion happens spontaneously. In reality, the most productive discussions occur because the faculty member has organized and structured the class session in a manner that facilitates it. One strategy for organizing a discussion is to provide students with written discussion questions associated with the reading assignment. One to three questions could be included in the calendar section of the syllabus, or a separate document could be created with discussion questions. By providing discussion questions and using them as a starting point for each class meeting, the instructor is helping students to see the logic or flow of the conversation. Introverted students, who require time to process their thoughts prior to speaking aloud in class, then have the opportunity to take notes on the reading and formulate responses to the discussion questions as they read. This provides them a basis for participating during class.

Instructors can also help students recognize the organization of a discussion by summarizing main points prior to moving on to the next question. For example, an instructor might summarize by saying, "Keesha made an excellent point when she pointed out how individuals' economic fortunes impact their voting behavior. Manuel followed up by noting that it is not merely one's geographic location, but also one's social location that influences their voting. Finally, Jasmine argued that perceptions of futility may cause entire groups of people to drop out of the election process. Everyone got that? Okay, let's move on."

Instructors can also signal the organization or flow of the discussion by affirming students as they make a significant point: "That's it! Did everyone hear what Calvin said? He just summarized the author's thesis. Calvin, say that again so that we all understand." Likewise, the instructor can write key concepts or terms on the whiteboard as Calvin repeats his point, again both affirming Calvin and making the organization of the discussion visible to the entire class.

Provokes

The third instructor behavior that Finn and Schrodt (2016) linked to productive discussions is "provokes." Faculty can provoke students' input by taking oppositional positions or offering a contrary response to student input. For example, when a student with a strong right-wing position immediately jumps into a conversation regarding the impact of gun control legislation, the instructor could thank the student for the input by saying, "Sean, you have done a great job articulating the conservative, right-wing perspective against gun control legislation of any sort. Thank you for helping us understand it. Now, let's assume you are a left-wing liberal. What argument would you offer and what evidence would you present to challenge the conservative perspective?" By following this strategy, you are inviting Sean and his classmates to assume a different perspective, and consider the evidence in support of it. You are not asking classmates to disagree with Sean per se, but to consider the arguments that would counter the conservative position on gun control. Rather than ask students to risk sharing their own opinions and to disagree with a classmate—something students are often loathe to do—you ask them to take on the role of someone who disagrees. This allows a safe means to challenge the position of a vocal, and perhaps unbending, classmate without appearing to "attack" the student.

If students are reluctant to challenge a classmate, the instructor can also gently assume the role of "devil's advocate." For example, we could respond to Sean by saying, "Let's take a look at the evidence in support of the conservative position that Sean has articulated for us, and allow me to play the devil's advocate for a moment. The conservative position holds that having more people carrying guns will lead to less crime. But does the evidence support that claim? What does the research in our reading assignment say about that assumption? When more citizens are carrying guns, does it correlate with a decrease in crime involving guns?" Again, this strategy allows the instructor and classmates to challenge a position without attacking the student who articulated the position. Ideally, it would be classmates who would respond to these questions and articulate the counterargument. But, if necessary, the professor can summarize the evidence and ask students, "Given this evidence, what types of laws or restrictions might result in less violent crime?"

Another strategy for gently provoking students' participation is to ask them to carry an argument or a position to its logical conclusion. If Hassam argues all forms of drug use should be legal, contending that the government should not seek to control what people choose to put in their bodies, an instructor can say, "Let's think about that for a moment. What do we know about the social costs of drug use and abuse? Is it fair to say that people can choose to put anything they wish in their bodies, but then expect other citizens, through their tax payments, to cover the cost of medical treatment if a person overdoses or becomes dependent on drugs? What do we know about crime rates in neighborhoods when recreational drug use and abuse becomes commonplace? If we end all restrictions on drug use, what happens to children whose parents become addicted or incapacitated through recreational drug use? Does society have an obligation to those children? What do others think?" By helping students begin to see some of the logical outcomes of their positions, we help them begin to develop the skills necessary to critique a position and evaluate evidence. By encouraging classmates to chime in, we encourage the development of their thinking skills while avoiding "attacking" Hassam.

Questions

Another instructor behavior that greatly assists in facilitating effective discussions is asking good questions. Open-ended questions without a single correct answer are much more effective than questions with a single correct answer. A question such as, "What motivated President Nixon to cover up the Watergate break-in?" does provide for multiple answers and perspectives. Questions with a single "correct" answer are much less effective in facilitating productive discussions. For example, "What sound caused Pavlov's dog to salivate?" is a much less effective question for discussion purposes than "How does Pavlov's training of his dog to salivate at the sound of a bell demonstrate the process of classical conditioning?" While there may ultimately be one right answer to this question, the answer is multidimensional and allows for varied input from students.

Corrects

Correcting students who have articulated incorrect or misleading answers without inadvertently "shutting down" discussion is a challenging task for instructors. There are clearly cases where instructors must correct false information in order to avoid confusing and misleading not only the student who voiced the incorrect answer, but also the rest of the class. Imagine a nursing student who offers an incorrect response on how to measure and administer a dosage of medicine. Such incorrect responses could, conceivably, have life or death consequences. In the social sciences, such consequences are not typically so dire. But a student arguing in favor of a policing "stop and frisk" policy by claiming it is both effective and legal could lead to infringement upon some peoples' civil rights. So we must address incorrect answers, but we must do so delicately.

One approach is to thank the student for the attempt, but gently identify it as a misconception. For example, "Jared, you are correct that people often assume a lack of any gun control laws leads to a lower incidence of crime. It seems quite logical on the surface, and many people believe it to be true. However, what does the evidence show when we compare states with stricter gun laws with states with few or no gun laws? Which is most likely to reduce violent crime rates?" Such an approach gently reminds Jared and the class that in higher education they must support arguments by evidence rather than assumptions or personal anecdotes. Another example, as evidenced by claims in the 2016 presidential election, is voter fraud. The average person, perhaps due to self-serving claims by candidates, assumes that voter fraud is much more common than it is in reality. So when a student claims voter fraud is common, the instructor could respond, "That is a good question. What evidence is there that supports claims of fraudulent voting? How many valid claims of voter fraud have been documented relative to the total number of votes cast? In what situations (e.g., very close elections) might this amount of voter fraud actually influence an election outcome?" Again, the instructor is taking the focus off of the student and placing it on the question or the topic itself while asking students to bring evidence to bear rather than rely on unsubstantiated claims or perceptions.

A related issue that sometimes arises in class discussion is responses that seemingly are unrelated to the question or topic at hand. How should an instructor respond to apparently irrelevant input? It often helps for the instructor to admit, "I do not see the connection between your comment and the question. Sorry, I have not had enough coffee this morning, and I am a little slow on the uptake. Can you explain for me the connection that I am missing?" By assuming the blame as the instructor, you provide the student with an opportunity to articulate the missing connection between their comment and the question. Sometimes it is simply a matter of the student having skipped over two or three steps that could show how the comment is related. In other cases, the comment really is only tangentially, if at all, related to the topic at hand. In these cases, a helpful response might be: "Can we 'table' that comment as it is taking us a bit far afield from the topic at hand? I would be happy to discuss it with you individually after class, but it is important with the exam coming up next week that we stay focused on the topic. Thanks for understanding."

CONCLUSION

Karp and Yoels (1976) first demonstrated that the norms of "civil attention" and the "consolidation of responsibility" work against effective classroom discussion. Civil attention allows students to come unprepared to participate in discussion without fear of being "called out" for their lack of preparation. The consolidation of responsibility means students know that five to seven classmates will assume responsibility for all students' contributions in class discussions, allowing the majority to be passive spectators. Finn and Schrodt's (2016) research offers us five teacher behaviors (affirms, organizes, provokes, questions, and corrects) that we can utilize to more effectively engage all students in class discussion whether classes are large or small.

In conclusion, I note that it is important to work on changing your students' assumptions about discussion norms in your course during the first class meeting. If, in that first class session, the instructors' voice is the only one heard as you read the roster to take attendance and read the syllabus to the students, you will have established that the norm of civil attention is in effect in your course. Instead, during the first class period, the instructor must get every student engaged in discussion whether it be whole class discussion or in pairs. It is imperative to get everyone talking.

One could ask every student to take one minute to introduce themselves by sharing their name, major, and some personal insight such as pets or favorite experience over the summer months. One could put students in small groups and collectively complete a multiple-choice quiz over the syllabus rather than reading the syllabus to students. As a part of this syllabus quiz activity, you could require students to introduce themselves and share contact information so that if they miss class, they have classmates whom they could contact and request a sharing of notes. By using such strategies on the first day of class, you are establishing new norms in your classroom. Students will understand that their participation in discussion is an expected, not an optional, part of the student role.

NOTE

1. Sue (2010) defines microaggressions as "the brief and commonplace daily verbal, behavioral, and environmental indignities, whether intentional or unintentional, that communicate hostile, derogatory, or negative racial, gender, sexual orientation, and religious slights and insults to the target person or group" (p. 5).

REFERENCES

Aagaard, Lola, Timothy W. Conner II, and Ronald L. Skidmore. 2014. "College Textbook Reading Assignments and Class Time Activity." *Journal of the Scholarship of Teaching and Learning* 14(3):132–45.

Aulls, Mark W. 2004. "Students' Experience with Good and Poor University Courses." *Educational Research and Evaluation* 10(4–6):303–35.

Auster, Carol J., and Mindy MacRone. 1994. "The Classroom as a Negotiated Social Setting: An Empirical Study of the Effects of Faculty Members' Behavior on Students." *Teaching Sociology* 22(4):289–300.

Bista, Krishna. 2011. "Why Some International Students Are Silent in the U.S. Classroom." *Faculty Focus,* June 23.

Brint, Steven, Allison M. Cantwell, and Robert A. Hanneman. 2008. "The Two Cultures of Undergraduate Academic Engagement." *Research in Higher Education* 49:383–402.

Burchfield, Colin M., and John Sappington. 1999. "Participation in Classroom Discussion." *Teaching of Psychology* 26(4):290–91.

Canada, Katherine, and Richard Pringle. 1995. "The Role of Gender in College Classroom Interactions: A Social Context Approach." *Sociology of Education* 68(3):161–86.

Crombie, Gail, Sandra W. Pyke, Naida Silverthorn, Alison Jones, and Sergio Piccinin. 2003. "Students' Perceptions of Their Classroom Participation and Instructor as a Function of Gender and Context." *Journal of Higher Education* 74(1):51–76.

Dallimore, Elise J., Julie H. Hertenstein, and Marjorie B. Platt. 2004. "Classroom Participation and Discussion Effectiveness: Student-Generated Strategies." *Communication Education* 53(1):103–15.

Eagan, M. Kevin, Ellen B. Stolzenberg, Jennifer Berdan Lozano, Melissa C. Aragon, Maria R. Suchard, and Sylvia Hurtado. 2014. *Undergraduate Teaching Faculty: The 2013-2014 HERI Faculty Survey.* Los Angeles: Higher Education Research Institute, UCLA.

Earl-Novell, Sarah. 2001. "The 'Chilly Climate' in the Seminar Room for Women: Are Temperatures Rising? An Assessment of Undergraduate Verbal Participation." Presented at the annual conference of the British Educational Research Association, September 13–15, University of Leeds. Retrieved July 5, 2016 (http://www.leeds.ac.uk/educol/documents /00001882.htm).

Eddy, Sarah L., Sara E. Brownell, and Mary Pat Wenderoth. 2014. "Gender Gaps in Achievement and Participation in Multiple Introductory Biology Classrooms." *CBE Life Sciences Education* 13:478–92. Retrieved June 29, 2016 (http://www.lifescied.org/).

Fassinger, Polly A. 1995. "Understanding Classroom Interaction: Students' and Professors' Contributions to Students' Silence." *Journal of Higher Education* 66(1):82–96.

Finn, Amber N., and Paul Schrodt. 2016. "Teacher Discussion Facilitation: A New Measure and Its Associations with Students' Perceived Understanding, Interest, and Engagement." *Communication Education* 65(4):445–62.

Fortney, Shirley D., Danette I. Johnson, and Kathleen M. Long. 2001. "The Impact of Compulsive Communications on the Self-Perceived Competence of Classroom Peers: An Investigation and Test of Instructional Strategies." *Communication Education* 50(4):357–73.

Freire, Paulo. [1968] 2006. *Pedagogy of the Oppressed: 30th Anniversary Edition.* New York: Continuum.

Fritschner, Linda M. 2000. "Inside the Undergraduate College Classroom: Faculty and Students Differ on the Meaning of Student Participation." *Journal of Higher Education* 71(3):342–62.

Hall, Roberta M., and Bernice R. Sandler. 1982. "The Classroom Climate: A Chilly One for Women?" *Project on the Status and Education of Women*. Washington, DC: Association of American Colleges.

Howard, Jay R. 2015. *Discussion in the College Classroom: Getting Your Students Engaged and Participating in Person and Online*. San Francisco: Jossey-Bass.

Howard, Jay R., and Roberta Baird, R. 2000. "The Consolidation of Responsibility and Students' Definitions of the College Classroom." *Journal of Higher Education* 71(6): 700–21.

Howard, Jay R., and Amanda L. Henney. 1998. "Student Participation and Instructor Gender in the Mixed-Age College Classroom." *Journal of Higher Education* 69(4):384–405.

Howard, Jay R., George James, and David R. Taylor. 2002. "The Consolidation of Responsibility in the Mixed-Age College Classroom." *Teaching Sociology* 30(2):214–34.

Howard, Jay R., Lillard B. Short, and Susan M. Clark. 1996. "Student Participation in the Mixed-age College Classroom." *Teaching Sociology* 24(1):8–24.

Howard, Jay R., Aimee Zoeller, and Yale Pratt. 2006. "Students' Race and Participation in Classroom Discussion in Introductory Sociology: A Preliminary Investigation." *Journal of the Scholarship of Teaching and Learning* 6(1):14–38.

Karp, David A., and William C. Yoels. 1976. "The College Classroom: Some Observations on the Meaning of Student Participation." *Sociology and Social Research* 60(4):421–39.

Laird, Thomas F. Nelson, Rick Shoup, George D. Kuh, and Michael J. Schwarz. 2008. "The Effects of Discipline on Deep Approaches to Student Learning and College Outcomes." *Research in Higher Education* 49:469–94.

Loftin, Collette, Lisa A. Davis, and Vicki Hartin. 2010. "Classroom Participation: A Student Perspective." *Teaching and Learning in Nursing* 5(3):119–24.

Lyman, Frank. 1981. "The Responsive Classroom Discussion: The Inclusion of All Students." Pp. 109–13 in *Mainstreaming Digest*, edited by A. Anderson. College Park: University of Maryland.

McKinney, Kathleen. 2008. "Correlates of Success in the Sociology Major." *International Journal for the Scholarship of Teaching and Learning* 2(1):9. Retrieved May, 26, 2017 (http://digitalcommons.georgiasouthern.edu/ij-sotl/vol2/iss1/9).

Nakane, Ikuko 2005. "Negotiating Silence and Speech in the Classroom." *Multilingua* 24(1):75–100.

Nunn, Claudia E. 1996. "Discussion in the College Classroom: Triangulating Observational and Survey Results." *Journal of Higher Education* 67(3):243–66.

Packard, J. 2011. "The Impact of Racial Diversity in the Classroom: Activating the Sociological Imagination." *Teaching Sociology* 41(2):144–58.

Pascarella, Ernest T., and Patrick T. Terenzini. 1991. *How College Affects Students: Findings and Insights from Twenty Years of Research*. San Francisco: Jossey-Bass.

Pascarella, Ernest T., and Patrick T. Terenzini. 2005. *How College Affects Students: A Third Decade of Research*. San Francisco: Jossey-Bass.

Pitt, Richard N., and Josh Packard. 2012. "Activating Diversity: The Impact of Student Race on Contributions to Course Discussions." *Sociological Quarterly* 53(2):295–320.

Rocca, Kelly A. 2010. "Student Participation in the College Classroom: An Extended Multidisciplinary Literature Review." *Communication Education* 59(2):185–213.

Smith, D. G. 1977. "College Classroom Interactions and Critical Thinking." *Journal of Educational Psychology* 69(2):180–90.

Sue, Derald Wing. 2010. *Microaggressions in Everyday Life: Race, Gender, and Sexual Orientation.* Hoboken, NJ: Wiley.

Tatar, Sibel. 2005. "Classroom Participation by International Students: The Case of Turkish Graduate Students." *Journal of Studies in International Education* 9(4):337–55.

Tiberius, Richard G., and Janet Mancini Billson. 1991. "The Social Context of Teaching and Learning." *New Directions for Teaching and Learning* 45:67–86.

Weaver, Robert R., and Jiang Qi. 2005. "Classroom Organization and Participation: College Students' Perceptions." *Journal of Higher Education* 76(5):570–601.

White, John W. 2011. "Resistance to Classroom Participation: Minority Students, Academic Discourse, Cultural Conflicts, and Issues of Representation in Whole Class Discussions." *Journal of Language, Identity and Education* 10(4):250–65.

Facilitating Learning and Leadership in Student Team Projects

Dennis O'Connor

Current college graduates cannot escape the reality of teams. As the pace of change and complexity increase, organizations need teams to pull together wide-ranging experiences and knowledge to fashion creative responses. The National Association of Colleges and Employers reported nearly 80 percent of employers surveyed indicated the ability to work in a team is an attribute of highly desired recruits (NACE 2011). The Association of American Colleges and Universities cites collaborative learning as a top-10, high-impact educational practice (Kuh 2008).

While many stunning examples of team success exist in organizations (e.g., Katzenbach and Smith 1993), achieving great team results has been vexing for many, if not most, organizations. Success for student team projects has proven problematic in the educational context as well. New students learn the ropes from others and pick up a variety of questionable behaviors and attitudes. The positive objectives of team projects are often undercut by the student culture (Richardson and Harper 1985). When I listened closely, I found rather uneven and often negative student feedback like: "I had to do all the work," "we couldn't find a time to meet," "we didn't have a leader," "I didn't want to fight," or "nobody listened to me." My team assignments were unwittingly reinforcing a "skilled incompetence" where students become unconsciously skilled in employing defensive routines antithetical to skilled team leadership (Holmer 2001).

Much remains to be done in bolstering students' competencies and attitudes toward collaborative team arrangements. The intricate challenge in helping teams respond to this complexity is illustrated by the wide range of reported efforts to improve their effectiveness: attention to composition, size, and grading (Bacon,

Stewart, and Silver 1999), establishing a positive vision (Holmer 2001), cooperative learning (Siciliano 2001), accountability (Hiller and Dunn-Jensen 2012), peer and self assessments (Kemery and Stickney 2013), team building (Tonn and Milledge 2002), mentoring and advising (Bolton 1999), and structuring tasks and progress reports (Holmer 2001; Bolton 1999).

Over the years, a close colleague and I had implemented many of the above ideas but in a piecemeal way. For each fix that worked, other problems became more apparent. We slowly realized that we had unwittingly underestimated the challenge: a great group is a marvelous human achievement and not the result of a quick fix or two. We needed both a deeper understanding of teamwork and a way to make teamwork a integral component of the course structure itself (Michaelsen, Knight, and Fink 2004).

A MODEL FOR BUILDING TEAM LEADERSHIP

Group projects have important content and deliverables, but too often these are the only foci of attention. In addition to *what* gets done, the project is a valuable opportunity to focus on: (1) *how* the work gets done in terms of tasks and people (project and group management), and (2) *who am I* in the process, the self-management of values, motivation, behavior, and outcomes (O'Connor and Yballe 2007).

Project management is perhaps the most accessible to students and involves coordinating the steps and timing of the various individual and group activities. We use a four-phase model that helps students visualize the arc of the project: startup / vision, mission / outline, rough draft, and paper / presentation.

Group management is complex, and building maps and skills to navigate its complexities is a lifelong challenge. Yet, small successes can lead to a feeling of hope in group endeavors and keep students on the path of team leadership. Required reflection assignments can make the "group" a topic for ongoing inquiry, rather than simply a context to meet an assignment. Reflection not only gives meaning to group work that students might perceive as arbitrary (Rafferty 2012), but also helps the team handle the emotional challenges of inclusion and influence central to moving to higher stages of group development (Tuckman 1965).

Self-management involves a deep commitment to reflection and learning, and to taking responsibility versus blaming others. The best leaders know who they are while also being aware of their personal strengths and weaknesses (Bennis 1989). With feedback and reflection, students learn about themselves and can have occasional "a-ha" experiences as they do serious work. They begin to learn how their habitual behaviors and attitudes impact others and the overall quality of group performance. Properly focused reflection builds emotional intelligence:

self-awareness and regulation, finding one's energy, and perseverance (Ainsworth 2016).

We believe that it is possible to create assignments that: (1) engage serious content and (2) bring the intangible elements of process and self to conscious attention. These normative, reeducative strategies (Chin and Benne 1969) involve the whole person in revising deeper assumptions, attitudes, values, and skills and build capacity for future teamwork and leadership.

PROJECT STEPS, TOOLS, AND ACTIVITIES

There is no one-size-fits-all for teamwork. Any model or tool must be constantly adapted to local and changing circumstances. For student projects, many factors call for custom tailoring: the scope of the project, the size of the class, the age and organizational experience of students, the institutional mission, the programmatic and course priorities, etc.

We begin with the three elements of the team leadership model and the importance of reflection and learning. Each of the model elements requires sustained attention and reflection pages. We want students to slow down and reflect during all phases of the project in order to improve the short-term results and to build sustainable leadership disciplines of visioning, action, and reflection. Our goal is to provide enough structure to reduce both the task and process uncertainties to manageable chunks.

After a brief sketch of basic details—scope, time frame, topic choices, and deliverables—we do some simple team building by asking students to share some information about themselves (see Appendix A) and stories from an appreciative inquiry into best teams (Cooperrider et al. 2008) (see Appendix B). As students share personal information, they see that no one is alone in their experience, nor are they exactly alike, and different pathways exist that can lead to good performance. Next, as team members listen to the various stories of best team experiences, the group builds a composite list of key elements of success that they will share later with the class at large. These lists always include some mix of task elements (timeliness, quality, etc.) and people elements (listening, fun, respect, etc.). Teams feel confident in their positive visions of group life, because they are based in the experiences of those present. We ask team members to formally sign off on the list as a psychological contract for the group. They add a team name and motto, and copies will be made for all.

They are not done yet! Each group is about to have its first performance. Each team is asked to take center stage, look over the class, notice their feelings as they stand before their peers and introduce themselves, share their composite list, team name, and motto. We remind them that they will return to the stage for a presentation, and the experience will be *far* more comfortable and rewarding for a group that achieves its vision, does good work, and is able to educate the rest of us about a useful topic.

In this first phase of group development, we want to immediately establish norms of sharing ideas, doing something useful, standing together as a team, and thoughtfully reflecting on important experiences. The structure helps all to participate and listen. Students feel included, capable, curious, and positive about successfully getting on and off stage.

Because the momentum of past experience propels students to only notice tangible project tasks, a startup reflection page (Appendix C) is due for the next class. Hundreds of final group reflection papers over the years confirm that this stage generally goes extremely well. The first reflection page focuses on the team, but also directs the student's attention to his or her feelings, personal behaviors, the sense of inclusion, and leadership. We want students to slow down and tackle these reflection pages with a spirit of inquiry and personal benefit, rather than write one more report that pushes accountability. All reflections will conclude with a focus on future actions for leadership and skill building. Such a cycle of learning activates the brain in complex ways (Zull 2002) and can be applied multiple times (five for us) to promote deeper learning (Border 2007).

Team members feel good after this first phase, but the initial burst of energy and enthusiasm will quickly dissipate if there are not follow-up activities. We have laid out several tasks for the next phase of the project: choosing a topic, assigning coordinators for the key tasks, completing annotated bibliographies, outlining the paper, and setting target dates.

If the instructor does not preassign a project topic, groups need to find and agree upon a topic or client that sufficiently taps their curiosity and personal learning goals. Every important decision must be handled with care and attention to the input and commitment of all. We ask each individual to brainstorm and share a list of their curiosities related to the course and project guidelines. As they notice commonalities and differences, our role vis-à-vis the team is to collaborate with them in finding worthwhile topics. In an appreciative way, we help to move students from "why does my supervisor assign boring work?" to an inquiry that asks about what makes a task challenging and exciting. Wanting to "know about motivation" can become an inquiry into the nature of peak performance.

The handling of each step affects later work and commitment. If one or two students pick a topic because they are extroverted, or they know each other, or it is deemed "easy," while others hesitate, then the possibility for those others to slowly withdraw their effort and commitment greatly increases over the life of the project. It becomes easy to step back and let the "leaders" do the work. "It's their project after all." Students need to discover that this first decision (and most remaining decisions and tasks) is not a race where finishing fast is good! Human interaction is often like fine craft work: we go faster by slowing down, focusing on quality, and attending carefully to each other and the important aspects of the task. The best groups find excitement and begin to build mutual trust in what they are doing.

We follow the topic choice with an overview of the remaining project management steps: outline / writing, rough draft, final paper, and presentation. We then ask groups to find a "coordinator" for each step. We strongly emphasize that the role of the coordinator is not to do all the work, but to make sure that the group completes that step according to its vision. A number of students now have a leadership opportunity to look forward to, and we give groups some time to discuss both the type and timing of leadership required. We encourage them to specifically describe what coordinators will need to do for the tasks to go well. There are benefits and pitfalls to both self-directed teams and teams with one leader (Rae 2011). The coordinator role puts the group somewhere in between. Several students can experiment with leadership, and the group is less likely to fall into the trap of one person doing almost all the work.

Leadership challenges arise with the first research task, an annotated bibliography. All are asked to find two sources of information from a list of specified journals and provide summaries of key points in preparation for a 15-minute meeting at the end of the next class. Inevitably, we see some floundering at this stage. Missing or poorly done work is surprising and annoying to the group, but it is also an unprecedented opportunity for the team to progress. It is important to face up to the shortcomings in work when the infractions are small, and positive momentum can be regained. We let teams know that this is not the first or last time in history that someone has fallen short on an agreed-upon assignment. Too often the initial response is to avoid the "confrontation," offer the usual excuses, and pretend that everything is within normal limits, and it will all work out. We want teams to establish a norm of accountability and learning.

From the group management point of view, a precedent of avoiding conflict would be set and further reinforced by the student culture. This negative work norm increases the chances that a free rider or slacker mindset will take root and grow in the group culture. We ask the coordinator of the outline step to help the group openly deal with the uneven results. The group must remind itself of its vision and openly discuss whose work is missing, too brief, or off the mark, and the timing of corrective actions.

A good outline sharpens everyone's effort and greatly reduces the emotion and work at the rough draft step. Yet, solid topic information creates a new challenge for the group. Sorting through a set of writings to build an outline is tough mental work for a group in an early stage of development. We have often used class time to help groups stay with the task longer than they might have if left on their own.

When they finish, we compliment them for sticking with such a difficult task. After creating an outline, the group is asked to discuss and agree on target dates and logistical details such as paper format. This second phase (mission / outline) has generally been more sobering than the first, and it is followed with another reflection task.

The third phase of the project requires individuals and pairs to further research the topic and compose a rough draft. The group needs some time for this work, but too much time between tasks will cause less experienced teams to lose focus and energy. We encourage students to check in on each other's progress to minimize the "last minute" syndrome. The coordinator can check up before or after class as well as online via texts, email, or Google docs. We strongly encourage students to experiment with virtual methods of communication (Bull Schaefer and Erskine 2012), as we are all increasingly embedded in a hybrid world of both face-to-face and virtual interaction.

At some point, the toughest task must take place: putting together and evaluating the rough draft. Even if the group navigates the first two phases well, quality and relevance issues inevitably crop up at this juncture. Outlines did not provide full guidance, honest misunderstandings occur, new ideas emerge, and some fall short in effort or simply lack the skill for this particular task.

The rough draft coordinator's job is to help the group honestly evaluate its work. Yes, the group has arrived at another key leadership opportunity! The best response is to deal with the quality issues openly and in a practical, unemotional way. The mission is to create a quality report, but the group finds itself in the strong currents of emotion tied to criticism and rejection. We encourage the coordinator to remind the group of its earlier hopes rather than blame individuals as a context to evaluate the writing for improvement. Team members must find a way to give and receive feedback. We remind the class that almost everyone stated that they would be able to accept "constructive" criticism. They need to see that this emotional work is inevitable, normal, and necessary.

We have asked students to tackle a very difficult task, and we let them know this and why. The recurring truth is that team leadership is hard work without a guarantee of immediate success. Learning can only be guaranteed with the proper attitude and discipline. This phase is followed with a third reflection. The professor, as always, has the option to devote class time to debriefing project activity. If possible, it is important to schedule course readings and activities that can highlight critical dimensions of group work as it occurs.

The last phase involves completing the project report and designing and delivering a presentation that actively engages the audience. At this point, many groups are feeling alive and invincible. They are pulling together, but still lack a consistent quality focus. We provide guidance and examples for an interactive presentation.

"The semester began with me in charge. Now the class is in *your* hands." Which findings or ideas are worth sharing? What would be great? Fun? Engaging?

After the presentation, teams receive written feedback from the professor and other students, but a critical step still remains. In addition to a final reflection, students must write a final paper where they consolidate and evaluate their overall experience from this project. They have a team data sheet, four reflection pages, and course and group topic readings to draw upon as they attempt to analyze the effectiveness of their group. We want an appreciative focus on what really worked and why, as well as an honest look at what fell short. Even a poor experience can be of lasting benefit, if it motivates the individual to take a more active, intentional role in future group experiences. We want some self-confrontation. Students need to examine their own personal contributions and leadership: What did I do that worked, what did others do that I could try, what leadership am I sure to provide in future teams? The goal of the final paper is to deepen understanding of the team and self and to build confidence in generating future leadership options.

CONCLUSION

Team leadership is an intricate process entailing many "real time" interconnected skills. It involves joining with complex others in a thoughtful, caring way to achieve mutually agreed upon, quality results. Failure is easy—it just takes one critical element to not work. Success is demanding—it takes all the pieces to work together over time.

Becoming a highly effective group member is not a quick fix, but rather a long journey of mastery. We believe that students learn more from good group experiences than bad (Bacon et al. 1999), and we have sought to boost their chances of success. Students in team projects need to slow down and learn about the logical steps in creating and executing a project *and* to establish personal leadership disciplines of reflection and action. Each tangible project activity affords opportunities to deepen knowledge about group dynamics and personal leadership.

It is important, however, to maintain realistic expectations. Students will not be "qualified" to be great leaders after one project. Still, as professors, we have seen more flashes of creativity and enthusiasm and fewer, if any, disasters. We see and read about deliberate efforts to understand and change teams, and we hear many satisfying reports by students who have always hated groups but found this experience productive and rewarding. The combination of structure and extra time has produced short-term results that we hope provide a foundation for long-term mastery.

Teaching team leadership is also a long-term journey of mastery for the professor. You will be challenged to become more competent in understanding the dynamics of teams, to consult with students about their teams, and to take the time to help teams manage their projects well. Our more active role in guiding team projects has been both difficult and satisfying. Continuous involvement with the various tasks has opened a window into student reality that has enriched our experience and raised our awareness. Through direct contact and reflection pages, we receive a tremendous amount of feedback, which helps guide our thinking and adjustments. Simply asking a few of the better students for mid-project updates provides clarity and motivation to address the larger class; carefully reading the final team analysis papers provides insights on both the positive and negative dynamics that occur. To maximize learning, the professors, like students, need to view this process as an opportunity for reflection and personal growth and not something to be discharged efficiently.

In summary, by following the guidelines below, professors can continuously improve their effectiveness in facilitating positive student team functioning, learning, and leadership.

1. Make sure you convey in all your actions that learning to be effective in teams is important. Effectiveness entails knowing about teams **and** yourself. It involves acquiring and sharpening task and people skills and developing a leadership mindset.

2. Be clear about your rationale for putting students in teams to work on a team project. Make clear statements about your expectations and about the exciting possibilities and outcomes. Verbalize your hopes for excellence, and return often to the positive visions the students have generated. The best assignment has a mix of structure and ambiguity.

3. Use reflection pages to encourage students to actively make sense of what is occurring in the team, to focus on their experience as a source of insights, and to identify skills needing work. Remind them that their learning and leadership is the project.

4. Be aware that teams need time and attention. Set aside time for start-up. A great start goes a long way toward a vigorous team experience. Have an open-door policy, and check periodically on how each team is doing by reviewing their reflections and asking for progress reports. You may have to intervene periodically, either with a single student or with the group. Try to reiterate their visions of excellence and hope. Remember, these are teaching moments.

5. The path of mastery is the same for both student and teacher. You will fall short and make numerous mistakes. Look outward and inward for help. Draw upon others' work to help craft your experiments. They can be great

resources for you (planning, interventions, etc.). Immerse yourself in the process of learning about and teaching about teams. See yourself on the path of mastery, and actively seek opportunities for personal and professional development.

REFERENCES

Ainsworth, Judith. 2016. "Student-Led Project Teams: Significance of Regulation Strategies in High- and Low-Performing Teams." *Journal of Management Education* 40(4): 453–77.

Bacon, Donald, Kim Stewart, and William Silver. 1999. "Lessons from the Best and Worst Student Team Experiences: How a Teacher Can Make the Difference." *Journal of Management Education* 23(5):467–89.

Bennis, Warren. 1989. *On Becoming a Leader.* New York: Addison Wesley.

Border, L. L. 2007. "Understanding Learning Styles: The Key to Unlocking Deep Learning and In-Depth Teaching." *NEA Higher Education Advocate* 24:5–8.

Bolton, Michele. 1999. "The Role of Coaching in Student Teams: A 'Just-In-Time' Approach to Learning." *Journal of Management Education* 23(3):233–50.

Bull Schaefer, Rebecca, and Laura Erskine. 2012. "Virtual Team Meetings: Reflections on a Class Exercise Exploring Technology Choice." *Journal of Management Education* 36(6): 777–801.

Chin, Robert, and Kenneth Benne. 1969. "General Strategies for Effecting Change in Human Systems." Pp. 32–59 in *The Planning of Change,* 2nd ed., edited by Warren G. Bennis, Kenneth D. Benne, and Robert Chin. New York: Holt Rinehart and Wilson.

Cooperrider, David L., Diana Whitney, and Jacqueline M. Stavros. 2008. *Appreciative Inquiry Handbook: For Leaders of Change,* 2nd ed. Brunswick, OH: Crown Custom.

Hiller, Janet, and Linda M. Dunn-Jensen. 2012. "Groups Meet . . . Teams Improve: Building Teams That Learn." *Journal of Management Education* 37(5):704–33.

Holmer, Lee. 2001. "Will We Teach Leadership or Skilled Incompetence: The Challenge of Student Project Teams." *Journal of Management Education* 25(5):590–605.

Katzenbach, Jon, and Douglas Smith. 1993. *The Wisdom of Teams: Creating the High-Performance Organization.* Boston: Harvard Business School Press.

Kemery, Edward, and Lisa Stickney. 2013. "A Multifaceted Approach to Teamwork Assessment in an Undergraduate Business Program." *Journal of Management Education* 38(3):462–79.

Kuh, George. 2008. *High-Impact Educational Practices: What They Are, Who Has Access to Them, and Why They Matter.* Washington, DC: Association of American Colleges and Universities.

Michaelsen, Lawrence, Arletta Knight, and L. Dee Fink. 2004. *Team-Based Learning: A Transformative Use of Small Groups in College Teaching.* Sterling, VA: Stylus.

NACE (National Association of Colleges and Employers). 2011. "Job Outlook 2012." Bethlehem, PA: NACE Research.

O'Connor, Dennis, and Leo Yballe. 2007. "Team Leadership: Critical Steps to Great Projects." *Journal of Management Education* 31(2):292–312.

Rae, Andre. 2011. "Using Leadered Groups in Organizational Behavior and Management Survey Courses." *Journal of Management Education* 35(5):596–619.

Rafferty, Patricia 2012. "Group Work in the MBA Classroom: Improving Pedagogical Practice and Maximizing Positive Outcomes with Part-Time MBA Students." *Journal of Management Education* 37(5):623–50.

Richardson, Alan, and Shelash Harper. 1985. "Group Work and Student Culture." *Journal of Management Education* 10(3):81–86.

Siciliano, Julie. 2001. "How to Incorporate Cooperative Learning Principles in the Classroom: It's More than Just Putting Students in Teams." *Journal of Management Education* 25(1):8–21.

Tonn, Joan, and Vicki Milledge. 2002. "Team Building in an MBA 'Gateway' Course: Lessons Learned." *Journal of Management Education* 26(4):415–29.

Tuckman, Bruce. 1965. "Developmental Sequence in Small Groups." *Psychological Bulletin* 63(6):384–99.

Yballe, Leo, and Dennis O'Connor. 2000. "Appreciative Pedagogy: Constructing Positive Models for Learning." *Journal of Management Education* 24(4):474–83.

Zull, James. 2002. *The Art of Changing the Brain: Enriching the Practice of Teaching by Exploring the Biology of Learning.* Sterling, VA: Stylus.

APPENDIX A: PERSONAL ASSESSMENT

1. Do I work better slowly or quickly?
2. Am I a good listener?
3. Do I like recognition and acceptance? Being counted on?
4. Do I work best alone or in groups?
5. Do I prefer to lead or follow?
6. Do I like to plan or jump in?
7. Do I meet deadlines or begin when work is due?
8. How do I react to criticism?
9. What are my strengths? What do I contribute to success?
10. What are my weaknesses? Where do I need to improve?

For class large group discussion options:

1. How many can deal with working with "good groups"? Are good groups simply a matter of luck?
2. What does it mean to "lead" in a student group?
3. Most can deal with constructive criticism, yet we hesitate to give feedback. Why?

APPENDIX B: APPRECIATIVE INQUIRY: BEST TEAM EXERCISE

Please take a minute and remember back to a successful group or team that you enjoyed being with, and then jot notes on: Why was this group the best? What qualities made this team special? What really stands out in your mind about this team? Break down general items like communication and leadership. What happened exactly? This exercise seeks to draw upon your individual experiences of success as a basis for collectively envisioning the type of team that you would like to create.

APPENDIX C: REFLECTION PAGES
First Reflection: Team Startup

- What were some of the important things that you saw happening as your team formed?
- What went well? What were key moments in your opinion?
- Where is your team's vision (as described on your Team Data Sheet) already coming to life?
- What did you do or say specifically? Or not do? What was the effect on the group and others?
- How are you feeling about your interactions so far? What are you feeling good about?
- How accepted do you feel by the group? Are you a part of what is going on? How "in" do you feel (rate 1–10)? Any concerns?
- What have you tried and what have you learned? What behaviors or skills can you work on or experiment with as we proceed? What's a good first step? Be specific!!

Second Reflection: Additional Questions

- What level of influence are you having, and how do you feel about it (rate 1–10)? Are others listening to what you say? Does the group seriously consider your ideas?
- Has your group maintained its initial positive momentum? What still needs to be done to help insure the success of this group? What would a leader do? What might you do? What will you do?

Third Reflection: Additional Questions

- How close is the group feeling at this stage? Are we feeling so good that we are not worried about quality? Or afraid to bring up issues of quality and disrupt the good cheer?
- How are you feeling about your section of the work? About the rough draft overall? What are you feeling good about? Not so good about?
- Were you able to accept performance feedback from others? Were you able to provide performance feedback that others could hear and act on? Or did you keep your concerns to yourself?

Fourth Reflection: Additional Questions

- What surprises were there? Could they have been foreseen?
- How are you feeling about your contributions? How do they stack up against your hopes and personal standards? What are you feeling good about?

- How are you feeling about the team now? What would you like to say to them individually and as a group?
- With perfect 20/20 hindsight, what will you do with future team projects to help insure a strong finish?
- What have you tried, and what have you learned? How could you exert more leadership? What would you like to experiment with on your next project team?

13

Courting Controversy and Allowing for Awkward

Strategies for Teaching Difficult Topics

Mari Plikuhn

For over two decades, scholars in the social sciences and beyond increasingly have focused on the need for instructors to foster active discussions on controversial or uncomfortable classroom topics and the preparation necessary for these discussions to be effective (Abbott 2009; Crabtree and Sapp 2003; Evans, Avery, and Pederson 2000; Ezzedeen 2008; Fredericks and Miller 1993; Goodman 1995; Jakubowski 2001; Roberts and Smith 2002). More recent scholarship has debated the necessity of "trigger warnings" (statements that alert students to potentially traumatic, controversial, or anxiety-provoking topics or material) and whether instructors should consider student discomfort with course content (Boysen, Wells, and Dawson 2016; Carter 2015; Dilevko 2015; Lockhart 2016; Rae 2016). Because of their focus on human behavior and the social world, the social sciences rarely can avoid controversial or uncomfortable topics and often must embrace difficult arguments in order to better understand the full scope of human experience. The value and need to court controversy and allow for the awkward, however, does not make it an easy task for instructors. Within a variety of classroom settings, the need to teach a diversity of perspectives and challenge students to engage with the material often conflicts with the desire to create a safe space for students (Rae 2016; Robbins 2016).

There are many reasons that a topic might be difficult to discuss. A topic may be politically or religiously controversial to some individuals, including topics that are polarizing for the majority of Americans (e.g., abortion, death with dignity) or topics that divide only the groups who feel directly affected (e.g., academic freedom in higher education). Beyond controversy, "difficult" topics may be those that make people uncomfortable to directly discuss or even witness the discussion.

These include both personal issues (whether they have occurred to the individual or not) or social issues. Often the personal and social levels are interconnected (Mills 1959); personal issues are (and should be) considered social issues and issues that confront society certainly are faced and experienced by the individual. For example, examining homelessness as a social problem forces society to consider how families with children negotiate activities of daily living, just as individuals who have been or are homeless are aware of the realities and can speak to ways that organizations can address these needs. Personal issues that make individuals uncomfortable to discuss are often sexual in nature (e.g., sexual orientation, rape, incest) (Lee 1993; Ogle, Glasier, and Riley 2008) or health related (e.g., physical or mental illness, suicide, death, disease, disability, pregnancy) (Alty and Rodham 1998; DiIorio, Kelley, and Hockenberry-Eaton 1999; Lee 1993), and uncomfortable social issues often include social injustice and issues of inequality (Brunsma, Brown, and Placier 2012; DiAngelo and Sensoy 2014; Rothenberg 2012).

In this chapter, I explore the types of topics that can be challenging to teach, what shapes this discomfort for students and for the instructor, and strategies for structuring and managing the classroom to make the presentation and discussion of difficult topics more fruitful.

COURTING CONTROVERSY

Controversial content can be difficult to navigate in traditional face-to-face classroom settings and in online formats. To be clear, "controversial" does not mean simply that people have different perspectives on an issue, but rather there exists contentious, bitterly divided sides of the perspective with little perceived middle ground. For example, debating whether a lengthened school year would narrow the test score gap between the United States and other nations may not be as controversial as debating the value of the nationwide legalization of marijuana. Yet sometimes controversy flares and other times it dissipates: the national legalization of marijuana is not as controversial for millennial students as it would have been for previous generations of students. One person's divisive controversy can be another person's shrug of indifference. Further, political alignment, religious upbringing, family socialization, and life experiences shape how individuals view their world and which values they hold (James et al. 2014; McAvoy and Hess 2013).

When topics are known to have polarized perspectives, instructors should prepare for the potential for hostility and brief students on tactics to engage effectively with the material, whether actively listening or participating in discussion (Fournier-Sylvester 2013). Instructors can acknowledge that conflicting or differing perspectives on an issue exist and provide a framework for students on all sides to feel that their views will be heard by acknowledging that the goal of learning and discussion is not to "win." This framework can be formal and predetermined, as through specific rules, guidelines, or expectations for discussions that take place in the classroom or on discussion boards, or informally constructed by the students through reflective conversation on what has and has not worked in previous classroom or online discussions. Outlining expectations at the start of a course sets the tone for open-minded engagement with controversial content and with others who have different perspectives, yet students often fail to meet these explicit expectations. Having been continuously socialized by family, cultural, political, or religious sources, "the grooves of the standard arguments are already worn into many students' minds" (Burkstand-Reid, Carbone, and Hendricks 2011:678), and it can be challenging to embrace a topic that is unknown or contrary to their values.

Despite these concerns, it is important for students to listen intently, debate respectfully, and learn openly from others, both in and beyond the classroom setting (Fallahi and Haney 2007). Though development of these skills may seem strictly the purview of interpersonal communication, the variety and type of content covered in courses across the range of the social sciences provide the need for the practical application and strengthening of these skills. Instead of competitive tactics for persuasive arguments and negative rebuttals as might be taught in a debate class, consider a broader framework for critical listening and evaluation, or what Johnson, Johnson, and Tjosvold (2006) refer to as "skilled disagreement." In their chapter on the value of intellectual conflict, they describe 11 skills necessary for engaging with controversial content and others who have differing views (Johnson et al. 2006:75–76):

1. I am critical of ideas, not people. I challenge and refute the ideas of the other participants, while confirming their competence and value as individuals. I do not indicate that I personally reject them.
2. I separate my personal worth from criticism of my ideas.
3. I remember that we are all in this together, sink or swim. I focus on coming to the best decision possible, not on winning.
4. I encourage everyone to participate and to master all the relevant information.
5. I listen to everyone's ideas, even if I don't agree.
6. I restate what someone has said if it is not clear.
7. I differentiate before I try to integrate. I first bring out all ideas and facts supporting both sides and clarify how the positions differ. Then I try to identify points of agreement and put them together in a way that makes sense.
8. I try to understand both sides of the issue. I try to see the issue from the opposing perspective in order to understand the opposing position.
9. I change my mind when the evidence clearly indicates that I should do so.

10. I emphasize rationality in seeking the best possible answer, given the available data.

11. I follow the golden rule of conflict. The golden rule is act toward opponents as you would have them act toward you . . .

Instructors can present these expectations, or ones they personally devise, to students in a variety of ways: inclusion in the syllabus, a separate handout given prior to structured classroom debates or discussions, or as the rules for discussion board participation in online courses. Presenting these expectations should go beyond a casual reference to them on the first day of class or a discussion board post. By providing students with a set of expectations for engaging with each other and with controversial content, instructors can shape how students view and learn the material, as well as their abilities to consider the perspective of others—a key component to understanding social science research.

Strategies such as these expectations can be useful in lower-level courses with students who are new to the discipline, the university, or discussion of complicated or controversial topics. These skills also are invaluable for upper-level courses where the deeper focus of the content delves into conflicting evidence and detailed analysis of issues. I use the set of expectations from Johnson et al. (2006) in all of my classes, regardless of level or topic. I present the expectations in my syllabus, as part of a section on the role and value of class discussions, and revisit this during the first week of class when I begin my content lectures. I provide the students with a context for why these guidelines are useful for constructive critical analysis, how they can shape the learning environment, and how a shared set of expectations in discussions provides the opportunity for exploration, growth, and understanding for all members of the discussion. I return to the list periodically across the semester to highlight how a student effectively used a strategy or as a reminder prior to teaching controversial content. Students have responded positively to the list of expectations, agreeing with the value of civility in creating a classroom climate that encourages all members to participate.

Finally, allowing students to engage with controversial topics highlights the importance of critical evaluation of information—as citizens, consumers, partners, and learners (Avery, Levy, and Simmons 2013; Hand and Levinson 2012). The core of critical evaluation is the ability to address ideas, whether currently held and not, to determine their merits and shortcomings. When individuals learn that holding an idea in one's mind does not necessarily mean embracing it as part of one's worldview, their ability to value empathy, awareness, and perspective can increase (Avery et al. 2013; Hand and Levinson 2012). In turn, they can engage thoughtfully in further discussions on perspectives that differ from their own. Thus, facilitating the discussion of controversial or uncomfortable topics is crucial both for learning about these issues and because these issues are more likely to lead to further discussions (Hand and Levinson 2012).

ALLOWING FOR AWKWARD OR UNCOMFORTABLE
TOPICS

Just as with "controversy," what makes a topic awkward or uncomfortable can vary by the audience. As described previously, issues that make individuals uncomfortable to discuss are often sexual in nature, health related, or issues of social injustice and inequality. Though topics like racial inequality, historically, have been uncomfortable for students to discuss in American classrooms (Goldsmith 2006; Haddad and Lieberman 2002; Harlow 2009), the greater awareness and presence of these topics in the media makes it even more important that instructors take on the challenge of addressing them. However, instructors must do some work prior to discussions on social inequality: providing historic context for the creation and continuation of inequality, explaining differences in and the value of lived experiences, describing privilege (whether asked for or not) and how it perpetuates inequality, and drawing attention to the lens society uses to frame arguments supporting inequality (for a detailed description of teaching race, see Brunsma et al. 2012).

Presenting a topic that falls into the awkward category often brings silence from students in a face-to-face classroom setting and a determined effort to appear engrossed in note-taking so as not to meet the eye of the instructor (Payne and Gainey 2003). Students may not want to participate because of perceived lack of knowledge on the topic or uncertainty in the amount of support they will receive from their instructor and classmates (Fassinger 1995). Classroom silence is uncomfortable for instructors, but can provide students a quiet moment to absorb the information presented, and it allows them time to reflect before responding, modeling effective discussion strategies in general. In addition, the silence can force them to end the tension by engaging with the material. Knowing how long to wait in silence when students do not answer is a more complicated question; for instructors standing at the front of a silent classroom, a few seconds' pause can feel like an eternity. But waiting to allow students to respond to a question posed, or to provide an example or interpretation from the readings, shifts the impetus of learning to the students and models active listening from the instructor (Schultz 2010). There are a variety of ways to encourage the conversation to continue: restate the question, ask for examples from the readings, media, or broader social institutions, or tie the new discussion to a topic previously covered in class. For example, probe the silence with questions such as: "what did today's readings say about this topic?" or "what might be a movie or song that highlights this issue?"

The previous situations involve more general topics that often cause students to squirm, but sometimes the topics are uncomfortable because students have firsthand experience with them. For example, rape is a terrible and too-frequent crime that can cause students to feel a strong empathetic compassion for victims, but it can be traumatic for the victims themselves to hear the topic come up within a classroom context. The national conversation on "trigger warnings" has criticized academics for coddling and infantilizing college students who want to avoid discomfort in the classroom (Boysen et al. 2016; Carter 2015; Dilevko 2015; Lockhart 2016; Rae 2016; Robbins 2016), yet it is important to distinguish between students requesting accommodations to dodge uncomfortable topics and students concerned about experiencing reactions to traumatic events they have faced (Carter 2015; Lockhart 206; Rae 2016).

One effective strategy I have employed is to provide opportunities for students to choose when to opt-out of material. If the course requires watching three documentaries, show four to allow students to choose which they will watch. Assign papers for each reading, but allow students to drop their lowest grade so they can choose to skip reading an article that would be difficult for them. Allow for an absence for any reason they choose that will not be counted against their grade. There are two important benefits to this strategy: (1) it allows the work of all students to be graded fairly in comparison to their peers; and (2) it does not require students to self-disclose a traumatic experience to the instructor to receive an exemption from that topic.

Topics sensitive in content are key components of the social sciences, yet when particular topics might elicit strong reactions, it is useful to have a brief discussion ahead of time on why it is important to discuss and understand this part of the social world. Instead of framing the argument for discussions of challenging topics as a need to be "stronger" or more objective (Rae 2016), structure the conversation around gaining insight into ourselves and the broader discourse of the topic. Include a section in the syllabus about the role of classroom participation and discussion in understanding the material. During the first class, highlight the type of content you will cover across the semester and the ways you will expect students to engage with the content (e.g., discussion, reading articles, watching documentaries, debates, etc.). This will allow students the chance to drop the class if they are concerned with the topics. By ensuring transparency in the content and expectations of the course from the beginning, students will be more prepared for addressing difficult topics (Rae 2016).

For a prolonged discussion or entire course on a potentially traumatic topic (e.g., Death and Dying; Domestic Violence; Child Psychology and the Law; Racism and Stereotyping; Terrorism; Human Rights), consider giving students information on counseling resources available on campus, help-line numbers, and website resources with information on the warning signs of becoming distressed. I distribute brochures from the university's counseling center to all students in courses on traumatic topics (e.g., Death and Dying) on the first day of class while discussing the course content and potential for distress. The reaction from students is frequently one of surprise, but it draws their attention to the gravity of the topic and possibility of challenges. Discuss as a class how students will keep themselves healthy and consider "check in" moments with all students across the semester, particularly when assignments or class discussions are especially challenging or with students who have discussed problems with the content with the instructor. These "check in" moments can be formal (e.g., required reflective component within assigned papers, periodic end-of-class writing prompts) or informal (e.g., asking students collectively or individually "how are you doing?"). Finally, for any type of difficult topic, have a plan for breaks, tension-breakers, and ways of defusing moments where students seem overwhelmed with the information presented (Mason and Briggs 2011). Instructors can plan a five-minute break after a difficult documentary to allow students to process the presented information. Instead of having a solid block of time allocated for a class discussion, consider interrupting the discussion to show a short clip on a different aspect of the topic. Finally, acknowledge in the moment that some conversations on content can be difficult. By saying "whew, this can be hard to talk about!" or "okay, let's take a moment to collect our thoughts on this topic!", an instructor affirms the students' need for reflection and provides space for that to happen (Rae 2016).

STRATEGIES FOR CLASS STRUCTURE AND MANAGEMENT

Classroom Policies and Procedures

One of the first steps in structuring space for effective discussions is to determine the type or form of policies or guidelines that the instructor will provide to the students for engaging with others. Instructors can construct these policies or guidelines in several ways. For example, the instructor can provide the ground rules for class discussion in the syllabus, such as the skilled disagreement strategies by Johnson et al. (2006) that were outlined above in the "Courting Controversy" section, and discuss with students the design and purpose of this structure at the start of the semester. Instructors and students both can benefit from a clear, mutual set of expectations for overall classroom behaviors, and outlining expectations for the instructor as well as the students will acknowledge the collaboration necessary to achieve a positive classroom atmosphere. The expectations for instructors might include items such as arriving on time and being prepared for class, respectfully listening to students, and announcing changes to the course as quickly as possible.

Alternatively, the instructor can have a core set of policies to start and then encourage students to discuss whether the instructor should include additional policies and then decide how the policies should be enforced. Instructors also may allow students to discuss and agree on the class policies and the enforcement of these policies, which allows them to take ownership of the process. For example, the instructor may ask students to construct a list of penalties if someone is disrespectful in the discussion and hold a vote to determine which penalties the class accepts. These more student-centered, active-learning strategies allow students to set the parameters for how they participate in the class and can lower their concerns for how their peers and professors will perceive them (Mason and Briggs 2011). Regardless of how the policies and enforcements are created, however, it is useful to refer back to them periodically throughout the semester, to remind students of the structure of good discussion.

Learning, Growing, and Patience

Occasionally, students may say things that are inappropriate, offensive, or disrespectful. Both at the beginning of the semester when discussing policies and across the semester, explain to the students that learning comes in fits, not in smooth arcs, and all members of the course need to be patient with each other as they grow in their understanding of how the world works while being respectful and courteous to each other. When a student says something that violates the policies of discussion, acknowledge why the particular response might be inappropriate, as most students do not realize they are being inappropriate, nor do they intend to be mean, offensive, or rude. Perhaps their statement draws on stereotypes that may not be true or their statement is intolerant or isolating to others in the discussion. Point out why stereotypes so often fall short of reality and where facts support a broader interpretation of that social issue. Draw on the readings or previous lecture materials to highlight the common misconceptions that arise from this topic. In an online setting, remind students that they are lacking the vocal tone, facial expressions, and hesitation present in a face-to-face setting and should consider how others in the discussion may have interpreted their words. Allow the student to come up with a more appropriate alternative to their original response. Returning the conversation to the student provides them the opportunity to learn from the experience, but also shows students that disagreement or differing viewpoints need not halt discussion in general or their participation in particular.

On the other hand, rare situations occur when a student's intent is to be intolerant, isolating, offensive, or disrespectful. Though it can disrupt the flow of the presentation or discussion of the content, it also can impact the classroom morale, hurting some students and making others less likely to share their ideas or perspective. When this situation arises, it is crucial to enforce the policies and procedures that had been discussed previously and periodically through the semester. Just as with an accidental offense, explain to the student why their statement was inappropriate. The instructor may find it less disruptive to the classroom discussion to address this concern in greater detail with the student after class or via email. If the student continues to argue the point in a hostile manner, it might be best to move on with the discussion. If the student still refuses to stop his or her hostile or offensive interjections, an instructor may find it necessary to ask the student to leave the class (Mason and Briggs 2011).

Consider, ahead of time, all of the options if the student refuses to leave. Should the instructor alert security? Would that risk escalating the situation? What are the university's policies on handling a disruptive student? Would it be better to halt and dismiss class to allow the situation to calm? If the instructor is concerned that he or she will be unable to ask a student to leave, an alternative strategy would be to have penalties within the instructor's control such as attendance or discussion point deductions for disrespectful participation. These deductions can be outlined as a part of the policies for classroom discussion that are detailed in the syllabus or constructed as a class. Include a statement in the syllabus along with the policies for classroom discussion or behavior that explicitly addresses what will happen to disruptive or disrespectful students; for example, those unable to remain respectful will be asked to leave the discussion and will be considered absent for that class period (or lose discussion points, be unable to complete class assignments, etc.).

Transparent Learning Objectives

When students are reluctant to engage with a topic, either because it is controversial or because it makes them uncomfortable, it can make the instructor seem cruel or unaware. For example, students might not want to consider the effects of cumulative physical disadvantage for minority elders, the abbreviated lives of impoverished children in developing countries, or the persistent threat faced by sexual minority youth. Requiring them to imagine uncomfortable scenarios like these might lead them to believe the instructor only wants them to feel guilty or ashamed of their privilege or their opportunities. Let the students know that the controversial or uncomfortable content is not just about "making them squirm," but has pedagogical value and ties into the course content, which can help the students see the importance of learning and discussing the material (Payne and Gainey 2003).

To mitigate the belief that the sole purpose of the content is their discomfort, explain why you chose the material or content to discuss and how it relates to the readings or course themes. As an example, for a course on death and dying, I show a documentary on end-of-life decisions for the terminally ill, including children. Students often respond emotionally to images of children dying or to the choice of removing life-sustaining support for a loved one. Yet the documentary highlights several key themes from the course: the importance of advanced directives, that dying happens across the life course and not just in old age, the value of hospice, and how funeral experiences bring comfort to grieving families. Pointing to segments or stories from the documentary as examples of each of these key themes reinforces the additional insight that material or discussion has provided and allows students to see that I subjected them to the uncomfortable film and discussion for a clear purpose. Include a section in written assignments that asks students to reflect on how the material tied to the material they were learning or extended their understanding of the content. For online classes, include a segment of the online lecture or a part of the discussion board prompt that explains your intent behind requiring students to tackle the challenging material or content. It normalizes the struggle students may have individually when they lack the non-verbal feedback in a classroom discussion.

Providing a Positive Frame for the Ending

Structure each discussion or presentation of difficult material to end in such a way that allows for a debriefing that acknowledges the level of discomfort and reiterates the importance of having uncomfortable discussions. For example, encourage them to reflect on the insights they gained from the discussion and interaction with the content. Ask students what the most difficult part of the discussion was or when they felt the most uncomfortable, and compose the list on the board. Normalize the experience by asking them to hypothesize why each of the listed items might be uncomfortable for "someone" to discuss and what steps "individuals" can take to alleviate this discomfort. This is not always easy to do: tensions and tempers can flare, ideas once held firm may have been reevaluated, and unpleasant sides of society may be discovered. Trying to end on an encouraging note does not mean glossing over social problems, the challenges facing the world, or feelings of hopelessness or disappointment that students may have. Instead, summarize the main points of the discussion or topic and highlight why knowing this information is valuable in understanding a broader social concern. For example, at the conclusion of a presentation or discussion on racial bias in the criminal justice system, the instructor or discussion leader could summarize why the topic remains divisive, how scholars and the broader public can benefit from learning more from all concerned, and the value in continuing the conversation and research on improving the system. If students seem unable to discuss what makes the conversations difficult as a larger group, consider breaking them into pairs or small groups to discuss it first, and then have them write their thoughts as a group and share them with the broader class.

It is crucial to model to students that uncomfortable topics of discussion provide them an opportunity to learn, both in and beyond the classroom. Framing the conclusion of the presentation or discussion as an acknowledgment of their ability and willingness to grapple with difficult issues reaffirms that the topic may be challenging, but that does not prevent its discussion or the work toward solutions. Remind them that this classroom discussion may have concluded, but the conversation may continue with friends, roommates, and in other classes. Encourage students to continue to work to see all sides of the arguments critically, including ones they hold. This final step of structuring the end of presentations and discussions of difficult topics influences whether instructors and students feel the discussion has been effective and how they will view discussions in the future.

CONCLUSION

It can be uncomfortable to discuss controversial or awkward topics, but that should not stop social science instructors from pursuing the topics central to their disciplines. By providing students with the skills for effectively engaging with difficult material and differing perspectives, participation both in and beyond the classroom can be more meaningful. By learning to approach difficult topics with open minds and ears, students will be able to broaden their perspectives and better understand the challenges and realities of the social world.

REFERENCES

Abbott, Traci B. 2009. "Teaching Transgender Literature at a Business College." *Race, Gender, and Class* 16(1–2):152–69.

Alty, A., and K. Rodham. 1998. "The Ouch! Factor: Problems in Conducing Sensitive Research." *Qualitative Health Research* 8(2):275–82.

Avery, Patricia G., Sara A. Levy, and Annette M. M. Simmons. 2013. "Deliberating Controversial Public Issues as Part of Civic Education." *Social Studies* 104:105–14.

Boysen, Guy A., Anna Mae Wells, and Kaylee J. Dawson. 2016. "Instructors' Use of Trigger Warnings and Behavior Warnings in Abnormal Psychology." *Teaching of Psychology* 43(4):334–39.

Brunsma, David L., Eric S. Brown, and Peggy Placier. 2012. "Teaching Race at Historically White Colleges and Universities: Identifying and Dismantling the Walls of Whiteness." *Critical Sociology* 39(5):717–38.

Burkstand-Reid, Beth, June Carbone, and Jennifer S. Hendricks. 2011. "Teaching Controversial Topics." *Family Court Review* 49(4):678–84.

Carter, Angela M. 2015. "Teaching with Trauma: Trigger Warnings, Feminism, and Disability Pedagogy." *Disability Studies Quarterly* 35(2).

Crabtree, Robbin D., and David Alan Sapp. 2003. "Theoretical, Political, and Pedagogical Challenges in the Feminist Classroom: Our Struggles to Walk the Walk." *College Teaching* 51(4):131–40.

DiAngelo, Robin, and Özlem Sensoy. 2014. "Getting Slammed: White Depictions of Race Discussions as Arenas of Violence." *Race Ethnicity and Education* 17(1):103–28.

DiIorio, Colleen, Maureen Kelley, and Marilyn Hockenberry-Eaton. 1999. "Communication about Sexual Issues: Mother, Fathers, and Friends." *Journal of Adolescent Health* 24:181–89.

Dilevko, Juris. 2015. "The Politics of Trigger Warnings." *Journal of Information Ethics* 24(2): 9–12.

Evans, Ronald W., Patricia G. Avery, and Patricia Velde Pederson. 2000. "Taboo Topics: Cultural Restraint on Teaching Social Issues." *Clearing House* 73(5):295–302.

Ezzedeen, Souha R. 2008. "Facilitating Class Discussions around Current and Controversial Issues: Ten Recommendations for Teachers." *College Teaching* 56(4):230–36.

Fallahi, Carolyn R., and Joseph D. Haney. 2007. "Using Debate in Helping Students Discuss Controversial Topics." *Journal of College Teaching and Learning* 4(10):83–88.

Fassinger, Polly A. 1995. "Understanding Classroom Interaction: Students' and Professors' Contributions to Students' Silence." *Journal of Higher Education* 66(1):82–96.

Fournier-Sylvester, Nicole. 2013. "Daring to Debate: Strategies for Teaching Controversial Issues in the Classroom." *College Quarterly* 16(3).

Fredericks, Marcel, and Steven I. Miller. 1993. "Truth in Packaging: Teaching Controversial to Undergraduates in the Human Sciences." *Teaching Sociology* 21(2):160–65.

Goldsmith, Pat António. 2006. "Learning to Understand Inequality and Diversity: Getting Students Past Ideologies." *Teaching Sociology* 34(3):263–77.

Goodman, Diane J. 1995. "Difficult Dialogues: Enhancing Discussions about Diversity." *College Teaching* 43(2):47–52.

Haddad, Angela T., and Leonard Lieberman. 2002. "From Student Resistance to Embracing the Sociological Imagination: Unmasking Privilege, Social Conventions, and Racism." *Teaching Sociology* 30(3):328–41.

Hand, Michael, and Ralph Levinson. 2012. "Discussing Controversial Issues in the Classroom." *Educational Philosophy and Theory* 44(6):614–29.

Harlow, Roxanna. 2009. "Innovations in Teaching Race and Class Inequality: 'Bittersweet Candy' and 'The Vanishing Dollar.'" *Teaching Sociology* 37(2):194–204.

Jakubowski, Lisa M. 2001. "Teaching Uncomfortable Topics: An Action-Oriented Strategy for Addressing Racism and Related Forms of Difference." *Teaching Sociology* 29: 62–79.

James, Jennifer Hauver, Simone Schweber, Robert Kunzman, Keith C. Barton, and Kimberly Logan. 2014. *Religion in the Classroom: Dilemmas for Democratic Education.* New York: Routledge.

Johnson, David W., Roger T. Johnson, and Dean Tjosvold. 2006. " Constructive Controversy: The Value of Intellectual Opposition." Pp. 69–91 in *The Handbook of Conflict Resolution: Theory and Practice, 2nd Edition,* edited by M. Deutsch, P. T. Coleman, and E. C. Marcus. San Francisco: Jossey-Bass.

Lee, Raymond M. 1993. *Doing Research on Sensitive Topics.* Thousand Oaks, CA: Sage.

Lockhart, Eleanor Amaranth. 2016. "Why Trigger Warnings Are Beneficial, Perhaps Even Necessary." *First Amendment Studies* 50(2):59–69.

Mason, Karen A., and Lisa T. Briggs. 2011. "Myths and Moral Panics: An Active Learning Approach to Controversial Topics." *Transformative Dialogues: Teaching and Learning Journal* 5:1–14.

McAvoy, Paula, and Diana Hess. 2013. "Classroom Deliberation in an Era of Political Polarization." *Curriculum Inquiry* 43(1):14–47.

Mills, C. Wright. 1953. *The Sociological Imagination.* London: Oxford University Press.

Ogle, Sharron, Anna Glasier, and Simon C. Riley. 2008. "Communication between Parents and Their Children about Sexual Health." *Contraception* 77(4):283–88.

Payne, Brian K., and Randy R. Gainey. 2003. "Understanding and Developing Controversial Issues in College Courses." *College Teaching* 51(2):52–8.

Rae, Logan. 2016. "Re-Focusing the Debate on Trigger Warnings: Privilege, Trauma, and Disability in the Classroom." *First Amendment Studies* 50(2):95–102.

Robbins, Susan P. 2016. "From the Editor—Sticks and Stones: Trigger Warnings, Microaggressions, and Political Correctness." *Journal of Social Work Education* 52(1):1–5.

Roberts, Alison, and Keri Iyall Smith. 2002. "Managing Emotions in the College Classroom: The Cultural Diversity Course as an Example." *Teaching Sociology* 30(3):291–301.

Rothenberg, Paula S. 2012. *White Privilege: Essential Readings on the Other Side of Racism.* 4th ed. New York: Worth.

Schultz, Katherine. 2010. "After the Blackbird Whistles: Listening to Silence in Classrooms." *Teachers College Record* 112(11):2833–49.

14

Becoming a Culturally Inclusive Educator

Dena R. Samuels

How do you respond when you hear a student make a racist, sexist, or heterosexist comment in class? Do you respond at all? How do you know if you have succeeded in transforming the environment from one of hostility to one of compassion, understanding, and connection? Chances are you have found yourself in this situation, and if you are like most educators, you may not respond at all because you have never been taught that it is important to do so, nor how to do so effectively. Unfortunately, not responding in such a situation condones the offensive behavior, and sets the foundation for a hostile environment, especially for students who come from traditionally marginalized identities. The result is an unsafe classroom where students are not likely to absorb the information you would like them to, and worse, are less likely to succeed.

Or, what if you make an offensive comment and do not realize that it is offensive? What might be the impact on the students who are offended? Will they articulate their concerns to you? If they do not feel like they can react or respond without repercussion, how are they likely to feel about coming to class in the future? Will they be able to receive the subject matter you may be incredibly passionate about teaching? Missteps around issues of social identities are not only inevitable, but required in order for us to be on the leading edge of culturally inclusive excellence. In order to engage with students, we must create an environment where they feel empowered to gently challenge / educate us without repercussion so that we can learn what "we don't know we don't know," and create a space where all students feel like they belong.

PREPAREDNESS

The changing demographics of the United States have created a substantive need to better prepare educators for diverse classrooms (Ladson-Billings 2005; Sobel, Iceman-Sands, and Basile 2007). Moreover, this need is widely considered one of the greatest challenges facing educators in today's society (Futrell, Gomez, and Bedden 2003; Hollins and Guzman 2005). It can be argued that faculty members are sometimes the strongest link between the university and the student (Hurtado 1992; Milem 1994).

Literature on this topic demonstrates a fundamental need for faculty members to be prepared to build cultural inclusiveness (Grant and Secada 1990; Howard 1999; Hurtado et al. 1998), but until now, there has been little empirical data available that assesses to what extent, if any, faculty members consider themselves to be prepared. In order to measure faculty preparedness for cultural competence, the current research uses a quantitative approach through the development of a survey instrument that was disseminated to a national, random sample of faculty members.

PREPAREDNESS STUDY

Campus climate surveys typically measure the cultural representation of campus members as well as the cultural environment, but often fail to delve into the actual attitudes and intentions of faculty members. Because I found no scales that specifically measured faculty preparedness to build cultural inclusiveness, it became incumbent upon me to create and test my own. My survey instrument (Samuels 2014) was informed by the literature as well as existing scales, and it attempted to measure the proposed latent construct of faculty *preparedness* to build cultural inclusiveness. The survey included 27 items that represented each of the five components of preparedness, all measured on a 7-point Likert-type scale, and concluded with demographic questions.

This instrument was tested on a national, random sample of 637 faculty members to determine how prepared they are to build cultural inclusiveness. The respondents were from two- and four-year colleges, universities, and academies and included a wide range of academic concentrations: social sciences, business, health sciences, physical sciences, education, and engineering, among others. Unlike other campus climate surveys, this instrument focuses on faculty members' attitudes, consideration of social group memberships, self-awareness of biases, intention, and behavioral outcomes. In addition, unlike other surveys, it is intersectional, covering issues of gender, race, sexual orientation, and disability, among others.

To analyze the data, I randomly split the sample into two groups. I conducted exploratory factor analysis (EFA) on the first subsample using principal axis factoring to identify factor structure. Consistent with the theoretical framework on which it was created, five factors emerged. Structural equation modeling (SEM) was utilized on the second group of the split sample to confirm the EFA findings, as well as to assess the resulting structural model. Results showed that a revised version of the structural equation model produced a good fit to the data, and the survey instrument demonstrated strong internal consistency (all alphas above .85).

PREPAREDNESS RESULTS

On average, faculty members scored relatively high on each of the five sub-latent constructs of preparedness, demonstrating that they perceive themselves to be prepared to build cultural inclusiveness. They were less likely, however, to actually behave in culturally inclusive ways in and out of their classrooms (behaviors that were derived from best practices as outlined by the Association of American Colleges and Universities, among other similar organizations). Additionally, faculty members admitted that they were not explicitly educated on diversity and inclusiveness, nor do their current institutions provide "meaningful education" on these topics.

If, on average, faculty members in this national study considered themselves prepared to build cultural inclusiveness, how do we reconcile these findings with the reality that they are less likely to behave inclusively, not to mention have not received the opportunity to learn how to do so?

Perhaps the discrepancy is in the confidence level of their preparedness. Social desirability theory postulates that survey-takers tend to present themselves in a positive light based on the socially constructed norms or standards of their culture or society (Crowne and Marlowe 1964; Ganster, Hennessey, and Luthans 1983). Based on the current cultural expectation to be respectful and accepting of diversity, respondents may have wanted to portray themselves as culturally inclusive, and moreover, wanted to believe that they are, in fact, culturally inclusive. Based on the robust nature of this study, it is reasonable to generalize these findings, which begs the question of every educator: How prepared are we to build cultural inclusiveness in and out of our classrooms? Challenging the notion that we are already culturally inclusive educators takes the courage to admit that "we don't know what we don't know," and the willingness to consider our own biases and behaviors through a social justice lens.

EIGHT TRANSFORMATIVE STEPS TO BUILD CULTURAL INCLUSIVENESS

In order to navigate this challenging path, I offer an eight-step transformative process that can be used to build authentic multicultural inclusiveness. The steps include: discovering our biases, reflecting on our (systemic) socialization, challenging our assumptions, reflecting on our identities, contemplating our emotions, reflecting on our behavior, considering our purpose, and committing to this work. Each step proposes specific questions we can ask ourselves along the way.

Step 1: Discovering Our Biases

What are the messages we have learned about women, gay people, lesbians, people in poverty, Latino/as, people with disabilities, older people, black people, large people, Muslims, etc.? We need to be aware of our implicit biases, making the invisible, visible to ourselves. In other words, we must acknowledge that we have learned misinformation about many different groups, even our own, and then shed light on those misperceptions. Without that explicit self-reflection, we do not know the extent of the challenge before us. We can tell ourselves and everyone else that "we don't have a prejudiced bone in our body," but the reality is that cultural stereotypes abound, and unfortunately, just by living in the culture, through osmosis, our perceptions about ourselves and others become severely impacted.

The Implicit Association Test can help with this task of raising our self-awareness. The IAT, an endeavor of Harvard University's Project Implicit, measures attitudes and prejudices toward specific groups based on various social group memberships (race, gender, age, sexual orientation, and so on), and it is available online. The test asks respondents to quickly categorize words or images as positive or negative by the click of one or another letter on the keyboard (Greenwald, McGhee, and Schwartz 1998). In empirical studies, McConnell and Leibold (2001), among others, found that discriminatory behavior correlated with more prejudiced IAT scores, demonstrating the validity of the IAT as a tool to predict behavior.

Powell (2012) asserts that our ideas and associations can be affected by the way we frame them. This is known as "priming." That is, providing counter-stereotypic information before engaging with someone who has been targeted by that stereotype can reduce bias. For example, when participants were asked to simply conjure a mental image that challenged a stereotype (e.g., a strong woman), Blair, Ma, and Lenton (2001) found that they were subsequently less likely to stereotype women as weak. This study has implications for the malleability of prejudice and the relative ease with which one can challenge bias. Moreover, increased exposure to a marginalized group tends to lead to less bias, suggesting that more intergroup contact, and specifically, intergroup friendships, can aid in overcoming bias (Aberson, Shoemaker, and Tomolillo 2004). These and other findings submit that if educators are given the opportunity to learn about their implicit, and often consciously unintended, biases, then they can learn to challenge those prejudices before they act on them.

Step 2: Reflecting on Our (Systemic) Socialization

Once we are more aware of the negative stereotypes we hold, we can ask: How do we know what we know? Where did the damaging myths we have bought into come from? Which institutions have misinformed us? Which of our own experiences have contributed to our assumptions about other people? Pinpointing the starting place (family, school, media, etc.) of our learned behavior can provide insight into the propaganda to which we have been exposed. Our attitudes are formed, at least in part, by social institutions. It is not necessarily a causal relationship, but rather a mutually perpetuating one since institutions are made up of individuals. Since these foundations exist in a society that perpetuates inequality, they not only tend to discriminate internally, but maintain and spread the notions. This, in turn, has dire consequences for our individual attitudes and often for our behavior.

For example, our culture teaches us primarily through the media that black men are dangerous and should be feared. Consider how that single assumption might impact how educators treat black students. Will they be less likely to trust black students? Will they be more likely to expect negative or even disruptive behavior from black students? In fact, many studies have shown that students of color are much more likely to receive much harsher disciplinary action, expulsion, and suspension than white students for the same or similar problem behavior, based primarily on implicit assumptions we have learned (Skiba et al. 2011; Wallace et al. 2008). Figuring out where these ideas come from helps us to understand how stereotypes are socially constructed and perpetuated, and reminds us that they can be unlearned.

In the same vein, it is useful to consider our past experiences and how they might affect our attitudes about people who are different from us. Sometimes we make assumptions about a whole group of people based on our experiences with a single member of a particular group. Making the leap to break away from stereotyping is, for some, an insurmountable challenge, but it has the potential to bring connection and understanding between people. Without understanding our or others' past experiences, it is difficult to fully comprehend the extent to which we adhere to our preconceived notions. Learning what these experiences are can help us understand more about our own or others' belief systems and can pave the way for relinquishing these stereotypes.

Step 3: Challenging Our Assumptions

Once we are more cognizant of where our biases come from, they become easier to confront. Best-selling author Byron Katie's (2002) work revolves around the notion of challenging our thoughts and thought processes. She proposes four questions we can ask to lead us through that process, which we can apply to stereotypes (with minor modifications). Katie's first question is: Is it true? The assumptions we make about ourselves and others may or may not be true. Regardless, we put a great deal of energy into maintaining those thoughts and beliefs without considering their veracity. Moreover, if we blindly consider stereotypes to be true, we deny the person about whom we are making assumptions the opportunity to defy our biases, and instead remain stuck in confirmation bias. Nevertheless, our unconscious biases and past experience may lead us to answer this first question in the affirmative.

The second question is: Can we absolutely know that it is true? This question asks us to consider how we came to know these "truths," and whether they are, in actuality, just assumptions. It also reminds us that even if the idea is sometimes true or true for one person based on our past experience, nothing is true for every single person in any socially constructed category. Thus, the answer to this question will almost always be *no*.

The third question takes the thought process a bit deeper by asking: What happens when we believe that idea? This question asks us to consider the consequences of believing what we believe. How does this "truth" or assumption affect us? Our emotions? How do those emotions manifest in our body and affect our behavior? How does this "truth" affect our relationships? How does it affect the way we interact with people we are just meeting?

Finally, the fourth question is: What would our life, thoughts, and actions be like without that idea? This last question can be incredibly transformative and freeing. It asks us to consider how our lives and interactions would be affected if we were to let go of our assumptions, liberating us from long-held misconceptions. This freedom from restrictive mythical notions allows us to treat others as individuals.

For some folks, it might be useful to add a fifth question to the list. It is not always necessary, but in some situations, it can help us move forward if we are stuck. My addendum to Katie's four questions would be: What might be a truth that supersedes the myth you just debunked? For example, if you had a notion about a certain group of people, and through this process you realized that the idea was only a stereotype, what might you teach yourself instead? Perhaps it could be something along the lines of, "Each individual has the potential to behave in a positive way or a negative way, regardless of their social identities." Or something more positive, such as, "Every person ultimately seeks peace and well-being."

Research shows that when we challenge a stereotype in our mind before we interact with someone who is a member of that particular social group, we can overcome our biases. Powell (2012) cites three ways that science has shown we can conquer negative biases. The first is viewing *positive* images of people from stereotyped groups; even simply invoking those images in our minds can overcome bias. Second, when an organization's members see a person of color in a leadership position, prejudice decreases throughout the organization. Third, cross-cultural relationships reduce implicit bias. These studies inform these transformational steps.

Step 4: Reflecting on Our Identities

How do our social identities (race, gender, sexuality, age, disability, etc.) affect our assumptions about ourselves and about others? How do our social identities affect how we interact with people who have different social identities than we do? Stereotypes run deep, and they can affect even our own perceptions of ourselves. The sociological term for this concept is *internalized oppression,* or conversely, *internalized privilege* (Samuels 2009). Internalized oppression occurs when people who are disadvantaged in society based on a particular social group membership believe the stereotypes and attitudes that are directed at their group. It can create a self-loathing that we may not even be aware of because it seeps in subconsciously from the negative messages we are exposed to in our culture on a daily basis.

One example of this is media bias. The media is more likely to portray people of color as lawbreakers and white people as law defenders (Dixon and Linz 2000). This leads to the increased likelihood that women will clutch their purses close to them in the presence of an African American man (Oliver 2003). As an educator, my biggest concern is how this affects black students. How would it feel to constantly be considered a threat? How does that stereotype squash a black male student's humanity, and what are the consequences to his self-esteem and efficacy to succeed? Moreover, how does internalized oppression manifest when the media spends a disproportionate amount of time emphasizing the school-to-prison pipeline rather than the 1.4 million black males in college, which is almost double the number of black males in prison (Fenwick 2013)?

The flip side of the coin is internalized privilege, which occurs when people are advantaged or given the benefit of the doubt based on a particular social group membership, and they come to believe the stereotypes and attitudes that are directed at their group. Internalized privilege breeds entitlement. In the example above, the fact that white people are more often portrayed as defenders of the law impacts all of us. It signals to everyone, especially to white people, that white people can be trusted. Thus, when a white person breaks the law, it is not at all uncommon for them to claim it was a person of color who actually committed the crime, and often, the authorities believe the white criminals (Russell-Brown 1998).

Internalized privilege also includes an element of invisibility. Those who are privileged in a certain category are the standard against which everyone else is measured and named, and therefore they do not typically see their status as privileged but rather as the norm. For example, even though we live in a heteronormative society, where the assumption and the expectation is that everyone is heterosexual, when we think or hear about sexuality, *homosexuality* is what comes to mind. In fact, heterosexuals are not typically cognizant of even having a sexual orientation and do not need to worry about stereotype threat based on their sexuality. That freedom from anxiety is an invisible privilege that is not accessible to most LGBTQ people (lesbian, gay, bisexual, transgender, queer / questioning).

Oppression and privilege are intertwined with exclusion and inclusion; thus it is important in this process to consider: How do institutionalized systems of inequality affect *me?* Which of my own social identities *allow* me access to benefits that are denied to others; and which *deny* me access to resources that are provided to others based on social group membership? How have I been socialized to think about and treat others, based on their social group memberships? Answering these questions honestly, in spite of the discomfort they may cause, is vital in this transformative process.

If we are unaware of the unearned advantages and disadvantages that our socially constructed society bestows on us, we may be missing the systemic ways privilege and oppression operate in our own lives. Based on our social identities, we are taught who to trust, who to avoid, who to idolize, and who to demonize. For example, do we see police officers as allies who will protect us and keep us safe, or as systemic profilers who we must hide from to keep *ourselves* safe? We must diligently consider how our own social identities have contributed to our ideas about ourselves and others. We must also scrutinize how we might, unintentionally, perpetuate systemic inequities at the individual level by being inclusive of some people at the expense of others.

Step 5: Contemplating Our Emotions

Which emotions arise when we think about people who have different social identities than we do? What feelings emerge when we think about people living in poverty? People with disabilities? Transgender individuals? Older people? These questions are certainly socially constructed since our culture has taught us how to feel about various groups. For example, some cultures consider aged individuals as wise, and treat them with the utmost respect or even revere them. Other cultures, such as mainstream U.S. society, consider senior citizens to be out of touch with current events, contemporary language, and present-day ideas. Therefore, the emotion that might arise when we see them is one of disdain or annoyance. Once again, it is important to acknowledge the emotions we have toward others.

Unfortunately, as mentioned, our unchallenged biases and assumptions about others serve to separate us from one another. Further, separation and fear are mutually perpetuating: the more we segregate ourselves from each other, the more misunderstandings occur, the more assumptions increase and fear arises. When we are afraid, we tend to withdraw even more, and not only do we miss the opportunity to challenge those assumptions, but we tend to exclude members of that group even more, in favor of the comfort of being around people who we perceive as more similar to us.

On the other hand, if we are aware that we have negative feelings toward members of a specific group, we can compassionately consider those feelings when they arise. We can even forgive ourselves for the misinformation we have systematically received, and go through the process of surrendering those negative feelings. Connecting with others in a genuine way can lead us from discomfort and anxiety to wholehearted feelings and inclusive attitudes and behaviors.

We must contemplate the feelings we have about others before we can truly connect with them. The goal is not to deny or stifle those feelings, but to acknowledge them and let them go. If we ignore them, we run the risk of allowing them to gain control over both our attitudes and behaviors, and doing so can cause us to unconsciously discriminate. Acknowledging those feelings, in contrast, gives us a choice about how we behave, and we are more likely to act inclusively.

For the faculty members who responded to my survey, they may never have been given the opportunity to consider or analyze their own emotions with regard to people whose social identities are different from theirs. Without deep self-reflection, they may have simply assumed they behave inclusively, despite the fact that their behaviors tended to paint a different picture. Perhaps if they considered their own emotions and biases, preparing themselves to interact cross-culturally, they may have realized that it is the implicit assumptions and emotions that, despite our best intentions, can contribute to our exclusion of others.

Step 6: Reflecting on Our Behavior

How have our false beliefs, assumptions, and stereotypes operated in our daily lives and/or in the classroom? The research by Skiba et al. (2011) mentioned in Step 2 above is a prime example of how our biases can lead to the excessive discipline of black students. These research findings demonstrate the depth of these preconceived notions, for it is likely that few, if any, of the teachers who were recommending expulsion or suspension for black students would do so knowing they were acting on stereotypes. It is also unlikely that they would consider themselves racist in any way. The disconnect here is between our unknown biases and our resulting actions.

This is where "microaggressions" and "stereotype threat" seep into our classrooms. We might be creating a "hostile" environment, one in which some students feel excluded, without even knowing it. Racial microaggressions are "brief and commonplace daily verbal, behavioral, and environmental indignities, whether intentional or unintentional, that communicate hostile, derogatory, or negative racial slights and insults to the target person or group" (Sue et al. 2007:273). The literature abounds with examples from the perspectives of students of color. Among others, they include: faculty making assumptions about the intelligence of students of color; ignoring, distorting, or stereotyping the experiences of people of color; and racial segregation of students in study/work groups (Solórzano, Ceja, and Yosso 2000).

Further, Kottler and Englar-Carlson (2009) clearly demonstrate that microaggressions do not occur only around issues of race, but also around gender, class, age, sexual orientation, religion, and so forth. It is unlikely that when people commit microaggressions against another person or a group of people, they mean to purposely insult or harm them. Mostly, microaggressions are the manifestations of stereotypes in the culture that are continually perpetuated through jokes, comments, and behavior. They often go unnoticed and, therefore, unchallenged (Sue 2010).

The most important aspect of microaggressions is their impact on those who are targeted by them (and their allies). Microaggressions lead to a rise in levels of cortisol (the stress hormone), and over time, this can cause mental and physical health problems and even an increase in mortality rates (Sue 2010). At the very least, in the classroom, microaggressions can trigger frustration, leading to feelings of marginalization and exclusion (Pierce 1988; Sue, Capodilupo, and Holder 2008). When looked at more broadly, students who are the targets of microaggressions may not even be getting an equitable education, compared with those who are not targets. Moreover, considering that a common goal of many colleges and universities in the past few decades has been to recruit, retain, and support a diverse student body, it is imperative for faculty to reflect on their own assumptions and actions so as to eliminate, or at least minimize, the microaggressions that they may, unknowingly, be perpetuating. As educators, we must be willing to learn more about what "we don't know we don't know."

Step 7: Considering Our Purpose

How do racism, sexism, heterosexism, ageism, disability, religious intolerance, etc., personally hurt me? How would I benefit if they no longer existed? It took me a very long time to understand the impact of these atrocities that we continue to tolerate in our society. As a Jewish person, I was keenly aware of how religious intolerance can devalue a person's beliefs and make a person feel excluded. As a woman, I knew that fighting for women's equality was incredibly important. As a white person, however, it was unclear to me how racism was hurting me, personally. I was aware of the damage it was doing to people of color, and I knew that I had the responsibility to be an antiracist advocate, but how was it affecting me?

I am not in any way insinuating that racism hurts white people as much (or more) than racism hurts people of color. Yet, it is important to consider the negative impact that racism has on white people; or sexism has on men; etc. For in so doing, we can be sure that the antiracist or antisexist or antiheterosexist (etc.) work we do serves us personally. For even if we believe we are passionate about helping other people, if we get busy with other things, we may put it off for another day. If we are only doing this work in service to members of traditionally marginalized groups, what happens when it gets difficult? What happens when we make a mistake? If, on the other hand, we understand that it is fundamental to healing our own pain, nothing will stop us from continuing to pursue it.

After considering this question for a very long time, I have learned that racism causes separation between people and, sometimes, distrust. I have learned that preconceived notions about me as a white person have sometimes led people of color (accurately or inaccurately) to treat me as an opponent rather than as a friend. I have learned that my skin color means something; it represents something, whether I want it to or not. I know that the times when I, even unintentionally, misuse my privilege by, for example, taking up more than my fair share of space (verbally or physically), and I become aware of my easily manifested entitlement, I tangibly feel the sting of inequality, the shame of unearned privilege. I remind myself that I have been socialized in a deeply rooted system of inequality and injustice, and I am a living legacy of this inequity. It is important that I have deeply felt this pain, not as white guilt, but as a reminder that these systems of inequality affect us all, obviously to different degrees. This sting makes me fervently renew my objective to dismantle these systems, to show up to build relationships across difference, and to keep showing up, in spite of the missteps I will make. Building relationships includes building trust and showing that you are someone other people can count on not to shy away from the work.

It is my job as an antiracist activist to confront the whiteness in the room when I see it. There are many ways to disrupt white supremacy, including verbal and nonverbal challenges. We can dismantle white supremacy slowly, relationship by relationship. It is a lifelong commitment and a practice that takes patience and faith, and I know I am not alone when I say it is well worth the effort (Samuels 2013).

Recognizing how systems of inequality affect us personally helps us to consider ways we might directly benefit from dedicating ourselves to social justice ideals and practices. The more we can identify the specific ways doing this work benefits us at a personal level, the more likely we will be to stick with it for the long haul. This is an opportunity to ask ourselves what kind of world we want to live in. I know I am creating that world every single time I stand up against injustice, especially when I do so both with purpose and compassion.

Step 8: Committing to This Work

How long are we willing to commit to learning about diversity and building inclusiveness? About which social identities do we know the least, and what kind of effort are we willing to make to continue our training? In the course of our education, we might have learned or taught ourselves important information about some social identities, but missed out on learning about others. Although we can never know everything about every social group, we can still make an effort to learn all we can. We can commit to learning a new language or listening to a radio station that is aimed at a culture that is different from our own. We can make an effort to attend multicultural events in our communities or go to meetings and get educated on the issues a particular culture faces at the local, regional, and/or global level.

This process also entails a certain amount of what is known in social psychology as *perspective-taking*. It is crucial that educators and administrators, in particular, go out of our way to understand the viewpoints and experiences of other campus members, especially students. Otherwise, problems can arise when "educators think they know about the lived experience of others; are in a position to speak on behalf of others' experiences; and do so through solely their own identities, experiences, and lens of privilege" (Arminio, Torres, and Pope 2012:187). In reality, we all have limited perspectives. Broadening those perspectives is fundamental to building inclusiveness, for this work cannot be done successfully in a vacuum.

When I began my own process of social justice work, I thought if I learned enough about other cultures (as though there is such a thing!), worked at it long enough, and challenged myself enough, I would suddenly become unbiased about all different social groups. I thought that perhaps one day I would wake up and no longer have preconceived notions about others. Many years later, it has not happened, and I have come to the conclusion that it never will. We are all constantly bombarded with racist, sexist, heterosexist, ageist, etc., messages through the culture, the media, the education system, etc. As Johnson (2006) explains, just simply being part of a system of inequality means we cannot escape these biased thoughts.

The good news is that the more we challenge these offensive ideas when they arise in our own minds, the more obvious they become everywhere else: in the media, in our culture, and in our classrooms, and the more we can make an effort to change these ideas. Unlearning misinformation, however, is a lifelong endeavor. The goal is not to figure out our preconceived notions and then blame ourselves for being bad people. Instead, the idea is to accept that there are certain stereotypes we have believed, acknowledge where they came from, and with compassion, challenge ourselves every single time we notice them. We can reframe our assumptions with counter-stereotypes. This is how we can create change. This process does take time and effort, but can be incredibly rewarding. The suggested eight steps lead us to the ultimate goal of being able to develop relationships across difference, for that is the key to building cultural inclusiveness and becoming a culturally inclusive educator.

REFERENCES

Aberson, Christopher L., Carl Shoemaker, and Christina Tomolillo. 2004. "Implicit Bias and Contact: The Role of Interethnic Friendships." *Journal of Social Psychology* 144(3):335–47.

Arminio, Jan, Vasti Torres, and Raechele L. Pope. 2012. "Integrating Student Affairs Values with the Elements of Inclusion." Pp. 187–93 in *Why Aren't We There Yet? Taking Personal Responsibility for Creating an Inclusive Campus,* edited by Jan Arminio, Vasti Torres, and Raechele L. Pope. Sterling, VA: Stylus.

Blair, I.V., J.E. Ma, and A.P. Lenton. 2001. "Imagining Stereotypes Away: The Moderation of Implicit Stereotypes through Mental Imagery." *Journal of Personality and Social Psychology* 81:828–41.

Crowne, Douglas P., and David Marlowe. 1964. *The Approval Motive: Studies in Evaluative Dependence.* New York: Wiley.

Dixon, Travis L., and Daniel Linz. 2000. "Overrepresentation and Underrepresentation of African Americans and Latinos as Lawbreakers on Television News." *Journal of Communication* 50(2):131–54.

Fenwick, Leslie T. 2013. "Upending Stereotypes about Black Students." *Education Week*, October 9. Retrieved March 21, 2014 (www.edweek.org/ew/articles/2013/10/09/07fenwick _ep.h33.html?qs = upending+stereotypes).

Futrell, Mary H., Joel Gomez, and Dana Bedden. 2003. "Teaching the Children of a New America: The Challenge of Diversity." *Phi Delta Kappan* 84(5):381–85.

Ganster, Daniel C., Harry W. Hennessey, and Fred Luthans. 1983. "Social Desirability Response Effects: Three Alternative Models." *Academy of Management Journal* 26(2): 321–31.

Grant, Carl, and Walter Secada. 1990. "Preparing Teachers for Diversity." Pp. 403–22 in *Handbook of Research on Teacher Education*, edited by W. Robert Houston, Martin Haberman, and John Sikula. New York: Macmillan.

Greenwald, Anthony G., Debbie E. McGhee, and Jordan L. K. Schwartz. 1998. "Measuring Individual Differences in Implicit Cognition: The Implicit Association Test." *Journal of Personality and Social Psychology* 74:1464–80.

Hollins, Etta R., and Maria T. Guzman. 2005. "Research on Preparing Teachers for Diverse Populations." Pp. 477–548 in *Studying Teacher Education: The Report of the AERA Panel on Research and Teacher Education*, edited by M. Cochran-Smith and K. M. Zeichner. Mahwah, NJ: Lawrence Erlbaum.

Howard, Gary R. 1999. *We Can't Teach What We Don't Know*. New York: Teachers College Press.

Hurtado, Sylvia. 1992. "The Campus Racial Climate: Contexts for Conflict." *Journal of Higher Education* 63(5):539–69.

Hurtado, Sylvia, Jeffrey Milem, Alma Clayton-Pedersen, and W. Allen. 1998. "Enhancing Campus Climates for Racial / Ethnic Diversity: Educational Policy and Practice." *Review of Higher Education* 21(3):279–302.

Johnson, Allan G. 2006. *Privilege, Power, and Difference*. 2nd ed. New York: Mayfield.

Katie, Byron. 2002. *Loving What Is: Four Questions That Can Change Your Life*. New York: Three Rivers Press.

Kottler, Jeffrey A., and Matt Englar-Carlson. 2009. *Learning Group Leadership: An Experiential Approach*. Thousand Oaks, CA: Sage.

Ladson-Billings, Gloria J. 2005. "Is the Team All Right? Diversity and Teacher Education." *Journal of Teacher Education* 56:229–34.

McConnell, Allen R., and Jill M. Leibold. 2001. "Relations among the Implicit Association Test, Discriminatory Behavior, and the Explicit Measures of Racial Attitudes." *Journal of Experimental Social Psychology* 37:435–42.

Milem, Jeffrey F. 1994. "Attitude Change in College Students: Examining the Effect of College Peer Groups and Faculty Normative Groups." *Journal of Higher Education* 69(2):117–40.

Oliver, Mary Beth. 2003. "African American Men as 'Criminal and Dangerous': Implications of Media Portrayals of Crime on the 'Criminalization' of African American Men." *Journal of African American Studies* 7(2):3–18.

Pierce, Chester M. 1988. "Stress in the Workplace." Pp. 27–34 in *Black Families in Crisis: The Middle Class*, edited by A. F. Coner-Edwards and J. Spurlock. New York: Brunner / Mazel.

Powell, John A. 2012. *Racing to Justice: Transforming Our Conceptions of Self and Other to Build an Inclusive Society*. Bloomington: Indiana University Press.

Russell-Brown, Katheryn. 1998. *The Color of Crime: Racial Hoaxes, White Fear, Black Protectionism, Police Harassment, and Other Macroaggressions*. New York: NYU Press.

Samuels, Dena R. 2009. "Introduction to Understanding Oppression and Privilege." Pp. 139–45 in *The Matrix Reader: Examining the Dynamics of Oppression and Privilege*, edited by Abby L. Ferber, Christina M. Jiménez, Andrea O'Reilly Herrera, and Dena R. Samuels. New York: McGraw-Hill.

Samuels, Dena R. 2013. "On White Privilege." *Stories on Diversity*. Beyond Diversity Resource Center. Retrieved February 19, 2014 (http://bdrcblogstories.wordpress.com/2013/07/28/).

Samuels, Dena R. 2014. *The Culturally Inclusive Educator: Preparing for a Multicultural World*. New York: McGraw-Hill.

Skiba, Russell J., Robert H. Horner, Choong-Geun Chung, M. Karega Rausch, Seth L. May, and Tary Tobin. 2011. "Race Is Not Neutral: A National Investigation of African American and Latino Disproportionality in School Discipline." *School Psychology Review* 40(1):85–107.

Sobel, Donna M., Deanna Iceman-Sands, and Carole Basile. 2007. "Merging General and Special Education Teacher Preparation Programs to Create an Inclusive Program for Diverse Learners." *New Educator* 3(3):241–62.

Solórzano, Daniel, Miguel Ceja, and Tara Yosso. 2000. "Critical Race Theory, Racial Microaggressions, and Campus Racial Climate: The Experiences of African American College Students." *Journal of Negro Education* 69:60–73.

Sue, Derald W. 2010. *Microaggressions in Everyday Life: Race, Gender, and Sexual Orientation*. Hoboken, NJ: John Wiley & Sons.

Sue, Derald W., Christina M. Capodilupo, and Aisha M. B. Holder. 2008. "Racial Microaggressions in the Life Experience of Black Americans." *Professional Psychology: Research and Practice* 39(3):329–36.

Sue, Derald W., Christina M. Capodilupo, Gina C. Torino, Jennifer M. Bucceri, Aisha M. Holder, Kevin L. Nadal, and Marta Esquilin. 2007. "Racial Microaggressions in Everyday Life: Implications for Clinical Practice." *American Psychologist* 62(4):271–86.

Wallace, John M., Jr., Sara G. Goodkind, Cynthia M. Wallace, and Jerald Bachman. 2008. "Racial / Ethnic and Gender Differences in School Discipline among American High School Students: 1991–2005." *Negro Educational Review* 59:47–62.

15

The Value of Games and Simulations in the Social Sciences

Amanda M. Rosen

Games, simulations, and other exercises in play have a mixed history in the college classroom. To those unfamiliar with these techniques, they are easily dismissed as fringe pedagogies that are inappropriate, time-consuming, difficult to do well, and an overall waste of valuable classroom time. At best, critics see them as an excuse to have fun but not particularly germane to academic learning. To the contrary, as a review of the literature and data analysis shows, simulations, games, and simulation games (SAGS) are mainstream tools used widely by instructors across disciplines to engage students and engender real—and even "real world"—learning. Numerous resources exist to make SAGS easy to use, of short duration, and an excellent complement to more traditional pedagogies. And yes, they can indeed be fun.

This chapter considers the collective risks and benefits of simulations, games, and simulation games, even while recognizing that these terms are neither exclusive nor exhaustive of all the active-learning techniques, analog and digital, that utilize role-play or gameplay. For our purposes we will use Dorn's (1989) definitions of simulations and games:

> A game is any contest or play among adversaries or players operating under constraints or rules for an objective or goal . . . a simulation is an operating representation of central features of reality . . . A simulation game is an exercise that has the basic characteristics of both games and simulations . . . Consequently, simulation games are activities undertaken by players whose actions are constrained by a set of explicit rules particular to that game and by a predetermined end point. The elements of the game constitute a more or less accurate representation or model of some external reality with which players interact by playing roles in much the same way as they would interact with reality itself. (P. 3)

Simulations, games, simulations games, and other similar activities differ from each other in many ways; indeed, even within a given category there is a high level of diversity to be found. For example, O'Brien, Lawless, and Schrader (2010) divide educational games into four categories: linear, competitive, strategic, and role-playing. Despite this diversity, the literature shows that there are many risks and benefits that SAGS collectively share, and these collective characteristics are the focus of this chapter.

While traditional lecture modules persist, a wide range of disciplines is starting to acknowledge the potential benefits of SAGS in the college classroom. Published work on SAGS can be found in areas including sociology (Paino and Chin 2011), psychology (Weisskirch 2009), political science (Asal 2005), and statistics (Chow, Woodford, and Maes 2011). In business, the military, and the corporate world, SAGS are incredibly commonplace and highly valued (Faria 1987; Kirriemuir and McFarlane 2004; Kumar and Lightner 2007). This chapter aims to examine the barriers and benefits to learning of using SAGS in the college classroom. I conclude with some best practices and tips for those new to SAGS use.

BARRIERS TO THE USE OF SIMULATIONS AND GAMES IN THE COLLEGE CLASSROOM

Moizer et al. (2009) cite three broad types of barriers to the adoption and use of innovative techniques such as SAGS in higher education: their suitability for the college classroom, limited resources, and the risk of failure or loss of control. Each of these three risks would give the most enthusiastic teacher pause in changing their teaching methods to incorporate games and simulations. These barriers, however, are hardly insurmountable, and the extensive literature on SAGS provides plenty of tips and techniques for overcoming them. Let us look at each of these barriers in turn.

Suitability Barriers

Some critics argue that SAGS are inappropriate for the college classroom. McGonigal (2011) cites a general cultural bias against games as a tool for learning, and Klopfer, Osterweil, and Salen (2009) and Green and McNeese (2007) note that there is a general reluctance and lack of support for bringing SAGS into the classroom. Meanwhile, Kirriemuir and McFarlane (2004) note that there are extensive concerns about the relevance and appropriateness of SAGS and that persuading stakeholders of their value remains a challenge. Whitton (2012) points out that students themselves may be the skeptics; indeed, Kumar and Lightner (2007) report that one student in their study called the games they used "silly, degrading . . . and childish" (p. 57). They also note that nonusers report fear of student resistance to SAGS. They may be right: Auman (2011) reports that prior to her simulation in educational psychology where students had to argue their case for different policies before a simulated school board, her students believed it would be a waste of their time.

Many of these concerns can be reduced. SAGS, particularly simulations, have a long history of use, and their acceptance is growing throughout higher education. A 2015 EDUCAUSE Center for Analysis and Research (ECAR) survey of more than 50,000 students at 161 institutions across 11 countries reported that 40 percent had played a game or simulation in at least one of their classes—compared to 8 percent in 2010 (Brooks et al. 2015; Smith, Caruso, and Kim 2010). Fifty-three percent expressed a wish that instructors would use these methods more frequently.

As for faculty, the 2015 ECAR survey of more than 13,000 instructors at 139 institutions of higher learning noted, "the only emerging technology for which a majority of faculty expressed an interest was simulations or educational games" (Brooks 2015:15). In particular, SAGS are common for communications and business instructors, with rates of use at 83 percent and 95 percent respectively (Faria 1987; Wiggins 2016).

Furthermore, as Stansbury Wheeler and Buckingham (2014) note, "educators using traditional lecture-style teaching methods struggle to keep digital-age learners engaged" (p. 105). Students do not want to see lectures disappear—Kumar and Lightner (2007) indicates they would like to see 50 percent of their class time remain as lecture—but there is certainly room and reason to incorporate more active-learning approaches into the classroom. Indeed, many SAGS combine more traditional methods such as reading, lecture, and writing papers with the interactive activity. Nishikawa and Jaeger (2011) require students to read Mancur Olson's *Dictatorship, Democracy, and Development* before participating in a computer simulation of that work, and Biziouras (2013) introduces his simulation of government coalition-building in Belgium with required readings, lectures, and written preparation reports.

Resource Barriers

SAGS can pose cost and resource requirements that are generally not found in lecture and discussion models (Stansbury et al. 2014; Whitton 2012). Online simulations such as Statecraft, ICONS, and most computer games require per-student or subscription fees, while physical games such as Monopoly, commonly used in sociology to teach income inequality, typically require a commercial purchase. Few professors or departments can justify these expenses. And as Sabin (2015) notes, it is unlikely that academic libraries have these resources already in circulation.

Many SAGS, however, are low or no cost. Online games on global issues, such as Climate Challenge, Against All Odds, and Ayiti: The Cost of Life, cost nothing to use. Meanwhile, blogs, websites such as Edutopia and the Serious Games Institute, professional associations, and academic pedagogy journals provide a wealth of resources for the newbie SAGS instructor. Some commercially available SAGS can be adapted and re-created without purchasing the original—the game Zendo, used to teach principles of research methods, is out of print, but can be re-created at little or no cost (Kollars and Rosen 2017). Many SAGS require no resources at all—except instructor time.

The amount of time it will take instructors to find, adapt, and design SAGS and their impact on content coverage is another potential barrier (Bonwell and Eisen 1991; Kirriemuir and McFarlane 2004; Kollars and Rosen 2016). While there are indeed many SAGS that are complex and require extensive time and energy to prepare and run, this is not the norm. SAGS can be run entirely outside of class, and preparation time can be minimal. Indeed, as the analysis shows later in the chapter, many SAGS require less than a week of class time.

As for reduced coverage of course concepts, this too lacks strength as an objection to SAGS. Every course must sacrifice content. This is why we have survey courses that dip into a subject that is later fleshed out in one or more courses. Thus, in intro to psychology, developmental psychology is a short component, later developed into a full class; meanwhile sociology majors may take an entire sequence on race and gender that is given no more than two weeks in their introductory course. Instructors are always making decisions about what content to include and cut. Sacrificing breadth for depth can actually bring benefits: as Sabin (2015) notes, "the time it takes out of class is worth it to give each individual player a rich and realistic decision experience" (p. 338).

Risk Barriers

The final set of barriers focuses on risk: the risk of losing control of the classroom and the risk of complete failure of the class session. When professors lecture, they control the flow of the class time, deciding how information is imparted and how much—if any—interaction to allow. With SAGS, success rests on the willing and quality participation of students. Lack of preparation, low enthusiasm, student resistance, confusion about tasks—all of these and more can spell disaster for SAGS (Kumar and Lightner 2007).

And yet, instructors report that the loss of control can be a good thing. Auman (2011) reports that giving over control of her classes to her students increased their motivation and enjoyment of the class. Students knew that the success of the lesson depended on them, and that failing to prepare or participate meant ruining the activity for their peers, motivating them to do a good job. Revere, Elden, and Bartsch (2008) also found that "social loafing"—free riding during group exercises—decreased in their use of Jeopardy-style group exams.

As for fearing SAGS failure, this is a natural but somewhat misguided fear. Yes, the activity may fail. But failure should be welcomed, not feared. As Whitton (2012) notes, "a crucial aspect of games, particularly in relation to their potential for learning, is that they provide safe and playful environments in which failure is an accepted part of the game dynamic, and learning through mistake-making is the norm" (p. 253). If a simulation or game fails, there is still something to be learned from the activity—whether it is the value of preparation, or how procedural rules structure substantive outcomes, or that time management is key.

LEARNING: THE REASON TO USE GAMES AND SIMULATIONS

The extensive literature on SAGS across disciplines is clear: at worst, these techniques are just as effective as traditional methods for student learning, and at best, they show marked improvement over simple reading and lecture models (Hake 1998; Herz and Merz 1998; Nishikawa and Jaeger 2011). While research on SAGS suffers from some fundamental issues such as small Ns, instructor bias as researchers, lack of controls, and overreliance on self-reporting of learning (Baronowski and Weir 2015), there is still a clear record of the positive impact SAGS have on student knowledge, skills, and attitudes.

Ranchhod et al. (2014) provide a framework we can use to categorize learning goals. Their three categories are: (1) *cognitive*, which focuses on knowledge, comprehension, and application of concepts; (2) *behavioral*, or development of skills; and (3) *affective*, which examines attitudes, motivation, engagement, and satisfaction. SAGS, as we shall see, thrive in all three areas.

Cognitive Learning

There is a strong record of SAGS increasing knowledge and comprehension of basic core concepts. Numerous studies show that compared to lecture and reading, SAGS show either similar (Auman 2011) or improved levels of objective learning (Baronowski and Weir 2015; Kahn and Perez 2009). This finding is confirmed across many disciplines, including political science (Biziouras 2013; Preston and Cottam 1997), statistics (Stansbury et al. 2014), and psychology (Weisskirch 2009).

Information retention is another area where SAGS shine. SAGS give students a concrete experience onto which they can map their understanding of course concepts, increasing the likelihood of retaining course content. Chow et al. (2011), for example, show that the use of an iterated Deal or No Deal game with their statistics students greatly increased the retention of the core concept of expected value; 95 percent of students who participated in the game retained their knowledge, while only 59 percent of nonparticipants did. Nishikawa and Jaeger (2011) and McCarthy (2014) confirm this kind of result, showing in retests taken one month after a simulation that participants maintained their initial learning.

SAGS can also connect academic theory to practice by giving students a common experience as a basis to critically evaluate theory. For example, Asal's (2005)

Survive or Die! exercise illustrates Thomas Hobbes's theory of how mankind behaves in a state of nature. Students are given life cards and told the rules regarding duels. At no point are they told that they must duel—and yet, inevitably, most students end up dueling anyway. This gives them a common experience in which to understand Hobbes and critique the limitations of his claims based not on pure theory, but their own experience of acting exactly as he predicted they would.

Finally SAGS, while often abstracting and simplifying the real world, help students engage in knowledge transfer by connecting course concepts to real-world situations (Chow et al. 2011; Gee 2003; Giraud-Carrier and Schmidt 2015; Kumar and Lightner 2007). As Laurel (1991) puts it, simulations "represent experience as opposed to information" (p. 113) and therefore have value in helping students see the connection between what they do in and out of class.

Behavioral Learning

SAGS are also known to augment behavioral learning and skill development (Aldrich 2004; Gee 2003; Lipman 2003). A wide range of skills can be developed and assessed using SAGS, several of which are cited as most valued by employers in a recent survey (Hart 2015). These SAGS skills include oral and written communication (Auman 2011; Bernstein 2008); team building (Daniau 2016); critical thinking (Kirriemuir and McFarlane 2004); strategic thinking and problem solving (Chow et al. 2011; Woodward, Carnine, and Gersten 1988); negotiation (Moore 2003); and professional behavior (Bradshaw and Harvey 2017).

Affective Learning

Finally, SAGS motivate and engage students and increase their enjoyment of learning (Hake 1998; McCarthy 2014; Moylan et al. 2015; Perrotta et al. 2013; Prensky 2001). Researchers have determined that learners are intrinsically motivated by activities or experiences that present a challenge, motivate them to learn, or give the learner control or evoke curiosity—as SAGS often do (de Freitas 2006; Lepper and Hodell 1989). Indeed, as Baronwski and Weir (2015) note, "In every instance students are surveyed, they evaluate the simulation in a positive manner, often overwhelmingly so" (p. 396).

This increased motivation can have real benefits, such as higher class attendance, increased attention spans, confidence, and self-esteem, and reduced stress (de Freitas 2006; Gareau and Guo 2009; Gorton and Havercroft 2012; Pan and Tang 2004). This is particularly true in courses on statistics and research methods. These benefits do not accrue simply to the individual student; scholars are quick to note that SAGS can also create a shared environment and community that enables collaborative learning (Foreman 2004; Hromek and Roffey 2009; Kirriemuir and McFarlane 2004). As McLellan (1994) argues, games can be seen as interactive stories in which students are the creators and the participants; this can build a strong social community in the classroom as students work together to produce knowledge (Gareau and Guo 2009). Certainly Daniau's (2016) focus on transformative role-playing games calls on students to do this, as do most role-playing simulations. As Herz (as cited in Foreman 2004:55) puts it: "the higher degree of social mesh you have, particularly in the game industry, the more learning you get, because the real power of the stuff is in peer-to-peer learning, not in what goes on between a single individual and a document." The mere process of engaging in gameplay can build social capital between students that can be expended on other activities—or translated into the building of genuine, lasting empathy for the lives of others (Bachen, Hernández-Ramos, and Raphael 2012).

The literature, therefore, is in strong consensus: SAGS have a record of increasing cognitive, behavioral, and affective learning. For further evidence, I now turn to an analysis of 18 years of pedagogical publications in a single discipline, to explore the extent to which simulations are readily available and pose barriers of time to adoption.

ANALYZING THE DISINCENTIVES TO USING GAMES AND SIMULATIONS

As discussed above, one of the most frequently cited barriers to the use of SAGS is the perceived amount of class time such activities take. To determine whether this is a well-founded belief, I conducted a review of all 39 SAGS published in the 10-year period between 2006 and 2015 in *PS: Politics and Political Science* (*PS*), one of the main venues for publishing games and simulations in political science. To these, I add Baronowski and Weir's (2015) review of 27 simulations in another pedagogy journal, *Journal of Political Science Education* (*JPSE*), published between 2005 and 2013. Using the authors' descriptions, I coded each *PS* simulation based on the amount of class time required to play the game: no class time needed (the SAG is run entirely online or outside of class), less than a single one-hour class session, one full class session of up to 1.5 hours, one week of class (two sessions or four hours), two weeks of class (four sessions or six hours), or more than two weeks of class (including full day, semester long, and weekend SAGS). When authors provided their own estimates, I always used the more conservative estimate. For the *JPSE* results, I used Baronowski and Weir's (2015:394) coding and translated it to the system I used for *PS*.

The results show that on average, SAGS require around one week to run. Roughly one third of SAGS require one class session or less; another third require between one and four sessions, and the final third take two weeks or more. On a 0–5 scale where 0 represents no class time and 5 more than two weeks of class, the mean across 66 SAGS is 3.3. Many of the published simulations do take a substantial amount of class time, as feared by many potential adopters—but the majority

(55 percent) need four hours of class time or less, and of those, 58 percent require a single class session or less.

Therefore, there are many options available to instructors that require only a small sacrifice of class time. Haynes (2015), for example, teaches the bargaining model for explaining why wars occur using a simple card game that takes 15 or 20 minutes to play; students can play Asal's (2005) Survive or Die! game teaching Thomas Hobbes's state of nature in five minutes. Displacement of content therefore can be quite minimal. Furthermore, the existence of 66 published SAGS in political science journals alone (not counting websites such as *Active Learning in Political Science*) indicates that instructors can draw on a rich body of pre-tested SAGS available in the public realm.

Of course, this analysis is preliminary and limited. Both journals are in the discipline of political science, leaving little room for cross-discipline comparison in resources. There is no reason to believe, however, that political science is unique in providing publishing venues for SAGS.

CONCLUSION: BEST PRACTICES IN SIMULATIONS AND GAMES

This chapter has argued that the barriers to the use of SAGS in the college classroom can not only be overcome, but are dwarfed by the benefits to learning that these techniques bring above and beyond those of traditional teaching methods such as lecture. The biggest fears—that SAGS are not a mainstream teaching technique, that few resources are available, and that they require too much class time—are mitigated by an analysis of publications in two political science journals, which shows that SAGS are widely used, that more than 60 exist in this discipline alone, and that the average amount of class time required is a single week of class, with many options for shorter games available. This discussion has hopefully convinced the reluctant adopter that SAGS, regardless of discipline, can be valuable tools to add to the pedagogical arsenal.

Let me conclude by considering some best practices and tips for new adopters. First, start small and smart. Use shorter SAGS to complement or supplement existing lessons; this will ease fears of sacrificing time and content while helping you gain experience in how to run a game. As Gareau and Guo (2009) point out, you have three options for choosing games: adopt an existing product; adapt an existing product for your own purposes; or develop something from scratch. Start with adoption before jumping into simulation creation. Try, perhaps, a review or exam game based around Jeopardy (Revere et al. 2008) or Bingo (Weisskirch 2009). These games are highly portable, meaning they can be used in multiple classes in different subject areas with only minor changes (Kollars and Rosen 2016). Next, adapt a simulation to work for your class: negotiation simulations such as Model

United Nations can be adapted to work for any large group, organization, government entity, or corporation. Seek out resources in your discipline, such as pedagogical journals, web resources and blogs, commercial pedagogical publishers, and professional associations. Once you have built up your resource base, experience, and skills, consider creating your own SAGS, possibly with the assistance of students (Druckman and Ebner 2008; Whitton 2012).

Strong SAGS depend on two key characteristics. First, the activity must be closely aligned with your course and learning outcomes (Prensky 2001; Smith, Caruso, and Kim 2010). The benefits of SAGS are striking, but they depend completely on having a good match between activity and learning objectives; otherwise you are simply using class time to let your students have a bit of fun. The Reacting to the Past simulation games, for example, are a great way to explore historical events such as Darwin's discoveries, the Protestant Reformation, or the founding of Athenian democracy. But if your course is really focused on understanding the findings of naturalism, religious conflict, or the challenges of democracy in a modern world, then these simulations might not have much value added.

Likewise, the benefits of SAGS are lost without a thorough debriefing session. Debriefing is the process of reviewing the events, strategies, outcomes, and emotions of the simulation and linking them back to the concepts under study. This is where the learning really occurs, and foregoing the debriefing due to time or other concerns is a rookie mistake to be avoided at all costs (Crookall 1995; Davidson et al. 2009; Preston and Cottam 1997). De Frietas (2006) notes that the debriefing is where the false world of the simulation or game and its connection to the real world are made. This is where students make the connection between theory and practice, and it allows them to critique theory on the basis of their learned experience via the SAG. Without it, students are likely to focus solely on the gameplay, and not actually achieve the learning goals of the exercise (Daniau 2016). Two studies (Druckman and Ebener 2008; Rieber and Noah 2008) found limited impacts of SAGS on learning, but in both cases, no debriefing occurred—raising the question of whether these activities, coupled with a debriefing, might have produced different results on the post-tests. Debriefing can also be an essential part of an assessment process, which can be used to evaluate student learning, provide ideas for revising the exercise, or as the foundation for publishing results (Chin, Dukes, and Gamson 2009).

In conclusion, the benefits of simulations and games in the college classroom are worth overcoming the perceived barriers against their use. To this we add one final incentive: the benefit to faculty themselves. SAGS can freshen up stale material, and even mitigate the emotional and intellectual draining that can occur after repeatedly teaching the same course year after year (Auman 2011). The positive benefits of SAGS, therefore, are not restricted solely to students.

REFERENCES

Aldrich, Clark. 2004. *Simulations and the Future of Learning: An Innovative and Perhaps Revolutionary Approach to E-learning*. San Francisco: Pfeiffer.

Asal, Victor. 2005. "Playing Games with International Relations." *Journal of International Studies Perspectives* 6(3):359–73.

Auman, Corinne. 2011. "Using Simulation Games to Increase Student and Instructor Engagement." *College Teaching* 59(4):154–61.

Bachen, Christine M., Pedro F. Hernández-Ramos, and Chad Raphael. 2012. "Simulating REAL LIVES: Global Empathy and Interest in Learning through Simulation Games." *Simulation and Gaming* 43(4):437–60.

Baranowski, Michael K., and Kimberly A. Weir. 2015. "Political Simulations: What We Know, What We Think We Know, and What We Still Need to Know." *Journal of Political Science Education* 11(4):391–403.

Bernstein, Jeffrey L. 2008. "Cultivating Civic Competence: Simulations and Skill-Building in an Introductory Government Class." *Journal of Political Science Education* 4(1): 1–20.

Biziouras, Nikolaos. 2013. "Bureaucratic Politics and Decision Making under Uncertainty in a National Security Crisis: Assessing the Effects of International Relations Theory and the Learning Impact of Role-Playing Simulation at the US Naval Academy." *Journal of Political Science Education* 9(2):184–96.

Bonwell, Charles C., and James A. Eison. 1991. *Active Learning: Creating Excitement in the Classroom*. Washington, DC: School of Education and Human Development, George Washington University.

Bradshaw, Kathlyn E., and Robert W. Harvey. 2017. "Accounting for Taste: Learning by Doing in the College Classroom." *College Quarterly* 20(2):1–15.

Brooks, D. Christopher. 2015. "Study of Faculty and Information Technology, 2015." *Student and Faculty Technology Research Studies*. Available at https://library.educause.edu /resources/2015/8/2015-student-and-faculty-technology-research-studies.

Brooks, D. Christopher, Eden Dahlstrom, Susan Grajek, and Jamie Reeves. 2015. "Study of Students and Information Technology, 2015." *Student and Faculty Technology Research Studies*. Available at https://library.educause.edu/resources/2015/8/2015-student-and-faculty-technology-research-studies.

Chin, Jeffrey, Richard Dukes, and William Gamson. 2009. "Assessment in Simulation and Gaming." *Simulation and Gaming* 40(4):553–68.

Chow, Alan F., Kelly C. Woodford, and Jeanne Maes. 2011. "Deal or No Deal: Using Games to Improve Student Learning, Retention and Decision-making." *International Journal of Mathematical Education in Science and Technology* 42(2):259–64.

Crookall, David. 1995. *Debriefing: The Key to Learning from Simulation/Games*. Thousand Oaks, CA: Sage.

Daniau, Stéphane. 2016. "The Transformative Potential of Role-Playing Games: From Play Skills to Human Skills." *Simulation and Gaming* 47(4):423–44.

Davidson, Jean H., Leanne Du Preez, Matthew W. Gibb, and Etienne L. Nell. 2009. "It's in the Bag! Using Simulation as a Participatory Learning Method to Understand Poverty." *Journal of Geography in Higher Education* 33(2):149–68.

De Freitas, Sara I. 2006. "Using Games and Simulations for Supporting Learning." *Learning, Media, and Technology* 31(4):343–58.

Dorn, Dean S. 1989. "Simulation Games: One More Tool on the Pedagogical Shelf." *Teaching Sociology* 17(1):1–18.

Druckman, Daniel, and Noam Ebner. 2008. "Onstage or Behind the Scenes? Relative Learning Benefits of Simulation Role-Play and Design." *Simulation and Gaming* 39(4):465–97.

Faria, A. J. 1987. "A Survey of the Use of Business Games in Academia and Business." *Simulation and Gaming* 18(2):207–24.

Foreman, Joel. 2004. "Game-Based Learning: How to Delight and Instruct in the 21st Century." *EDUCAUSE Review* 39(5):50–66.

Gareau, Stephen, and Ruth Guo. 2009. "'All Work and No Play' Reconsidered: The Use of Games to Promote Motivation and Engagement in Instruction." *International Journal for the Scholarship of Teaching and Learning* 3(1):1–12.

Gee, James Paul. 2003. *What Video Games Have to Teach Us about Learning and Literacy.* New York: Palgrave MacMillan.

Giraud-Carrier, François C., and Glen M. Schmidt. 2015. "Learning in the Fast Lane: The Freeway Game." *Decision Sciences Journal of Innovative Education* 13(3):273–87.

Gorton, William, and Jonathan Havercroft. 2012. "Using Historical Simulations to Teach Political Theory." *Journal of Political Science Education* 8(1):50–68.

Green, Mary, and Mary Nell McNeese. 2007. "Using Edutainment Software to Enhance Online Learning." *International Journal on E-Learning* 6(1):5–16.

Hake, Richard R. 1998. "Interactive-Engagement vs. Traditional Methods: A Six-Thousand-student Survey of Mechanics Test Data for Introductory Physics Courses." *American Journal of Physics* 66(1):64–74.

Hart Research Associates. 2015. *Falling Short? College Learning and Career Success.* Washington, DC: Association of American Colleges and Universities.

Haynes, Kyle. 2015. "Simulating the Bargaining Model of War." *PS: Political Science & Politics* 48(4):627–29.

Herz, Bernhard, and Wolfgang Merz. 1998. "Experiential Learning and the Effectiveness of Economic Simulation Games." *Simulation and Gaming* 29(2):238–50.

Hromek, Robyn, and Sue Roffey. 2009. "'It's Fun and We Learn Things': Promoting Social and Emotional Learning with Games." *Simulation and Gaming* 40(5):626–44.

Kahn, Melvin A., and Kathleen M. Perez. 2009. "The Game of Politics Simulation: An Exploratory Study." *Journal of Political Science Education* 5(4):332–49.

Kirriemuir, John, and Angela McFarlane. 2004. *Literature Review in Games and Learning. A NESTA Futurelab Research Report.* Available at https://telearn.archives-ouvertes.fr/hal-00190453/document.

Klopfer, Eric, Scot Osterweil, and Katie Salen. 2009. "Moving Learning Games Forward: Obstacles, Opportunities, and Openness." *Education Arcade: Massachusetts Institute of Technology.* Available at http://www.educationarcade.org/.

Kollars, Nina, and Amanda M. Rosen. 2016. "Bootstrapping and Portability in Simulation Design." *International Studies Perspectives* 17(2):202–13.

Kollars, Nina, and Amanda M. Rosen. 2017. "Who's Afraid of the Big Bad Methods? Methodological Games and Roleplay." *Journal of Political Science Education* 13(3):333–45.

Kumar, Rita, and Robin Lightner. 2007. "Games as an Interactive Classroom Technique: Perceptions of Corporate Trainers, College Instructors and Students." *International Journal of Teaching and Learning in Higher Education* 19(1):53–63.

Laurel, Brenda. 1991. *Computers as Theatre*. Menlo Park, CA: Addison-Wesley.

Lepper, Mark R., and M. Hodell. 1989. "Intrinsic Motivation in the Classroom." Pp. 73–105 in *Research on Motivation in Education*, edited by Carol Ames and Russell Ames. New York: Academic Press.

Lipman, Matthew. 2003. *Thinking in Education*. Cambridge: Cambridge University Press.

McCarthy, Mary M. 2014. "Role of Games and Simulations to Teach Abstract Concepts of Anarchy Cooperation and Conflict in World Politics." *Journal of Political Science Education* 10(4):400–13.

McGonigal, Jane. 2011. *Reality Is Broken: Why Games Make Us Better and How They Can Change the World*. London: Jonathan Cape.

McLellan, Hilary. 1994. "Magical Stories: Blending Virtual Reality and Artificial Intelligence." Pp. 76–80 in *Imagery and Visual Literacy: Selected Readings from the Annual Conference of the International Visual and Literacy Association,* edited by D.G. Beauchamp, R.A. Braden, and R.E. Griffin, October 12–16, Tempe, AZ.

Moizer, Jonathan, Jonathan Lean, Michael Towler, and Caroline Abbey. 2009. "Simulations and Games: Overcoming the Barriers to Their Use in Higher Education." *Active Learning in Higher Education* 10(3):207–24.

Moore, Christopher. W. 2003. *The Mediation Process: Practical Strategies for Resolving Conflict*. 3rd ed. San Francisco: Jossey-Bass.

Moylan, Gina, Ann W. Burgess, Charles Figley, and Michael Bernstein. 2015. "Motivating Game-Based Learning Efforts in Higher Education." *International Journal of Distance Education Technologies* 13(2):54–72.

Nishikawa, Katsuo A., and Joe Jaeger. 2011. "A Computer Simulation Comparing the Incentive Structures of Dictatorships and Democracies." *Journal of Political Science Education* 7(2):135–42.

O'Brien, Dan, Kimberly A. Lawless, and P.G. Schrader. 2010. "A Taxonomy of Educational Games." Pp. 1–23 in *Gaming for Classroom-based Learning: Digital Role Playing as a Motivator of Study,* edited by Y.K. Baek. Hershey, PA: Information Science Reference.

Paino, Maria, and Jeffrey Chin. 2011. "Monopoly and Critical Theory: Gaming in a Class on the Sociology of Deviance." *Simulation and Gaming* 42(5):573–90.

Pan, Wei, and Mei Tang. 2004. "Examining the Effectiveness of Innovative Instructional Methods on Reducing Statistics Anxiety for Graduate Students in the Social Sciences." *Instructional Psychology* 31(2):149–59.

Perrotta, Carlo, Gill Featherstone, Helen Aston, and Emily Houghton. 2013. *Game-Based Learning: Latest Evidence and Future Directions*. NFER Research Programme: Innovation in Education. Slough: NFER.

Prensky, Marc. 2001. *Digital Game-Based Learning*. New York: McGraw-Hill.

Preston, Thomas, and Martha Cottam. 1997. "Simulating U.S. Foreign Policy Crises: Uses and Limits in Education and Training." *Journal of Contingencies and Crisis Management* 5(4):224–30.

Ranchhod, Ashok, Călin Gurău, Europides Loukis, and Rohit Trivedi. 2014. "Evaluating the Educational Effectiveness of Simulation Games: A Value Generation Model." *Information Sciences* 264(20):75–90.

Revere, Lee, Max Elden, and Robert A. Bartsch. 2008. "Designing Group Examinations to Decrease Social Loafing and Increase Learning." *International Journal for the Scholarship of Teaching and Learning* 2(1):1–17.

Rieber, Lloyd P., and David Noah. 2008. "Games, Simulations, and Visual Metaphors in Education: Antagonism between Enjoyment and Learning." *Educational Media International* 45(2):77–92.

Sabin, Phillip. 2015. "Wargaming in Higher Education: Contributions and Challenges." *Arts and Humanities in Higher Education* 14(4):329–48.

Smith, Shannon, Judy Caruso, and Joshua Kim. 2010. "ECAR Study of Undergraduate Students and Information Technology." *EDUCAUSE Center for Applied Research (ECAR)*. Available at https://library.educause.edu/resources/2010/10/ecar-study-of-undergraduate-students-and-information-technology-2010.

Stansbury, Jessica A., Evangeline Wheeler, and Justin T. Buckingham. 2014. "Can Wii Engage College-Level Learners? Use of Commercial Off-the-Shelf Gaming in an Introductory Statistics Course." *Computers in the Schools* 31(1–2):103–15.

Weisskirch, Robert S. 2009. "Playing Bingo to Review Fundamental Concepts in Advanced Courses." *Scholarship of Teaching and Learning* 3(1):1–14.

Whitton, Nicola. 2012. "The Place of Game-Based Learning in an Age of Austerity." *Electronic Journal of E-Learning* 10(2):249–56.

Wiggins, Bradley E. 2016. "An Overview and Study on the Use of Games, Simulations and Gamification in Higher Education." *International Journal of Game-Based Learning* 6(1):18–29.

Woodward, John, Douglas Carnine, and Russell Gersten. 1988. "Teaching Problem Solving through Computer Simulations." *American Educational Research Journal* 25(1):72–86.

16

Putting the Student at the Center

Contemplative Practices as Classroom Pedagogy

Tracy Wenger Sadd

Both religious and nonreligious people have used contemplative practices for more than four thousand years to benefit human well-being, and in the last 20 years, scholars across academic disciplines have piloted a plethora of projects applying contemplative practices as classroom pedagogy across many academic disciplines, including the liberal arts and sciences, as well as pre-professional programs. According to Zajonc (2013), contemplative practices now constitute a quiet revolution in pedagogy. While Fisher (2017) critiques contemplative pedagogy for valuing first-person experience over analytical reasoning, the *Chronicle of Higher Education* ("Innovators" 2017) includes the University of Pennsylvania's Justin McDaniel as one of ten featured innovative and trailblazing professors for his utilization of contemplative pedagogies in the classroom.

Contemplative practices can be visual, auditory, cognitive, affective, kinesthetic, or physical. We may associate some of these practices more directly with religion (e.g., *lectio divina*, yoga) than others (e.g., improvisation, journaling). At the same time, none of these practices are solely religious, and many of these practices have been used by artists, activists, athletes, leaders, medical practitioners, and teachers throughout history. Educational theorists such as John Dewey, Jean Piaget, Paulo Freire, Daniel Kolb, and others include experiential or reflective components as part of their systems. Many readers of this chapter already incorporate contemplative practices into classes, whether or not they realize it or wish to identify those practices as contemplative.

The Center for Contemplative Mind in Society (CCMIS) dominates the recent literature, specifically focusing on contemplative pedagogies in higher education. Bush (2011) documents a timeline beginning as early as 1995, to Brown University establishing a Contemplative Studies Initiative in 2005, to 600 educators attending the "Uncovering the Heart of Higher Education" conference in San Francisco in 2007. Morgan (2015) sees the work of CCMIS in partnership with the American Council of Learned Societies (1995–present) as a reemergence of a contemplative focus in education, which was present in both Classical Greece and Classical India. She views the current movement as the third of three significant stages of contemplative education in the United States, with the first two waves in 1840 and 1960–70.

According to Barbezat and Bush (2014), contemplation involves making a space for observation (historically in temples) and gazing attentively (either literally or metaphorically), while introspection is noticing what is occurring within. A comprehensive diagram, "The Tree of Contemplative Practices," is available for download at the website for the Center for Contemplative Mind in Society.

GOALS FOR USE OF CONTEMPLATIVE PRACTICES IN THE CLASSROOM

One of the strongest arguments for contemplative pedagogies is the goal of placing the "whole" student at the center of learning, so that the student can engage the inner world (introspection) and more deeply and effectively understand the outer world (contemplation). To speak in student-learning outcome language, Bloom's Cognitive Taxonomy (Anderson 2013) takes us only part of the way. Logic, reason, analysis, and critique are not the only important modes of higher thinking. Believing, valuing, prioritizing, imagining, choosing, and appreciating also are significant aspects of higher thinking, and Krathwohl's Affective Taxonomy has proven useful in my pursuit of conveying these skills to my students (Krathwohl and Bloom 1999). The objectivist way of knowing is limited, and while the dangers of subjectivity are real, students' affect does matter in the classroom, whether or not we acknowledge it and engage it. Students do have powerful and highly influential inner worlds, as do we, whether or not we choose to engage these inner worlds consciously and intentionally.

A second reason to use contemplative pedagogies relates to the students' skills in application of knowledge and action for the good of the world. Barbezat and Bush (2014) note that real-world problems and practical solutions require personal involvement, focused attention, deep understanding and connection, compassion and creativity, personal meaning, and insight. Barbezat (2009) has demonstrated that students majoring in economics make different decisions about economic systems and the welfare of others after they participate in contemplative practices. Moreover, in recognition that science alone fails to fully prepare doctors for patient care in the twenty-first century, the MCAT now has a fourth section to the exam, entitled "Psychological, Social, and Biological Foundations of Behavior."

The application of scientific knowledge to human systems requires the integration of knowledge and analysis from multiple fields.

A third reason to utilize contemplative practices in classrooms (as well as outside of classrooms) relates to the rising rates and severity of students' anxiety (Kadison and DiGeronimo 2005; Voelker 2003) and the extent to which meditation and mindfulness support psychological well-being, self-regulation, positive emotional states, and decreased stress (Brown and Ryan 2003). Deckro et al. (2002) conducted a six-week mind / body intervention on college students and found significantly greater reductions in psychological distress, anxiety, and perceived stress in the experimental group. Perhaps we might reduce our students' stress and even increase their test scores by inviting them to do a five-minute deep breathing exercise or meditation before quizzes and exams.

A fourth goal for integrating contemplative pedagogies is to improve cognitive learning and course content. Cranson et al. (1991) conducted a longitudinal study finding that transcendental meditation improved performance on intelligence-related measures. Barbezat and Bush (2014) summarize their review of recent research by saying it has shown the use of contemplative practices in the classroom can help students increase attention and awareness, health and well-being, self-understanding and compassion, deepened connection with others, and deeper understanding of and appropriation of course material.

SPECIFIC OUTCOMES OF CONTEMPLATIVE PEDAGOGY

In literature specific to academic disciplines, LaForge (2004) connected meditation practices and the development of moral imagination in a business course. Sellers-Young (2013) has integrated contemplative practices into the performing arts classroom. In a study of mindfulness in a sociology classroom, Song and Muschert (2014) found the practice benefited students' self-awareness, appreciation of differences, and social connection.

Giorgino (2015) uses meditation in sociology classes as a counter to feelings of being caged and impotent from pervasive constructivist approaches and in support of the embodied, interactional, and presence-based nature of human experience. He writes: "Currently, as a matter of social concern, questions about the meaning of our life—which in the near past were relegated to the private existential sphere—arise and take a relevant place in the collective agenda" (p. 479). Giorgino (2015) calls for self-observation of inner states through contemplative practices as we begin to rethink our epistemologies.

Contemplative pedagogies have been connected to the work of transformative learning pedagogy (Mezirow et al. 2009) and integral education (Esbjörn-Hargens 2007). Lange's (2009) work with transformative pedagogy as creating a sanctuary space and a pedagogy of hope aligns with sociologist Giorgino's (2015) call for pedagogies that move students beyond feelings of impotence. Lange (2009) describes her dialectic transformative pedagogy as both personal and social, creating "a container for the dialectics between a pedagogy of critique and a pedagogy of hope" (p. 197).

Kronman (2008) traces how the rise of secular humanism, the developing research ideal of the academy, and the dominance of the scientific method have obscured the understanding of the role of higher education in shaping the souls and spirits of students. On the other hand, Martinez (2015) has critiqued Steel's (2015) call for a reform of education based on a triad of knowledge, happiness, and contemplation as too personal and subjective, and for its failure to account for larger issues and concerns of social justice. However, Berlia (2012) found contemplative practices enhanced outcomes of personal empowerment among students in women's studies. Solloway (2000) found connection between contemplative practices and content related to social justice and feminism. Blinne (2014) connects contemplative pedagogy with compassionate engagement addressing social problems in a communications course.

Gortner (2013) has demonstrated the existence of a phenomenon he calls "personal theology," a personal operating theory of the entire cosmos, which, like a self-concept, is an amalgamation of perceptions, expectations, and goals. Parks (2000) speaks of what might be called both cognitive-learning goals (e.g., critiquing assumptions and social conventions, pursuing truth) and also affective learning goals (e.g., awareness, self-consciousness, trust, valuing, determining what counts).

Craig (2011) conducted a mixed-methods research design on the outcomes of the 130 courses integrating contemplative practices into academic courses ranging from chemistry, physics, engineering, and business to art, literature, religious studies, economics, and social work, taught by 158 fellows at more than 107 colleges and universities, supported by scholarly grants from the American Council of Learned Societies from 1997–2009. While 82 percent of the fellows reported a "deeper sense of personal and professional integration," about 65 percent still use contemplative pedagogies, and 25 percent have done so for more than 10 years. Two-thirds of the faculty fellows in Craig's study reported institutional acceptance and support for the use of contemplative practices in the classroom. Craig also found that 80 percent of the fellows said that students expressed appreciation; 75 percent of the fellows said students reported contemplative practices helping them in their lives outside of the classroom; and less than half of the fellows indicated any student discomfort.

Shapiro, Brown, and Astin (2011) have compiled and analyzed the outcomes research related specifically to meditation in the classroom. For a large-scale study on the broadly construed "spiritual life" of college and university faculty, see Lindholm (2014).

USING FOUR CONTEMPLATIVE PRACTICES IN
INTRODUCTORY COURSES

I used contemplative practices, primarily in the form of inquiry-based pedagogies, in an introductory course in religious studies and compared those outcomes to three other first-year introductory courses not taught with these pedagogies in the subject areas of math, science, and literature (Sadd 2015). When initial results seemed promising, I asked another faculty in religious studies to try the pedagogies, and I included those outcomes. Astin, Astin, and Lindholm (2012) found that when instructors challenged students to engage in big questions of life, meaning, and purpose, the students' scores in ecumenical worldview were higher, and my research focused specifically on big questions inquiry (an inquiry-based pedagogy related to contemplating unknowing), appreciative inquiry journaling, and contemplative free writing.

Big Questions Project Assignment (Contemplating Unknowing)

Each student in the class named a big question about existence, meaning, purpose, or life in general that he or she wished to explore. Unlike the topic of the research paper for the course, students could not answer or research the big question by using any known disciplinary methodology or any current peer-reviewed literature. Indeed, finding an "answer" might not be possible, but the important point was for students to find an engaging question and articulate a way to make progress on it. I divided students into small groups, called big question groups, and they met throughout the semester to help each other understand why their questions mattered to them and to think creatively about how each one might go about finding an answer to this question, or at least "make progress" on the big question. In consultation with the instructor, students confirmed a "plan" for exploring the big question, implemented the exploration, and presented to their peers a final product related to the process at the end of the semester (e.g., poem, video, screenplay, sculpture, collage, rock collection, and hendecagram).

Appreciative Inquiry Contemplative Journals Assignment

I briefly introduced the students to the major themes of appreciative inquiry, which is based theoretically on the principles of constructionism, simultaneity, poetic, anticipatory, positive, wholeness, enactment, free-choice, narrative, and awareness, and more practically, includes inquiring into and investigating the positive, or what is working, appreciating and valuing it, and dreaming, designing, and building on the strengths of what is (Cockell and McArthur-Blair 2012; Cooperrider and Whitney 2005). The primacy of intentional focus of attention, choice of language, and phrasing of questions in creating reality and outcomes is central to the pedagogy.

Throughout the semester, each individual student had to attend out-of-class events, programs, and experiences of their own choosing, on or off campus. For 13 of these events, students wrote a two-page contemplative journal using appreciative-inquiry question-based prompts: What do you think the presenter(s) really wanted you to think about, learn, know, or understand? What did you really appreciate and value about this experience? What surprised you, made you curious, or made you wonder? What questions would help you gain a deeper understanding of things?

The Appreciative Inquiry Class Session Structure

In a typical class period, we followed a three-movement experience adapted by me from Appreciative Inquiry (AI). Students shared the author they read and their key points with the class, followed by naming several things they really appreciated about that theologian or philosopher's thoughts. Sometimes I asked them variations on this question: What really resonated with you? What will linger with you? What positives might you build on? Then, we moved into a time of critical thinking, in which students used logic, personal experience, and/or knowledge from science or another academic discipline to critique the theologian or philosopher's work. Finally, students shared questions they would like to ask the person they had read, or what new thoughts or questions they had due to their encounter with this specific theologian or philosopher.

Contemplative Free Writing Assignments

Many times, as listed in the syllabus, at either the beginning or the very end of class, I asked the students to do a contemplative free writing:

- Take a few deep breaths, and then write a response to any of the readings for today, perhaps focusing on what you appreciate, what bugs you, or what questions are most pressing for you.
- Now that we have concluded our discussions and lectures related to the topic, write a contemplative and thoughtful response to this question: How do you "know" what you claim to know?
- Considering the totality of your head and heart, the material we have read, the comments from others in the class, and your experiences, write a reflection in answer to this question: How do you make sense of the bad things that have happened in your life and to others in the world?

OUTCOMES ASSESSMENT OF FOUR CONTEMPLATIVE PRACTICES IN INTRODUCTORY COURSES

The study involved 76 students (including Christians, atheists, and those with no religious affiliation across all courses), and I carried out pre-course and post-course surveys. I also conducted four sets of in-depth interviews with a subset of the students over a two-year period—from the students' entry into college until the end of the students' sophomore year. According to both surveys and interviews, students in the inquiry-based and contemplative pedagogy courses reported increased development of their inner lives and also greater frequency of engaging students of different religions (or of no religion) and different cultures, as opposed to comparison group students.

Qualitative Outcomes Assessment

In interviews, students reported that because of the inquiry-based and contemplative pedagogy, a certain type of space was created in the classrooms, and it felt relaxed. They felt it recharged them, and at the same time, they learned as much or even more than in other classes. Students responded to a question about any changes in ethics or beliefs by saying that they had become more open, tolerant, and curious. They reported knowing more about religions, and they also reported their realization about how much more there was to know and wanting to know it.

Many students reported that the format of the contemplative and appreciative inquiry-based classes engaged not only their minds, but also their hearts (emotions and motivations). They made progress on identity and clarity about what they valued and why.

> I definitely changed completely . . . not so much religiously but like mentally. I definitely figured out a lot of problems that were kind of like sitting there and I didn't really know what to do with them and first-year seminar has kind of given me tools, so I'll be like okay, this is what I'm questioning so that's what I'm going to do for my research paper or this doesn't make sense so this is what I'm going to do for my basic theological question like, I feel like it really gave me the opportunity to be creative and start understanding myself instead of just like learning facts. (ID#63972652)

Students also reported skill development as significant, related to the continuing practice of listening, gaining clarification, and practicing appreciative inquiry throughout the entire semester. Students reported learning how to listen well, ask clarifying questions, and really trying to understand the other. They noticed increasing skill over the semester. A couple of students in the comparison noncontemplative pedagogy course on literature mentioned this type of skill development, but it was not reported as widely as in the contemplative pedagogy classes and was not reported at all in the noncontemplative math or science courses. Students reported that the big questions and appreciative inquiry conversations continued out of class in a really positive way. The appreciative inquiry exercises started a pattern and began to establish a habit or discipline.

Students reported that by the end of the semester, they were listening to each other and building from what each other said—constructing new ideas, new possibilities, and new questions.

[In the contemplative practice course] people were listening and didn't have the risk of being completely disregarded or interrupted. It was a good environment for feeling comfortable speaking and knowing other people would hear you ... A lot of times it would spur off into different discussions and people would ask for clarification ... They were paying attention enough to realize that they didn't really understand things so, there would always be someone searching for more after you would say something instead of just you saying it end up being dropped. There was always like a condition or question or clarification to show that there was attention being put onto it. (ID#27422648)

Dr. Christina Bucher, Professor of Religious Studies and a former Dean of Faculty who also used the pedagogies, said that the big question project was the "big" one in terms of influence on her students. As a professor of biblical studies, she had rarely, if ever, assigned a project that was not a research paper. The big question project required students to contemplate unknowing, to be creative and to think big. She said the big question project required them to reflect on their own views, to seek other ways of seeing (including "authority"), to consider, to deliberate, and then to create the end product. She concluded that while the big question project was not research, it was more than just opinion, and in some ways, was almost the opposite of a research topic. In research, we nearly always end up telling students: narrow it down, refine it, manage it, utilize standard disciplinary methods, or it has not been done by anyone before, so you cannot do it. With the big question project, we were always telling them to think even bigger, to look across disciplines, to look to wisdom outside the academy, to think of creative ways to make even a little progress on something so big, so complex, and quite possibly truly unanswerable. I had intended that the big question project would take the entire semester, and for most students, it really did.

Quantitative Outcomes Assessment

The quantitative outcomes of the inquiry-based and contemplative courses as opposed to the comparison courses (Pearson chi square, $\alpha = .05$) suggest that an inquiry-based and contemplative pedagogy applied to the teaching of theology and religion can advance students' spiritual development or enhance their "inner lives" if spiritual development and inner lives are defined in the following ways: be more aware of who I am, state clearly what I believe, listen to others' points of view, appreciate what others believe, engage diverse religious and cultural viewpoints, treat others with respect, form friendships with people different than me, and initiate conversations with people of other religions and cultures. Other survey results of this study suggest that a contemplative and inquiry-based pedagogy applied to the teaching of theology and religion can lead to positive changes in students related to curiosity, search for meaning and significance, epistemology, and engagement with family about religion and spirituality, regardless of whether or not the students were Christians, atheists, or those with no religious affiliation.

Interview reports of frequency of engaging diversity showed that the contemplative pedagogy course students had higher levels of engaging diversity in 10 of 10 areas. The types of engagement Patel (2007) calls pluralistic, civic, bridge-building behaviors included: having class with, speaking to, eating with, having meaningful conversation with, doing a service project together with, discussing religion outside of class, sharing a friendship, choosing as a roommate, advocating for, and visiting a house of worship.

In summary, the effectiveness of the inquiry-based and contemplative pedagogy used in teaching theology and religion in the students' words seemed to center on the concept that inquiry-based and contemplative practices integrated in multiple ways throughout the course challenged them to hold the cognitive and critical in tension with the affective and appreciative. Students valued the new cognitive knowledge as much as the contemplation of beliefs and values. They noted the importance of thinking critically and gaining new knowledge about religion, but also the value of digging deep in terms of the subjective—listening, questioning, valuing, appreciating, challenging, creating, and constructing. The results of this research challenged me to consider the possibility of a null curriculum in higher education (Flinders, Noddings, and Thornton 1986) related to the advancement of students' inner lives and engaging the affect and subjectivity of the learner.

IDENTIFYING DISCIPLINE-SPECIFIC CONTEMPLATIVE PEDAGOGIES

The process of identifying content, entire courses, or specific class periods for the use of contemplative pedagogies in a specific academic discipline requires care and contemplation. Faculty interested in pursuing contemplative practices in the classroom might review the definitions and pedagogical application of selected contemplative practices, selecting several for further consideration. The questions below may aid faculty in identifying discipline-specific content that might be most easily enhanced through the use of contemplative pedagogies. Some faculty might think about the questions cognitively and analytically, while other faculty might process a subset of these questions as a contemplative exercise, perhaps as a loving-kindness visualization or a walking meditation.

- Which disciplinary content involves any sort of values, choice, and decision-making?
- At what points does our curriculum require any future application to human systems or interaction with clients, co-workers, teams, or supervision of employees?
- Which data, research, diagram, theory, or text could be enriched by observing more attentively, seeing differently, making connections to a larger perspective, paying attention, or engaging personally or affectively?

- Which disciplinary or course content requires application, creativity, imagination, generativity, experimentation, challenge, risk, or failure?
- Which parts of any specific course do students seem least interested in engaging, or at what points in the semester do we just need to have some fun and do something different?
- For which courses would a parallel experience of journaling about mood, consumption, observations of personal choices, emerging questions, possible research topics, or potential solutions be useful to students?

BASIC GUIDELINES FOR CONTEMPLATIVE PRACTICES

Once you decide to move ahead with contemplative pedagogies, here are a few guidelines to keep in mind:

1. Decide what you actually are willing to take time to do, and what you really have time to do (e.g., five-minute deep breathing meditation before exams, a carefully selected contemplative pedagogy embedded into selected course activities, or a sustained contemplative pedagogy integrated with course content for the entire semester).
2. Rehearse before class.
3. Make all exercises accessible to all students, with an option for not participating as well.
4. Be clear that you know this requires a degree of risk and trust, and articulate clearly how grading will occur (e.g., general participation, overall level of engagement, actual content and product). Determine a system of grading that includes the broadest possible definition of and multiple criteria for assessing "thinking" (Minnich 2003).
5. Be ready to adapt in the moment as you engage the contemplative pedagogy, and allow students to process and debrief in conversation or in writing and to provide the instructor feedback and evaluation.
6. Be sure you are ready to give up control and that you are ready to adapt to unexpected things happening (conflict, anger, tears, laughter, humor, joy, insight, etc.).

CONCLUSION

The use of contemplative practices in education has a history of thousands of years, and the recent burgeoning of literature in the field suggests multiple benefits for both students and instructors in terms of decreased stress and increased focus, attention, and integration of knowledge, self, and world. In general, students and faculty respond positively to contemplative practices in the classroom, as well as possible discomfort and unease that may initially occur. Primarily through the work of the Center for Contemplative Mind in Society, as well as independent research published in academic journals in a variety of disciplines, instructors can find a plethora of examples, possible pitfalls, data on outcomes, general "how to" guidelines, and even a "frequently asked questions" article (Coburn et al. 2011). Least-studied areas include contemplative practices in math and science, contemplative pedagogies beyond meditation and mindfulness, contemplative pedagogies and discipline-specific content-learning outcomes, contemplative practices most useful with particular academic disciplines, and the differences between integrating contemplative practices in an entry-level or upper-level course within a major and in a general distribution course.

REFERENCES

Anderson, Lorin. 2013. *A Taxonomy for Learning, Teaching, and Assessing: A Revision of Bloom's Taxonomy of Educational Objectives.* Abridged Edition. Upper Saddle River, NJ: Pearson Education.

Astin, Alexander, Helen Astin, Rebecca Chopp, Andrew Delbanco, and Sam Speers. 2007. "A Forum on Helping Students Engage the 'Big Questions.'" *Liberal Education* 93(2):28–33.

Astin, Alexander W., Helen S. Astin, and Jennifer A. Lindholm. 2011. *Cultivating the Spirit: How College Can Enhance Students' Inner Lives.* San Francisco: Jossey-Bass.

Barbezat, Daniel. 2009. "Regret." Pp. 7–9 in *Fifth Annual Summer Session on Contemplative Curriculum Development* by B. Wadham. Northampton, MA: Center for Contemplative Mind in Society.

Barbezat, Daniel, and Mirabai Bush. 2014. *Contemplative Practices in Higher Education: Powerful Methods to Transform Teaching and Learning.* San Francisco, CA: Jossey-Bass.

Berlia, Beth. 2012. "Embodied Learning: Integrating the Body into Feminist Pedagogy." Unpublished manuscript referenced on p. 83 in *Contemplative Practices in Higher Education: Powerful Methods to Transform Teaching and Learning*, by Daniel Barbezat and Mirabai Bush. San Francisco: Jossey-Bass.

Blinne, Kristen C. 2014. "Awakening to Lifelong Learning: Contemplative Pedagogy as Compassionate Engagement." *Radical Pedagogy* 11(2):1.

Brady, Richard. 2007. "Learning to Stop, Stopping to Learn: Discovering the Contemplative Dimension in Education." *Journal of Transformative Education* 5(4):372–79.

Brown, Kirk, and Richard Ryan. 2003. "The Benefits of Being Present: Mindfulness and Its Role in Psychological Well-Being." *Journal of Personality and Social Psychology* 84(4):822–48.

Bush, Mirabai. 2011. "Mindfulness in Higher Education." *Contemporary Buddhism* 12(1): 183–97.

Coburn, Tom, Fran Grace, Ann Carolyn Klein, Louis Komjathy, Harold Roth, and Judith Simmer-Brown. 2011. "Contemplative Pedagogy: Frequently Asked Questions." *Teaching Theology and Religion* 14(2):167–74.

Cockell, Jeanie, and Joan McArthur-Blair. 2012. *Appreciative Inquiry in Higher Education: A Transformative Force.* San Francisco: Jossey-Bass.

Cooperrider, David, and Diana Whitney. 2005. *Appreciative Inquiry: A Positive Revolution in Change*. San Francisco: Berrett-Koehler.

Craig, Barbara. 2011. *Contemplative Practice in Higher Education: An Assessment of the Contemplative Practice Fellowship Program, 1997–2009*. Northampton, MA: Center for Contemplative Mind in Society.

Cranson, Robert, David Orme-Johnson, Jayne Gackenbach, Michael Dillbeck, Christopher Jones, and Charles N. Alexander. 1991. "Transcendental Meditation and Improved Performance on Intelligence-Related Measures: A Longitudinal Study." *Personality and Individual Differences* 12(10):1105–16.

Deckro, Gloria, Keli Ballinger, Michael Hoyt, Marilyn Wilcher, Jeffery Dusek, Patricia Myers, Beth Greenberg, David Rosenthal, and Herbert Benson. 2002. "The Evaluation of a Mind / Body Intervention to Reduce Psychological Distress and Perceived Stress in College Students." *Journal of American College Health* 50(6):281–87.

Duerr, Maia, Arthur Zajonc, and Diane Dana. 2003. "Survey of Transformative and Spiritual Dimensions of Higher Education." *Journal of Transformative Education* 1(3):177–211.

Esbjörn-Hargens, Sean. 2007. "Integral Teacher, Integral Students, Integral Classroom: Applying Integral Theory to Education." *Journal of Integral Theory and Practice* 2:71–103.

Fisher, Kathleen. 2017. "Look Before You Leap: Reconsidering Contemplative Pedagogy." *Teaching Theology and Religion* 20(1):4–21.

Flinders, David J., Nel Noddings, and Stephen J. Thornton. 1986. "The Null Curriculum: Its Theoretical Basis and Practical Implications." *Curriculum Inquiry* 16(1):33–42.

Giorgino, Vincenzo. 2015. "Contemplative Methods Meet Social Sciences: Back to Human Experience It Is." *Journal for the Theory of Social Behaviour* 45(4):461–83.

Gortner, David. 2013. *Varieties of Personal Theology: Charting the Beliefs and Values of American Young Adults*. Burlington, VT: Ashgate.

"Innovators: 10 Classroom Trailblazers." 2017. *Chronicle of Higher Education* 64(9): B1–40.

Kadison, Richard, and Theresa DiGeronimo. 2005. *College of the Overwhelmed: The Campus Mental Health Crisis and What to Do about It*. San Francisco: Jossey-Bass.

Krathwohl, David, and Benjamin Bloom. 1999. *Taxonomy of Educational Objectives, Book 2: Affective Domain*. Upper Saddle River, NJ: Longman.

Kronman, Anthony T. 2008. *Education's End: Why Our Colleges and Universities Have Given Up on the Meaning of Life*. New Haven, CT: Yale University Press.

Lange, Elizabeth. 2009. "Fostering a Learning Sanctuary for Transformation in Sustainability Education." Pp. 193–204 in *Transformative Learning in Practice: Insights from Community, Workplace, and Higher Education*, edited by Jack Mezirow, Edward Taylor, and Associates. San Francisco: Jossey-Bass.

LaForge, Paul. 2004. "Cultivating Moral Imagination through Meditation." *Journal of Business Ethics* 51(1):15–29.

Lindholm, Jennifer A. 2014. *The Quest for Meaning and Wholeness: Spiritual and Religious Connections in the Lives of College Faculty*. San Francisco: Jossey-Bass.

Martinez, Maria. 2015. "The Pursuit of Wisdom and Happiness in Education: Historical Sources and Contemplative Practices (Book Review)." *Journal of Catholic Education* 18(2):242–44.

Mezirow, Jack, Edward Taylor, and Associates. 2009. *Transformative Learning in Practice: Insights from Community, Workplace, and Higher Education.* San Francisco: Jossey-Bass.

Minnich, Elizabeth. 2003. "Teaching Thinking: Moral and Political Considerations." *Change* (September–October):19–24.

Morgan, Patricia Fay. 2015. "A Brief History of the Current Reemergence of Contemplative Education." *Journal of Transformative Education* 13(3):197–218.

Parks, Sharon Daloz. 2000. *Big Questions, Worthy Dreams: Mentoring Young Adults in Their Search for Meaning, Purpose, and Faith.* San Francisco: Jossey-Bass.

Patel, Eboo. 2007. *Acts of Faith: The Story of an American Muslim, the Struggle for the Soul of a Generation.* Boston: Beacon Press.

Sadd, Tracy Wenger. 2015. "Big Theological Questions: Using Inquiry-Based Pedagogy in Teaching Theology and Religion to Undergraduate Students." DMin dissertation, Virginia Theological Seminary. Retrieved from WorldCat Database, Accession No. 939715309.

Sellers-Young, Barbara. 2013. "Motions in Stillness-Stillness in Motion: Contemplative Practice in Performing Arts." Pp. 75–90 in *Embodied Consciousness: Performance Technologies*, edited by Jade McCutcheon and Barbara Sellers-Young. New York: Palgrave Macmillan.

Shapiro, Shauna, Kirk Warren Brown, and John Astin. 2011. "Toward the Integration of Meditation into Higher Education: A Review of Research Evidence." *Teachers College Record* 113(3):493–528.

Solloway, Sharon. 2000. "Contemplative Practitioners: Presence or the Project of Thinking Gaze Differently." *ENCOUNTER: Education for Meaning and Social Justice* 13(3):30–42.

Song, Kirsten Younghee, and Glenn Muschert. 2014. "Opening the Contemplative Mind in the Sociology Classroom." *Humanity and Society* 38(3):314–38.

Steel, Sean. 2015. *The Pursuit of Wisdom and Happiness in Education: Historical Sources and Contemplative Practices.* Albany: State University of New York.

Voelker, Rebecca. 2003. "Mounting Student Depression Taxing Campus Mental Health Services." *Journal of the American Medical Association* 289(16):2055–56.

Zajonc, Arthur. 2013. "Contemplative Pedagogy: A Quiet Revolution in Higher Education." *New Directions for Teaching and Learning* 2013(134):83–94.

PART III

Out-of-Class Situations

17

Student Reading Compliance and Learning in the Social Sciences

Jay R. Howard

Textbooks are nearly ubiquitous in college and university courses. In a study of faculty teaching beginning courses in mathematics, sciences, social sciences, and humanities at a large research university, Wambach (1998) found that over 80 percent of instructors used textbooks for at least some of the required reading. All the science and mathematics faculty included in the study reported using a textbook for half or more of assigned reading in the course. A strong majority of faculty in social science (88 percent) and humanities (65 percent) disciplines assigned textbooks as well.

While textbooks were heavily utilized across disciplinary areas, Wambach (1998:23) discovered that faculty use them to achieve different goals. Mathematics and social science faculty most commonly use textbooks to increase familiarity with a topic and thereby aid students' understanding during in-class lecture and discussion. Science faculty also frequently cited this goal, but their most-cited purpose is to help students acquire knowledge that they could recall later. Thus mathematics, science, and social science faculty tended to use textbooks to help students master, and to a significant extent memorize, content. In contrast, humanities faculty were more likely to stress the facilitation of critical and analytical thinking as well as developing a healthy skepticism in assigning texts, with a secondary goal of teaching students to critique an argument.

Wambach (1998:23) also found a close link between textbooks and lectures, though with some variation by discipline. All of the science faculty agreed or strongly agreed that students could gain at least 75 percent of the knowledge over which they will be tested by attending lecture and participating in class. A majority (72 percent) of mathematics faculty, but only half (50 percent) of social science and a minority (38 percent) of humanities faculty, agreed or strongly agreed with the statement. These results suggest that faculty in the sciences and mathematics primarily use textbooks to reinforce material presented in class. Social science and humanities faculty are more likely to use textbooks as a source of additional information or perspective that goes beyond the material presented or discussed in class.

Instructors also frequently use textbooks to frame and structure courses (Wambach 1998). In a study of introductory psychology courses, chapter topical coverage in introductory textbooks closely aligned with lecture topics, and the authors concluded that psychology faculty tend to "teach the text" (Griggs and Bates 2014:144). Such an approach leads students to expect their instructor to be a walking, talking human highlighter, who signals to them which material in the encyclopedic textbook they need to know for the exam.

While faculty often want to "blame the student" for failing to read assignments, by "teaching the text," faculty members themselves may be quite unintentionally facilitating students' lack of reading compliance. Again as Wambach (1998) showed, if the vast majority of material that students will be expected to learn is covered during class meetings, demonstrating what the faculty member views to be the most important material in the textbook, and, therefore, most likely to be included in exams, students determine there is less need to read assigned textbooks. Faculty members may be their own worst enemies when it comes to motivating students' reading compliance. The silver lining in this dark cloud is that faculty members have the opportunity and ability to structure courses in a manner that will encourage greater reading compliance.

While we do not have similar research from other fields beyond psychology, neither do we have reason to suspect that instructors utilize textbooks in a significantly different manner in other social science disciplines. The increasing political pressure for articulation agreements, particularly from community colleges to four-year institutions, can easily lead to a "teach to the text" approach in an attempt to ensure courses at different institutions are similar in content and level of academic rigor. Likewise, the growing emphasis on assessment in higher education encourages standardization across course sections within institutions. One way to avoid battles among faculty members regarding idiosyncratic approaches to a particular course is to teach to the text. Both the trends toward greater articulation between institutions and increasing assessment of learning outcomes within institutions, for better or worse, likely lead to a greater emphasis on textbooks to frame teaching, particularly in introductory-level courses in the social sciences.

SOCIAL CONTEXT, ACADEMIC CULTURES, AND TEXTBOOKS

While there are pressures toward greater uniformity within courses, differences in the uses of textbooks by discipline point to divergent academic cultures between humanities and social science disciplines versus that found in natural science, engineering, and mathematics. Tiberius and Billson (1991) noted that teaching and learning has a social context that is not completely under the control of either faculty members or students. The aforementioned emphases on articulation and assessment are examples of expectations placed on faculty members to adjust their approach to a social context. Articulation agreements work against novel approaches to teaching and textbooks in courses for which students commonly seek transfer credit between institutions. Students', parents', and politicians' concerns about postgraduation employment are another element of the social context that shapes how students see and value different disciplines and majors, which topics they perceive as valuable or not valuable in a given course, and whether or not students perceive reading for class is necessary. In addition, students' prior experience in educational settings shapes their expectations for higher education. If, in their prior experience, students have learned they can earn top grades without reading assigned texts, they bring that assumption to other higher education classrooms. Students may have learned through their secondary education experience that being a successful student amounts to memorizing what teachers say in class and remembering it long enough to repeat it back on exams and in writing assignments. Students may come to the college classroom with the assumption that their role is a relatively passive one—attend class, listen attentively, take notes, and be respectful toward others. Critically engaging with texts, and perhaps even reading those texts, may be considered an optional and unnecessary activity for success in college and in future careers.

Brint, Cantwell, and Hanneman (2008) argued that two distinct cultures of engagement in higher education exist, which both faculty and students often take for granted. Arts, humanities, and social science disciplines tend to have a classroom culture that focuses on interaction, student participation, and interest in ideas—which, incidentally, requires that students read prior to class in order to be most effective. In contrast, the academic culture of the natural science disciplines, mathematics, and engineering places greater emphasis on quantitative skills through collaborative study as students have an eye toward future career rewards. Each of these cultures of engagement has strengths as well as weaknesses (Brint et al. 2008). The approach more commonly used in the natural sciences and related disciplines can easily lead to hardworking students, who collaboratively seek to solve problems and address case studies, while developing technical competencies. Yet, it can also lead to students who have little interest in grappling with and critiquing competing perspectives found in reading assignments. The approach more typically found in the humanities and social sciences can generate student interaction, discussion, and insightful contributions, but also may reward extroverted, verbal students who can "shoot from the hip" without requiring hard work and investigation in preparation for a class discussion or activity.

Laird et al. (2008) found further empirical support for diverse academic cultures. They concluded that students majoring in fields with less consensus about content and methods, sometimes referred to as "soft" disciplines, tend to utilize deeper approaches to learning and reading than students majoring in "hard" disciplines with a greater consensus on content and methods. The academic culture in the social sciences and humanities, therefore, places greater emphasis on theoretical work, critical thinking, connecting ideas, and intellectual growth (see for example, Parpala et al. 2010). This approach also leads to an emphasis on application of course content, from both texts and lectures, to society and to students' experiences. In order to be most successful in this academic and social context, social science students are required to thoughtfully and reflectively read assigned texts, utilizing a deep approach. A deep approach involves reading for long-term retention and for comprehension at a level that potentially can transform one's perspective (for example, see Roberts and Roberts 2008). Reading at this level requires the difficult work of constructing meaning as one reads. Will students read and take a deep approach to learning? What steps can social science instructors take in order to make it more likely that students will do so?

ARE STUDENTS LIKELY TO READ ASSIGNMENTS?

The 2013 National Survey of Student Engagement (NSSE) reported that first-year students spend, on average, six hours per week reading for classes, while seniors spend seven hours per week reading assigned material. If we assume that full-time students enroll in 12–15 credit hours per semester, that is an average of no more than 30 minutes per credit hour spent invested in reading assignments each week. However, these overall averages do not tell us how many or which students read assigned texts, how often, or to what effect.

Student reading compliance is a topic that has been frequently investigated over the past two decades. Burchfield and Sappington (2000) conducted, arguably, the most often cited study of reading compliance. They looked at student compliance with reading assignments in psychology courses at a small Southeastern university from 1981–97. They concluded that, on any given day, only about one third of students will have completed reading of assigned texts prior to class. They also found a statistically significant and dramatic decline in reading compliance over the nearly two decades included in the study.

One of the challenges for both instructors and researchers investigating reading compliance is exactly when, if at all, do students read? Do students read texts prior to the day they are assigned for class as professors typically expect? Do they wait until after their instructors discuss the readings in class in hopes of better understanding the text when they read? Or do they read immediately prior to exams as a result of procrastination or in hopes that the recent activity will facilitate greater recollection for the exam? As Wambach (1998) suggested, while faculty members, particularly those in mathematics and the social sciences, may expect the former approach—students should read in preparation for class—students most often utilize the latter approach.

Slightly more encouraging than the results found by Burchfield and Sappington (2000) are the results of a study of eight courses across a range of disciplines at a regional university. Aagaard, Conner, and Skidmore (2014) found that half (52 percent) of students reported that they read textbook material when assigned. Interestingly, only 30 percent of students surveyed felt they "should be" required to read material in the textbook prior to class, which again is completely counter to typical faculty expectations for students and evidence of a social context that may discourage reading compliance. Baier et al. (2011), in a study of students at two Midwestern universities, the majority of which were teacher education majors, found that 25 percent of students completed readings prior to coming to class; 15 percent read after the material was covered in class; 40 percent read when preparing for exams; and 19 percent never completed the readings. A study of undergraduates at Northwestern University by Clump, Bauer, and Bradley (2004) found very similar results, with 27 percent of students reporting they read before class and 70 percent reading prior to an exam. This suggests that even students who are well prepared for college and who attend highly selective institutions are not particularly likely to complete readings prior to class. There is some evidence that this pattern is not unique to higher education in the United States. In a study conducted in Swedish universities (Pecorari et al. 2012), only 25 percent of students reported that they read assignments prior to class. About half (52 percent) indicated they would read after the material was covered in class, and 17 percent indicated they did not intend to complete reading assignments.

With such disappointing percentages of students actually reading for class, we must ask: Why are so many students choosing not to complete assigned reading for class? Nearly two thirds of the students surveyed in Baier et al. (2011) reported that they perceived they could earn an A or B in the course without reading the assigned texts. Students believe this is true because they perceived the instructor had an obligation to review material during class and to tell them what is important to learn or remember from the reading (see Clump, Bauer, and Bradley 2004). As cited above, Wambach (1998) suggests that students are correct in assuming that faculty will cover the vast majority of material to be learned in class. Gurung and Martin (2011) note that if students believe they can succeed in a course without reading the book, they will not read. This problem is likely exacerbated by those faculty who require students to purchase expensive textbooks, but do not make use of or refer to the textbook during class. Even if students purchase required textbooks, reading may become the casualty of a cost-benefit analysis conducted by students who rationally determine the additional benefit that comes from the reading is not worth the cost in terms of time and effort.

A study that compared introductory psychology student reading compliance in a large, research intensive university setting with students at a regional university found that 82 and 78 percent of students, respectively, reported either not reading a text or reading it sparingly after purchasing it for at least one course (Sikorski et al. 2002). Students at both institutions perceived that taking notes and studying notes (without reading the textbook), attending class, and listening to lecture were more important to academic success in the typical course than reading the text. A majority of students at both institutions reported they would not begin reading the assigned text until shortly before an exam.

Academic cultures play a role in students' decisions regarding whether or not to read. The students in the study by Pecorari et al. (2012) reported that they saw their textbooks as a valuable contributor to their learning, but nonetheless, they often chose not to read them. Instead, students depended upon the faculty member's lecture to define important course content, seeing the reading as a somewhat helpful, but entirely optional, aid to learning. Reflecting the aforementioned academic culture of the social sciences and humanities, Pecorari et al. (2012) found that reading assignments were more common and students were more likely to complete reading assignments in these disciplines. Wambach (1998) also found that students in "soft" academic disciplines had higher levels of intrinsic reading motivation.

Of course, reading assigned texts does not guarantee increased learning will result. Students must read thoughtfully and deeply. The majority of students included in a study of undergraduates at a regional four-year university readily admitted to multitasking (e.g., watching TV, texting, using the internet, etc.) while reading for academic purposes even while acknowledging that such activities interfered with their ability to focus (Kouider, Delello, and Reichard 2015). A study of students enrolled in first-year seminar courses at a small Midwestern, two-year university revealed that 46 percent of students reported that they read assigned texts. However, of those who reported completing the assigned reading, only slightly more than half (55 percent) were able to demonstrate the most basic level of comprehension (Hoeft 2012). Thus, we not only need to find ways to structure courses that encourage student reading compliance, but we also need to find ways to encourage deep reading that facilitates learning.

INCREASING READING COMPLIANCE

How can an instructor increase the likelihood that students will read assigned texts? The first and most important strategy is to utilize the readings in class and cover material from the readings in exams and writing assignments. Some researchers have suggested that as many as one third of professors assign and require students to purchase textbooks that are not used in the course (see Gurung and Martin 2011). It seems obvious that requiring students to buy and read textbooks that are not utilized in the course is a waste of students' money and will lead students to conclude that reading the assignments is not necessary in many courses. Professors may argue that readings that are unrelated to class presentations and are not covered in writing assignments or exams are still valuable developmentally for students. However, students are likely to perceive the professor as engaging in unethical behavior by requiring the purchase of materials that are not necessary for success in the course.

In order to foster students' reading, another basic step faculty members may take is to ensure that assigned texts are appropriate for the course level and are engaging and relevant to students (Weir 2009). Are the textbooks aiding in the achievement of learning goals in the course? Are they necessary, or only ancillary, to achievement of those goals? Hobson (2004) argues that not every course is well served by requiring a textbook and that requiring fewer readings that focus on the most important material, rather than more readings covering a wider breadth of topics, is likely to increase students' reading compliance. Hobson (2004) also advises explaining the importance and relevance of the reading for student success and learning during an in-class preview prior to the day it is assigned.

Students included in a focus group study conducted by Sharma, Van Hoof, and Pursel (2013) identified a number of factors that reduced their motivation for reading. First, a lack of demonstrated enthusiasm for the course topic by the instructor during class meetings reduced motivation to read outside of class. Second, if the majority of time in class consisted of the instructor reviewing and summarizing the readings, students perceived that reading compliance was less necessary. Finally, when students found reading assignments to be interesting and useful, it increased their reading compliance. These findings suggest that instructor behaviors and course structure can impact reading compliance rates.

Using Quizzes to Increase Reading Compliance

The most frequently studied strategy for increasing reading compliance is to quiz students over the reading (Aagaard et al. 2014; Burchfield and Sappington 2000; Clump et al. 2004; Connor-Greene 2000; Howard 2004; Marcell 2008; Marchant 2002). Students themselves report they are more likely to complete assigned readings if they know the instructor will quiz them on the material (Aagaard et al. 2014). In a study of students enrolled in psychology courses, Clump et al. (2004) found that only about 28 percent of students read assignments before class, although 70 percent read before an exam. When they added quizzes associated with the daily reading, student reading compliance increased to levels similar to reading before a test. Marcell (2008) compared student reading compliance within the same course in units that included daily quizzes and in units without daily quizzes. Results indicated that not only were students more likely to read the assignment when they expected a quiz, but students were also more likely to ask questions and make comments related to the reading when they expected a quiz. This suggests that an external motivation, such as a quiz, can lead to some of the results we hope come from intrinsic motivation for reading, such as participation in discussion by asking questions and making comments.

Connor-Greene (2000) conducted a comparative study of courses featuring daily quizzes over assigned readings versus courses with four scheduled exams instead of daily quizzes. In the exam condition, the majority of students (72 percent) postponed reading until immediately prior to the exams. Only 12 percent of students reported that they usually or always read assignments for class. In sharp contrast, 92 percent usually or always read for class when they expected daily quizzes. Howard (2004), in a multiple semester study of introductory sociology students, found similar results when utilizing an online, just-in-time quiz associated with readings as 98 percent of students reported usually or always completing reading assignments. Ruscio (2001) utilized randomly occurring quizzes (based on a coin flip at the start of class) to motivate reading compliance and found that 75 to 90 percent of students reported reading the assignment prior to class.

Not only does assigning quizzes over reading material increase reading compliance, but there is evidence that it also increases student learning. In a study of students in educational psychology courses, Marchant (2002) compared student scores when instructors told students they would be quizzed over assignments with scores when instructors told students that the reading was "important for their professional development" but quizzes were unannounced. He found a statistically significant improvement in scores when students knew of the forthcoming quiz, concluding that while professors hope students will be intrinsically motivated to read, their reading compliance ultimately depends on whether it will affect their grade (Marchant 2002).

Using Writing to Increase Reading Compliance and Deep Learning

While Marchant (2002) recommends a pragmatic approach over an idealistic approach, the use of quizzes as a motivational tool to increase reading compliance has its critics. Roberts and Roberts (2008) argue that this approach encourages a surface-level reading of assigned texts. They advocate instead for the use of written responses to reading assignments designed not only to motivate reading compliance but also to facilitate deep learning objectives. Likewise Weir (2009) and Hobson (2004) advocate for developing strategies that use writing to ensure reading. These strategies are not necessarily mutually exclusive. Faculty members could combine a mix of written responses to assigned readings, which likely requires a greater investment in terms of grading time, with short answer or objective question quizzes, which require less time in terms of grading. Nor is it the case that quizzes can only be used to facilitate surface learning. Short answer questions can be written in such a way as to require students to summarize the evidence in support of a thesis or to critique an argument, thus facilitating a deep learning approach to the reading assignment.

Other studies have demonstrated the positive impact of a variety of types of writing assignments designed to increase reading compliance. When Uskul and Eaton (2005) utilized long-answer graded questions associated with readings, students reported they were more likely to read the assignment, and they performed significantly better on exam questions related to topics covered by the long-answer questions than on exam questions related to other topics. Maurer and Longfield (2015) created reading guides associated with assignments for students in multiple sections of a child development course and compared daily quiz scores with students in sections without reading guides. They found students in the reading guide sections scored significantly better on the daily reading quizzes. Lineweaver (2010) utilized an online discussion assignment in a cognitive psychology course to increase student reading compliance. Students completing the online discussions were more likely to read the textbook in advance of class, and they reported reading it more carefully, having a better understanding of lectures, and feeling more prepared for exams. However, participation in online discussions did not have a significant impact on students' performance on multiple-choice items on exams.

READING COMPLIANCE AND STUDENT LEARNING

Should instructors be concerned when students do not complete reading assignments? Can we show that there is an objectively demonstrated link between reading compliance and learning? The answer to these questions is mixed. Of course, if reading compliance is associated with greater learning, faculty should be concerned when students do not read. However, there are challenges in demonstrating a relationship between reading compliance and learning. A key part of the difficulty is the measure used to estimate student learning. For example, Prohaska (1994) found that students, at all GPA levels, enrolled in advanced courses in psychology tended to overestimate their grades, with low and medium GPA students making the greatest overestimations. Others have also argued that self-reported measures of learning can be misleading. Gurung, Daniel, and Landrum (2012) found that teacher behavior predicted students' self-reported learning, but it did not impact an objective measure of learning. Conversely, they found that total time studied and online quizzes predicted an objective measure of learning, but not students' self-reported learning. Thus, students may not be good judges of which behaviors and activities actually facilitate their learning. Gurung et al. (2012) also reported that student ratings of textbook quality and helpfulness did not predict either self-reported or objective measures of learning. Because we cannot rely on the accuracy of students' self-perceptions regarding the utility of reading in facilitating learning, we must look at more objective measures of learning.

Additionally, it is not merely a matter of whether students read or do not read. How and when students read is likely to impact whether they learn from the experience of reading.

If students are reading, but doing so in a superficial manner, rushing through simply to "get it done," then there is little reason to expect reading compliance to predict learning (Jolliffee and Harl 2008). Faculty members must strive to select textbooks and readings that students will find intrinsically interesting; prime students for close reading by previewing the value and importance of readings for students (particularly those that students will find challenging to understand); and structure their courses in such a way as to encourage deep reading in order to facilitate greater learning.

In a study of the relationship between textbook usage and student performance, Landrum, Gurung, and Spann (2012) identified three factors associated with students' evaluation of textbooks. Students preferred textbooks that: (1) featured practical application to their lives, (2) were accessible in terms of the level of reading difficulty, and (3) included graphs and tables. Students liked textbooks when they perceived the material included was relevant to their lives and future careers and was readable. However, the authors were not able to demonstrate a direct relationship between student attitudes about textbooks and their associated pedagogical aids with actual performance in the course (Landrum et al. 2012). The authors did find a significant, positive correlation between percentages of textbook read with quiz scores and course grade. The authors concluded that the role of the instructor likely moderates the relationship between the textbook and student learning, suggesting that the shortcomings of a textbook poorly suited to a particular course or group of students may be overcome by high-quality instruction by the professor. Conversely, a textbook of outstanding quality with strong pedagogical aids well suited to the course and students may help overcome poor instruction by the faculty member.

In a study of student behaviors and exam scores in introductory psychology, Gurung, Weidert, and Jeske (2010) found that attendance, use of a study guide, use of practice exams, and use of class material to explain problems were each positively correlated with exam scores. Most of their measures related to textbook usage (i.e., reading difficult material slowly, taking notes while reading, creating and answering questions about the material while reading, relating reading to lecture, and reading and evaluating figures and tables in the text) did not have a statistically significant relationship with exam scores. Two measures of student behavior related to reading were actually significantly and negatively correlated with exam scores: highlighting information while reading and reviewing the chapter after lecture on the topic. In other words, students who highlighted what they perceived to be important material to review later and students who reviewed the chapter after the lecture on the topic performed more poorly on the exam than students who did not engage in these behaviors.

Gurung et al. (2010) then grouped students by cumulative GPA to determine if differences existed between high ability and lower ability students. They found that among those identified as high ability, only one student behavior was significantly correlated (though still negatively) with exam scores—highlighting information while reading. For the low ability students, a number of behaviors were negatively correlated with exam scores. These included highlighting, looking over notes after class, and reviewing the chapter after lecture on the topic—all strategies that faculty commonly suggest to students who are struggling!

These findings are consistent with Dunlosky et al.'s (2013) review of research in cognitive psychology on student-learning techniques. They found that in most situations, highlighting and underlining have little impact on performance and, when dealing with difficult texts, highlighting may harm performance. Dunlosky et al. (2013) also rated rereading of texts as having low utility in facilitating student learning as most studies of the effectiveness of rereading have focused on recall as opposed to comprehension. Somewhat more surprising, Dunlosky et al. (2013) found summarization, having students write summaries of key points in texts, to be a low utility learning strategy. In their view, summarization is a skill that requires extensive training in order to be effective, and available research has resulted in mixed findings, presumably due to students' lack of expertise in effective summarization.

Another reason for the lack of effectiveness of summarization of key points in a reading assignment as a learning strategy is students' inability to identify important information in their textbooks. Gallo and Rinaldo (2012) compared sentence by sentence highlighting of a primary research article by freshmen and senior biology students with that of faculty members. Both faculty and students were instructed to highlight information they believed to be important. Faculty members had a very high level of agreement (80 percent) among themselves regarding which sentences they highlighted. Senior-level students had less agreement among themselves regarding what to highlight, and freshmen students had even less agreement. Freshmen students typically highlighted a much higher percentage of the sentences, implying that they have not yet developed the ability to discern the most important material in a reading assignment. There was no significant association between particular sentences highlighted by faculty and those highlighted by freshmen. Seniors, on the other hand, were more likely to highlight sentences identified by faculty as important. Thus, seniors, while showing evidence of skill development, were not at the expert level demonstrated by faculty members. Pedagogically speaking, summarization of key points within assigned readings would logically lead to greater learning. However, students' lack of expertise, and their still developing skills in identifying the most important material within a text, limits the effectiveness of this strategy. For summarization to be effective, faculty members need to demonstrate this process and intentionally seek to assist students as they develop the skill necessary to identify important information for summarization.

In sum, the research suggests that simply reading is not sufficient. How and when students read matters. As Roberts and Roberts (2008) argue, faculty want students to read closely and deeply in a manner that can be transformational for them. Only when students do so will reading texts maximally facilitate learning.

CONCLUSION

The research on reading compliance and learning makes it clear that some strategies are ineffective in promoting student learning. In particular, relatively passive strategies, such as highlighting or underlining while reading, may facilitate students' sense of familiarity with the material, which is easily mistaken for an understanding of the material. Likewise, superficially rereading assignments prior to an exam may create an increased sense of familiarity—but not the long-term ability to recall (Weimer 2014).

A likely reason why these highlighting and rereading strategies are so ineffective is students' inability to identify what is important in an assigned reading. Weimer (2014) points out three problems with rereading. First, it is time-consuming. Second, it does not result in durable memory. And third, it can lead to students' mistaking a vague familiarity for mastery of material. Students' tendency to equate familiarity with mastery, at least in part, explains why students who perform poorly on exams frequently complain, "But I knew the material prior to taking the exam!" Students wrongly assumed that because they had a sense of familiarity with the content in a superficial sense, they were ready and able to demonstrate mastery in a learning assessment.

Instead of relatively passive and superficial approaches, faculty need to structure courses in a manner that encourages students to engage with the assigned reading material in a deeper fashion. As we have seen, using quizzes can both increase reading compliance and students' learning. Similarly, using writing assignments to increase reading can facilitate a deeper understanding of the material. Strategies include requiring response papers connected to the reading assignments, requiring long-answer written responses to questions, or providing study guides to help students identify the most important points in the reading.

By continually requiring students to read closely and reflect upon the content, faculty provide the opportunity for students to develop and practice the ability to discern what is most important in a particular assignment and the ability to critique an argument. Such structuring will require a more reflective approach to how we utilize textbooks in our courses and will require greater effort on the part of instructors in developing quizzes, writing assignments connected to reading, and discussion questions or study guides to facilitate students' development. By providing frequent low-stakes opportunities to practice these skills as students read, we can expect better performance and greater demonstration of learning on high-stakes assessments of learning.

REFERENCES

Aagaard, Lola, Timothy W. Conner II, and Ronald L. Skidmore. 2014. "College Textbook Reading Assignments and Class Time Activity." *Journal of the Scholarship of Teaching and Learning* 14(3):132–45.

Baier, K., C. Hendricks, K. Warren Gorden, J. E. Hendricks, and L. Cochran 2011. "College Students' Textbook Reading, or Not!" *American Reading Forum Annual Yearbook* 31:1–8.

Brint, Steven, Allison M. Cantwell, and Robert A. Hanneman. 2008. "The Two Cultures of Undergraduate Academic Engagement." *Research in Higher Education* 49:383–402.

Burchfield, Colin M., and John Sappington. 2000. "Compliance with Required Reading Assignments." *Teaching of Psychology* 27(1):58–60.

Clump, Michael A., Heather Bauer, and Catherine Bradley. 2004. "The Extent to Which Psychology Students Read Textbooks: A Multiple-Class Analysis of Reading across the Psychology Curriculum." *Journal of Instructional Psychology* 31(3):227–32.

Connor-Greene, Patricia A. 2000. "Assessing and Promoting Student Learning: Blurring the Line between Teaching and Testing." *Teaching of Psychology* 27(2):84–88.

Dunlosky, John, Katherine A. Rawson, Elizabeth J. Marsh, Mitchell J. Nathan, and Daniel T. Willingham. 2013. "Improving Students' Learning with Effective Learning Techniques: Promising Directions from Cognitive Psychology." *Psychological Science in the Public Interest* 12(1):4–58.

Gallo, Mark, and Vince Rinaldo. 2012. "Towards a Mastery Understanding of Critical Reading in Biology: The Use of Highlighting by Students to Assess Their Value Judgment of the Importance of Primary Literature." *Journal of Microbiology and Biology Education* 13(2):142–49.

Griggs, Richard A., and Scott C. Bates. 2014. "Topical Coverage in Introductory Psychology: Textbooks versus Lectures." *Teaching of Psychology* 41(2):144–47.

Gurung, Regan A. R., David B. Daniel, and R. Eric Landrum. 2012. "A Multisite Study of Learning in Introductory Psychology Courses." *Teaching of Psychology* 39(3):170–75.

Gurung, Regan A. R., and Ryan C. Martin. 2011. "Predicting Textbook Reading: The Textbook Assessment and Usage Scale." *Teaching of Psychology* 38(1):22–28.

Gurung, Regan A. R., Janet Weidert, and Amanda Jeske. 2010. "Focusing on How Students Study." *Journal of the Scholarship of Teaching and Learning* 10(1):28–35.

Hardin, Garrett. 1968. "The Tragedy of the Commons." *Science* 162:1243–48.

Hobson, Eric H. 2004. "Getting Students to Read: Fourteen Tips." IDEA Paper No. 40, 1–10.

Hoeft, Mary E. 2012. "Why University Students Don't Read: What Professors Can Do to Increase Compliance." *International Journal for the Scholarship of Teaching and Learning* 6(2):Article 12. Retrieved June 28, 2016 (http://digitalcommons.georgiasouthern.edu /ij-sotl/vol6/iss2/12).

Howard, Jay R. 2004. "Just-in-Time Teaching in Sociology or How I Convinced My Students to Actually Read the Textbook." *Teaching Sociology* 32:385–90.

Jolliffee, David A., and Allison Harl. 2008. "Texts of Our Institutional Lives: Studying the 'Reading Transition' from High School to College: What Are Our Students Reading and Why?" *College English* 70(6):599–617.

Kouider, Mokhtari, Julie Delello, and Carla Reichard. 2015. "Connected Yet Distracted: Multitasking among College Students." *Journal of College Reading and Learning* 45(2): 164–80.

Laird, Thomas F. Nelson, Rick Shoup, George D. Kuh, and Michael J. Schwarz. 2008. "The Effects of Discipline on Deep Approaches to Student Learning and College Outcomes." *Research in Higher Education* 49:469–94.

Landrum, Eric R., Regan A. R. Gurung, and Nathan Spann. 2012. "Assessments of Textbook Usage and the Relationship to Student Course Performance." *College Teaching* 60(1):17–24.

Lineweaver, Tara T. 2010. "Online Discussion Assignments Improve Students' Class Preparation." *Teaching of Psychology* 37(3):204–9.

Marcell, Michael. 2008. "Effectiveness of Regular Online Quizzing in Increasing Class Participation and Preparation." *International Journal for the Scholarship of Teaching and Learning* 2(1):Article 7. Retrieved October 24, 2016 (http://digitalcommons.georgiasouthern.edu/ij-sotl/vol2/iss1/7).

Marchant, Gregory J. 2002. "Student Reading of Assigned Articles: Will This Be on the Test?" *Teaching of Psychology* 29(1):49–50.

Maurer, Trent W., and Judith Longfield. 2015. "Using Reading Guides and On-line Quizzes to Improve Reading Compliance and Quiz Scores." *International Journal for the Scholarship of Teaching and Learning* 9(1):Article 6. Retrieved June 28, 2016 (http://digitalcommons .georgiasouthern.edu/ij-sotl/vol9/iss1/6).

National Survey of Student Engagement. 2013. *A Fresh Look at Student Engagement—Annual Results 2013.* Bloomington: Indiana University Center for Postsecondary Research. Retrieved June 28, 2016 (http://nsse.indiana.edu/NSSE_2013_Results/pdf/NSSE_2013 _Annual_Results.pdf).

Novak, Gregor M., Evelyn T. Patterson, Andrew D. Gavrin, and Wolfgang Christian. 1999. *Just-in-time Teaching: Blending Active Learning with Web Technology.* Upper Saddle River, NJ: Prentice Hall.

Parpala, Anna, Sari Lindlom-Ylanne, Erkki Komulainen, Topi Litmanen, and Laura Hirsto. 2010. "Students' Approaches to Learning and Their Experiences of the Teaching-Learning Environment in Different Disciplines." *British Journal of Educational Psychology* 80: 269–82.

Pecorari, Diane, Philip Shaw, Aileen Irvine, Hans Malmström, and Špela Mežek. 2012. "Reading in Tertiary Education: Undergraduate Student Practices and Attitudes." *Quality in Higher Education* 18(2):235–56.

Prohaska, Vincent. 1994. "'I Know I'll Get an A': Confident Overestimation of Final Course Grades." *Teaching of Psychology* 21(3):141–43.

Roberts, Judith C., and Keith A. Roberts. 2008. "Deep Reading, Cost/Benefit and the Construction of Meaning: Enhancing Reading Comprehension and Deep Learning in Sociology Courses. *Teaching Sociology* 36(2):125–40.

Ruscio, John. 2001. "Administering Quizzes at Random to Increase Students' Reading." *Teaching of Psychology* 28(3):204–6.

Sharma, Amit, Bert Van Hoof, and Barton Pursel. 2013. "An Assessment of Reading Compliance Decisions among Undergraduate Students." *Journal of the Scholarship of Teaching and Learning* 13(4):103–23.

Sikorski, J. F., K. Rich, B. K. W. Buskist, O. Drogan, and S. F. Davis. 2002. "Student Use of Introductory Texts: Comparative Survey Findings from Two Universities." *Teaching of Psychology* 29(4):312–13.

Tiberius, Richard G., and Janet Mancini Billson. 1991. "The Social Context of Teaching and Learning." *New Directions for Teaching and Learning* 45:67–86.

Uskul, Ayse K., and Judy Eaton. 2005. "Using Graded Questions to Increase Timely Reading of Assigned Material." *Teaching of Psychology* 32(2):116–18.

Wambach, Catherine A. 1998. "Reading and Writing Expectations at a Research University." *Journal of Developmental Education* 22(2):22–24.

Weimer, Maryellen. 2014. "Is Rereading the Material a Good Study Strategy?" *Faculty Focus,* May 14. Retrieved June 6, 2016 (http://www.facultyfocus.com/articles/teaching-professor-blog/rereading-material-good-study-strategy/?utm_campaign = shareaholic& utm_medium = email_this&utm_source = email).

Weir, Rob. 2009. "They Don't Read!" *Inside Higher Ed,* November 13. Retrieved June 6, 2016 (https://www.insidehighered.com/advice/2009/11/13/they-dont-read#.VuCBhhLf5NA .mailto).

18

Cultivating Engagement and Deepening Understanding While Leaving the Textbook Behind

Robin G. Isserles

When asked in a *New York Times Book Review* interview which book she most hated as a student, the comedian Tig Notaro responded, "any and all textbooks" (Notaro 2016). A funny retort, indeed, though Notaro is certainly not alone in this indictment. An abundant literature on textbooks exists—both research driven and commentary, supportive and critical, from across the disciplines—highlighting their effectiveness at content delivery and student learning. Numerous studies examine the ways faculty and students use textbooks (Berry et al. 2010; Carpenter, Bullock, and Potter 2006; Landrum, Gurung, and Spann 2012; McGee, Vaughan, and Baker 1985; Starcher and Proffitt 2011). Others focus more on the purpose and structure of textbooks (Babchuk and Keith 1995; Persell 1988; Thomas and Schmidt 2011). Efforts have been made to include student voices in the conversations around textbooks (Knecht and Najvarová 2010) and to connect these preferences to student learning (Durwin and Sherman 2008; Gurung and Landrum 2012). Additionally, numerous articles demonstrate how and why teachers have moved away from using textbooks (Castellano, DeAngelis, and Clark-Ibanez 2008; Howard 2004; Klymkowsky 2007; Martell and Martell 2011). More recently, research has examined the move toward Open Educational Resources or OERs, in large part to address the rising costs of textbooks (Hilton 2016).

This literature provides an important backdrop as I reflect on my own teaching and my students' classroom experiences. I teach Sociology at the Borough of Manhattan Community College, one of the seven community colleges that are part of the City University of New York. In the spring of 2015 when this study was conducted, there were 25,336 students enrolled, and from self-reported data, 57 percent identified as women, 31 percent Black, 13 percent White, 41 percent Latino/a, and 15 percent Asian. The vast majority of students are eligible for Pell grants (*BMCC Factbook* 2014–15). With such incredible diversity, BMCC is an exciting place to teach, notwithstanding the challenges of teaching so many students who are economically fragile.

Reflecting on my pedagogy after each semester, I returned to the same, persistent concerns: the students continually provided feedback that the assigned textbook was really quite uninspiring—"boring" in fact, and class discussions made clear the majority of the students were not reading it anyway. Consistent with the research, my students tended to use the textbook as a source of information (Knecht and Najvarová 2010) or as a study aid, rather than something they *read* (Starcher and Proffitt 2011).

Despite my efforts to make the textbook a centerpiece of class discussions to increase the number of students who read it, students consistently shared with me that they did not read it. An additional concern was the cost. According to the U.S. Accountability Office, "textbook costs increased by 82% from 2002–2012, triple the rate of inflation" (USGAO 2013:6). So, not only were they failing to read it, they were spending a great deal of money on something that did not provide much benefit.

But what really troubled me was how textbooks seemed to disengage students. From informal written and oral feedback, students shared that they tried to read the textbook, but got bored and turned off. Others found the textbooks confusing or difficult to understand. These comments were pretty consistent among the vast majority of my students—mostly working-class and lower-income students who never pictured themselves being in college someday.

Deeply influenced by Dewey ([1938] 1997), Freire (1970), and hooks (1994), among others, my pedagogical orientation is about guiding students on a journey of self-discovery and intellectual growth. Students spend 15 weeks with me, against a great many odds; forefront in my mind is making this learning experience meaningful so they are inspired to come back and continue their college education. I take seriously my role of cultivating for them an interest, a curiosity, perhaps even a love for thinking, reading, and writing—as much as that is possible. The more I thought about how to do this, the more I knew I had to leave the textbook behind.

However, this was a rather daunting proposition. Don't students *need* the structure of a textbook, as some have argued (Hess 1988; Kammeyer 1988)? Would I be able to provide such structure without one, especially for students with less academic preparation and those for whom this is their first introduction to the discipline (Persell 1988)? If I made this move, how would I present the conceptual language I want them to learn? Moreover, could the learning objectives I care about be realized, and what challenges would emerge by moving away from a conventional textbook?

THE STUDY

In the fall of 2013 I restructured my introductory course without a textbook. Since then, I have had countless informal conversations and email exchanges with students about their experiences in the course. During the spring 2016 semester, I received IRB approval to study the experience of using an alternative to a textbook in an Introduction to Sociology Writing Intensive class. The data presented here come from an analysis of students' work and responses to an open-ended survey administered toward the end of the semester. In a class of 24 students, 21 students signed consent forms and completed the survey. As the analytic frame, I chose three important student-learning objectives (Castellano et al. 2008) and demonstrated how these were met in the course. For this discussion, I draw primarily on the weekly journal entries submitted by students while reading the book, and student responses to the survey. In the next section, I share the process of shedding the textbook and introduce the book I chose to replace the textbook, offering some examples of how I incorporated it into the course material.

THE PROCESS: A STEPPING-STONE

Before leaving behind the textbook entirely, one change I made was to incorporate supplemental readings with each chapter. Students continued to reject the textbook, but came to class eager to discuss the supplemental readings. Horace Miner's (1956) "Body Rituals among the Nacirema," William Chambliss's (1973) "The Saints and the Roughnecks," and Jean Anyon's (1980) "Social Class and the Hidden Curriculum of Work" are some examples of readings students came prepared for class ready to discuss. This suggested to me most students *will* read course material if they had felt connected to it in some way, which gave me the impetus to find an alternative. As Goode (1988) suggests, "first, it is wise to know our audience, to be aware of students' interests and tastes, so that we can gear our teaching methods and materials accordingly" (p. 386).

 While I was aware I could have just switched to a reader to anchor my course (Howard 2004), I was troubled by offering only a "fragmented picture of the discipline" (Babchuk and Keith 1995:223). But more than that, I really wanted my students to have the experience of reading an entire book, and I wanted the pedagogical challenge of accomplishing this effectively.

THE PROCESS: CHOOSING THE BOOK

In thinking of alternatives, I had a few stipulations. First, I wanted a book to demonstrate to my students what solid, sociological research entails. I needed something not overburdened by quantitative jargon or conceptual language that could potentially turn them off. Ideally, I was looking for an authentic voice to speak to my students, an increasing number of whom are majoring in Criminal Justice. I often consult the resources *Teaching Sociology* and *Contemporary Sociology,* and more recently the Facebook page *Teaching with a Sociological Lens,* to gather teaching ideas—whether texts, articles, films, and the like.

Around the time I was considering alternatives, a new book by sociologist Randol Contreras was inspiring a great deal of conversation. Intrigued, I read *The Stickup Kids: Race, Drugs, Violence and the American Dream,* and became convinced this book could serve as the primary text in my course. While ideal for an Introductory Sociology class as I will discuss, I think that other undergraduate sociology courses (i.e., Urban, Sociology of Work / Informal Economy), as well as courses in criminology, gender studies, and social psychology, could utilize this book.

The Stickup Kids is an ethnographic study of a group of Dominican men coming of age in the South Bronx during the 1990s, the time period marking the rise and fall of the crack epidemic. These young men, many with early prison records and no high school degrees, first engaged in dealing crack, and then, as the crack era began to wane, switched their economic enterprises to robbing drug dealers. Contreras was not an outside researcher—he grew up with two of the main subjects and dabbled in the underground drug economy in his teens. C. Wright Mills's concept of the sociological imagination (1959) is a prominent theme in the book, demonstrating how one's surroundings and history deeply influence one's actions.

Each chapter easily relates to the major concepts I cover in an introductory course—culture, socialization, ideology, gender, hypermasculinity, class, race, ethnicity, intersectionality, marginality, deviance, cultural capital, the formal and informal economy, institutions, and the school to prison pipeline. The reading and terminology are quite accessible, not overly fraught with jargon. Contreras's subjects' experiences bring these concepts to life in a way that cannot be done with bold-typed definitions and examples in a textbook.

To illustrate, when I cover methods, we see this book in its methodological context. In fact, the book invites some really important discussions regarding methodological ethics given Contreras's insider status and the conflicts that, at times, emerged between his responsibilities as an objective researcher and those as a good friend to those he was studying. Contreras shares some of these internal struggles around his multiple standpoints, enabling my students to see the person behind the researcher, an important experience that students would miss in a course centered on a traditional textbook. In fact, I have found questions about methodology remain a constant theme to return to regarding evidence and what we know to be true.

There were other important, albeit tangential, reasons I chose this book beyond its substantive contributions. Contreras's Dominican and South Bronx identities are ones many of my students share. He also began his educational trajectory at a community college (then went on to the City College of New York [CCNY] and the CUNY Graduate Center). As so many of my students experience and internalize the stigma surrounding attending a community college (i.e., referring to it as "grade 13"), I hoped reading this book would broaden their perspectives about the possibilities that lie ahead of them.

Since I began using *Stickup Kids,* I have been collecting anecdotal evidence from students about their experiences of the book and learning sociology without a conventional textbook. Students frequently wrote some feedback in their journals or along with their final paper submissions. Occasionally, I heard from former students, as in this email:

> I took your Sociology 100 course in fall 2013 and learned an incredible exponent [*sic*] of knowledge. Reading The Stick-up Kids, chatting with Contreras and taking a course that was both challenging and enlightening is something that has stuck around with me throughout my college career.

In fact, while writing this chapter, I received an email from a former student who asked me to send him the journal questions I had assigned so he could review them while rereading the book. He wrote, ". . . I have placed the book in at least four people's hands and they have yet to put it down. Their ignorance and lack of empathy toward those who come from lower socioeconomic backgrounds pushed me to doing so, they have to read it." Clearly, this book has made its mark on many of my students.

THE PROCESS: WRITING, REFLECTING, AND SCAFFOLDING

Each week, I assign a chapter or two in the book and ask students to keep a weekly reading journal on Blackboard, our course management system. I give them a guided question to reflect on, as well as an opportunity to react to each chapter, modeled after TIERs—Thoughtful Intellectually Engaging Responses (Starcher and Proffitt 2011). These are private journals, and I am the only reader, to encourage students to write freely without worrying about sharing personal details with classmates they do not know very well. While the primary objective of these journal submissions is to help the students synthesize material in the book with concepts and ideas we discuss in class, the questions are also designed to develop their sociological imaginations, to connect their own private orbits with larger social forces. As this is a prominent theme of the book itself, my hope is seeing these connections in the stickup kids' lives will help them see similar connections in their own lives. In this way, these journals play a vital role in developing critical-thinking skills as well as inviting self-discovery (Everett 2013).

The journal entries are due the night before we meet as a class to ensure students are prepared for class and the content is fresh in their minds. (The class meets weekly for 2 hours and 45 minutes.) I usually start each class by asking them to share any reactions to the assigned chapter and then move the discussion to the question prompts. I encourage them to share their journal entries, and many of them do. Invariably, the vast majority of the students are engaged in these discussions. After allowing about 15–20 minutes for discussion, I segue to the unit under discussion, referring back to the chapter where appropriate.

In class each week, I present PowerPoint discussions highlighting the conceptual language, theories, and research on each unit. Students then connect these with the assigned reading. For example, the book's third chapter, which I assign during the unit on socialization, chronicles the two main subjects' experiences after they are sent to Riker's Island on drug and weapons convictions. This follows a unit on culture, norms, and values. Students are able to connect those concepts to socialization, resocialization, and total institutions and to unpack how norms and values are often context-specific.

In addition to helping students develop their understanding of course content, journal entries serve as a scaffolding mechanism toward the final paper, an exploration of the sociological idea that our individual lives are *contextual*. They must choose one of the subjects (Gus or Pablo) and write about how the choices they made were deeply affected by the circumstances in which they found themselves.

At three different points in the semester, I respond to the journal submissions (usually three entries at a time), pushing their thinking further. I do not expect the students to respond to my comments, but instead, I encourage students to consider these comments while they write the first drafts of their papers. When I discuss the paper in class, I draw on their posts and my responses.

On the final day of class, the students read aloud their paper's conclusion, sharing with each other their experiences reading this book. I jot down the sociological terms and concepts they invoke, ones they have clearly mastered in their papers (i.e., marginalization, family socialization, structured inequality, internalized racism, hypermasculinity, to name but a few). Following their presentations, I read this list aloud to show them the concepts they have learned over the last 15 weeks. Consistently, this is a pretty powerful class, and I have received such positive feedback from students who relay how proud they are of how much they learned in the course.

ANALYTIC FRAME: THREE GENERAL STUDENT-LEARNING GOALS

In a 2008 article in *Teaching Sociology*, Ursula Castellano and her colleagues discuss how they used nontraditional texts and the positive impact this had on three general learning objectives: promoting student engagement, increasing student understanding, and improving student analytic abilities. In the next section, I discuss some of the ways leaving the traditional textbook behind helped to foster these same meaningful learning objectives in my classes, drawing on the data generated from the student survey I distributed as well as the weekly journal entries that students wrote throughout the semester. Due to length limitations, I have cut out some of the less relevant parts below, but I have not altered their words or grammar (and will refrain from using [sic]), as I want to honor and highlight the authenticity of their voices. Because I am particularly interested in how students experience these learning goals, this article does not focus on conventional student-learning outcomes as measured by exam scores or final grade in the course.

Student-Learning Objective: Promoting Student Engagement

The students in my class shared many negative characterizations of textbooks that Martell and Martell (2011) found. In fact, not one student said they would have preferred a textbook, speaking from experiences of taking many classes that utilize textbooks. Student responses on the survey described textbooks as boring, offering broad, generic explanations, difficult to understand, disconnected to their lives, and expensive. This student captured the sentiment well:

> A textbook is so broad and has so many topics. With this book we covered everything that I think a sociology class should cover and it went straight to the point. The story of someone else's life taught us so many things that I think a textbook would've never served the purpose.

While students may find a course interesting, even if they are not completing the readings, it is likely that their level of understanding and analytical abilities may be undermined if they are disengaged from the content.

In contrast, the students reported finding the Contreras book much more engaging and interesting, able to hold their attention, and accessible. Further, students remarked that they enjoyed learning the subject material through the real-life experiences of people in the book. Even this student, who identifies as a "non-reader," wrote the following:

> This book was perfect for introducing both sociology and a new perspective in life and how we see others. It was a great insider to the life of a criminal, their lifestyle and social factors that influenced them to make the choices they made. For anyone who isn't into reading, like me, would enjoy reading this book.

When Howard (2004) changed his core text to a reader to respond to his students' rejection of the assigned textbook, he found not only an increase in the number of students completing the weekly assigned readings, but as he wrote, "students had a much higher degree of emotional reaction to the reader" (p. 388) than he ever saw with a textbook. As one of my students writes in support of this idea:

> Learning should add emotion so we have something to hold on to, textbooks do not provide that. This book touched all subjects we discussed in class and I would not have chosen any other method above this book.

This response speaks to the emotional connection students seem to crave to make the course more interesting to them. In this next example, reading about other Hispanics deepened the connection to the material for this student:

> I did learn more from reading this book because in general, reading from a textbook is more difficult to understand when it's not connected to us personally or something we can relate to individually. When we are able to relate to something we become more interested. For example, I connected well with Gus and Pablo because we are Hispanic and their culture is the same as mine.

There were other ways students identified their connection to the book. Students who live in the Bronx often comment on how this book helped them to understand the history of where they call home. But even among non-Bronx natives, students indicate new understanding of the historical realities that explain the burned-out, abandoned residential building and factories they remember from their childhood. Others have shared they remember seeing groups of boys—like the stick-up kids—as they walked to school or to the corner bodega in their own neighborhoods. This book has given them a conceptual language for understanding their daily lives in ways they never had before.

Another important dimension of student engagement that emerged from the surveys is the number of students who discussed the book outside of class with people in their lives. Discussing the book or passing it along to others suggests students are thinking about and appreciating the material they are learning. In some cases, this could mean using the book to teach others about what they are learning. This, too, is consistent with conversations I have had over the last several semesters. Very few of my students sell the book back to the bookstore, and I hear from a great many students that they intend to keep the book. Clearly, this underscores the level of interest and engagement in the material.

Of the 21 students who answered the survey, an overwhelming number of them (18 or 86 percent) responded that they had discussed the book with family and/or friends during the semester. Two students mentioned they intended to give the book to someone after the semester ends. Only one student said they did not share nor do they intend to, and only one student did not respond to the question.

Two students were taking the class for the second time, having previously failed it. Both commented that this had been a much better experience, in large part because the course was not tethered to a traditional textbook. As one of them wrote:

> Not sticking to the normal textbook routine helped a lot this semester. I took SOC 100 last semester and my professor was interesting but with the regular sociology textbook he could only teach but so much outside the book. So most of the time I fell

asleep . . . I took way more interest than I did before, and I didn't fall asleep the whole semester. I had every reason to come to back to class.

There were clear indications of student engagement fostered by using this book as a centerpiece of the course. The students enjoyed the readings, even when they do not agree with the main subjects' choices and decisions. Contreras shows these young men to be morally complex, whole people—who share a great many values and aspirations with so many others in our society but choose alternative paths, which encourages students to think in complicated ways about human behavior. Their deep emotional engagement with the material makes them want to share what they are learning with others who are important in their lives.

Student-Learning Objective: Increasing Student Understanding of the Material

I was particularly interested in asking the students what they thought they had learned in the course. The question I included to address this did not specifically ask them to consider whether this learning could have been done with a textbook, but their words certainly imply that the book offered them a way to understand the material at a much deeper level. As one student responded on the survey, "I came, I read, I learned."

Several students responded to this question in a way that made clear they increased their understanding of the course content. These two examples demonstrate comprehension of the sociological imagination:

> I understood the sociological imagination idea. An example could be that we can't understand Pablo's actions without understanding his society, culture, and government that he lived in.

> After reading this book, I now understand what it means to view an individual life contextually. I also understand the importance of C. Wright Mills quote, and how you cannot understand one aspect without knowing and understanding the other.

In the first instance, the student demonstrates her understanding by way of an example from one of the book's primary subjects. In the second, the student correctly uses the word "contextually" and defines the term "sociological imagination."

In another example, the student evokes core course concepts—marginalization and norms—and refers to the book in helping to develop understanding. The student clearly appreciated learning these concepts through learning about the lives of real people.

> Because I'm a visual type of person, such great detail allowed me to grasp the link between reality and the concept. For example, I was able to really understand what it means to be marginalized by understanding Gus and Pablo. Also, social norms came alive as I read of their time at Rikers.

Last, a few students offered responses suggesting their understanding of ideas or concepts had deepened and developed over the semester. As one student wrote, "It has changed my perspective about people and why they do violent things," and another wrote, "This semester I got a full understanding that social class we are already born into sometimes affects how one views self and others." This student sums up her own development:

> When I entered this class, I didn't even know what the term sociology meant. Along the way, I learned to understand that, to think as a sociologist, and even life lessons. I never expected to learn as much as I did from an introductory class.

Student-Learning Objective: Improving Analytic Abilities

Fourteen students—or two thirds of the students who submitted consent forms—submitted weekly journal submissions that revealed increased analytic abilities. I include two strong examples of developed analytic abilities in this section, excerpted from longer submissions. In this first example, we see a student recognize how her own beliefs and opinions were altered by what she learned, an important element of critical thinking:

> The chapters more than caught my attention, it touched my feelings . . . But, further than that is because in one way or another they mentioned how their past or situations influenced how limited they were . . . As is explained by Pablo in a part of chapter eleven: he did not have someone who leads him, teach him or give him a good purpose to follow in life, which in addition to his background, cultural position, and disadvantages where he and his friends were born were main factors to their in life and failures . . . I really was impressed to know that out are still people who have lived or are still living this kind of life and not only by choice but also because of necessity and lack of opportunities. Thinking about it, something changes in my mind and it was that I use to think that drugs were easy money and after read the story of those young men I learn that that is not easy.

This second entry weaves together so many of the concepts discussed over the course of the semester. This student's understanding of how people are categorized by society and how these categories affect the way people are perceived and treated is well developed. Even more than that, the student's analysis of the categorization is sociological in that the behaviors of a few—despite the pervasive stereotypes—do not mean an entire group conforms to those stereotypes. The student discusses this concept, beyond the context of the book:

> It all depends on how certain groups are characterized or shown into society, it all depends on how the public itself portrays that particular group. It doesn't necessarily mean that just because the majority of people incarcerated are blacks and Puerto Ricans that all Puerto Ricans and blacks are characterized as criminals, it's all based on how others classified a certain group. Certain groups are characterized and looked

down in a certain way that classifies the entire population of that group. It can based on race, economic status, or simply they're place of origin. Many say that Colombia is a country of drugs and cocaine and because many simplify this statement many Colombians are looked down upon. Just because a certain minority group is looked down in a specific that does not mean the entire population are in a drug industry. Many say that groups that practice the religion of Islam are mostly terrorist which is not true at all. Its assumptions through, the sharing of ideas and a way to characterize a certain group. It's the way a group is marginalized.

There was a great deal of evidence of deepening analytic abilities coming through these journal entries. In some, students quoted from the book (without my prompting) and began to make connections to material we were learning in the course and/or their own lives. In other submissions, students addressed the questions asked of them, but then asked follow-up rhetorical questions. Sometimes they were critically thinking about their own ideas, ideas challenged by what they learned from the book. This was also evidenced through the maturing of one's thinking, and the awareness that this was happening. True too, there were occasions when students demonstrated an ability to see both commonalities and differences between their experiences and those about which they were reading. Finally, what emerged from journal entries were expressions of ideas that stretched their thinking to everyday phenomena and human experiences.

SOME CHALLENGES

While leaving the textbook behind has been a predominantly positive experience, some challenges have arisen. One lingering concern has been the impact on students who are not native English speakers. I worry their reading and comprehension skills are not at the levels required to understand the book. However, I had the same concern when I used a textbook, and I think the rich discussions to which this book lends itself help with this. For the students who shared these struggles with me, I suggested they reread the material after we discussed it in class. Because the material was more interesting to them, it seemed many more of these students were willing to push themselves in this way.

There is a great deal of work in this class and the pace is rather fast, so falling behind can be quite difficult to overcome given students' heavy course loads in addition to work and family obligations. It has been difficult to track students who withdraw from the class, but I am concerned I do lose students who just cannot handle the workload given their myriad responsibilities. However, this is another concern I had prior to using this book. I should note that the class highlighted in this paper had a very low attrition rate. The semester began with 25 students enrolled (though one never showed up and subsequently withdrew). By the end of the semester, 23 students were consistently coming to class—only one student stopped attending. This high retention pattern is consistent since I began using the book.

A final challenge is a structural one. As a community college faculty member, with a teaching load of nine courses per year and expectations for research and college service, my ability to maintain a *weekly* response around the journal entries throughout the semester is constrained. Such a continuous dialogue would be ideal, and I suspect if that were possible, students would gain even more from the experience.

CONCLUDING REMARKS

The purpose of this chapter was to chronicle the experience I have had over the last few semesters replacing the conventional textbook. The fact that I teach in New York City, where most of my students live, has made *The Stickup Kids* particularly salient. However, I do think it could be used just as effectively in another college setting and / or even in another social science or humanities course. While I appreciate the contributions of textbook authors, the way these texts deliver course content easily becomes uninspiring and disengaging. Whether there is a way to construct textbooks differently is an interesting question, and I hope these findings may, in some way, contribute to these discussions.

Reading *The Stickup Kids* has been a very important experience for many of my students, as well as for me. I learn so much from their reactions—both verbal and written—as well as the connections they make to their own lives and the world around them. More than what a textbook can often offer, my students seem to gain a deeper understanding of the course concepts, which they take with them when the semester ends. Increasing one's understanding is certainly an important learning goal and engagement with the book and the course material is just as significant, for I submit that when engagement is stronger, the other two important goals—understanding and greater analytic abilities—follow.

For the community college students who enter my class with a vast array of skills, interests, and lived experiences, I hope to cultivate a thirst and curiosity for learning and thinking differently. This comes with an attunement to the way they connect with the course material. Over the last several semesters, I have found a way to engage them by leaving the textbook behind.

REFERENCES

Anyon, Jean. 1980. "Social Class and the Hidden Curriculum of Work." *Journal of Education* 162(1):64–96.

Babchuk, Nicholas, and Bruce Keith. 1995. "Introducing the Discipline: The Scholarly Content of Introductory Texts." *Teaching Sociology* 23(3):215–25.

Berry, Thomas, Lori Cook, Nancy Hill, and Kevin Stevens. 2010. "An Exploratory Analysis of Textbook Usage and Study Habits: Misperceptions and Barriers to Success." *College Teaching* 59(1):31–39.

BMCC Factbook. 2014–15. Borough of Manhattan Community College, Office for Institutional Research and Assessment.

Carpenter, Philip, Adrian Bullock, and Jane Potter. 2006. "Textbooks in Teaching and Learning: The Views of Students and Their Teachers." *Brookes eJournal of Learning and Teaching* 2(1). Retrieved June 6, 2016 (http://bejlt.brookes.ac.uk/article/textbooks_in_teaching_and_ learning/).

Castellano, Ursula, Joseph DeAngelis, and Marisol Clark-Ibanez. 2008. "Cultivating A Sociological Perspective Using Non-Traditional Texts." *Teaching Sociology* 36(3):240–53.

Chambliss, William. 1973. "The Saints and the Roughnecks." *Society* 11(1):24–31.

Contreras, Randol. 2012. *The Stickup Kids: Race, Drugs, Violence, and the American Dream.* Berkeley: University of California Press.

Dewey, John. [1938] 1997. *Education and Experience.* Reprint. New York: Free Press.

Durwin, Cheryl Cisero, and William M. Sherman. 2008. "Does Choice of College Textbooks Make a Difference in Students' Comprehension?" *College Teaching* 56(1):28–34.

Everett, Michele C. 2013. "Reflective Journal Writing and the First-Year Experience." *International Journal of Teaching and Learning in Higher Education* 25(2):213–22.

Freire, Paolo. 1970. *The Pedagogy of the Oppressed.* New York: Continuum.

Goode, Erich. 1988. "Sociology Textbooks: A Teaching Perspective." *Teaching Sociology* 16(4):384–89.

Gurung, Regan, and R. Eric Landrum. 2012. "Comparing Student Perceptions of Textbooks: Does Liking Influence Learning?" *International Journal of Teaching and Learning in Higher Education* 24(2):144–50.

Hess, Beth. 1988. "In Defense of the Introductory Textbook." *Teaching Sociology* 16(4):403–4.

Hilton, John. 2016. "Open Educational Resources and College Textbook Choices: A Review of Research on Efficacy and Perceptions." *Educational Technology Research and Development* 64:573–90.

hooks, bell. 1994. *Teaching to Transgress: Education as the Practice of Freedom.* London: Routledge.

Howard, Jay. 2004. "Just-in-Time Teaching in Sociology or How I Convinced my Students to Actually Read the Assignment." *Teaching Sociology* 32(4):385–90.

Kammeyer, Kenneth. 1988. "Are Sociology Textbooks Really So Bad?" *Teaching Sociology* 16(4):424–27.

Klymkowsky, M. W. 2007. "Teaching without a Textbook: Strategies to Focus Learning on Fundamental Concepts and Scientific Process." *CBE Life Sciences Education* 6:190–93.

Knecht, Petr, and Veronika Najvarová. 2010. "How Do Students Rate Textbooks? A Review of Research and Ongoing Challenges for Textbook Research and Textbook Production." *Journal of Educational Media, Memory and Society* 2(1):1–16.

Landrum, R. Eric, Regan Gurung, and Nathan Spann. 2012. "Assessments of Textbook Usage and Relationship to Student Course Performance." *College Teaching* 60(1):17–24.

Martell, Christopher, and Erin Hashimoto-Martell. 2011. "Throwing Out the History Textbook: Changing Social Studies Texts and the Impact on Students." Presented at the annual meeting of the American Educational Research Association, April 9, New Orleans, LA.

McGee, Reece, Charlotte Vaughan, and Paul Baker. 1985. "Introductory Instruction for a Discipline in Decline: A Critique and Proposals for Reorientation." *Teaching Sociology* 13(1):12–33.

Mills, C. Wright. 1959. *The Sociological Imagination.* Oxford: Oxford University Press.

Miner, Horace. 1956. "Body Rituals among the Nacirema." *American Anthropologist* 58: 503–7.

Notaro, Tig. 2016. Interview. *New York Times Book Review,* June 5. Available at https://www.nytimes.com/2016/06/05/books/review/tig-notaro-by-the-book.html.

Persell, Caroline Hodges. 1988. "Reflections on Sociology Textbooks by a Teacher, Scholar, and Author." *Teaching Sociology* 16(4):399–402.

Starcher, Keith, and Dennis Proffitt. 2011. "Encouraging Students to Read: What Professors Are (and Aren't) Doing about It." *International Journal of Teaching and Learning in Higher Education* 23(3):396–407.

Thomas P. L., and Renita Schmidt. 2011. "Challenging Texts: Challenging Textbooks: Servants, Not Masters of Our Classrooms." *English Journal* 100(3):91–96.

USGAO (United States Government Accountability Office). 2013. *College Textbooks: Students Have Greater Access to Textbook Information.* Report to Congressional Committees, GAO 13-368 (June). Available at https://www.gao.gov/assets/660/655066.pdf.

PART IV

Assessment

19

(Re-)Creating Your Course

Backward Design and Assessment

Melinda Messineo

WHERE TO START? ASSESSING THE CURRICULUM

Because you have this book in your hands, you obviously care about your teaching. Perhaps you have been teaching for years and want to take a fresh approach to a familiar course. But before you dive into course (re)design, we want you to consider initiating a series of conversations (or joining them if they already exist in your department) because your course should not exist in an institutional vacuum. Depending on the climate of your department, your colleagues may welcome your questions or you may find yourself in the role of a pioneer. Even if there is resistance from colleagues, know that your efforts will not only benefit your students, but others knowledgeable about curriculum design will appreciate and take notice of your work.

STEP ONE: PLACE YOUR COURSE

Departments exist to deliver the best curriculum possible. Each course is a part of that curriculum, and programs that are intentional about their course offerings are more likely to be successful than those whose curriculum is a loosely connected series of courses.

Departments should start by crafting a mission statement (McKinney 2004). Departments that have a mission statement articulate their curricular goal(s) and often make it public. In the "best-case-scenario," the department's mission is aligned with the institution's overall mission, and the strategic plan reflects these values.

Question #1: Does Your Department Have a Mission Statement?

If your department does not have a mission statement, that is a task that needs to be addressed but not solely by you. The department mission statement must be crafted through community discussion. In the meantime, you can begin with the student-learning objectives for the curriculum.

Question #2: Does Your Department Have Student-Learning Objectives for the Curriculum?

Because assessment has become a prominent part of the academic landscape, most departments now have student-learning objectives at the program level. If so, examine the document that articulates these objectives. If your department does not, that is another task that your entire department must address. Until that time, you can proceed to the next step of course learning objectives.

Question #3: Does Your Department Scaffold or Map Courses in the Curriculum?

Departments that have been thoughtful and thorough about their curriculum may have created a curriculum map. A curriculum map is a matrix that contains all the courses in the curriculum along one axis and the curriculum's student-learning objectives along the other axis. Each cell will contain a mark that indicates whether or not that course exposes students to that particular skill. Scaffolding refers to the degree to which supports present early in a curriculum are removed as students develop mastery in those areas and skills as they progress through the program.

That said, it is a rare department that regularly follows a process when it comes to developing new or revising existing courses. In order for that to happen, departments need to meet regularly to discuss the curriculum. Without that, it is difficult to have a coordinated and intentional curriculum. Many campuses also have connections, and even obligations, to other programs. This is especially true in joint programs, so it is important to establish early on where your course fits into these interdisciplinary cross-departmental offerings. Numerous opportunities exist for programs that venture into partnerships. However, it is also important to keep your department's central values and objectives at the forefront so your unit does not become subsumed within a partnering area.

Question #4: Does Your Department Have Learning Objectives for Your Course?

Ideally your course is placed in an intentional curriculum that is informed by broader learning goals, which ultimately support a department's mission. Short of that, instructors may find themselves entering the course design process at the course level, therefore, we offer step two.

STEP TWO: ARTICULATE THE OBJECTIVES—
A SOCIAL PROBLEMS EXAMPLE

My early career experiences may sound familiar. As a graduate student, I was invited to teach a Social Problems course. Having no idea how to begin, I turned to the persons most eager to help—the local publishing representatives. They gave me a dozen texts to review that were all surprisingly different while at the same time strikingly similar. I was relieved to see that the books had 16 chapters that perfectly coincided with the number of weeks in the term. I thought to myself, "A chapter a week, how convenient! Course design task complete!" After creating my PowerPoint presentations and tests, my chairperson asked me to provide my learning objectives. I had not given this any thought. When designing my course, I had been most worried about coverage. I assumed that the more material I presented, the better my course would be and that learning was an inevitable consequence of the exposure. I had not thought of starting at the end, partly because I did not know where I was going. As you can imagine, writing learning objectives after designing the course was a haphazard task of fitting a framework around something that had already been built.

Learning Objectives: What Does Success Look Like?

I sought support on how to write objectives and learned that faculty are often encouraged to word their learning objectives in the form of a sentence that is phrased: "At the end of this course students will . . ." Faculty then complete the sentence with words taken from Bloom's taxonomy or a similar active-learning frame (Anderson et al. 2001; Bloom 1956; Bloom, Hastings, and Madaus 1971; Marzano 2001). The objectives typically have the conditions of the performance as well as the degree of mastery (Nilson 2010). As a result of this approach, learning objectives can, at times, feel forced and awkward to write (Harden 2002). The exercise produced grammatically accurate statements that were not authentic to the learning I was hoping to facilitate. I felt that there had to be a better approach to objectives, and I learned from peers that I should begin at the end. This is referred to as "backward design" (Wiggins and McTighe 1998).

To help make the task of writing objectives more authentic, I encourage colleagues to begin with their vision of how students change as a result of engaging with the learning. To do this, I have faculty draw a picture of what a successful student looks like at the end of the term. Some faculty members are tempted to simply write descriptive words, but it is helpful to take the time to actually draw an image. What do the successful students know? What are they able to do? What are their attitudes and dispositions at the end of the term? When we think about the impact of a course, we often imagine how students will be changed as a result of their experience in the course. If they are not changed, perhaps they experience clarification of their beliefs or knowledge in some way. This change we seek represents the learning objectives we envision for the course. The change typically falls into three domains: content mastery, skills development, and affective / dispositional change. This image of the successful student at the end is the embodiment of your learning objectives for the course. Once you have this image, tease out the learning objectives that you hope to help your students achieve.

Thinking back to that early course, when asked what I wanted my students to be like at the end of the semester, I would have stated that I wanted them to understand the range of problems in the United States (content mastery). I wanted my students to know how to read newspaper accounts to determine how power was involved in defining and responding to social problems (skill development). Last, I wanted students to be passionate about creating social change related to problems they cared about in the world (affective / dispositional change). In fact, it was toward this attitudinal change that I felt most passionate. However, if you were to look at my actual course, you would be hard-pressed to see anything other than multiple-choice vocabulary tests along with essays that asked students to match social problems to examples they generated, rounded out with some uninformed opinions masquerading as discussion posts. A gap existed between what I wanted my students to achieve and what they were actually doing. Hoping that students would change through the learning experience is not the same thing as designing learning experiences that facilitate that change (Kegan 2000). It requires intentional design (Mezirow et al. 2009).

STEP THREE: IDENTIFY THE BEST MEANS—GETTING STUDENTS TO SUCCESS

To succeed, we must identify what needs to happen in order to get students to move from where they are to where we want them to end up. We often think about what we are doing in the classroom, but it is more impactful to think of the course as a whole, inclusive of all participants' roles. Fink (2013) uses the "Castle Top" approach to help contextualize the path to this final outcome. To design a course in this manner requires a faculty member to diagram the in-class and out-of-class activities sequentially over the term. The "castle" part refers to the resulting blocks that resemble the crenellations of a castle that archers would shoot arrows through during battle. As you design a course, ask yourself, what am I, as the instructor, doing in class, out of class, and in the virtual spaces to advance students to this end point? Similarly, what are students doing in class, out of class, and in the virtual spaces to reach those goals? What do students need to do, read, and experience? Instead of calculating how many pages students need to read in a week, ask yourself, "What foundational material does a student need to know about this topic in order to be able to move to the next step?" Instead of thinking that this class needs 10 quizzes at 10 points each so that the math works out evenly, think, "Where do I need to test for understanding so I know we can move forward in the course?" The U. S. Department of Education (n.d.) has determined that most course time exists outside of the physical classroom space. For example, my home institution tells students to expect to put in two to three hours of work per week for every credit hour. While it is not clear that all instructors follow this guideline, the message is clear: most of students' courses involve activity outside of the classroom (Light 2001).

Deciding on Learning Activities

How do we, as instructors, structure and guide student activity outside of the classroom walls? To succeed, instructors need to remember what it is like to be a student, experiencing the material for the first time. Of course, over time with greater experience, faculty can lose track of the steps it takes a learner to get from point A to point B. Perhaps you have experienced this yourself. The first literature reviews I received from my students were lists of book report–like summaries of what this author said followed by what this other author said, etc. My initial reaction was that my students did not try very hard, so I asked them to revise the literature reviews by stressing how they needed to connect the readings to one another. The next drafts were the same book reports with varied transition sentences spliced in between. I asked my students why their reviews looked like this, and they reported back that they did not know what literature reviews were supposed to look like. I was shocked. In the preparation for the assignment, the students had presumably read at least 20 literature reviews in the peer-reviewed pieces they had identified as relevant to their topics. However, the students did not realize that they had read reviews of the literature. In fact, many students incorrectly cited results from the literature review section as the findings of the articles themselves.

Discouraged, I lamented how unprepared the students were; however, what I should have noticed was that it was actually the difference between novice and expert learners being revealed. As an expert learner, I was demonstrating a wide range of skills as I prepared to write a literature review. I had lost track of all of the skills I was using and, as a result, I had glossed over the steps critical for novice learners to learn (Ross et al. 2005). I needed to be explicit and transparent about the various steps of an assignment and to provide scaffolding support as students developed these skills (Wood, Bruner, and Ross 1976). Over the course of a department's curriculum, instructors could eventually remove those scaffolds or supports. The result: the literature review assignment in an introductory sociology course would look quite different than the one required in capstone. Knowing the steps in between and being cognizant of the assumptions we have as instructors make for critical elements to course design.

As the above example illustrates, understanding where your course fits into a curriculum helps you better understand what scaffolding you need to provide students. Knowing the steps of various projects and tasks helps teachers better understand where the gaps exist when students are only partially prepared for the tasks at hand. Often the gaps are only revealed when students submit their work, so getting students active early in the semester is critical to effective course design.

As discussed, most faculty inherit a course and a location in the curriculum, but if you have the opportunity to (re)design, you will want to ask some additional questions.

Questions to ask as you design your course:

1. Is my course required or an elective?
2. What level is this course?
3. Is the course sequenced?
4. Who is most likely to enroll?
5. Will other departments use this course?
6. What resources are needed to meet the objectives of this course?
7. What campus units can help support this course?
8. What taken-for-granted assumptions am I making about this course and my students?

So again . . . What are you doing? What are your students doing? Early in my career I was told that the most active person in the classroom is the one who is learning the most. At the time, I was clearly working the hardest of anyone present, and I realized that my investment was not translating into student success. I was lecturing, describing, asking, connecting, and critiquing while my students were listening, watching, answering, sleeping, and daydreaming. Effective course design intentionally structures the "in-class" and "out-of-class" activity as supports for the ultimate learning objectives. If we think of the course as primarily what we are doing during the scheduled class time, we miss out on where the exploration and learning for students occurs. Much has been written about the power of active learning, deep learning, and the need to create authentic learning tasks (AAHE 1993). Intuitively we know that active learning works and that practice is a powerful part of the learning process. It is more effective to learn piano by actually sitting at the piano as opposed to reading about how to play a piano. Similarly, trying your hand at creating a survey and administering a survey is more effective than only reading about successful surveys (Committee on Developments in the Science of Learning 2000). Sometimes we cannot create active authentic experiences, so faculty find other ways to design learning experiences that bring students to successful learning outcomes.

Consider Virtual Spaces in Your Course

Just as much of the class experience happens outside of classroom walls, much of it can also occur outside of the physical space as we know it. Virtual spaces such as those provided by course management systems and social media should be integrated into course designs from the beginning. Developing proficiency in these spaces is relevant not only to online and hybrid courses but to face-to-face classes as well. These virtual spaces create opportunities to connect with students in a place where students "reside." Consider how attendance at office hours has changed over the past 20 years. When I started teaching, I would have students lined down the hallway seeking assistance. Today I probably spend equal, if not more time, engaging with students in digital spaces. Once class and office hours were over, engagement with students was closed. Now engagement and learning opportunities are unencumbered by space and time. Similarly, students are connecting more with each other in these virtual spaces, and research suggests that increased student-to-student engagement increases learning (Swann 2002). How can these interactions be structured to maximize learning and protect faculty time? A change in orientation is useful. Instead of thinking of these as either / or (face-to-face or virtual space), we should think of digital platforms as teaching modalities and tools along a continuum that extend the learning experience. Faculty cannot ignore this space as it is the critical space of engagement for students and is an increasingly important contact point for faculty and students. Needless to say, these virtual spaces represent that most likely point of enrollment growth in higher education, so faculty must master the pedagogy of virtual space. Also, faculty must understand the strengths and limitations of these spaces in order for departments to justify the value-added benefits of the brick-and-mortar experience.

Connecting to Course (Re)Design

As you consider your learning objectives, to what degree can digital spaces facilitate student engagement? Can virtual spaces give students access to content, people, data, and experiences that would not be available in a more traditional classroom design? Have you considered the degree to which the "backchannels" of your course are impacting learning? By backchannel I am referring to the student-to-student engagement that occurs around a course that is not typically tied to formal course activities. In the past, this communication took the form of whispered comments, passed notes, knowing looks, and after-class commentary. This communication now occurs in texts, posts, and social media. While often experienced as disruptive, these tools can enhance and extend the learning space. Ignoring the backchannel environment does not make it go away, so leveraging these spaces in course design can be beneficial (Yardi 2006).

Role of Technology

While technology can be a powerful tool to assist in learning, it can also be a distraction (Bowen 2012). When approaching the adoption of technology in a course, keep in mind the question, "What is the pedagogical challenge that this technology solves?" When discussion boards first emerged, faculty eagerly added them to their courses only to quickly learn that they take a great deal of work to monitor and assess. Before adopting something like a discussion board, instructors want to ask, "What are the learning objectives that discussion boards most effectively address?" "What do discussion boards do well?" For example, discussion boards can create engagement between students. They give quieter students a chance to engage in discussion over the course material and seek support and clarification. It extends the course discussion beyond classroom meeting times. It gives students a chance to formulate their thoughts and consider other people's positions before responding. It gives practice with evidence-based discourse and can be a safe space to try out ideas and explore perspectives. If these benefits advance learning objective in your course, the adoption of discussion board technology may be the answer. This applies to other technological add-ons as well. What does Twitter do well? Snapchat? Slack? Pinterest? Technology can help facilitate learning and maintain continuity between the face-to-face portions of the class experience. Faculty often state that they require less and less work from students during the in-between times because students will not do the work. This is a fair critique that deserves further exploration.

Being "The Fire"

One of the reasons that students do not utilize the out-of-class course time is that faculty often compensate when students are not prepared. If the discussion is slow and the instructor infers that students have not done the reading, the instructor will fill in and start offering more information from the text. Students quickly learn that faculty will review the reading during class time, which influences the way they approach the text in the future. It is not a *lazy* approach as much as it is an *efficient* approach. Students quickly determine which classes require what degree of preparation and invest accordingly. They, like faculty, spend their days putting out the "fires" in their schedule. What is most pressing right now? What must I do immediately? For this reason, faculty need to design their courses to hold students accountable in a supported way. Similarly, faculty need to be responsive and engage in best practices that make the most of the faculty-student partnership (Chickering and Gamson 1991). Be "the fire" in your students' schedules. Online quizzes about the main points of the reading that occur before class are a good way to encourage students structurally to prepare before class. Breaking up assignments into chunks with numerous deadlines as opposed to one end-of-term due date keeps projects moving along and students cognitively engaged. Activities in class that require out-of-class preparation also create momentum and immediacy in a course. Project management strategies and programs such as Scrum, Agile, and Gantt charts not only help make your class a "fire" in a student's schedule, but also help develop transferable skills that can extend beyond the classroom.

Co-Curricular Activities

When you expand your understanding of the course, you realize that the responsibility of reaching the objectives is shared more broadly than by just you. Students, their peers, university support resources, campus and community programming, etc., all can be tapped to help move students toward the learning objectives. Again, think of what resources, contacts, experiences, or activities students need in order to meet learning objectives successfully? I have worked with colleagues to bring more co-curricular activities into our curriculum, and a common barrier we face is that we do not know early enough which events will be happening the next semester in order to plan. To address this challenge, we have developed flexible assignments that are general enough to use a wide variety of experiences but specific enough to advance student learning. For example, in my Introduction to Sociology course, I utilize a "Fine Arts / Speaker Essay" assignment. Students attend an arts or speaker event and complete a write-up that requires them to analyze the experience from a disciplinary perspective and use relevant concepts correctly. Another assignment asks students to attend a student government or city council public meeting and analyze the issues discussed from a variety of theoretical perspectives. I encourage students to share their experiences with their peers in class and provide feedback to each other online about upcoming events and ridesharing opportunities.

At the end of the semester I ask students what they think they will remember about the class in five years. The mostly frequently cited element is experiencing the new outside event. I generally think this is a positive response, although I suppose I would like them to say more about how deftly the learning objectives were reached. But why would they mention learning objectives at all unless they knew those were the goal?

Communicating Objectives to Students and Other Audiences—The Syllabus

Students may not mention the learning objectives because they do not perceive them as elements worth noting. I see this absence of comment more as a weakness of the course design than the students' learning experience. Students do note how the course changed them, and by helping them connect this change to the learning objectives, we can easily communicate the utility of the experience. Take a look at your syllabus, and ask yourself what it communicates to students and other audiences about what happens in the course. In many contexts the syllabus is described as a contract, a roadmap, and more (Parkes and Harris 2002). Faculty present the learning objectives of the course in the syllabus, along with the transferable skills students will gain from the course. It is clear, explicit, and extremely useful, if anyone were to look at it after the first day. Of course, the fact that students do not look at the syllabus after the first day is a course design issue. Faculty can create course elements that bring students back to the syllabus and the objectives regularly. A transparent approach is to tell students regularly which objectives are connecting to what they are doing that day or what an assignment is designed to accomplish. We assume students can tell why we are doing what we are doing, but this is an expert's perspective, not a novice's experience.

The syllabus communicates a great deal to students and other audiences beyond the assignments, readings, resources, and policies. The syllabus also communicates the teaching and grading philosophies of the instructor, even if not explicitly stated. The tone of the syllabus communicates whether or not the instructor considers the faculty-student relationship to be hierarchical, collegial, adversarial, or any number of possible frames. It also communicates the temperature of the anticipated engagement. I was asked recently how "warm" (Slattery and Carlson 2005) my syllabus was this semester? I found lots of warmth in terms of offers of support, a willingness to make appointments outside of office hours, and a desire to help the students reach their goals. But it lacked the campus's diversity statement, and the accommodations statement was so mundane that I cannot imagine a student finding it supportive. Campus cultures vary in terms of what is required to be on a syllabus, so the degree to which an instructor can shape a syllabus to be an effective communication tool may vary. However, thinking critically about the message you want to communicate is an important part of course designs because it helps define and shape expectations of effectiveness.

STEP FOUR: ASSESS IF IT WORKS

I recall, as an undergraduate, that my classes consisted of attending lectures, completing a paper, a midterm, and a final. This can be an effective strategy if students are prepared and motivated, but many of us were not in that position. The risk of these assessments was that they were extremely high stakes. They provided no way for faculty to assess how the students were doing and if the instruction needed to be modified. This lack of feedback (known as formative assessment) prevented students and faculty from making necessary adjustments. Effective course design includes both formative and summative assessment in order to provide feedback for faculty and student improvement (Angelo and Cross 1993; Walvoord 2010).[1] These high-stakes assessment approaches can have the deleterious effect of encouraging students to compromise their academic integrity.

The assessment movement met with significant resistance and understandably so. Much of the early emphasis was on meeting external guidelines and expectations. The fear was that lots of data would be gathered and reports would be written and either nothing would be done or, in a worst-case scenario, resources redirected based on the results. In this initial panic, we lost the idea that assessments can be a helpful tool to facilitate more effective instruction. If someone were to ask you to summarize what your students learned in your classes this week, what would you say? How would you respond if they asked, "How do you know?" At the end of the semester, programs do overall assessment and ask the same questions, "What have our students learned this semester and how do we know?" These big assessment questions are fed by the smaller formative and summative assessment opportunities we construct through the semester. There are benefits of knowing in real time how things are going so adjustments can be made instead of waiting until accreditations to learn that things are not going well. In many ways, our teaching efforts are like our discovery scholarship efforts. We ask questions and use data to come to conclusions. Once you know your course or your program has weaknesses, you cannot un-know it, so assessment encourages action that can benefit learning. The challenge is that thorough assessment can be a great deal of work, and the resources needed to make appropriate adjustments may not exist. In this case, efficiency is needed.

Embedded Assessment

Some resistance to assessment stems from the perception that it is an additional service task on top of already heavy workloads. However, effective course design and assessment design bring the two together so that the assignments of the course are used for the program assessment. You do not add assessments for the purpose of curriculum review. Instead, you use existing assignments as evidence of the course and program learning objectives being met. This is easier to do when you know the objectives in advance and design the course accordingly. It is more difficult to find evidence of learning objectives when you are working with preexisting assignments. For program assessment, it is important to note that a weak outcome does not mean the faculty member was a terrible teacher and unsuccessful in teaching the material. It does mean that students did or did not master the material. Careful programs de-identify student papers and pick from multiple sections so that no one faculty member is the sole representative.

Alignment

Thinking back to the Social Problems example, if I had been asked the question about what my students had learned, I would have been hard-pressed to show that my course objectives had been met. In fact, when I went to do that very task I ran into this problem: I identified learning objectives that were not connected to any means of assessment, and I had assessments that were not connected to any learning objectives. And sadly, the objective I cared most about—that students would experience agency and motivation to create positive social change—was never revisited at all. I discovered that my class was not aligned. To not have an aligned course means that the learning objectives and assessments of learning are not connected. This is a common error in early course design efforts. Similarly, I had no embedded assessments that would contribute to the program objectives. To put it bluntly, the course was a mess and what complicated my repair efforts was that my assessment was ineffective because I did not know why I was assessing, or more specifically, grading, in the first place.

Grading Philosophies and Why We Grade

One consistent theme I hear from faculty is that they find grading to be the least enjoyable part of the job. Many have uttered words like "chore," "hate," and "abhor," and the task is frequently described as tedious and nonproductive. This intense investment does not seem to benefit student learning. I confess that I have spent much emotional energy frustrated with grading, but a transition in my grading philosophy has helped me view the task in a different light.

First, take a moment to contemplate your own grading philosophy or philosophy of grading. Ask yourself, "Why do I grade?" Perhaps you might say it is a way to measure learning or a way to motivate students. The "carrot" or "stick" nature of grading is an integral part of the U.S. educational system (Kohn 1999). Some describe the norming, ranking, comparative utility of grades, which is also an important part of the way we do business in higher education. But why else do we grade? Stated another way, what are grades, and what do grades *do?*

Grades are one of the ways that we communicate and hopefully dialogue with students about their learning. This conversation is where we clarify, challenge, support, and direct our students to success. Think of graded assignments not as student workload that results in faculty workload, but instead consider them as evidence of progress toward learning objectives. As mentioned earlier, as a novice instructor, I would select reading based on what I thought seemed like the right number of pages in a week, not based on what the students needed to be successful. Similarly, I would space the quizzes based on what seemed like an appropriate workload in that particular level of course. But if "proper" spacing of quizzes and making the points work in the grading computation are *not* your primary deciding factors, then how do you know when to give quizzes or how many points to give an assignment?

For a potential remedy let me start with a proclamation that I am a fan of the idea of mastery-based learning. I remember experiencing this type of learning as a student in elementary school where students completed self-paced units. Embodied in workbooks, if you finished the lesson at a mastery level, you were able to go forward. If you did not meet the threshold, you would study more, and then try again. Students only moved forward when they mastered the unit. I use this approach in many classes, which results in some students doing numerous drafts of an assignment while other students do just one. Peer and self-grading can help with the grading load. Careful consideration needs to be given to how each assignment is scored. Since these skills and competencies are necessary later in the course, it is critical that all students reach the objective. This orientation to learning greatly impacts how we think about things like the "normal curve." Developing units with mastery-based opportunities demonstrates a learning-centered approach to course design. Seeing where students thrive and struggle helps you adjust future iterations of your assignments.

STEP FIVE: REFLECT AND ADJUST

Adjusting course design is inevitable. As a general rule, I think that faculty are tinkerers. We tweak and adjust our courses regularly, perhaps nonproductively, with the intent of improving the course. We may feel external pressure to adjust courses as well. Many states have supported legislation that rewards schools and universities based on student performance. The stakes are high, and teachers at all levels are keenly aware of how their student performance reflects on them as instructors. This fear can temper the course (re)design efforts toward defensive or protective responses that discourages risk-taking and potentially even rigor.

As mentioned earlier, there are benefits of knowing in real time how things are going, so adjustments can be made instead of waiting until accreditations to learn that things are not going well. The challenge is to reflect as close to the class session as possible. If we wait too long to reflect and make changes, the issues become distorted. I have found that breaks have magical restorative powers, making once clunky or ineffective course elements appear flawless again. Effective course design incorporates habits of reflection. Even well-designed courses can benefit from reflection, so they stay fresh and relevant. I have learned to write notes after each class, each assignment, and each assessment about what went well and what needs to change. I also have a note on my calendar to remind me to actually look at the notes before I change the dates on the syllabus the following semester. These notes prompt me to find solutions from the literature and peers so that I do not keep replicating poor course design.

STEP SIX: SHARE WHAT YOU HAVE LEARNED

If you have made it this far in the chapter, you are deserving of congratulations and appreciation for your commitment to course (re)design. If you implement insights from these chapters, you can indeed be considered a scholarly teacher. A scholarly teacher is one who uses evidence from student performance and best practices and scholarship findings to advance their teaching. It is a critical and noble pursuit. I have never taught a perfect course, and I learn constantly from my students and colleagues. If you have found valuable insights in this piece, thank those amazing teachers who have come before us and "pay it forward" by sharing your experiences and insights through the scholarship of teaching and learning. Share with your campus, present at conferences, participate in research, design your own SoTL studies, and engage in the inquiry.

CONCLUSIONS

This goal of this chapter has been to discuss course design at all levels. Beginning with a step-by-step, to-do list, instructors can (re)design their courses for increased learning and integration into the department curriculum. As faculty we need to articulate where we want our students to go in order to design learning elements that help students reach those goals. Our assessments are not simply progress checks through a course, but they are integrated in the course design itself. Our philosophies of grading inform the choices we make and help us navigate the reflection and revisions process. It is my hope that you have gained practical tips for implementation as well as macro-level principles that can guide future development efforts.

NOTE

1. "Formative assessments" refer to the feedback that faculty receive from student work that helps shape instruction and student behavior. These typical low-stakes assessment experiences give students and faculty an idea of how the learning is coming along. Examples are: quizzes, minute papers, journal entries, discussion board posts, etc. "Summative assessments" are the high-stakes assessments that give faculty and students a final evaluation of whether or not the learning objective has been met. Examples are: final exams, final projects, end-of-term presentations, etc.

REFERENCES

AAHE (American Academics and Higher Education). 1993. *Deep Learning, Surface Learning.* Bulletin 45 (April):10.

Anderson, Lorin, David Krathwohl, Peter Airasian, Kathleen A. Cruikshank, Richard E. Mayer, Paul Pintrich, James Raths, Merlin C. Wittrock, and Benjamin Samuel Bloom. 2001. *A Taxonomy for Learning, Teaching, and Assessing: A Revision of Bloom's "Taxonomy of Educational Objectives" Complete.* Boston: Allyn & Bacon.

Angelo, Thomas, and K. Patricia Cross. 1993. *Classroom Assessment Techniques: A Handbook for Faculty.* San Francisco: Jossey-Bass.

Bain, Ken. 2004. *What the Best College Teachers Do.* Cambridge, MA: Harvard University Press.

Bloom, Benjamin Samuel. 1956. *Taxonomy of Educational Objectives: The Classification of Educational Goals.* 1st ed. Essex, England: Longman Group.

Bloom, Benjamin, J. Thomas Hastings, and George Madaus. 1971. *Handbook on Formative and Summative Evaluation of Student Learning.* New York: McGraw-Hill.

Bowen, Jose Antonio. 2012. *Teaching Naked: How Moving Technology Out of Your College Classroom Will Improve Student Learning.* San Francisco: Jossey-Bass.

Chickering, Arthur, and Zelda F. Gamson. 1991. "Applying the Seven Principles for Good Practice." *Undergraduate Education New Directions in Teaching and Learning* no. 47 (J-B TL Single Issue Teaching and Learning). San Francisco: Jossey-Bass.

Committee on Developments in the Science of Learning. 2000. *How People Learn: Brain, Mind, Experience, and School.* Washington, DC: National Academy Press.

Fink, Dee. 2013. *Creating Significant Learning Experiences.* Revised and updated. San Francisco: Jossey-Bass.

Harden, Ronald M. 2002. "Learning Outcomes and Instructional Objectives: Is There a Difference?" *Medical Teacher* 24(2):151–55.

Kegan, Robert. 2000. "What 'Form' Transforms? A Constructive-Developmental Approach to Transformative Learning." Pp. 35–70 in *Learning as Transformation: Critical Perspectives on Theory in Progress,* edited by J. Mezirow & Associates. San Francisco: Jossey-Bass.

Kohn, Alfie. 1999. *Punished by Rewards: The Trouble with Gold Stars, Incentive Plans, A's, Praise, and Other Bribes.* New York: Mariner Books.

Light, Richard. 2001. *Making the Most of College, Students Speak Their Minds.* Cambridge, MA: Harvard University Press.

Marzano, Robert. 2001. *Designing a New Taxonomy of Educational Objectives.* Thousand Oaks, CA: Sage.

Mezirow, Jack, Taylor Edward, and Associates. 2009. *Transformative Learning in Practice.* San Francisco: Josey-Bass.

McKinney, Kathleen. 2004. "The Scholarship of Teaching and Learning: Past Lessons, Current Challenges, and Future Visions." *To Improve the Academy* 22(1):3–19.

Nilson, Linda. 2010. *Teaching at Its Best: A Research-Based Resource for College Instructors.* 3rd ed. San Francisco: Jossey-Bass.

Parkes, Jay, and Harris, Mary. B. 2002. "The Purposes of a Syllabus." *College Teaching* 50(2):55–61.

Pascarella, Ernest T., and Patrick T. Terenzini. 2005. *How College Affects Students: A Third Decade of Research.* San Francisco: Jossey-Bass.

Ross, Karol, Jennifer Phillips, Gary Klein, and Jonathan Cohn. 2005. "Creating Expertise: A Framework to Guide Technology-Based Training." Final Technical Report for Contract #M67854-04-C-8035 for the Marine Corps Systems Command / Program Manager for Training Systems. Fairborn, OH: Klein Associates.

Slattery, J. M., and J. F. Carlson. 2005. "Preparing an Effective Syllabus: Current Best Practices." *College Teaching* 53:159–64.

Swann, Karen. 2002. "Building Learning Communities in Online Courses: The Importance of Interaction." *Education Communication and Information* 2(1):23–49.

U.S. Department of Education. N.d. "Program Integrity Questions and Answers—CreditHour." Retrieved January 8, 2017 (https://www2.ed.gov/policy/highered/reg/hearulemaking/2009/credit.html).

Walvoord, Barbara. 2010. *Assessment Clear and Simple: A Practical Guide for Institutions, Departments, and General Education.* San Francisco: Jossey-Bass.

Wiggins, Grant, and Jay McTighe. 1998. *Understanding by Design.* Alexandria, VA: Association for Supervision and Curriculum Development.

Wood, Davis, Jerome Bruner, and Gail Ross. 1976. "The Role of Tutoring in Problem Solving." *Journal of Child Psychology & Psychiatry & Allied Disciplines* 17(2):89–100.

Yardi, Sarita. 2006. "The Role of the Backchannel in Collaborative Learning Environments." Pp. 852–85 in *ICLS* 2006 *Proceedings of the 7th International Conference on Learning Sciences*, June 27–July 1, Bloomington, IN.

20

"Am I Grading Consistently and Effectively?"

Developing and Using Rubrics

Shirley A. Jackson

About 15 years ago, I decided to expand my course repertoire by changing my undergraduate courses to writing-intensive courses. At that time, I had a great deal of experience grading essay exams and both short and long (research paper length) writing assignments. These were the types of assignments I had learned to write while a graduate student. I have always been a fast grader, so grading quickly was not a real concern for me. Nonetheless, I was not always sure if I was being too harsh when grading my students' papers, but I did want to be fair. Thus, when the opportunity came to take a workshop on grading assignments for writing-intensive courses, I was a ready and willing participant.

The workshop for writing-intensive courses offered by my university introduced me to the grade rubric. This went beyond the tools I had grown so comfortable using since my days in graduate school. These had included placing checks on key words or sentences and using symbols in the margins and body of papers to denote where a new paragraph should be or if something should be omitted. The rubric meant reconsidering my use of extensive edits, including comments that I had relied so heavily upon because I saw them as "quick" ways to impart to students what needed to be revised in their work. Little did I know that other more useful and time-saving techniques existed. More specifically, there was the grade rubric.

To be honest, I cringed at the mere thought of using a tool that I perceived as taking away my freedom when grading. Any skilled professor or graduate student can clearly distinguish between a B and a B+, right? Not so. I was soon transported to the world of rubrics.

Many of us who lacked knowledge of and / or experience in using rubrics had to first learn *what* they were and *why* we should use them. I had the nagging feeling that I would be losing, not gaining, something in the process. In the end, I did lose something—wasted time. Consequently, I gained the opportunity to decrease grading time while focusing on the core of what I expected students to know based on the assignment. In this way, I was able to show my students why they earned the grades they did, and in those rare instances where students challenged their grades, I did not have to re-grade the assignment. Rather, I was able to see the amount of weight I had placed on specific elements of the assignment and my summary comments. It became a win-win situation.

WHAT IS A RUBRIC?

Rubrics are an assessment tool that tells the professor how well a student has accomplished a particular skill (Rom 2011). Yet, research findings have varied with regard to how well rubrics can accurately and consistently assess student performance when used for large classes (Davis 2011; Jönsson and Svingby 2007). Goodrich (1966 / 1997) defines the rubric as "a scoring tool that lists the criteria for a piece of work, or 'what counts' (for example, purpose, organization, details, voice, and mechanics are often what count in a piece of writing); it also articulates gradations of quality for each criterion, from excellent to poor" (p. 14). In a nutshell, a rubric should tell the professor and student what they did and how well they did it.

Rubrics have been used to assess K–12 student performance for many years, but only in the last two decades have found an audience outside of teacher education programs at colleges and universities (Hack 2015). Rost Rublee (2014) states that "rubrics are now used to score not only writing products, but also oral presentations, video production, graphic design, debates, wiki contributions, and more" (p. 199). They have frequently been employed in higher education to assess student performance in English courses (Parr and Timperley 2011) or in writing-intensive courses in a variety of disciplines (Almagno 2016). Rubrics are useful across disciplines, pedagogical styles, and assignment types from grading students in music on their class participation (Matthews 2012), dance (Mcgreevy-Nichols 2001), and writing (Anderson and Speck 1997), to teaching students sociological concepts through fiction writing (Lackey 1994). Kain (1999) shows the usefulness of grade rubrics when grading student presentations.

Nonetheless, Reddy and Andrade (2010) find that much resistance to the use of rubrics in higher education still exists. Additionally, Brookhart (1993, 1994) and Rom (2011) explore how grading is sometimes more about the professor and the professor's perceptions than the student. This can have unfair consequences for some students while muddying the waters when it comes to professors' measurements of student learning.

Although rubrics are used most often in English and education departments at the college level, professors in other disciplines also use them (Anderson and

Speck 1997; Lackey 1994; Matthews 2012; Mcgreevy-Nichols 2001; Trepagnier 2004). However, evidence exists that some perceive rubrics as being too "touchy feely" and, thus, are hesitant to use them. This may be as a result of having little knowledge of or experience with rubrics. Reddy and Andrade (2010) report in their study of the literature on rubric use:

> Professors' limited conception of the purpose of a rubric might contribute to their unwillingness to use them. College and university teachers might be more receptive if they understand that a rubric can be used to enhance teaching and learning as well as to evaluate. (P. 439)

For students, the rubric is a helpful tool in knowing where one's strengths and weaknesses lay (Hendry and Anderson 2013; Reddy and Andrade 2010). Students may find the rubric helps provide them not only with guidance in determining how they will be graded but offers feedback on those areas in which the student has shown strengths and / or weaknesses (Brookhart 1994). Furthermore, rubrics can guide both students in their own performance and peers during peer reviews.

For the professor, a rubric is a good way to discern whether students have not only done well, but whether they have accomplished the objectives of the assignment. Thus, the rubric can be a useful guide in shedding light on assignment structure for both professor and student. The rubric is based on the skill sets the professor hopes to accomplish. However, if either the assignment or the rubric is poorly written, the rubric may not be as useful as it could be (Goodrich 1996 / 1997; Jönsson and Svingby 2007).

As an assessment tool, a rubric can help us to focus on the concepts we really expect our students to learn and evaluate them accordingly.

WHY USE A RUBRIC?

Research shows that teachers have higher expectations for students whom they expect to do well in their class (Rosenthal and Jacobson 1968). There is persistent evidence that implicit bias (Holroyd 2015; Skiba, Kavitha, and Rausch 2016; Waller, Lampman, and Lupfer-Johnson 2012) may result in expectations that students will exhibit higher or poorer skills based on their race / ethnicity, gender, or class, as well as other attributes. Ramos and colleagues (2012) found that stereotype trait inferences can impact perceptions of an individual's abilities. It is important to be aware of the potential for biases when it comes to grading since the goal is to be fair and consistent. Rom (2011), Matthews (2012), and Hodges (2014) show the usefulness of grade rubrics to ease problems associated with grading by increasing accuracy and decreasing grade inflation respectively. The rubric does not mean that the professor gives up making remarks outside of "scoring" with numbers or letters the skills exhibited. These can be included in a summary on the rubric sheet.

Rubrics can be beneficial when grading writing assignments (Parr 2010; Parr and Timperley 2011), in-class presentations (Kain 1999), and classroom performance— anywhere the professor provides feedback to students. Ramos et al. (2012) state, "Stereotypes allow perceivers to draw inferences about others based on their group membership" (p. 1248). Because students can vary greatly in their ability to give effective presentations or write persuasively and clearly due to cultural or language competency, even when addressing the elements asked for in the assignment, using a rubric can stave off tendencies to reward or punish students as a result of their group membership.

Rubrics can also decrease the amount of time required for grading without decreasing the quality of feedback (Stevens and Levi 2005). One of my biggest fears in using rubrics was the belief that I would give up my ability to give the kind of feedback I had been giving for so many years. It was a surprise to find that once I used rubrics, I decreased the amount of time spent giving feedback. My feedback was more concise, but the combination of the grades and comments on the rubric I developed resulted in students having clearer notions of both my expectations and their errors. This was particularly helpful when it came to revision assignments.

While rubrics can be of great value to the professor, particularly due to their time-saving capability, they can be intimidating or unclear to use (Turley and Gallagher 2008) or judged as incapable of fulfilling our pedagogical needs (Wilson 2007). This is due, in large part, to the fact that a well-developed rubric can assess whether or not professors have accomplished the goals they have set for themselves. Particularly those who believe they are good teachers do not want to find out that what they thought they were teaching was not what the students were learning. The rubric, therefore, is apt to shed light on the professors' abilities, just as much as it does on their students.

It is crucial that we consider the myriad ways in which we can look at rubrics and use them in all-encompassing ways. This applies to program reviews and individual courses. The more comfortable faculty are with the purpose and benefits of rubrics, the more accepting they are likely to be. Additional research on language and clarity of rubrics is needed to make this happen (Reddy and Andrade 2010; Turley and Gallagher 2008). Just as important, the clearer professors articulate their expectations, the smoother the grading process. Rubrics can help us to rethink how we write our assignments in the first place. The clearer we are in our written expectations for an assignment, the easier it is for us to use the rubrics we develop to grade our students.

In her work on grading, Susan Brookhart (1993, 1994) addresses the role of value judgments used by teachers in grading and the degree to which this can result in stress about impartiality. Rubrics may address cultural, class, or gender biases in grading where students may be treated differently because they do not conform to a stereotype of how students should behave and what they should know. Group membership is not the only source of bias in grading. I noticed that my own grading tendencies, prior to using rubrics, included focusing on poor sentence structure and spelling errors in students' writing assignments. I was not aware of the grade penalty I gave to students because I was focusing on areas students were not asked to address in the assignment. As a result, I gave these elements a degree of primacy in my grading whereby students who otherwise were answering questions correctly received lower grades. If I wanted students to write papers that were organized, without typos, and addressed the goals of the assignment thoroughly, I should tell them of my expectations and grade them accordingly.

According to Popham (1996), although many educators embrace rubrics, when rubrics are poorly developed and used, they have little impact on teacher or student. Over the years, professors have designed a number of tools that have both pitfalls and benefits. Some of these are packaged with course management platforms. It can be difficult to use rubric templates unless the user knows how to use the rubric and what they want to measure. The purpose and format of the rubric must be clear to the user. The variables on which students are graded must actually be ones that the professor sees as necessary and measurable. If the assignment is not clear, the rubric will not be clear either. I, for one, rely on developing my own rubric because I have clear ideas of the types of skill sets I want my students to use or show, which are based on the type of course or assignment.

GAINING COMFORT WITH RUBRICS

Learning Management Systems and Rubrics

One of the things I found to be most valuable is that I could be flexible in my choice of rubric once I gained familiarity in what I wanted my rubric to measure. For instance, although it appears to be mandatory to use the rubric that might be attached to your university's learning management system (LMS), you are not necessarily bound to it. If you are a user of Blackboard or Desire2Learn (D2L), you can use some of their built-in rubric tools. Users of D2L will find their rubrics may be either analytic or holistic and can use text, points, or percentages depending on the type of rubric selected. There is even an option for competencies and ePortfolio. LMS rubrics have changed over the years and are much more user friendly than in the past as they provide more choices for the user. While learning management systems may have upsides with regard to the tools they offer, you may find that the built-in rubric system does not work for you. Here is where it becomes important to really think about the skills you want your rubric to measure.

If you have some basic comfort with the use of rubrics and are interested in developing your own, there are online tools that may help to ease your anxiety. This is most helpful to the novice user who may have also used "canned" grade scales for assignments since the development of a rubric takes just a few more steps when using your own grade scheme or one found on your course delivery platform (which can be used by on-ground, hybrid, and online courses). Regardless of which course management system you use, simply reviewing the instructor video tutorials will help you begin building your rubric, so it is a useful tool for you and your students.

VALUE Rubrics

Rubric development can also be learned through participation in university or systemwide initiatives. I received some of my rubric training while participating in the Multi-State Collaborative sponsored by the State Higher Education Executive Officers Association (SHEEO). Similarly, Liberal Education and Promise (LEAP), an initiative of the Association of American Colleges and Universities (AAC&U), offers a variety of materials, webinars, and workshops designed to help higher education institutions and faculty engage in rubric development in a variety of areas, including those in which they have very little or no expertise. I have found LEAP's VALUE Rubric especially useful as it addresses a broad range of skill sets and learning outcomes by which students are measured (Association of American Colleges and Universities a N.d.).

There are three substantive areas and 16 rubrics with related learning outcomes under the AAC&U's VALUE Rubric: (1) Intellectual and Practical Skills (inquiry and analysis, critical thinking, creative thinking, written communication, oral communication, reading, quantitative literacy, information literacy, teamwork, and problem-solving), (2) Personal and Social Responsibility (including civic engagement—local and global, intercultural knowledge and competence, ethical reasoning, foundations and skills for lifelong learning, global learning), and (3) Integrative and Applied Learning (integrative learning) (Association of American Colleges and Universities b N.d.).

RUBRIC DEVELOPMENT

There are many ways to construct a rubric. One's approach to rubric development depends on one's comfort level with using the technological tools that provide templates through course management platforms or one's comfort level with developing a rubric in their own format and words. Many, if not all, course management systems have rubric templates. I personally find these to be cumbersome and overly complicated to use and a constant source of frustration. Newcomers to rubric development may find developing their own rubric tool easier than using canned ones. Because templates are available, they are not the focus of this chapter. Instead, I focus on creating one's own rubric from scratch, which allows for the addition of elements that are absent from preformatted rubrics. Also, while rubrics should be updated from time to time, I discuss developing a rubric that does not require major overhauls.

Assignment Purpose

The first step in developing a rubric is to think about your assignment. It plays a central role in the information you should include in your rubric. Is the assignment oral? Written? Is it a music, dance, or theatre performance? Does it involve revision? Does it involve lab work? Is the assignment a group assignment or an individual assignment? A rubric can be used for any of the above. Once you determine the type of assignment for which you are developing a rubric, it is important to consider next the goal of the assignment. This is the step where, I believe, most professors face their primary dilemma.

What kinds of things must the student show based on the assignment directions? A rubric should consider the primary purpose of the assignment because it sets the stage for the professor's expectations about the knowledge students are expected to show they have learned or accomplished. Almagno (2016) advises that rubric development should be transparent so that students know the professor's expectations of them. Likewise, Roever and Manna (2005) state that not only do grading sheets (rubrics) assist them with accurate grading, but they also "provide helpful feedback to students who genuinely want to improve their work" (p. 317). There must be something that the professor expects the students to have learned in the course. The assignment is the opportunity for students to show this.

Professors should clearly demonstrate that the assignment and the rubric are interconnected. When building the rubric, the assignment should constantly be referenced to ensure that it explains what is to be done and how. The rubric, just as the assignment, can also include an explanation of the expected learning outcome(s). Doing the initial groundwork helps you to stay on track as you move from the initial stage of assignment development to the actual grading of the assignment. This can also be done if one plans to reuse a rubric for another assignment and would like to avoid spending time on rubric revision.

In developing the rubric, the professor must decide on the aspects of the assignment for which students will be graded. These can be broken down accordingly, but at the very least, should incorporate three elements: the purpose of the assignment, clear directions on how to undertake the assignment, and the weight of the assignment. In other words, the assignment purpose explains *the knowledge students are expected to show they have gained*. The directions show *what the students are expected to do* in order to complete the assignment. This can include explaining what materials students are to use (i.e., particular terms, concepts, readings, or other material), the format they are to follow (e.g., double- or single-spaced, word count, page length, disciplinary style format such as MLA, APA, etc.), and how they are to present their completed assignment (e.g., in a folder, on time, handed in during class or on the course LMS, proofread, with a specific cover page). The assignment weight is *the full and/or portion of the grade allocated to content, style, page length, word count, etc.; whichever elements the instructor wants to use as the basis for the grade.* If the assignment is one third of the course grade, then what elements make up this one third? Once the required elements are listed in order of importance, they should be weighted accordingly on the rubric. By thinking carefully about how to create the assignment and link it to course materials and expectations, students and the professor are able to ascertain the elements the professor wants the students to show they have learned.

Rubric Details

A rubric can be as simple or as detailed as necessary. The important thing is to provide enough information so students know not only the purpose of the assignment, but also how they will be graded. I provide this information on the syllabus when I explain the structure of assignments because I want my students to know what they have signed on for at the start of the term. I include the same information in the rubric, thereby providing no surprises to students. The assignment is given separately to students with a clear list of expectations. These expectations are also included in the criteria for the various elements on the rubric.

Not only do I include the rubric with the assignments after I have graded them, but I also inform students of the general categories and weights for which assignments are graded on the course syllabus. The rubric I use for writing-intensive courses where revisions are expected shows the original and revised grades for each entry on the rubric sheet and a space for my comments. It is simple in that it requires only three grades that combine to give a total grade for the assignment. Yet, it is also detailed enough so that I can see the criteria to be used to grade each section.

The grade format I have chosen to employ gives students a clear picture of ways to improve their grades. I use letters as on a standard grade scale rather than points (although either can be used). It is simple enough to show students their performance on the original version of the assignment and the revised version. Before revising an assignment, students can read through the rubric and the grades provided for each element for the original version. The grades for the distinct area or areas of evaluation serve as indicators of the strengths and weaknesses of their work. Because students are revising their work, it is easy for them to review the questions for each of the grade elements and determine whether they are on track or not.

By adding a comments section, I am prevented from reverting to my old format of revising statements and inserting correct punctuation or stylistic changes in the assignments students have submitted. Instead, I do a summary of the overall paper and make clear in the separate entries of the graded elements where they have done well or can improve. This does not mean that I do not make comments on their papers. Rather, I read the paper first, make brief comments in the margins, and then use the rubric to tell the rest of the story. It is important to mention that by using the rubric's comments section, I summarize my overall "take" on the assignment, instead of giving students detailed information in the margins where I am fixing errors for them. Students are forced to find these areas of concern themselves using the graded entries, brief comments in the margins, and summary comments at the bottom of the rubric. This aids in teaching students to learn from their mistakes and understand the grading process without my serving as their personal editor.

Weighting

Rubric details can vary greatly from one assignment to the next. They are dependent on the elements you have determined to be most important for your students. Let us take, for example, an assignment that asks students to use only course material (rather than outside material) in their response. The assignment might further ask students to show their understanding of material for specific weeks. Next, determine how much weight you will give them for this part of the assignment. For example, I designate 50 percent of the rubric to content, 25 percent to professionalism / style, and 25 percent to structure / organization. You should use as many elements as you see fit, but you should ensure they are the components you want to use as the basis of your assignment grade(s).

Are there certain terms that the student must incorporate? Are there websites that should be used or excluded, and if so, did the student follow these directions? I look at content and the ability to follow my directions as key related elements, and thus I assign more weight to this portion of the rubric. If this is the most important part of the assignment, then I allocate more weight to questions on the rubric related to the content of the assignment. Will students be expected to include steps or stages in their assignment? These should be clearly explained in the assignment so that the content grade is comprehensive in its inclusion of what the assignment should contain.

While I also take into consideration the organization of an assignment, it carries less weight for me than does the content. The higher weight for content is based on my belief that students may have developed other skill sets that appear in the other elements on the rubric. Because I want them to show their understanding of the material assigned for the course, they have the potential to earn a higher grade based on this one component. The other skill sets may be strengths they bring to the course; thus, I give them less weight but still expect them to show they are accomplished in these areas.

Related to organization and the last component, style, is professionalism. Here, students must be able to write in a fashion that shows they can use terminology correctly, speak to a specific audience, organize paragraphs appropriately, and write clear sentences. Students who receive lower grades on this section of the rubric may have done well in other areas, but can see the areas they need to improve.

Finally, is there a particular style of writing the student is required to use (i.e., ASA, APA, MLA, Chicago, or Turabian)? Are these cited properly in the body of the paper as well as in the reference page? For my style section, I not only go over the appropriate style students must use throughout the term, but I require the appropriate style for all assignments in order to reinforce the information. Additionally, I include links to style guide sites on the course-learning management system site. I expect that students will continue to develop in this area throughout the term.

I have also developed rubrics for students to use when engaging in peer reviews, oral presentations, and both group and individual presentations. Once again, depending on your rubric's grade elements, they can be simple or complex. If you have others who are assisting with or grading for your classes, a rubric tool can be a helpful guide to instruct them on the most important elements to you. If you have one or more people grading for you, your rubric may be used to test for inter-rater reliability—addressing potential problems with those who grade more leniently and those who grade more harshly.

WHAT I LEARNED

When I first started using grade rubrics, I was astounded by the higher grades my students received. According to the literature, there can be biases in how professors grade their students based on language skills, writing skills, etc., while excluding from consideration whether or not they have grasped knowledge of the material or concepts required for the assignment (Bay and Kotaman 2011; Rezaei and Lovorn 2010) and I certainly found this to be true in my case. I was not grading students based on the actual information they showed me they had gained; rather, I focused on the subjective elements of their assignments. In other words, I found that if a student consistently misspelled words, I would grade them more harshly than I would have if they had not misspelled words or used poor grammar or weak sentence structure. My bias against misspelled words impacted students negatively even when they answered the assignment correctly. I know some of you are thinking: "But that is how they should be graded!" Perhaps. However, rubrics should specify the set of skills or requirements on which you are assigning points or letters to the students. The absence of or a poorly written rubric that does not include the variables on which students are being graded can result in biased and unfair grading. One is restrained from penalizing students or, on the contrary, rewarding them, if the rubric is adhered to during the grading process.

CONCLUSION

My use of rubrics has changed over the years depending on what I expect students to learn in each course. It is quite possible to use the same rubric again and again, yet, in the end, it is about developing a style of rubric that works best for you. If you are not going to use it, it does not make a difference how well conceived it was. I urge those professors who are looking for a way to make their grading less of a chore to consider using rubrics. The benefits far outweigh the time spent in developing a rubric. The biggest challenge for many is taking the first step. I may not use rubrics for every assignment, but I find my life much easier when I do. Finally, using a rubric provides me (and hopefully, my students) with the knowledge that I have given my very best effort to assign grades fairly and consistently.

REFERENCES

Almagno, Stephanie. 2016. "Rubrics: An Undervalued Teaching Tool." *Faculty Focus*, Magna Publications. Retrieved February 15, 2017 (http://www.facultyfocus.com/articles /effective-teaching-strategies/rubrics-an-undervalued-teaching-tool/).

Anderson, Rebecca S., and Bruce W. Speck. 1997. "Suggestions for Responding to the Dilemma of Grading Students' Writing." *English Journal* 86(1):21–27.

Association of American Colleges and Universities a. N.d. "About LEAP." Retrieved January 6, 2017 (https://www.aacu.org/leap).

Association of American Colleges and Universities b. N.d. "VALUE Rubrics." Retrieved January 6, 2017 (https://www.aacu.org/value-rubrics).

Banerjee, Jayanti, Xun Yan, Mark Chapman, and Heather Elliott. 2015. "Keeping Up with the Times: Revising and Refreshing a Rating Scale." *Assessing Writing* 26:5–19.

Bay, Erdal, and Hüseyin Kotaman. 2011. "Examination of the Impact of Rubric Use on Achievement in Teacher Education." *New Educational Review* 24(2):283–92.

Brookhart, Susan M. 1993. "Teachers' Grading Practices: Meaning and Values." *Journal of Educational Measurement* 30(2):123–42.

Brookhart, Susan M. 1994. "Teachers' Grading Practices: Practice and Theory." *Applied Measurement in Education* 7(4):279–304.

Davis, Jan. 2011. "Taking a Practical Approach: A Pilot Study on Grading Nursing Students' Performance in Practice Has Revealed Pros and Cons." *Nursing Standard* 26(10):64.

Goodrich, Heidi. 1996/1997. "Understanding Rubrics." *Educational Leadership* 54(4):14–17.

Hack, Catherine. 2015. "Analytical Rubrics in Higher Education: A Repository of Empirical Data." *British Journal of Educational Technology* 46(5):924–27.

Hendry, Graham D., and Judy Anderson. 2013. "Helping Students Understand the Standards of Work Expected in an Essay: Using Exemplars in Mathematics Pre-Service Education Classes." *Assessment and Evaluation in Higher Education* 38(6):754–68.

Hodges, Linda C. 2014. "Demystify Learning Expectations to Address Grade Inflation." *College Teaching* 62(2):45–46.

Holroyd, Jules. 2015. "Implicit Bias, Awareness and Imperfect Origins." *Consciousness and Cognition* 33:511–23.

Janssen, Gerriet, Valerie Meier, and Jonathan Trace. 2015. "Building a Better Rubric: Mixed Methods Rubric Revision." *Assessing Writing* 26:51–56.

Jönsson, Anders, and Gunilla Svingby. 2007. "The Use of Scoring Rubrics: Reliability, Validity, and Educational Consequences." *Educational Research Review* 2:130–44.

Kain, Ed. 1999. "Evaluating Students' Presentations with the COPS Form." *Teaching Sociology* 20(4):302–8.

Lackey, Chad. 1994. "Social Science Fiction: Writing Sociological Short Stories to Learn about Social Issues." *Teaching Sociology* 22(2):166–73.

Matthews, Aaron. 2012. "Rubrics: The Universal Grade-Leveling Device." *MTNA e-Journal* 4(2):4–5.

Mcgreevy-Nichols, Susan. 2001. "Dance in K–12: Understanding Rubrics." *Dance Teacher* 23(12):63–64.

Parr, Judy M. 2011. "Repertoires to Scaffold Teacher Learning and Practice in Assessment of Writing." *Assessing Writing* 16:32–48.

Parr, Judy M., and Helen S. Timperley. 2010. "Feedback to Writing, Assessment for Teaching and Learning and Student Progress." *Assessing Writing* 15:68–85.

Popham, W. James. 1997. "What's Wrong and What's Right with Rubrics." *Educational Leadership* 55(2):72–75.

Ramos, Tânia, Leonel Garcia-Marquez, and David L. Hamilton. 2012. "What I Infer Depends on Who You Are: The Influence of Situational Spontaneous Inferences." *Journal of Experimental Social Psychology* 48:1247–56.

Reddy, Y. Malini, and Heidi Andrade. 2010. "A Review of Rubric Use in Higher Education." *Assessment and Evaluation in Higher Education* 35(4):435–48.

Rezaei, Ali Reza, and Michael Lovorn. 2010. "Reliability and Validity of Rubrics for Assessment through Writing." *Assessing Writing* 15:18–39.

Roever, Sally, and Paul Manna. 2005. "Could You Explain My Grade?: The Pedagogical and Administrative Virtues of Grading Sheets." *PS: Political Science and Politics* 38(2):317–20.

Rom, Marl Carl. 2011. "Grading More Accurately." *Journal of Political Science Education* 7(2):208–23.

Rosenthal, Robert, and Lenore Jacobson. 1968. "Pygmalion in the Classroom." *Urban Review* 3(1):16–20.

Rost Rublee, Marie. 2014. "Rubrics in the Political Science Classroom: Packing a Serious Analytical Punch." *PS: Political Science and Politics* 47(1):199–203.

Skiba, Russell J., Mediratta Kavitha, and M. Karega Rausch, eds. 2016. *Inequality in School Discipline: Research and Practice to Reduce Disparities.* New York: Palgrave Macmillan.

State Higher Education Executive Officers Association. "MSC: A Multi-State Collaborative to Advance Learning Outcomes Assessment." Retrieved January 6, 2017 (http://www.sheeo.org/projects/msc-multi-state-collaborative-advance-learning-outcomes-assessment).

Stevens, Dannelle D., and Antonia J. Levi. 2005. *Introduction to Rubrics: An Assessment Tool to Save Grading Time, Convey Effective Feedback and Promote Student Learning.* Sterling, VA: Stylus.

Trepagnier, Barbara. 2004. "Teaching Sociology through Student Portfolios." *Teaching Sociology* 32(2):197–205.

Turley, Eric D., and Chris W. Gallagher 2008. "On the 'Uses' of Rubrics: Reframing the Great Rubric Debate." *English Journal* 97(4):87–92.

Waller, Tabitha, Claudia Lampman, and Gwen Lupfer-Johnson. 2012. "Assessing Bias against Overweight Individuals among Nursing and Psychology Students: An Implicit Association Test." *Journal of Clinical Nursing* 21(23–24):3504–12.

Wilson, Maja. 2007. "Why I Won't Be Using Rubrics to Respond to Students' Writing." *English Journal* 96(4):62–66.

21

Defining and Implementing the Scholarship of Teaching and Learning

Jeffrey Chin

The scholarship of teaching and learning (SoTL) has become a recognized area of study both within disciplines and as a stand-alone area. Witness the growth of journals that publish SoTL, both discipline-specific and discipline-agnostic journals. In addition, many institutions, particularly liberal arts colleges whose mission revolves around teaching, have made SoTL an explicit part of their tenure and promotion criteria. Some schools, such as the University of Central Florida and Illinois State University, have created professorships with SoTL as the area of specialization.

SoTL has emerged from recognition of the value of good teaching. Thanks to the groundbreaking work by Boyer (1990), we now accept that good teaching is the product of systematic research and practice. The old-school perspective that "good teachers are born" is patently false; rather, "good teachers are made." Like the process of engaging in discovery research, good teaching is the product of consistent and intentional work (Bain 2004).

Boyer (1990) contended that there are multiple ways to define scholarship outside of a narrow conception of scholarship as "basic research." He argued that there are four types of scholarship:

1. The scholarship of discovery (e.g., basic research)
2. The scholarship of integration (e.g., writing textbooks)
3. The scholarship of application (e.g., applied research or what in our discipline we call "public sociology")
4. The scholarship of teaching

Boyer's "scholarship of teaching" is what we now refer to as scholarly teaching, that is, teaching that is informed by scholarship (Kreber 2001; McKinney 2004).

In this chapter, I will focus on the SoTL that has evolved beyond scholarly teaching (Schulman 2000). For those wishing to engage in SoTL work or who wonder if their research questions constitute SoTL, this chapter provides a step-by-step guide. For those new to SoTL, this chapter will also demonstrate how this work can help departments with assessment (Boyer 1995). Boyer (1990) and Glassick, Huber, and Maeroff (1997) discuss how the scholarship of teaching and learning is connected with assessment.

DOES THIS SOUND FAMILIAR?

It was soon after starting a tenure-track job with a brand new PhD that I attended my first workshop on teaching and learning. It was a transformative experience (Mezirow 1991). Suddenly I was surrounded by like-minded individuals who cared about their teaching, despite not necessarily being very good at it, and who were committed to becoming better. We all threw great ideas around, and as is typical with most teaching and learning workshops, everyone went home with great energy and plans to make changes in their courses, individual class periods, or their curricula.

However, once back at our home institutions, the glow began to fade with the reality of everyday tasks, and our colleagues were not always as impressed with the idea that it might be worthwhile to consider how to become a better teacher and, more importantly, spend the time to make it happen. Even at many small liberal arts colleges like mine, the goal was to be an adequate teacher, avoid service as much as possible, and publish to get tenured, promoted, and recognized in our disciplinary worlds. So we labored in our isolated worlds, and if we were lucky, we had a colleague or two at our home institutions with whom to share ideas. If we were really lucky, our institution had the foresight to create a center for teaching and learning (Gaff et al. 2003).

One of the realities of academic life is that the research agenda that I had developed as a graduate student was difficult to maintain at an institution where teaching is the primary mission. Whether one is teaching a 3–3 load at a liberal arts college, 5–5 at a community college, or something in between, the reality of life as a junior faculty member looks very different than what I may have envisioned. A significant disjunction exists between the hopes I had for my research agendas and the reality of what I could manage to do after completing my duties in teaching, advising, serving on committees, etc. This is where SoTL becomes relevant.

Many young faculty who end up at teaching-intensive institutions find themselves there as the result of a targeted job search and because they enjoy teaching. Once there, I suspect that the scenario goes something like this: you start teaching using the tools you acquired as a graduate student, which range from fairly competent to abysmal. But you work on your craft because you care and because it is your first job. You have some good classes, and you have classes that flop. Sometimes it defies explanation: for example, maybe you have two sections of the same course, maybe even around the same time of day, and one is lively—you cannot get your students to shut up—and one is so dead you think you could keel over and no one would say anything. Or maybe it is even more perplexing: you are well prepared for class, and it goes over like a lead balloon, and then on another day, you rush to a class totally unprepared, and it goes incredibly well. You wonder why this occurred. You tinker and eventually you create a couple of winning class periods. Students are engaged. It is clear that they learned something. The activity seems to work pretty consistently. Everyone you tell thinks it is a good idea. You think you are onto something.

If your institution will reward you for publishing your ideas on teaching, your next step, like any other research project, is to search the literature. If you are in sociology, you start with *Teaching Sociology (TS)*; if you are in psychology, it is *Teaching of Psychology*; for philosophy, it is *Teaching Philosophy*, and so on. Next, you move on to interdisciplinary journals on SoTL, such as the *Journal of the Scholarship of Teaching and Learning* or the *Journal of Higher Education* and many more. If your search appears to confirm that your idea is in fact new, you think about writing it up and looking for a place to send it.

But your next step is to turn your great idea into professional capital. In most academic worlds, this means publication. In some institutions, publication may not be the only way to demonstrate scholarship, and in fact Schulman (1999) argues that taking this position privileges individuals and institutions that support the traditional model of scholarship and that this is counterproductive to making SoTL more accessible. Schulman argues that there are multiple ways to define scholarship and that there is no such thing as "one size fits all." We can see this by simply looking across disciplines and witnessing how promotion and tenure committees struggle when comparing portfolios from candidates in disciplines such as the social sciences versus, say, performing arts.

However, I have made the argument (Chin 2002:60) that while it may be limiting to require that SoTL be published, publication in scholarly journals is still the coin of the realm, and if an individual ever wishes to be on the job market, publishing your SoTL work provides currency that is universally understood. While some institutions may recognize other forms of scholarship such as roundtable presentations, poster sessions, invited talks, facilitating workshops, etc., not all institutions do. I always advise junior faculty to remain relevant for a possible foray into the job market and to focus on publication. It is better to be safe.

My discipline, sociology, recognizes multiple options, and these options settle into essentially three categories:

1. Publications in scholarly, peer-reviewed journals that most tenure and promotion committees will recognize as scholarship, with *TS* serving as an example of what "counts" as legitimate in my discipline; most disciplines have peer-reviewed journals on pedagogy.

2. Publications in places that will require some convincing in order for tenure and promotion committees to consider them, or they will "count" only to support an already adequate portfolio; examples include chapters in edited volumes, refereed presentations, and in my discipline, TRAILS (Teaching Resources and Innovations Library for Sociology), the American Sociological Association's digital library of teaching resources.

3. Publications that will probably not "count" other than as evidence of scholarly activity except in the most inclusive definitions of scholarship— examples include invited presentations at conferences and newsletter articles; in my discipline, these might include the newsletter for the American Sociological Association's section on Teaching and Learning, *Teaching and Learning Matters,* or perhaps the discipline's general newsletter (in sociology that is *Footnotes*) or book reviews (in my discipline, *TS* accepts reviews of books related to teaching including textbooks, but there is an ASA journal called *Contemporary Sociology,* and reviews in *CS* are highly valued).

Please recognize that I make these generalizations with my own discipline and my particular institutional context in mind. For some schools, the criteria for what will "count" will be more stringent; for others, it may be more flexible.

DISCIPLINARY CONTEXT

I completed a three-year term as Editor of *Teaching Sociology* from 1997–99, and it was a life-changing experience. During that time, *TS* and other disciplinary journals on pedagogy were pushing authors to make sure their papers went beyond a model of: "I tried it, and I liked it." Rather, we wanted the authors to include assessment data. We wanted our authors to demonstrate that their presented technique would actually work if the reader was motivated to try it out.

Common Errors

Much of what appeared in the 1970s and 1980s in *Teaching Sociology,* especially in the section we called "Notes," were great ideas for how to conduct a particular activity, but they lacked information that we would never omit if we were submitting a paper to a research journal. For example, one of the first things I would look at was the list of references. Did the author see if there were similar papers published on that topic? Too often, papers came in with virtually no literature review.

The more egregious examples were papers not only without references but also without citations from *TS*.

The second major weakness of papers in the early years of *TS* was the absence of empirical evidence. As we have documented, the number of papers published in *TS* with no assessment data has gradually decreased (Baker 1985; Chin 2002; Paino et al. 2012). This series of papers suggests that in my discipline, SoTL is becoming more widely understood and being conducted more rigorously. Weimer (2006:19–39) provides an insightful overview of similar changes in other disciplines.

Moreover, while more papers now come in with assessment data, the quality of these data has improved. In the early days of the journal, we were pretty lenient on what constituted assessment data. For example, *TS* editors might accept examples of indirect learning like student reports that they had learned something (but had they, really?). Examples of indirect learning include surveys of current students or graduates that ask whether or not they felt that they had learned something. Since that time, more papers now use direct measures of learning such as portfolios, reading student papers and assessing them with rubrics, pre-/post-tests or exit exams. Concurrently, the push to do assessment work in our home institutions has made us more aware of the need for better measures of student learning.

Although Institutional Review Boards (IRBs) were mandated beginning in the mid-1970s, papers often came into my editorial office that were based on original data but without IRB approval. It is unlikely that any editor today would accept a paper without IRB approval and rightly so. My campus now requires all research-ers working with human subjects, including student researchers, to complete a free online training program called Collaborative Institutional Training Initia-tive (CITI, https://about.citiprogram.org/en/homepage/). It is a long and extensive training program, and while it takes a significant amount of time to complete, it does provide researchers with insights into how their research design might create significant, even if unintentional, hardships on their subjects. Some institu-tions also require completion of the National Institutes of Health (NIH) Protecting Human Research Participants Training (https://phrp.nihtraining.com/users/login .php).

HOW DO YOU MAKE SURE YOUR WORK IS SOTL?

Turning your great teaching ideas for in-class or out-of-class activities, pedagogi-cal techniques, curricular strategies or innovations into SoTL is easy if you follow the same steps as you would for any research project. Your next step is to design a strategy for collecting empirical evidence. For most readers of this volume, train-ing in a social science means having a basic understanding of how to construct instruments that will collect useful assessment data.

To turn your idea into SoTL, it is best to try to develop instruments that will collect data on direct assessment of learning. These are instruments that measure any changes in what the student knows. Examples of direct measures of student learning include pre- / post-tests, assessing written work with the use of a rubric (see chapter 20), portfolios, and more. The best direct measures for assessing SoTL will depend on what is being assessed (Walvoord 2010).

In comparison, the most common versions of indirect measures are self-reported measures. Examples of indirect measures include surveys of current students and graduates about whether or not they felt that they had learned anything or that they had enjoyed the class or activity. Other examples of indirect measures include measures of retention rates, pass / fail rates, course repeat rates, etc. All of these measures raise questions of causality. While indirect measures may be easier to administer, they provide less compelling evidence of effectiveness.

The last step is what is referred to in assessment as "closing the loop." Closing the loop refers to taking the information gained during the assessment process and using it to improve whatever is being assessed. In the case of SoTL, it might be a tweak to the experimental class activity, a change in a course or a curriculum. The strongest SoTL is work that shows that these changes had a measurable impact on student learning.

By now, the astute reader can see that much of what I have been discussing here on how to assess SoTL can be easily transferred into the type of assessment activities we are increasingly asked to perform on our home campuses. Typically, faculty are asked to assess student learning (this is different from institutional assessment), and paying attention to teaching with the use of SoTL will automatically propel the process of assessing student learning forward. The skills used for SoTL can benefit one's department and indeed one's institution as well. These include developing surveys, rubrics, or assignments that measure student learning.

CONCLUSION

The experience of academic training in postgraduate programs makes us content specialists. Although this is changing, many graduate training programs offer little education or information on how to become a better teacher. Programs like "Preparing Future Faculty" (http://www.preparing-faculty.org/) and the establishment of centers on teaching excellence try to address this shortcoming. These types of programs often offer courses on how to prepare and deliver courses and individual classes. We assume that many of you who are reading this volume are doing so as part of one of these courses.

We applaud institutions that develop these programs or support centers for teaching and learning because they will not only elevate the quality of teaching at the local level, but they help to augment the discussion in the respective disciplines. I hope that this chapter will help the reader see the ways in which your work can also be transformed into SoTL research and perhaps also assist with efforts to satisfy questions about student-learning assessment at your institution.

REFERENCES

Bain, Kenneth. 2004. *What the Best College Teachers Do*. Cambridge, MA: Harvard University Press.

Baker, Paul. 1985. "Does the Sociology of Teaching Inform *Teaching Sociology?*" *Teaching Sociology* 12(3):361–75.

Boyer, Ernest. 1990. *Scholarship Reconsidered*. San Francisco: Carnegie Foundation for the Advancement of Teaching.

Boyer, Ernest. 1995. "From Scholarship Reconsidered to Scholarship Assessed." *Quest* 48(2):3–14. Retrieved March 15, 2017 (http://boyerarchives.messiah.edu/files/Documents4/1000%20 0001%2064870cr.pdf).

Chin, Jeffrey. 2002. "Is There a Scholarship of Teaching and Learning in *Teaching Sociology?* A Look at Papers from 1984–1999." *Teaching Sociology*. 30(1):53–62.

Gaff, Jerry G., Anne S. Pruitt-Logan, Leslie B. Sims, and Daniel D. Denecke. 2003. *Preparing Future Faculty in the Humanities and Social Sciences: A Guide for Change*. Washington, DC: Association of American Colleges and Universities.

Glassick, Charles, Mary Taylor Huber, and Gene Maeroff. 1997. *Scholarship Assessed*. San Francisco: Jossey-Bass.

Hutchings, Pat, ed. 1998. *The Course Portfolio*. Washington, DC: American Association for Higher Education.

Hutchings, Pat, ed. 2000. *Opening Lines: Approaches to the Scholarship of Teaching and Learning*. Menlo Park: Carnegie Foundation for the Advancement of Teaching.

Kreber, Carolin. 2001. *Scholarship Revisited: Perspectives on the Scholarship of Teaching*. San Francisco: Jossey-Bass.

Maki, Peggy L. 2004. *Assessing for Learning: Building a Sustainable Commitment across the Institution*. Sterling, VA: American Association for Higher Education.

McKinney, Kathleen. 2004. "What Is the Scholarship of Teaching and Learning in Higher Education?" Retrieved April 11, 2017 (http://uca.edu/cte/files/2011/06/6whatdefinesotl .pdf).

McKinney, Kathleen. 2007. *Enhancing Learning through the Scholarship of Teaching and Learning*. Bolton, MA: Anker.

Mezirow, Jack. 1991. *Transformative Dimensions of Adult Learning*. San Francisco: Jossey-Bass.

Paino, Maria, Chastity Blankenship, Elizabeth Grauerholz, and Jeffrey Chin. 2012. "The Scholarship of Teaching and Learning in *Teaching Sociology*, 1973–2009." *Teaching Sociology* 40(2):93–106.

Schulman, Lee S. 1999. "Professing Educational Scholarship." Pp. 159–65 in *Problems and Possibilities: Issues in Educational Research*, edited by E. D. Lagemann and L. S. Schulman. San Francisco: Jossey-Bass.

Schulman, Lee S. 2000. "From Minsk to Pinsk: Why a Scholarship of Teaching and Learning?" Presented at the annual meeting of the Carnegie Academy for the Scholarship of Teaching and Learning (CASTL), March 29, Anaheim, CA.

Walvoord, Barbara E. 2010. *Assessment Clear and Simple: A Practical Guides for Institutions, Departments and General Education.* San Francisco: Jossey-Bass.

Weimer, Maryellen, ed. 2006. *Enhancing Scholarly Work on Teaching and Learning.* San Francisco: Jossey-Bass.

CONTRIBUTORS

CRAIG DOUGLAS ALBERT, PHD, is Associate Professor of Political Science and Graduate Director of the MA program in Intelligence and Security Studies program at Augusta University. He also serves as Director of the Model United Nations and is the past President of the Georgia Political Science Association.

JEFFREY CHIN is Professor of Sociology at Le Moyne College and a Carnegie National Scholar, a program of the Carnegie Foundation for the Advancement of Teaching. He is a former editor of *Teaching Sociology* and currently serves as the Secretary-Treasurer of Alpha Kappa Delta, the international honor society for sociology.

SHANNON HALEY-MIZE is Assistant Professor of Education at Elizabethtown College. Dr. Haley-Mize completed doctoral study in special education at The University of Southern Mississippi in Hattiesburg. Dr. Haley Mize's areas of research include technology and social media in teacher education, inclusion, and Universal Design for Learning.

JAY HOWARD, Professor of Sociology and Dean of the College of Liberal Arts and Sciences at Butler University, is the author of *Discussion in the College Classroom* and, with Nancy Greenwood, coauthor of *First Contact: Teaching and Learning in Introductory Sociology*.

ANDREA N. HUNT is Assistant Professor of Sociology at the University of North Alabama. Her research focuses on effective online pedagogy, gender bias in instructor evaluations, the role of academic advising in student retention, mentoring undergraduate research, and learning experiences that promote information and media literacy.

ROBIN G. ISSERLES is Professor of Sociology at Borough of Manhattan Community College, CUNY. Her current research focuses on community college students and the institutional factors that help shape their initial college experiences. She is also training undergraduate students to collect and analyze data for a user study in New York City.

SHIRLEY A. JACKSON, PHD, is Professor and Chair of the Black Studies Department at Portland State University. She received her doctorate in sociology from the University of California, Santa Barbara. Her areas of teaching and research include race/ethnicity, gender, social movements, and inequality.

KRISTY L. KENYON is Associate Professor in the Biology department at Hobart and William Smith Colleges. Her scholarly work is focused across the fields of developmental biology, neuroscience and STEM education. She teaches courses in genetics, developmental biology, stem cell biology, and reproductive politics.

BRENDA J. KIRBY is a Professor of Psychology at Le Moyne College in Syracuse, New York, where she teaches courses in social psychology, psychology and law, research methodology, and stereotyping. She received her BA from Midland University and her PhD from the University of Nebraska—Lincoln.

MICHELE LEE KOZIMOR-KING, Associate Professor of Sociology at Elizabethtown College, received her PhD from The Pennsylvania State University. She is the recipient of the National Resource Center for the First-Year Experience and McGraw-Hill Excellence in Teaching First Year Seminars Award. She is Deputy Editor of *Teaching Sociology* and past President of Alpha Kappa Delta.

MELINDA MESSINEO, PHD, is an award-winning teacher and has been the lead coordinator of numerous national and regional Teaching and Learning pre-conference workshops on behalf of ASA and AKD. She is an active SoTL scholar and serves on the editorial boards of numerous teaching and learning outlets.

RENEE MONSON is Associate Professor of Sociology at Hobart and William Smith Colleges. Her research on welfare reform, child support enforcement policy, presidential elections, collaborative pedagogy, and curricular interdisciplinarity has appeared in several journals and edited volumes. She teaches courses in research methods, gender, family, social policy, and reproductive politics.

CHRISTINE OAKLEY is the Director of International Programs' Global Learning and Associate Clinical Professor in Sociology at Washington State University. She received a Masters of Public Health in 1979 and her PhD in Sociology in 2000. She teaches in and administers a Global Leadership Certificate program.

DENNIS O'CONNOR earned a PhD in Organizational Behavior from CWRU. He is Professor and Chair of Management and Leadership at Le Moyne College and has published numerous articles in the Journal of Management Education as well as pieces on Ignatian pedagogy. He currently facilitates leadership workshops for local nonprofits.

SARA PARKER earned her PhD in International Relations from the University of Delaware. She is Dean of Social Sciences at Chabot Community College, where she taught Political Science as tenured faculty. She is a Fulbright Scholar and chair of the American Political Science Association Status Committee on Community Colleges.

STACIE PETTIT, PHD, is an Assistant Professor and Middle Grades Program Coordinator in the Department of Teaching and Leading at Augusta University. Her research interests include teaching English Language Learners, using social media in education, and Professional Development School partnerships.

DIANE PIKE, Professor of Sociology, received her PhD from Yale University and teaches at Augsburg University. Her scholarly work focuses on the scholarship of teaching and learning in sociology and on faculty development. Dr. Pike is the 2012 recipient of the American Sociological Association's Distinguished Contributions to Teaching Award.

MARI PLIKUHN, PHD, is Associate Professor of Sociology in the Department of Law, Politics, and Society at the University of Evansville. Her research focuses on the role of family in educational outcomes and opportunities, and specifically on first-generation college students and their unique educational pathways and challenges.

BARBARA PRINCE is an Assistant Professor of Sociology at Morningside College. She earned her MA from West Virginia University and her PhD from Bowling Green State University. Her research interests include sexual minorities, work-family conflict, and community-based research. She teaches courses in statistics, family, and minority groups.

AMANDA ROSEN is an associate professor of politics and international relations at Webster University. She is the recipient of several innovative teaching awards. Her research focuses on the politics of climate change, human rights of the family, and the design and use of simulations and games in the college classroom.

TRACY WENGER SADD teaches religious studies at Elizabethtown College. Dr. Sadd's interests include contemplative pedagogies, interfaith leadership, personal theologies and secular philosophies of life. She was featured in the *New York Times* for leading an interdisciplinary effort to create the first academic major in interfaith leadership studies in the nation.

DENA R. SAMUELS, PHD, is Associate Professor in Women's and Ethnic Studies at the University of Colorado—Colorado Springs. She provides keynotes, seminars, and executive coaching consultation nationally and internationally as Director of UCCS's Matrix Center for the Advancement of Social Equity and Inclusion and through www.DenaSamuels.com.

MONICA R. SYLVIA is a developmental psychologist with a BA from Fairfield University and an MS and PhD from the University of Massachusetts. Her teaching and research time centers on cognitive development and includes an examination of the impact of shared book reading on literacy skill development.

CHRISTOPHER TERRY is Assistant Professor and Assistant Chair of the Department of Mathematics at Augusta University. His research interests include student engagement, general education curriculum, and commutative algebra.

INDEX